Air Force Officer's Guide

36th Edition

Col. Stephen E. Wright, USAF (Ret.)

STACKPOLE
BOOKS

Copyright © 2014 by Stackpole Books
First edition published 1948. Thirty-sixth edition 2014.

Published by
STACKPOLE BOOKS
5067 Ritter Road
Mechanicsburg, PA 17055
www.stackpolebooks.com

Printed in the United States of America

10 9 8 7 6 5 4 3 2 1

Library of Congress has cataloged this serial publication as follows:

Air Force officer's guide / by Jeffrey C. Benton
[Mechanicsburg, Pa.] Stackpole Books

    v.:ill.;23 cm.
    Began with: 23rd ed.
    Description based on: 26th ed.
    Continues: Air Force officer's guide.
  ISSN 0739-635X=Air Force officer's guide.

1. United States. Air Force—Officer's handbooks.

UG633.A1A49   358.4'00973—dc19   83-644873
                                                AACR2 MARC-S

36th Edition
ISBN: 978-0-8117-1377-1
ISBN: 0-8117-1377-6

Contents

Preface

Air Force Officer's Guide is designed to help Air Force officers in their professional careers. The guide dates back to 1948, after the U.S. Air Force became independent of the U.S. Army. Its genesis, however, lies in the parent *Officer's Guide* (now *Army Officer's Guide*, in its 52nd edition), which first appeared in 1930, and which since then has been an indispensable source of reference for hundreds of thousands of officers. Our hope is that this 36th edition of *Air Force Officer's Guide* will be an equally indispensable reference for you.

The United States Air Force is an instrument available to the people of this republic for our common defense and for the advancement of the interests of the United States throughout the world. Insofar as the Air Force is strong, sharp, and ready, its existence tends to deter the potential aggressor, giving warning of swift punishment for the lawless. A great and historic interest of the American people lies in our desire for a world of peace and justice. The U.S. Air Force, through prompt and efficient completion of its assigned missions, can help ensure the arrival of that long-hoped-for day when all human beings may walk in freedom and in fear of none save God . . . or, by slipshod and indifferent performance on its part, the Air Force can cause the American people to lose what Abraham Lincoln called the last, best hope of earth. The issue is in the balance. You, as an officer of the U.S. Air Force, may tip the scales for better or for worse.

The U.S. Air Force seal bears a bald eagle with wings elevated and displayed in front of a cloud. The eagle is looking to the right, the field of honor.

The striking power of the Air Force is from above the clouds and is represented by the winged thunderbolt taken from the shield of Mars, which is placed above the cloudlike base represented by the nebular partition line and white background.

Thirteen stars surround the seal, and the Roman numerals MCMXLVII (1947) indicate the year of the Air Force's founding as a separate service.

The Air Force developed and released a new symbol in 2000 on a trial basis and made it the official USAF symbol in 2004. The symbol is composed of elements common to the Air Force identity. It is intended to bind airmen together, to capture the Air Force heritage, and to signify the service's aspirations for the future.

The Air Force symbol has two main parts. The upper half's stylized wings represent the stripes of the Air Force's strength—its enlisted men and women.

U.S. AIR FORCE

The stripes are drawn with great angularity to emphasize swiftness and power, and they are divided into six sections, which represent the Air Force's core competencies—aerospace superiority, global attack, rapid global mobility, precision engagement, information superiority, and agile combat support.

In the symbol's lower half, the sphere within the star represents the globe, which reminds us of our challenges as a worldwide expeditionary force. The star's five points represent the components of our force—our active-duty, civilians, guard, reserve, and retirees. The star is framed with a diamond and two trapezoids, which represent the Air Force's Core Values—integrity first, service before self, and excellence in all we do.

The two elements come together to form one symbol that presents two powerful images—it is both an eagle, the emblem of our nation, and a medal, representing valor in service to our nation.

Airmen may use the Air Force symbol on personal items. Although it is used as a trademark on a variety of official marketing goods, it may not be used for unauthorized endorsements, retail sales, or advertisement without Air Force approval.

PART I

The Profession of Arms

1

The Professional Officer

OATH OF OFFICE

The Air Force oath is essentially the same as that taken by American officers since George Washington. On taking the oath, young officers join a long line of dedicated and talented officers in khaki, olive drab, and blue who have gone before in upholding our nation's security. Their watchwords—Duty, Honor, Country—do not belong to West Point alone.

Service as an Air Force officer is much more than a job. Officers are professionals whose duties are of great importance to the government and people of the United States. If they accept their calling as professionals, the nation will be well served by them. It is tradition for officers to repeat this oath of office at each promotion ceremony throughout their careers.

> I, _____ (name) _____ , having been appointed a _____ (grade) _____ , United States Air Force, do solemnly swear (or affirm) that I will support and defend the Constitution of the United States against all enemies, foreign and domestic; that I will bear true faith and allegiance to the same; that I take this obligation freely, without any mental reservation or purpose of evasion; and that I will well and faithfully discharge the duties of the office upon which I am about to enter, SO HELP ME GOD.

THE LEARNED PROFESSIONS

There are several ways to think about the traditional learned professions: theology, the law, the various academic disciplines, and medicine. To one degree or another, the learned professions govern themselves. In the United States, the clergy is almost totally self-regulating; university-level teachers, physicians, and attorneys are less so. The professions also can be thought of as service organizations—the clergy to serve individuals' and society's spiritual needs, teachers to help individuals develop their intellectual potential, attorneys to help ensure justice for individuals and for society as a whole, and physicians to cure physical injuries and disease. Professions are also defined by a specialized

2

expertise: the clergy by theology; attorneys by the law; teachers by various academic disciplines; and physicians by medicine. The degree of self-regulation—controlling admissions to the profession, defining professional expertise, and maintaining professional ethics—gives each of the learned professions a sense of corporate identity.

THE PROFESSION OF ARMS

Although serving as an officer was generally a prerogative of Europe's aristocracy during the Old Regime, the officer corps was not really professionalized until the Napoleonic Wars, when the requirements of mass armies, logistics, and artillery demanded professional expertise in addition to leadership skills. Only then did soldiering become one of the learned professions—joining theology, the law, teaching, and medicine.

The officer corps is fairly self-regulating internally, but it has significant external controls and governmental oversight. After all, in many countries the armed forces are the major threat to liberty and government by law. The nation has constituted the armed forces of the United States to serve the republic; they exist for no other purpose. Regulation of the armed forces, the corporate nature of the institution, and its overriding mission are well understood, and need not be belabored here. The expertise of the officer corps, however, is somewhat confusing and does require explanation.

MILITARY EXPERTISE

Each Air Force officer serves two roles. One is as a technical specialist, and the other is as a military professional. Most young officers understand their roles as technical specialists—as pilots, engineers, and maintenance, logistics, or personnel officers, for example. Perhaps their academic majors have some connections to their Air Force specialties. Certainly each officer's initial training is directly related to his or her first job in the Air Force. Some officers identify with their specialties exclusively, never coming to understand that they are first and primarily Air Force officers—professionals—and only then specialists. This is rather difficult to understand because most, if not all, of the duty time of junior officers is devoted to their specialties. Many officers complete their careers as specialists, never having served as generalists. But even this does not change the fact that all Air Force officers are professionals first and specialists second. Why?

The armed forces exist to serve the United States by providing the military wherewithal to deter war and, should that fail, to fight and conclude war to the advantage of the United States. The armed forces do not exist for themselves, as a source of employment, as a market for American industry, or as a social welfare tool for social engineering. Nor do they exist as a domestic police agency. Planning, equipping, and training to employ military force, what many call managing violence, is an extremely complicated and demanding task. Unlike the other learned professions, the officer corps requires a very broad spectrum of specialties. And each one of these specialties exists, not independently in its own right, but to contribute to the armed forces' warfighting capabilities. This professional role demands that each Air Force officer understand the purpose of war, the capabilities of air and space power, the roles of air and space forces in warfare, and how the officer's specialty contributes to unit mission accomplishment. With understanding of the ultimate objectives of armed force and how organizations and functional specialties interact, units, specialties, and officers can maximize their potential contributions to mission accomplishment. Each Air Force officer's duty is to acquire and maintain professional expertise. Professional military education (PME) aids in achieving this responsibility, but because the breadth and depth of professional military expertise is so great, no officer can depend on PME alone. Career-long self-study is required to attain real professionalism. The place to begin is with AFDD1, Air Force Basic Doctrine and, if you can obtain a copy, with volume one of AFM 1-1, *Basic Aerospace Doctrine of the United States Air Force* (1992).

ETHICS
Each learned profession is bound by a code of ethics. Some are written; others are expressed only in traditions and customs. The profession of arms is bound by both. Traditional military virtues include integrity, initiative, loyalty, physical and moral courage, and self-sacrifice. These virtues may be honored by American society as a whole; some of them—integrity, moral courage, and especially self-sacrifice—have strong religious sanctions. Few would deny that these personal characteristics are worthy of honor. However, the ultimate interest of the armed forces in these virtues is not that they are honorable and not that they are morally right; rather, the interest of the armed forces is that these virtues are practical. The nature of the everyday work of the armed forces, and especially the nature of wartime duty and mission, demands that each individual have integrity, initiative, loyalty, and physical and moral courage, and maintain the interest of service before self. The profession of arms is, ultimately, a profession of service. There is not only an ethical demand on individuals in the armed forces, but also ethical restraint on how military violence is employed. Without individual and institutional ethics, servicemembers and the armed services would be without honor.

RESTRAINTS ON THE USE OF MILITARY FORCE
Although war is violent by its very nature, its violence should be restrained for two reasons. One is obviously practical: War is an instrument of political policy, and unrestrained violence can work against achieving the political ends sought. The other is also practical, but many would say it is "merely" moral. The United States cannot use unrestrained violence without altering the very essence of our national being. The United States represents justice and right; to act to the contrary would repudiate what we are as a nation. This is not to say, of course, that the United States cannot morally use violence at all. Ultimately,

our government exists to protect the citizens of the United States. Not to do so would be immoral, and also impractical. The United States, being a sovereign power, does not allow others to bind it to when and how it uses its military power. Rather, it has chosen to restrict its use of military force for practical reasons, and because to do so is morally right.

The basis of the restriction, customary international law and the Charter of the United Nations, is legally binding on the United States. Although the United States is a sovereign, secular state, these restrictions and historic just-war theories exert a strong influence on states whose moral and philosophical foundations rest on the Western tradition. Just-war theory is concerned with both when to enter or engage in war and how combatants wage war. Combatants must pursue war only for a just cause, such as self-defense or to defeat evil. A competent authority must declare and direct it; that is, states, not sub-state actors, should conduct war. War comes only after peaceable means have failed; it is a last resort. Furthermore, war must have a probability of success; if there is no probability of success, there is no purpose in suffering the inevitable horrors of military violence. The good to be achieved must outweigh the damage done; war must be proportional. Finally, war must discriminate between combatants and noncombatants, avoiding harming noncombatants where possible. President George H. W. Bush did not cite just-war theory before the United States employed military force violently in the Gulf War, but he did explain the need to go to war in just-war terms, and much scholarly debate in the United States centered on whether liberation of Kuwait was a "just cause."

Although not legally bound by just-war theory, the United States is bound by the Law of Armed Conflict (LOAC), which is composed of customs and international laws, treaties, and conventions. The purposes of the LOAC are to diminish the adverse effects of conflict, to protect people from unnecessary suffering, to safeguard fundamental rights, to prevent degeneration of organized conflict into savagery and brutality, and to facilitate restoration of peace. The principle of military necessity guides military operations. This principle requires the amount or level of force used to correspond to desired objectives. The principle of humanity requires that targeting be as accurate as possible so that collateral damage can be avoided to the greatest extent possible. Force should be concentrated so as to end the conflict faster and to reduce lives lost. Maximization of military advantage can also end the conflict faster.

The United States Air Force is bound to the LOAC by national law and Department of Defense and Air Force directives (DOD Directive 2311.01E, *DOD Law of War Program* [2010] and AFI 51-401, *Training and Reporting to Ensure Compliance with the Law of Armed Conflict* [2011]). Air Education and Training Command is responsible for initial LOAC training; personnel complete refresher training using the Advanced Distributed Learning System once at first duty station. Adhering to the LOAC reduces potential for breakdown in discipline, reduces the likelihood that American servicemembers will commit war crimes, and helps avoid worldwide outrage, congressional investigations, and adverse media attention. Adherence to the LOAC is practical in the politico-military sense, and it ensures that the Air Force maintains the moral high ground.

THE BOTTOM LINE

The United States will go to war in the future. Our nation's success will rest in great part on the strength of its officer corps. If the officer corps is professional—that is, if individual officers have prepared themselves to use their specialties to contribute to the overall military capabilities of the armed forces and if they hold fast to the military virtues—the nation can count on victory. However, if individual officers define their duties too narrowly and if they think only of serving themselves, the nation should be prepared for defeat.

Professionalism is the bottom line of each officer and airman's service in the Air Force and the way we accomplish the Air Force mission. Former Air Force Chief of Staff General Ronald R. Fogelman summarized this point well:

> The Air Force is not a social actions agency. The Air Force exists to fight and win wars. That's our core expertise; it is what allows us to be called professionals. We are entrusted with the security of our nation. The tools of our trade are lethal, and we engage in operations that involve much national treasure and risk to human life. Because of what we do, our standards must be higher than those of society at large. The American public expects it of us and properly so. In the end, we earn the respect and trust of the American people because of the professionalism and integrity we demonstrate.

2

The Code of Air Force Service

This chapter sets down principles to which all officers aspire, both in their official duties and in their personal concerns, in actions seen and known by the world and in the privacy of the mind. These ideals are encapsulated in the Airman's Creed, initially articulated in 2007 by then Air Force Chief of Staff General T. Michael Moseley. This creed captures the heritage, honor, and faith airmen profess to themselves and to each other. The Air Force had earlier codified its core values with the 1997 publication of *The Little Blue Book*. This chapter presents extracts from that official publication, as well as selections from an older, unofficial compilation of ideals titled *Principles of the Air Force Code*. The Airman's Creed and the Core Values define the character of officers and enlisted personnel as airmen in the United States Air Force. These are so important to the Air Force that they are codified in its doctrine; refer to Air Force Doctrine Document AFDD1-1, *Leadership and Force Development*. It and other Air Force doctrinal publications can be downloaded at www.au.af.mil/au/lemay/main.htm.

THE AIRMAN'S CREED
I am an American Airman.
I am a Warrior.
I have answered my Nation's call.

I am an American Airman.
My mission is to Fly, Fight, and Win.
I am faithful to a Proud Heritage,
A Tradition of Honor,
And a Legacy of Valor.

I am an American Airman.
Guardian of Freedom and Justice.
My Nation's Sword and Shield,
Its Sentry and Avenger.
I defend my Country with my Life.

> I am an American Airman.
> Wingman, Leader, Warrior.
> I will never leave an Airman behind,
> I will never falter,
> And I will not fail.

AIR FORCE CORE VALUES

Whoever you are and wherever you fit on the Air Force team, this is your basic guide to the Air Force Core Values of *Integrity first*, *Service before self*, and *Excellence in all we do*. The Core Values exist for all members of the Air Force family: officer, enlisted, and civilian; active, reserve, and retired; senior, junior, and middle management; civil servants; uniformed personnel; and contractors. They are for all of us to read, to understand, to live by, and to cherish.

The Core Values are much more than minimum standards. They remind us what it takes to get the mission done. They inspire us to do our very best at all times. They are the common bond among all comrades in arms, and they are the glue that unifies the force and ties us to the great warriors and public servants of the past. Study them, understand them, follow them, and encourage others to do the same.

Integrity First. Integrity is a character trait. It is the willingness to do what is right, even when no one is looking. It is the "moral compass," the inner voice, the voice of self-control, and the basis for the trust imperative to today's military. Integrity is the ability to hold together and properly regulate all the elements of a personality. A person of integrity, for example, is capable of acting on conviction. A person of integrity can control impulses and appetites. But integrity also covers several other moral traits indispensable to national service. *Courage.* A person of integrity possesses moral courage and does what is right even if the personal cost is high. *Honesty.* This is the hallmark of the military professional, because in the military, our word must be our bond. We don't pencil-whip training reports, we don't cover up tech data violations, we don't falsify documents, and we don't write misleading operational readiness messages. The bottom line is, we don't lie, and we can't justify any deviation from the truth. *Responsibility.* No person of integrity is irresponsible; a person of true integrity acknowledges his or her duties and acts accordingly. *Accountability.* No person of integrity tries to shift the blame to others or take credit for the work of others; "the buck stops here" says it best. *Justice.* A person of integrity practices justice. Those who do similar things must get similar rewards or similar punishments. *Openness.* Professionals of integrity encourage a free flow of information within the organization. They seek feedback from all directions to ensure they are fulfilling key responsibilities, and they are never afraid to allow anyone at any time to examine how they do business. *Self-respect.* To have integrity also is to respect oneself as a professional and a human being. A person of integrity does not behave in ways that would bring discredit upon himself or herself or the organization to which he or she belongs. *Humility.* A person of integrity grasps and is sobered by the awesome task of defending the Constitution of the United States of America.

Service before Self. Service before self tells us that professional duties take precedence over personal desires. At the very least, it includes the following behaviors. *Rule following.* To serve is to do one's duty, and our duties are most commonly expressed through rules. While it may be the case that professionals are expected to exercise judgment in the performance of their duties, good professionals understand that rules have a reason for being, and the default position must be to follow those rules unless there is a clear, operational reason for refusing to do so. *Respect for others.* Service before self tells us also that a good leader places the troops ahead of his or her personal comfort. We must always act in the certain knowledge that all people possess a fundamental worth as human beings. *Discipline and self-control.* Professionals cannot indulge in self-pity, discouragement, anger, frustration, or defeatism. They have a fundamental moral obligation to the persons they lead to strike a tone of confidence and forward-looking optimism. More specifically, they are expected to exercise control in the following areas. *Anger.* Military professionals and especially commanders at all echelons are expected to refrain from displays of anger that would bring discredit upon themselves and/or the Air Force. *Appetites.* Those who allow their appetites to drive them to make sexual overtures to subordinates are unfit for military service. Likewise, the excessive consumption of alcohol casts doubt on an individual's fitness, and if an officer is found to be drunk and disorderly, all doubts are removed. *Religious toleration.* Military professionals must remember that religious beliefs are a matter of individual choice. Professionals, and especially commanders, must not try to change or coercively influence the religious views of subordinates. *Faith in the system.* To lose faith in the system is to adopt the view that you know better than those above you in the chain of command what should or should not be done. In other words, to lose faith in the system is to place self before service. Leaders can be very influential in this regard. If a leader resists the temptation to doubt the system, then subordinates may follow suit.

Excellence in All We Do. Excellence in all we do directs us to develop a sustained passion for continual improvement and innovation that will propel the Air Force into a long-term, upward spiral of accomplishment and performance. *Product and service excellence.* We must focus on providing services and generating products that fully respond to customer wants and anticipate customer needs, and we must do so within the boundaries established by the taxpaying public. *Personal excellence.* Military professionals must seek out and complete professional military education, stay in physical and mental shape, and continue to refresh their general educational backgrounds. *Community excellence.* This is achieved when the members of an organization can work together to successfully reach a common goal in an atmosphere free of fear that preserves individual self-worth. Several factors influence interpersonal excellence. *Mutual respect.* Genuine respect involves viewing another person as an individual of fundamental worth. This means never judging a person on the basis of his or her possession of an attribute that places him or her in some racial, ethnic, economic, or gender-based category. *Benefit of the doubt.* Avoid making snap judgments about a person or his or her behavior; it is important to get the whole story. All coworkers should be considered innocent until proven guilty. *Resources excellence.* It is important to aggressively implement policies to ensure the best possible cradle-to-grave management of resources. *Material resources excellence.* Military professionals have an obligation to ensure that all of the equipment and property they ask for is mission essential. This means that residual funds at the end of the year should not be used to purchase "nice to have" add-ons. *Human resources excellence.* We should recruit, train, promote, and retain those who can do the best job for us. *Operations excellence.* There are two kinds of operations excellence: internal and external. Internal operations excellence pertains to the way we do business internal to the Air Force, from the unit level to Headquarters Air Force. It involves respect on the unit level and a total commitment to maximizing the Air Force team effort. External operations excellence pertains to the way we treat the world around us as we conduct our operations. In peacetime we must be sensitive to the rules governing environmental pollution, for example, and in wartime we are required to obey the laws of war.

Why These Core Values?

> Core Values make the military what it is; without them, we cannot succeed. They are the values that instill confidence, earn lasting respect, and create willing followers. They are the values that anchor resolve in the most difficult situations. They are the values that buttress mental and physical courage when we enter combat. In essence, they are the three pillars of professionalism that provide the foundation for military leadership at every level. With the incredible diversity of our organization and the myriad of functions necessary to make it work efficiently and effectively, Core Values remain unifying elements for all our members. They provide a common ground and compass by which we can all measure our ideals and actions.

> —Former Secretary of the Air Force Dr. Sheila E. Widnall

There are four reasons why we recognize the Core Values and have developed a strategy to implement them. First, the Core Values tell us the price of admission to the Air Force itself. Air Force personnel—whether officer, enlisted, civil servant, or contractor—must display honesty, courage, responsibility, openness, self-respect, and humility in the face of the mission. All of us must accept accountability and practice justice, which means that all Air Force personnel must possess *integrity first.* At the same time, the individual's desires must take a backseat to Air Force service. Rules must be acknowledged and followed faithfully; other personnel must be respected as persons of fundamental worth; discipline and self-control must be in effect always; and there must be faith in the system. In other words, the price of admission to the Air Force demands that each of us place *service before self.* And it is imperative that we all seek *excellence in all we do*, whether it be product and service, resources, community, or operations excellence.

Second, the Core Values point to what is universal and unchanging in the profession of arms. Some are bothered by the fact that different branches of the service recognize different values; other people are bothered by the fact that the Air Force once recognized six values and has now reduced them to three. But they need not worry. It is impossible for three or six or nine Core Values to capture the richness that is at the heart of the profession of arms. The values are road signs inviting us to consider key features of the requirements of professional service, but they cannot hope to point out everything. By examining integrity, service, and excellence, we also eventually discover the importance of duty, honor, country, dedication, fidelity, competence, and a host of other professional requirements and attributes. The important thing is not the three road signs our leaders choose; what is important is that they have selected road signs, and it is our obligation to understand the ethical demands these road signs place upon us.

Third, the Core Values help us get a feel for the ethical climate of the organization. How successful are we in trying to live by the Core Values? Our answer to this question may not be the one we'd like to give. All of us have heard about the sensational scandals—senior officers and NCOs engaged in adulterous fraternization; the exchange of acquisition information for post–Air Force employment; issues like prisoner abuse in Iraq; or sexual assault upon any person, male or female. We all have read about these incidents and experienced the shame associated with them. But these big-ticket scandals don't just happen in a vacuum, and they aren't always caused by evil people acting on impulse. The people involved knew the difference between right and wrong, and they knew what professionalism demanded in these situations. These scandals grew out of a climate of ethical erosion. Because we believe our operating procedures or the requirements levied upon us from above are absurd, we tend to cut corners, skate by, and get over. As time goes by, these actions become easier and even habitual, until one day we can no longer distinguish between the important taskings or rules and the stupid ones. Lying on official forms becomes second nature. Placing personal interests ahead of the mission seems sensible. And we develop a "good enough for government work" mentality.

In such a climate of corrosion, the Core Values are like a slap in the face. How far have you strayed from integrity, service, and excellence? What about the folks with whom you work?

Fortunately, there is a fourth reason for recognizing the Core Values. Just as they help us evaluate the climate of our organization, they also serve as beacons to keep us on the path of correct professional conduct. The Core Values allow us to transform a climate of ethical erosion into one of ethical commitment. That is why we have developed the Core Values Strategy.

The Core Values Strategy

1. The Core Values Strategy exists independently of and does not compete with chapel programs. The Core Values Strategy attempts no explanation of the origin of the Values except to say that all of us, regardless of our religious views, must recognize their functional importance and accept them for that reason. Infusing the Core Values is necessary for successful mission accomplishment.
2. You don't need to be a commander in order to be a leader.
3. The leader of an organization is the key to its moral climate. As does the commander, so does the organization. But a commander must enlist and insist upon the help of all organizational supervisors and all assigned personnel in the effort to ensure a culture of conscience for the organization.
4. Leaders cannot just be good; they also must be sensitive to their status as role models for their people and thus avoid the appearance of improper behavior.
5. Leadership from below is at least as important as leadership from above in implementing the Core Values.
6. A culture of conscience is impossible unless civilians, officers, and enlisted personnel understand, accept, internalize, and are free to follow the Core Values.
7. To understand, accept, and internalize the Core Values, our people must be allowed and encouraged to engage in an extended dialogue about them and to explore the role of the Values at all levels of the Air Force.
8. Our first task is to fix organizations; individual character development is possible, but it is not a goal. If a culture of compromise exists in the Air Force, it is more likely to be the result of bad policies and programs than to be symptomatic of any character flaws in our people. Therefore, long before we seek to implement a character development program, we must thoroughly evaluate and, where necessary, fix our policies, processes, and procedures.

Further information on the Values can be found at the U.S. Air Force's e-Publishing website, which contains a copy of *The Little Blue Book* (www.e-publishing.af.mil/shared/media/document/AFD-070906-003.pdf). The "Our Values" section of the Air Force website (www.airforce.com/learn-about/our-values) also has a feature by which you may submit questions about the Core Values.

REQUIREMENT FOR EXEMPLARY CONDUCT

All commanding officers and others in authority in the Air Force are required by §10 USC 8583 of the U.S. Code

- to show in themselves a good example of virtue, honor, patriotism, and subordination;
- to be vigilant in inspecting the conduct of all persons who are placed under their command;
- to guard against and suppress all dissolute and immoral practices, and to correct, according to the laws and regulations of the Air Force, all persons who are guilty of them; and
- to take all necessary and proper measures, under the laws, regulations, and customs of the Air Force, to promote and safeguard the morale, the physical well-being, and the general welfare of the officers and enlisted persons under their command or charge.

PRINCIPLES OF THE AIR FORCE CODE

In addition to the official Air Force Core Values and the Requirements for Exemplary Conduct, there are other principles of the Air Force code; although unofficial, they have withstood the test of time. They express an attitude of the spirit, rarely arrived at consciously, but strongly governing the reactions of Air Force officers to all the many aspects of Air Force life.

The printed word cannot capture the code of the Air Force in its entirety, for this code is a living reality that an officer must experience to fully understand. Yet, we can identify some of the deep foundations upon which our code rests. These are criteria by which we have lived and fought and many have died; these are values we have sought to uphold, the true hallmarks of the U.S. Air Force.

Patriotism. Patriotism as practiced in the Air Force is an intelligent devotion to the interests of the United States. It rests upon the conviction that preservation of the American way of life, with its noble traditions, free institutions, and infinite promise, is both practical morality and enlightened self-interest. American patriotism is not jingoism, blindly unaware of faults of our system. Rather, our patriotism works to remove faults that exist, while remaining confident that here in America the hands and minds of humans have done their best work, that ours is a most promising road toward a goal of maximum human welfare, toward freedom, dignity, and justice for each individual, and peace for the world.

Not only in the high drama of war does patriotism invoke a readiness to make personal sacrifices, but also in routine duties, during off-duty hours, and in the thousands of small choices that confront us in daily life. Patriotism in the Air Force is intelligent devotion to the interests of the United States day by day, at work and at leisure, in war and in peace, in life and, if need be, in death.

Honor. Honor is the highest form of self-respect. You must live with your-self alone for a very substantial part of your life. It is imperative to peace of mind and soul that you respect your own character. Thus, honor is that code of conduct that springs not only from a "do unto others as you would have them do unto you" philosophy but also from a determination to do only those things about which your conscience is clear. A person of honor does not lie, steal, cheat, or take advantage of another. The question here is not whether you would be seriously hurt if someone did such things to you, but whether you could be proud of such practices. Service in the U.S. Air Force is honorable duty, and Air Force personnel seek to be counted as such.

Courage. Courage is ascendancy over fear. Note that where there is courage, there must be fear. The Air Force wants no officers who are unafraid. The perils that threaten the United States are such that a person who is without fear is either foolish or ignorant. The Air Force *does* want officers who can conquer their fears, suppress them in the interests of the nation, and coura-geously carry on despite fear. We need officers whose courage is steady and long enduring, and who can steel themselves for the long pull over the years.

Loyalty. Loyalty is the quality of sincere confidence in and support for the purposes, methods, and capabilities of one's superiors, peers, and subordinates. Loyalty is a quality that precludes sneering comment on the faults of your com-mander or complaints about the errors of your fellow airmen. It is an attitude of warm friendship toward your comrades. If you look carefully, you will find that most of your associates well deserve your loyalty.

Discipline. Discipline is the cement that binds together any military force. Without it, the Air Force would be a mob. Obeying orders to the letter—and, more important, the spirit—is the heart of discipline. Air Force officers who grudgingly, complainingly, or unenthusiastically obey orders are poorly disci-plined officers who encourage poor discipline in the airmen they are supposed to lead. Such officers do not build and maintain an effective fighting force. Almost everyone agrees that discipline is a fine thing—for everyone else. Too many of us are tempted to believe that orders and regulations were meant for the masses, but not for the Great Me. Yet we all should be aware that unless we practice discipline in our routine conduct, the stress of combat, of emergency, and of violent uncertainties can easily force us from the iron path of obedience to orders, with results disastrous to our cause and to ourselves. One thing seems certain: We will have disciplined officers of our Air Force, or we will one day have no Air Force, no nation, and no freedom.

Readiness. One of the most striking qualities of Air Force officers is their relative readiness to meet whatever tasks arise. In 1950 the Far East Air Forces transformed themselves overnight from a slow-paced occupation force to the combat arm of the United Nations over Korea. Yet two days before the entry of U.S. air forces into combat in Korea, not an officer of the Far East Air Forces had an inkling such a task would arise. Eight days later, they had destroyed the North Korean air force of more than three hundred aircraft. The nation once again called upon the Air Force for a quick reaction to the combat situation in Vietnam. Thousands of Air Force members deployed into battle in Southeast Asia to fight a bitter, difficult war. Our officers can be ready, as they were in the Gulf War. They can be well-trained, well-informed, clear-headed, and physically fit masters of their duties. We must maintain such readiness, for someday a bigger warning than Korea, Vietnam, the Gulf War, the Balkans, Afghanistan, or Iraq may suddenly ring out a dreaded alarm, calling Air Force officers to a greater trial. For this possibility, each of us must stand prepared.

Frugality. The Air Force represents a large expenditure in the U.S. budget. We are an expensive force, using extremely costly equipment and supplies. In fairness to all American taxpayers, we ought to hold this expense to the minimum consistent with national safety. This quality of frugality involves more than just these measures, however. Air Force units have sometimes found to their sorrow that the cost of wastefulness was ineffectiveness and that the price of ineffectiveness was a longer war with more lives lost. One of the dark hopes of our enemies is that the United States will bankrupt itself through its far-flung national security programs. Let us not contribute to that enemy hope.

Caution. Caution has a proper place in the code of the Air Force. The great strength we hold poised is the chief defense of the United States. Although there is no one massive, national power that threatens our survival, as did the Soviet Union during the Cold War, the situation is still dangerous and explosive. A mistake can still lead to war. Has any condition of affairs ever more strongly recommended caution? Moreover, Air Force officers operate equipment noted for its great speed and powerful effects. Recklessness often costs lives; it certainly costs millions of dollars annually. These circumstances do not justify an Air Force officer to abandon caution. A famous Air Force combat ace once said, "When I get in an airplane, I slow down."

Sense of Responsibility. Responsibility is one of the most valued characteristics in an officer. Its most frequent evidence is the execution of work that should be done whether or not you are directly charged with that work. How many times can you hear the phrase from the substandard officer: "Oh, well, it's not my headache"? But it *is* your headache, if it hurts the Air Force. The sense of responsibility found in the best of Air Force officers will not be satisfied with a job merely well done. The question is: Has the job been done to the best of my ability? If not, it isn't finished.

Teamwork. Teamwork is the means by which officers do the impossible more rapidly. Teamwork makes football champions of eleven people who, if they all insisted on being ball carriers, would gain nothing. Teamwork makes every officer's task easier, and yet the overall result is greater success. It is the nearest thing to getting something for nothing. If you insist on playing a lone hand, always want to carry the ball, and feel that associates should do their own work without bothering you, you will find that your path is rough and does not go very far. Cooperation with others is essential, as the Air Force is a team organization.

Ambition. To be ambitious is the mark of a superior officer. Every officer has a right to be ambitious and will be a better officer for it. People will tend to assess you according to the evaluation you place upon yourself. If you exert yourself to become qualified for higher positions and greater responsibilities, you will eventually become convinced that you are ready for advancement. Thus, ambition based on qualification will give you confidence and aggressiveness, qualities indispensable to superior officers. Stonewall Jackson said, "You can be what you determine to be." When Jackson used the word *determine*, he meant willingness to do the work, gain the qualifications, and seek the opportunity necessary for advancement to your goal. Ambition can and should be a driving force for self-improvement. Only one caution is relevant: set the sights of your ambition no higher than the level of your willingness to work, for the two are linked.

Adaptability. One of the qualities that Air Force officers must employ the most is adaptability, the ability to make the best of any situation. Life in the Air Force is a rough-and-tumble of widely varying conditions. Officers serve in all parts of the world, in an almost infinite number of differing conditions. Equipment and technology change frequently, new maintenance problems arise, and all things are subject to change. As an officer, you must be prepared to adapt to the conditions you may find in any assignment. Living accommodations, offices, operational facilities, the quality of superiors and subordinates—all may differ radically from your previous assignment, yet you must work with these new factors. You, not they, must adapt. Adaptability and flexibility are essential to meet such different situations.

Ascendancy of the Civil Power. It is important that you know where your loyalty lies. Under our system of government, you have a dual allegiance to the U.S. Constitution, which you swore to uphold, and to the president as commander in chief.

In this system of divided civilian supremacy—between the president and Congress—over our armed forces, you must not allow yourself to become involved in the tug-of-war between an administration and Congress. You should keep informed about politics, and it is your duty to vote, but on active duty, you should not speak publicly about your personal views on political policy. If you cannot support established policy, you should take the honorable course and resign your commission.

Relations with Civilians. One of the most important responsibilities expected of Air Force officers is the maintenance of favorable relations with civilians. This is very important when you realize that a significant part of the American public's attitude toward the Air Force is a reflection of the impression individual Air Force servicemembers make. The continued strength of the Air Force demands that American citizens hold a favorable view of the Air Force. The future of the service depends in large measure on the relations of Air Force personnel with their civilian neighbors.

All Air Force officers are public affairs officers, sources of information about the Air Force to civilians with whom they come in contact. As an Air

Force officer, if you are irresponsible for your debts, conduct yourself in an obnoxious manner in your civilian neighborhood, display yourself in a drunken condition, or ignore the laws and the customs of the community, then how much confidence would you expect a civilian observer of these antisocial behaviors to place in the Air Force you are a part of? On the other hand, if you conduct yourself as a sober, responsible citizen of the civilian community, your civilian acquaintances will tend to feel that the Air Force is an organization in which they can have confidence. Thus, by your *pattern of conduct*, you form important impressions regarding the Air Force.

Your civilian friends are interested in their Air Force. They have a right to be. It is one of their best hopes for averting war and one of their most effective instruments to win the nation's wars. The Air Force is close to their vital interests, for it is a force that stands between their homes and the enemy. As citizens and taxpayers, they have a lively and legitimate interest in the Air Force, and they frequently turn to the individual Air Force officer for information. The manner in which you meet that interest will have a decided effect on the future of the Air Force. Accordingly, each officer should welcome the opportunity to provide factual information about the Air Force to civilian friends, taking care always, of course, to avoid classified matters. If your civilian friends point with alarm to a report that an aircraft has crashed, explain how such things happen and how infrequently they happen. If civilians ask whether your quarters allowance is tax exempt, tell them yes. Also, explain to them the *overall* financial status of Air Force personnel. In other words, so far as security considerations permit, give your civilian friends the *whole* truth. Throughout, remember that the U.S. Air Force is the property of American citizens. They have built it, manned it, and paid for it. They have an awful lot of blue chips riding on its wings.

Air Force officers should seek to take a full part in the life of the civilian community. Be sociable with your neighbors. Become a member of their clubs, societies, and religious institutions. Take your share in community enterprises. In short, be a good citizen, a respected and desired neighbor. While doing so, you will not only perform a duty expected of you as an Air Force officer but also add greatly to your own enjoyment of life.

CODE OF CONDUCT IN WARTIME

The Code of Conduct for Members of the U.S. Armed Forces, which appears on the next page, was designed specifically for prisoner-of-war (POW) situations, so that POWs can survive honorably while resisting their captors' efforts to exploit them to the advantage of the enemy's cause and to the disadvantage of the POWs and the United States. However, the spirit and intent of the code are also applicable to servicemembers subject to other hostile detention; servicemembers can use the provisions of the code to avoid discrediting themselves and the United States.

Adherence to the Code of Conduct can help military personnel who are detained by unfriendly governments or groups survive with honor. Those

CODE OF CONDUCT FOR MEMBERS OF THE
U.S. ARMED FORCES

I

I am an American, fighting in the forces which guard my country and our way of life. I am prepared to give my life in their defense.

II

I will never surrender of my own free will. If in command I will never surrender the members of my command while they still have the means to resist.

III

If I am captured I will continue to resist by all means available. I will make every effort to escape and to aid others to escape. I will accept neither parole nor special favors from the enemy.

IV

If I become a prisoner of war, I will keep faith with my fellow prisoners. I will give no information or take part in any action which might be harmful to my comrades. If I am senior, I will take command. If not, I will obey the lawful orders of those appointed over me and will back them up in every way.

V

When questioned, should I become a prisoner of war, I am required to give my name, rank, service number, and date of birth. I will evade answering further questions to the utmost of my ability. I will make no oral or written statements disloyal to my country and its allies or harmful to their cause.

VI

I will never forget that I am an American, fighting for freedom, responsible for my actions, and dedicated to the principles which made my country free. I will trust in my God and in the United States of America.

Notes: The secretary of defense has directed training under the code in three main phases: a general citizenship type of orientation; a formal course for combat crews likely to fall into enemy hands, which could include training in avoiding capture, survival while evading or during captivity, resistance to giving information and making false "confessions," and escape attempts; and a specialized course for selected students, which could include prisoner interrogation, and treatment courses of definite duration designed to toughen individual students and to let them test their resistance ability and determine their physical and mental weaknesses.

Because of the special status given them under the Geneva Convention, chaplains and medical personnel are granted a degree of flexibility with regard to some of the specific provisions of the code so that they are able to perform their professional duties.

detained during peacetime must take every reasonable step to prevent exploitation of themselves or the U.S. government. If one cannot avoid exploitation completely, every step must be taken to limit exploitation as much as possible. Detained U.S. military personnel often are catalysts for their own release, based on their ability to become unattractive sources of exploitation; in other words, one who resists successfully may expect detainers to lose interest in further exploitation attempts. Detainees, or captives, very often must make their own judgments as to which actions will increase their chances of returning home with honor and dignity. Without exception, military members must say honestly that they have done their utmost in detention or captivity to resist exploitation, uphold DOD policy, the founding principles of the United States, and the highest traditions of military service.

Once in the custody of a hostile government, regardless of the circumstances that preceded the detention situation, detainees are subject to the laws of that government. Detainees should maintain military bearing and should avoid any aggressive, combative, or illegal behavior. The latter might complicate their situation, their legal status, and any efforts to negotiate a rapid release.

Capture by terrorists is generally the least predictable and structured form of captivity. The captors qualify as international criminals. The possible forms of captivity vary from spontaneous hijacking to a carefully planned kidnapping. In such captivities, hostages play a greater role in determining their own fate, since the terrorists in many instances expect or receive no rewards for providing good treatment or releasing victims unharmed. If U.S. military personnel are uncertain whether captors are genuine terrorists or surrogates of a government, they should assume that they are terrorists.

AMERICA'S COMMITMENT TO POWS
The U.S. government also has responsibilities under the Code of Conduct. The government promises
- To keep faith with you and stand by you as you fight in its defense;
- To care for your family and dependents; and
- To use every practical means to contact, support, and gain release for you and all other prisoners of war.

3

Leadership

Leadership is the art of influencing and directing people to accomplish the mission. Management is the manner in which one uses both human and material resources to achieve objectives. As an Air Force officer, you should be aware of your responsibility as a leader and manager. British Field Marshal William Slim, who led troops in both world wars, made a clear distinction between the terms:

> There is a difference between leadership and management. The leader and the men who follow him represent one of the oldest, most natural, and most effective of all human relationships. The manager and those he manages are a later product with neither so romantic, nor so inspiring a history. Leadership is of the spirit, compounded of personality and vision—its practice is an art. Management is of the mind, more a matter of accurate calculation, statistics, methods, timetables, and routine—its practice is a science. Managers are necessary; leaders are essential.

In essence, you lead people, and you manage things. The Air Force needs people who can do both. The requirement is for the proper division of attention between the two, with the proportion dependent on the situation.

Leadership is essential to a successful officer. When considering other attributes of successful officers, there are specific exceptions to all but leadership. Ulysses S. Grant rarely wore his uniform properly and sometimes used liquor to excess, yet he knew how to win a war. Robert E. Lee had every desirable attribute of an officer, but of all his military attributes, that which shone brightest was leadership. Renowned Air Force officers such as Henry "Hap" Arnold, Hoyt Vandenberg, and Curtis LeMay were men of many talents, but their outstanding talent was leadership.

A young officer should recognize that all officers are leaders, not just those in command positions. Leading is the most exciting and interesting experience the service can offer. The Air Force does not expect that every officer will equal Arnold, Vandenberg, or LeMay, but who can tell? Some writers have described the good, common, garden-variety leaders as officers who can inculcate those under them with knowledge of their tasks and imbue them with the spirit to do them well. That goal is not impossible for any airman. With application, a person who meets the standards for commissioned officers can be that sort of good leader.

A *leader* is one fitted by force of ideas, character, or genius or by strength of will or administrative ability to arouse, incite, and direct individuals in conduct and achievement.

Leadership means the art of imposing one's will upon others in such a manner as to command their respect, their confidence, and their wholehearted cooperation. The core of the definition is that leaders must impose their will on others, who must do what their leaders direct them to do.

Martinets accomplish this goal by simple reliance upon their positions of authority and their power of punishment. Leaders accomplish it through the quality of leadership the Air Force seeks. In the case of martinets, the people commanded do what the martinets direct them to do, but often in a sullen and grudging manner. In the case of leaders, the people carry out directions with enthusiasm, contributing their own ingenuity and drive to the task at hand. Many of the key concepts of leadership are discussed in Air Force doctrine. A good starting point is Air Force Doctrine Document (AFDD) 1-1, *Leadership and Force Development*. You can find this doctrine publication and other Air Force doctrine documents at www.au.af.mil/au/lemay/main.htm.

THE AIR FORCE LEADERSHIP CONCEPT

The Air Force concept of leadership encompasses two fundamental elements: the mission and the people. All facets of Air Force leadership should support these two basic elements.

The Mission. The primary task of a military organization is to perform its mission. This is paramount, and everything else must be subordinate to this objective. As a leader, your primary responsibility is to lead people to carry out the unit's mission successfully. Most missions involve many tasks that a unit must complete if it is to fulfill its responsibilities. Commanders set priorities for the mission's various components, but all officers, as leaders, support their commanders to accomplish their units' missions. General LeMay emphasized, "No matter how well you apply the art of leadership, no matter how strong your unit or how high the morale of your men, if your leadership is not directed completely toward the mission, your leadership has failed." Yet, you must never forget the importance of the unit's personnel.

The People. People perform the mission. They are the heart of the organization, and without their support, a unit will fail. You cannot be totally successful at getting the most out of people without first knowing their capabilities and what motivates them. Your responsibilities also include the care and support of your unit's personnel. To be a successful leader, you must continually ensure that you promptly and properly meet the needs of the people in your unit.

Clearly, the two "simple" parts of the leadership concept—mission and people—are actually two very complicated elements. Finally, a leader ensures the people behind the members, their families, are equally well cared for, too. Successful leaders who effectively deal with this complex concept have certain characteristics or traits.

LEADERSHIP TRAITS

There is a long list of qualities desirable in a leader. Although these characteristics are expected of all members of the military profession, six traits are vital to Air Force leaders: integrity, loyalty, commitment, energy, decisiveness, and selflessness.

Integrity. Integrity is a total commitment to the highest personal and professional standards. As a leader, you must be honest and fair. Integrity means establishing a set of values and adhering to those values. Air Force Chief of Staff General Charles Gabriel said, "Integrity is the fundamental premise of military service in a free society. Without integrity, the moral pillars of our military strength—public trust and self-respect—are lost."

Loyalty. Loyalty includes faithfulness to superiors, peers, and subordinates. You must first display an unquestionable sense of loyalty before you can expect members of your unit to be loyal. General George Patton highlighted the importance of loyalty when he said, "There is a great deal of talk about loyalty from the bottom to the top. Loyalty from the top down is even more necessary and much less prevalent."

Commitment. Commitment means complete devotion to duty. As a leader, you must demonstrate total dedication to the United States, the Air Force, and your unit. Plato said, "Man was not born for himself alone, but for his country." Dedicated service is the hallmark of the military leader.

Energy. Energy is an enthusiasm and drive to take the initiative. Throughout history, successful leaders have demonstrated the importance of mental and physical energy. You must approach assigned tasks aggressively. Your preparation should include physical and mental conditioning that will enable you to look and act the part. Once a course of action is determined, you must have the perseverance and stamina to stay on course until the job is completed.

Decisiveness. Decisiveness is a willingness to act. As a leader, you must have the self-confidence to make timely decisions. You must then effectively communicate the decisions to your unit. British admiral Sir Roger Keyes emphasized that "in all operations a moment arrives when brave decisions have to be made if an enterprise is to be carried through." Of course, decisiveness includes the willingness to accept responsibility. You are always accountable—when things go right and when things go wrong.

Selflessness. Selflessness requires sacrificing personal requirements for a greater cause. You must think of performing the mission and caring for the welfare of the men and women in your organization. As an Air Force leader, you cannot place your own comfort or convenience before the mission or the people. Willingness to sacrifice is intrinsic to military service. Selflessness also includes the courage to face and overcome difficulties. Although courage is often thought of as an unselfish willingness to confront physical dangers, equally important—and more likely to be tested on a daily basis—is the moral courage you need to make difficult decisions. General of the Army Douglas MacArthur said, "No nation can safely trust its martial honor to leaders who do not maintain the universal code which distinguishes those things that are right and those things that are wrong." It requires courage and strength of character to confront a tough situation head-on rather than avoid it by passing the buck to someone else.

These traits are essential to effective leadership. Developing these characteristics will improve your ability to employ the principles of leadership.

LEADERSHIP PRINCIPLES

Leadership principles are guidelines that have been tested and proven over the years by successful leaders. The most important of these principles are discussed below. Although some aspects of these principles apply only to commanders, most are universally applicable to all officers. Not all officers are commanders, but all are leaders.

Know Yourself. Knowing your own strengths and weaknesses is important to successful leadership. You, the leader, must recognize your personal capabilities and limitations. Former Chief Master Sergeant of the Air Force Robert Gaylor put it this way: "Sure, everyone wants to be an effective leader, whether it be in the Air Force or in the community. You can and will be if you identify your strengths, capitalize on them, and consciously strive to reduce and minimize the times you apply your style inappropriately."

Know Your Job. People will follow you if you are a competent person who has the knowledge needed to complete the mission successfully. You should have a broad view of your unit's mission, and you must make sure all members of your unit understand how their jobs relate to mission accomplishment.

Between World War I and World War II, the United States Army Air Corps was fortunate to have men like General Arnold and General Carl Spaatz. These men learned their jobs and knew how they could enhance the Air Corps mission. Their preparation and vision paid substantial dividends when they were charged with building a force to fight and win the air battles of World War II.

Just as important as your own competence is ensuring that assigned people know their responsibilities. Former Chairman of the Joint Chiefs of Staff General Maxwell Taylor stated, "One expects a military leader to demonstrate in his daily performance a thorough knowledge of his own job and further an ability to train his subordinates in their duties and thereafter to supervise and evaluate their work."

Set the Example. You must help set the standard for professional competence in your unit. People will emulate your standards of personal conduct and appearance. They will observe your negative characteristics as well as your positive ones. If you are arrogant or domineering, you will get no respect, only resentment. If you violate basic standards of morality, you will invariably end up in a compromising situation. If you drink excessively or abuse drugs, you send a dangerous message: "I cannot control myself; how can I control you?" Lack of self-discipline in a leader destroys the unit's cohesion and, ultimately, impairs its ability to perform the mission.

Self-discipline also pertains to physical fitness. When you are in good physical condition, you are better prepared for any assigned mission. Setting the right example includes supporting your unit's fitness program and enforcing Air Force fitness standards. As a military leader, you must be a positive example of professional conduct, appearance, and physical conditioning. As General Patton once remarked, "You are always on parade."

Care for People. General of the Army George Marshall believed, "A decent regard for the rights and feelings of others is essential to leadership." Take care of the people. Find out what their requirements are and be sensitive to human needs. Are the people housed adequately? Are they well fed? Are there personal problems with which they need help? When people are worried about these conditions, they cannot focus their full attention on their jobs, and the mission will suffer. If people believe they are cared for as well as circumstances will permit, you, as leader, are in a position to earn their confidence, respect, and loyalty.

Communicate. Information should flow continuously throughout the organization. Former Air Force Chief of Staff General Thomas White believed, "Information is the essential link between wise leadership and purposeful action." Communication is a two-way process. Only as an informed leader will you be able to evaluate realistically your unit's progress toward mission accomplishment. You must listen to what your people have to say and always look for the good ideas that can flow up the chain. It is also key to emphasize the importance of feedback. The worker who is well informed concerning the quality of the work and its importance to the mission will be more effective and highly motivated. It is your job to keep all channels open. The more senior you become, the more listening skills will be required.

Educate and Train. People should be properly educated and trained to do their jobs. Professional military education, technical training courses, and on-the-job training are formal means by which Air Force personnel are prepared. Informal training, practice, and personal experience at the unit level are crucial reinforcements to formal training. General MacArthur observed, "In no other profession are the penalties for employing untrained personnel so appalling or so irrevocable as in the military."

Equip. It is also your responsibility to ensure that your subordinates are equipped properly. Just as an aircrew should never be expected to engage in combat without a well-armed aircraft, personnel should not be sent ill-equipped to the office, shop, or flight line. Your leadership responsibilities include identifying needs, securing funds, and then obtaining the necessary weapons, tools, and equipment.

Motivate. Your greatest challenge is motivating subordinates to achieve the high standards set for them. Motivation is the moving force behind successful leadership. In fact, the ability to generate enthusiasm about the mission may be the single most important factor in leadership. Recognition of the efforts people put forth is one positive way in which motivation toward mission accomplishment pays dividends. When you publicly applaud the efforts of unit personnel, you build a cohesive organization that will accomplish the mission.

To motivate people, you must understand their needs and work to align these needs with unit requirements. Most people will work for an organization that they know cares about them, and one in whose mission they believe. Remember, the most powerful form of lasting motivation is self-motivation. One of your goals as a leader should be to provide an environment that fosters and rewards self-motivation.

Accept Your Responsibility. General LeMay was once asked to provide a one-word definition of leadership. After some thought, he replied, "If I had to come up with one word to define leadership, I would say *responsibility*." As a leader, you are responsible for performing the unit's mission. If you fail, you are accountable for the consequences. Any unwillingness to accept responsibility for failure destroys your credibility as a leader and breaks the bond of respect and loyalty. Accountability also includes the requirement for discipline within a unit. A leader should reward a job well done and punish those who fail to meet their responsibilities or established standards. The former is easy and enjoyable; the latter is much more difficult, but equally necessary. George Washington observed, "Discipline is the soul of an army. It makes small numbers formidable, procures success to the weak, and esteem to all."

Develop Teamwork. As a leader, you must mold a collection of individual performers into a cohesive team that works together to accomplish the mission. The unit's mission will suffer if each person in your organization is doing his or her own thing. As the leader, you should know how the various functions within the unit fit together and how they must work in harmony. You should create and maintain an atmosphere of teamwork and cooperation to meet mission demands. Teamwork comes when people are willing to put the unit's mission before all else.

Be Flexible. There is no one perfect leadership style. Rather, the most effective style is the one that the leader tailors to the mission, the people, and the environment. You should carefully consider the environment in which you work. Leadership methods that worked in one situation with one group may not work with the same group in a different environment. Consider the squadron that is permanently based in the United States but deploys overseas for an extended period of temporary duty. Billeting or food service difficulties, equipment or parts shortages, family separation problems, challenging weather conditions, hostile local populations, or other problems may occur. Any of these situations creates an entirely new environment with which you must cope. As a unit leader, you must alter your leadership behavior, as necessary, to accommodate changes in the environment of the given mission. Be sensitive to your surroundings.

Successful military leaders adapt their leadership styles to meet mission demands and use approaches that capitalize on their strengths. For example, if you are able to communicate effectively with people on an individual basis but are uncomfortable when speaking to large groups, then use personal conferences as much as possible. If you write well, take advantage of this skill by writing letters of appreciation or using other forms of correspondence. If you are a good athlete, organize and participate in unit sports activities.

In addition to capitalizing on your strengths and minimizing your weaknesses, your style of leadership must correspond to the people's job knowledge. When they lack sufficient knowledge to do the job at hand, you must spend much of your time directing their efforts to accomplish the mission.

On the other hand, if people have the requisite training or experience, you are not required to direct their every action and should not do so. Still, you must motivate them to complete the task. Work with them, but keep your eye on the objective.

Occasionally, you may discover that people are only moderately motivated to do a job they are capable of completing. In such circumstances, let them participate in planning the task. Motivate them by maintaining a job-related working relationship. Their capabilities will do the rest.

When the people have extensive experience and are enthusiastic about the task, you should provide them greater freedom to complete it the way they choose. Nevertheless, you, as the leader, are still ultimately responsible for the mission, so stay informed of the group's progress.

LEADERSHIP PREPARATION

Now that we have examined some of the basics of Air Force leadership, here is how you can best prepare yourself to lead:

Think about Leadership. What would you do in a given situation, and why? If leadership placed you in charge of your work unit tomorrow, how would you act? Remember the concepts, traits, and principles of Air Force leadership.

Observe Leaders in Action. How does your boss handle a given situation? Why did a particular action succeed or fail? How do your wing commander, squadron commander, first sergeant, and supervisor lead?

Study Leadership and the Profession of Arms. The military has a long tradition of leadership. Read about the successful leaders in our history and how they led. Alfred Thayer Mahan wrote, "The study of history lies at the foundation of all sound military conclusions and practice." You must have detailed professional knowledge to develop perspective and to meet the challenges of the future.

Practice Leadership. Look for opportunities to exercise leadership. It can be as simple as taking the initiative and leading one person to complete a task. Learn from your efforts, seek feedback, and evaluate your efforts. Always lead by positive example. Do not confuse leadership with management. Leadership is about people; management is about things.

The United States was fortunate that between the two world wars, several members of its military services prepared themselves to be leaders. Their preparation resulted in strong leadership during some of the most crucial years in our history. The Air Force has inherited a legacy of strong, dynamic leadership from the early air pioneers. As one of today's leaders, you must continue this tradition of excellence.

The Air Force depends on positive, effective leaders at all levels to perform the mission. Leadership is not the private domain or responsibility of senior officers. Every member of the Air Force must prepare for a responsibility like this one. General LeMay's words continue to serve us well: "I'm firmly convinced that leaders are not born; they're educated, trained, and made, as in every other profession." To ensure a strong, ready Air Force, we must always remain dedicated to this process.

4

Responsibilities of Command

To most junior officers of the Air Force, nothing seems more remote from current or prospective duties than does command of an Air Force unit. Command is indeed a rare assignment for Air Force officers of any grade. The officer strength of the Air Force is many times the number of Air Force units available to command, hence the rarity of command jobs. Yet consider another aspect of command. Command is not a function exercised solely by one officer, such as the squadron commander. The squadron commander cannot exercise command other than through the officers and noncommissioned officers of the squadron. Each officer of the squadron not only is subject to command, but also helps exercise command. Thus, every officer participates in the function of command. For this reason, all officers, whatever their grades, ranks, or assignments, should understand the basic elements and objectives of the command function. They are part of the command operation, and it is one of their most important responsibilities. The command function has to do with the mission of the unit, with training, discipline, supply, and morale. How could an officer not be involved in these factors? All officers should appreciate the responsibilities of their unit commanders to better comprehend the reasons for their commanders' decisions. One of the hallmarks of a professional is the ability to appreciate the responsibilities of other members of the team and to assist in the discharge of those responsibilities.

During the Cold War, the Air Force became accustomed to operating from large, fixed bases with extensive infrastructure. Missions became almost inflexible, operations routine; leadership gave way to management. Foreign officers occasionally voiced their contempt of American officers as clerks, not officers—clerks whose expertise was confined to knowing the applicable regulation or standing operating procedure. The Korean and Vietnam wars temporarily brought us back to the timeless nature of all wars—confusion, unpredictability, uncertainty, and unreliability. But these "limited wars" and contingency operations were largely dismissed as aberrations and sideshows. For those who are still caught up in the Cold War mentality, much of this chapter may seem anachronistic. For those, however, who have focused on Grenada, Panama, the Gulf, Haiti, the Balkans, Afghanistan, and Iraq the prospects of assuming command and operating semiautonomously—modern communications notwithstanding—may seem more descriptive of the present and the future than of the past. Commanders may find themselves left to their own resources and forced to act without the enormous "tail" that has defined the Air Force for much of its independent existence. And wise young officers will prepare themselves to operate in this uncertain, changing environment.

ASSUMPTION OF A COMMAND POSITION

Almost every Air Force officer must anticipate being assigned without warning to assume command of an Air Force unit. By U.S. law, chaplains may not command, and medical corps officers may command only medical units. All other officers are eligible to command. This opportunity may arise as a result of combatlike situations, or less dramatically, a sudden need to shift personnel. As an Air Force officer in such a situation, you may find that the command position given is a larger one than normally associated with your grade. Therefore, you should develop the habit of getting to know the problems of command of your unit whenever you assume any new assignment. Commanders should learn the problems of command of the next higher unit.

Assumption of Command in Combat. During operations in a hostile environment, your superior may become a casualty. If you are the next senior officer down the chain of command, your immediate duty is to take over the responsibility of your senior. This need could result from any one of several situations, such as a flight leader's plane going down, the commander of a security forces squadron being struck by hostile gunfire on the ground, or the commander of a maintenance squadron becoming ill. In any case, you, as the next in command, must act at once to ensure that the unit continues to perform its mission. Although such assumption of command under conditions of combat may prove to be only a temporary expedient, you must never allow a break in the continuity of command during combat. Like almost every other officer, you must be prepared to step in and take over when necessary.

Assumption of Command Under Conditions Other than Combat. Whenever the commander of an Air Force unit is detached from command of the organization for any reason, the next senior officer present for duty automatically assumes the command function, pending orders from higher authority. In such a situation, the officer assuming the command function shoulders the responsibility and the authority previously held by the officer replaced. Such a situation is, of course, extremely rare.

Transfer of Responsibilities. Other than under conditions of combat, officers assuming command take over all standing orders, the unit fund, all government property pertaining to the unit, and the organization's records. The transfer of these responsibilities, especially for property and funds, should proceed in a careful and thorough manner, with the outgoing and the incoming commanders reaching jointly acceptable conclusions. As the new commander, you should decline to accept responsibility until you have satisfied yourself that the property, the funds, and the records of the unit are in an understandable and proper order.

Do Not Hasten to Change Things. Sometimes officers assuming command of an Air Force unit are overly quick to disrupt standing operating procedures (SOPs), to radically modify policies the unit personnel have become familiar with, and generally to create confusion. As the new commander, you should allow a reasonable period of time to study the organization, the personnel, and the practices that preceded your command before launching into major changes.

THE SQUADRON COMMANDER

The commander is responsible for the execution of all activities pertaining to the unit, including the successful accomplishment of all missions assigned in either training or war. Commanders are responsible in every way for all that their organizations do or fail to do.

To a greater degree than commanders at higher levels, squadron commanders must be in intimate touch with their people and know their individual characteristics and capacities, their degree of training, their morale, and their discipline. They must provide for the welfare of their people under all conditions. In training, they must prepare their own people to succeed despite the most rigorous hardships. In war or even in training, they must save them from all unnecessary trials to preserve their stamina. The conditions airmen experience in their own squadrons determine their opinions of the Air Force as a whole.

There are several duties commanders cannot decentralize, such as responsibility for organization property, responsibility for the unit fund, nonjudicial punishment under Article 15 of the Uniform Code of Military Justice (UCMJ), and the authentication of many records.

Use of Subordinate Leaders. Highly successful commanders are adept at obtaining maximum efficiency from subordinate leaders. These subordinates' responsibilities should be clearly defined so that each may proceed with confidence.

Events that depart from routine must be disclosed to subordinate leaders in time to permit them to make their plans and prepare to do their parts. A meeting may be held at which the requirement is discussed. Thought should be given to the manner of presenting the project before the group assembles. At the assembly, the commander should state the mission, with its time and place of execution. Opportunity to ask questions should be provided. At the end of the meeting, the commander will probably have announced the decision and plan for the execution of a mission for which the commander alone is responsible.

Meetings of the key officers of a squadron should be held frequently. This is an opportunity for the commander to announce new work to be undertaken, specific small tasks to be completed in anticipation of a later action, and inspections and other matters that affect the squadron as a whole. Opportunity to make suggestions for improvement in conditions should be extended. A healthy reaction is obtained by asking opinions as to matters of general concern and interest. These meetings should be informal and brief. They provide an opportunity for the commander to obtain the cooperation of all subordinate leaders, because they will know exactly what is wanted.

Understudies and Replacements. The services of key persons are often lost to an organization with surprising suddenness. The Air Force must maintain itself so that any officer, noncommissioned officer, or specialist may be immediately replaced without adversely affecting the efficiency of the unit. The training of understudies must be continuous.

The best people must convince themselves that they will receive consideration for appointment to higher responsibility or position if they prepare themselves for the task. Some regular procedure must be followed for the training of ambitious airmen who wish to demonstrate their capacity for advancement. As opportunities arise, airmen should be given a chance to exercise leadership or control of others to provide a means of further development. When this is done, the selection of the best people for advancement or for replacements is made more likely.

Preparations to Be Relieved of Command. The conditions of military service often result in a limited tenure of command by individual officers. Although one should approach each current duty as if it would continue for a lifetime, commanders know well that one day they must turn their units over to their reliefs.

The efficiency of commanders can be better judged after their relief from command. When command is relinquished, it should be clean, with no hidden skeletons, no loose ends to confound a successor unfamiliar with the problems. Property should be in good condition, with no shortages. All required entries should be made in official records, and the unit fund should be built up and its exact status made entirely clear.

It would seem to be a questionable practice for an officer about to be relieved to embark upon a program of expenditure of the unit fund. The successor may have ideas on these matters and be prevented from carrying them into execution.

The new commander should not be embarrassed by requests that are just within permissible practices. It is an imposition to ask a new commander to receipt for overages or shortages, and if such request is made, it should be refused. The successor should not be asked to complete transactions that should be finished by the officer being relieved.

It is reprehensible to criticize the predecessor in command. Even in those few instances when it may be well deserved, it should be strictly avoided. But the officer being relieved can eliminate much of the chance of such criticism by being certain to complete every required transaction, to inform the successor of every helpful bit of information (not forgetting the special desires and requirements of the immediate commander), and finally, to transmit to the new commander an organization to be proud of.

THE SOUND OF COMBAT

Air Force officers who have seen the sights and heard the sounds of battle understand the reactions of untried Air Force officers. Most experienced officers state that inexperienced officers show more bravery, more unconcern for enemy fire than do those who have sweated through more deadly circumstances on a number of earlier occasions.

Combat is too often described as being only the event of deadly encounters between two adversaries. Not so. Combat is more often the tiresome struggle to supply aviation materiel, such as fuel, at the proper time and place in the combat zone. Combat is frequently the effort to produce sanitary water and food in an area where it is almost impossible to do so; to build revetments around aircraft; to operate a decent eating facility in indecent surroundings; to furnish needed parts for inoperable aircraft when the parts are many miles away. In today's warfare, especially in unconventional warfare, frustration can build because of the near impossibility of distinguishing friend from foe or the seeming ingratitude or hostility of the local population. Combat is doing the best you can under the circumstances. It is a sharp realization that your life or death or someone else's hangs in the balance between your performance and that of your enemy.

Air Force officers need not be unduly afraid of combat, provided they have done their best to prepare themselves professionally, physically, emotionally, and spiritually for the test.

IMPORTANCE OF THE MILITARY MISSION

In the exercise of command, the first necessity is to perform the mission. Orders may assign the mission. If so, just go ahead and do it. Occasionally, the assignment is general with an overall objective. You may then need to select and adopt successive missions, the sum of which will accomplish the requirement. Successful commanders are the ones who accomplish their missions on time, with minimal expenditures of personnel and other resources, and in a professional manner.

TRAINING

Purpose of Military Training. The ultimate purpose of all military training is the assurance of victory in war. We want a fighting Air Force composed of officers and enlisted people who can do their complex jobs better than the enemy. If we train well, the task of winning will require far less time than that which will be necessary if we train poorly.

One of the outstanding lessons derived from experiences in World War II, Korea, Vietnam, the Gulf War, and the wars in Afghanistan and Iraq is that the state of training of units is the governing factor determining the combat capability of a military unit. Air Force equipment in general is excellent in quality and adequate in quantity. Air Force morale is high. Supply and maintenance standards are superior. Discipline is commendable. Leadership, from the top down to the lowest unit, is superb. In training, however, lapses may be noted. Every commander should recognize this: *Training is never good enough; improvement is always possible.* Training is a round-the-clock function for the unit. A great deal of it may seem dull and tiresome. Nonetheless, it must be accomplished thoroughly, for it pays off in lives saved and in missions accomplished.

War also points up the tremendous importance of the less dramatic aspects of Air Force training. Officers controlling support activities, such as the supply of munitions and aviation fuel, actually hold the throttle of the Air Force. It is of critical importance that officers commanding support organizations realize the controlling nature of their units' performance and bring those units to the highest possible state of readiness and performance. Aircrews cannot fly without fuel, ammunition, spare parts, operable weapons, well-maintained air bases, and in-commission aircraft. The Air Force is a chain made of many links, only one of which is the operating combat force. Air depots, engineers, researchers, administrators, hospital staffs, maintenance crews, tactical control parties, intelligence agencies—all of these and many more are absolutely indispensable links in the chain of airpower. Everyone has a crucial job to do; everyone must be highly trained to do it.

Joint Training. Most commanders of combat units will sooner or later find their units engaged in some form of joint training with the Army, Navy, or Marine Corps. In the past, there was too little emphasis given to joint training. This attitude stemmed in part from a false belief that the Air Force could win wars alone, that joint training was superfluous. Many felt that there was already too much to be accomplished in the training program without adding joint training. If any single fact stood out in Korea, Vietnam, and again in the Gulf War, it was the need for more and better joint training. The Air Force, Army, Marines, and Navy fight in close coordination. Each depends upon the others.

For the unit commander, the point is this: Wars are won by teamwork among the services. Your unit not only must want to take part in this teamwork, but also must be well trained in joint operations. Mere willingness to cooperate in an emergency will never take the place of practiced know-how. It would be a sickening thing to think that Americans were dying because of a low state of joint training of *your* unit; nor would you find it any solace to reflect that such Americans were in the Army, the Navy, or the Marines rather than in the Air Force.

THE CONDUCT OF INSTRUCTION
Every commander has responsibilities for the conduct of instruction. Airmen will have received instruction in their specialties, through the formal training

processes of the Air Force. But instruction never ceases. All airmen should be brought to a higher state of competence as rapidly as possible, particularly in respect to the specific tasks they must perform in their unit of assignment. Commanders must engage themselves in this process, either through direct participation or through supervision of the noncommissioned instructors who perform the training tasks.

Instruction includes explanation, demonstration, practice, and correction. It is the responsibility of all officers to ensure that within their areas of responsibility instruction is carried on constantly and well. They cannot safely assume that this will be automatically accomplished by noncommissioned officers or that the formal training of airmen is sufficient. In the Air Force, change is constant, and almost every change requires new instruction of airmen. This is a prime responsibility of command.

LOGISTICS

The United States has been lavish with money and effort to make our armed forces the best equipped and maintained. Most individuals understand this point clearly when they consider outstanding single items. The total number of separate items is infinite, and the cost is prodigious. The job of commanders is to obtain the items allowed for their units, see that they are issued to their people, and see that they are maintained in top-notch condition.

Supply officers can provide all the necessary information on what is authorized. The unit commander, however, must supply the energy, care, and attention to detail that are necessary to attain the required results. Unit commanders must find out the equipment authorized for their units, and then ensure that it is obtained, distributed, inspected, and maintained, always ready for use.

Supply in the United States. Unit commanders constantly face supply problems. The supply procedures require considerable bookkeeping and responsibility. It cannot be otherwise. The whole problem revolves around accomplishing two primary objectives: first, to equip the unit with the items needed; and second, to keep every item of equipment in serviceable condition.

Supply in the Field. As soon as a unit enters field conditions, it faces a different sort of supply problem. But if any officers conclude that their responsibility has been left behind, they are in for a rude awakening. An officer is responsible for seeing that the enlisted personnel are provided with the items of equipment they require, in combat especially. The penalty for carelessness or inefficiency may be to do without, which in combat may mean the difference between life and death, victory and defeat.

Even if a unit reaches an overseas area fully equipped, at once things will happen that must be handled promptly. People are careless and lose things. Property is pilfered. Sympathetic American airmen may be tempted to give clothing, food, and other necessities to poverty-stricken locals. The airmen may feel that they can obtain replenishment or have more equipment than they will need. There is even the temptation to sell articles to locals. In any event, the commander is responsible for having personnel of the unit fully equipped. Impressing personnel with the importance of jealously guarding their equipment will help. Frequent property checks will also reduce losses and inform the commander of the unit's situation.

Wear and tear is a most difficult problem, especially in combat zones. The unit commander must reduce waste and present the needs in time for the supply or repair machinery to respond.

The problems of supply of food, ammunition, fuel, and clothing are with unit commanders day and night. Commanders must provide for these problems and plan for them. In combat, supply lines are lifelines. Most items are in short supply. Squadrons unaccustomed to frugality with supplies pay for this failing in inconvenience, inefficiency, and sometimes lives.

Importance of Maintenance. In combat, any failure to maintain equipment in safe and operable condition may be disastrous. A gun that fails to fire may result in loss of life. Missiles or bombs that malfunction can waste the effort and increase the risk involved in a mission. A landing gear that is improperly maintained will be subject to unnecessary breakage and wear. It may fail in a crucial moment. Continual training and inspection are necessary. Adequate maintenance will reduce the necessity for returning vast quantities of supplies to the United States for extensive overhaul. Unit commanders, who are in direct charge of the equipment and the people who use it, must understand the whole problem, see the need for maintenance, and acquaint themselves with the condition of their equipment through unremitting inspections and corrective action. Maintenance may mean the difference between success and failure.

MILITARY SECURITY

There is always the problem of security. Personnel must be ready to detect attack from the air or the ground, on and off military installations. The repeated sudden attacks in Afghanistan and Iraq are sufficient examples of the necessity for vigilance. Security in combatlike situations, such as those that have proliferated since the end of the Cold War, pose many hazards, especially if airmen are complacent. Teach your people thoroughly the difficult art of security. The Royal Air Force concept that all airmen are soldiers first has its merits.

UNIT ADMINISTRATION

Administration begins in the squadron. That is where the airmen work and where changes in their status take place. That is where they are disciplined and trained to become efficient, high-spirited fighting teams. The entire process of administering their affairs depends in large measure upon the initial action of the commander. If that first action by the commander and his staff is speedy and accurate, the administrative process may then become a smooth-running operation of which the tactical commander is scarcely conscious.

Command of a unit includes a diversified responsibility over several different but interdependent phases of operation: organization, morale, discipline, training to develop battle efficiency, security, administration, and supply. The breakdown of one will have an injurious effect upon the others. Balance is required.

Classification and Assignment. The Air Force has an excellent classification system that identifies special skills possessed by airmen. After classification, people are assigned to units or other assignments in accordance with these skills. This knowledge is of inestimable value, because the use of skills reduces the training burden. Classification follows airmen wherever they go.

The Air Force is vitally interested in placing all members where they can best use their talents. In so doing, we use the training of our industry, our schools, and our colleges. Don't be guilty of hiding an experienced computer expert or an airplane mechanic.

TAKING CARE OF THE TROOPS

Next to the mission, welfare of the troops, especially in combat situations, is a leader's most important responsibility because of its effect on their morale and their consequent ability to perform the mission. Leaders must interest themselves in all matters affecting the welfare of their people, including food, adequate clothing and equipment, health and sanitation, recreation and entertainment, career guidance, and personal problems. This responsibility involves planning, procuring and distributing necessary supplies, training, frequent inspections, and corrective measures, which may include disciplinary action.

Consideration and, when possible, help must be given in dealing with personal problems. Young people away from home for the first time will most likely need unsolicited advice.

The spirit behind the leader's interest must be one of genuine helpfulness and thoughtfulness. In matters involving the proper care of government property, protection of health, and fitness of the airmen to perform assigned duties, stern measures should be taken, if necessary.

MORALE

Personal Appearance and Morale. The service prescribes the uniform to improve the appearance and standing of the wearer. It will do so only to the extent that it is clean, pressed, and worn properly. Airmen cannot feel pride in their service unless they look the part of good airmen.

Health as an Aid to Morale. Commanders are responsible for the health and physical well-being of the members of their units. In this responsibility, they are assisted by the medical officers. Medical officers serve as staff officers and advisors of the commanders in all matters that pertain to the care of the sick and wounded and the evacuation of the wounded, as well as in matters of sanitation or hygiene, all in addition to their professional duties within medical facilities serving the needs of the armed forces. There is nothing so destructive to the morale of service personnel as the knowledge or even the suspicion that the sick or wounded are being inadequately attended. In the execution of normal command functions, officers of the Air Force have, in the medical officers, a material source of assistance upon which they may draw.

Athletics and Morale. Provision for athletics is an important factor in the physical fitness of the individual airman and in maintaining high morale. In addition to the mandated Air Force Fitness Program, commanders must sponsor and develop athletic facilities. For the most part, airmen are young, strong, and energetic. They need constructive outlets for their energies. A variety of fitness and athletic facilities should be available to meet the varying preferences of members of the unit. The use of the facilities should be encouraged.

Religion and Morale. Freedom of religion and of religious belief is one of the most important principles in our national philosophy. This principle must be extended to the airman and proper respect extended to religious convictions. The religious and spiritual welfare of the members of a command is an important factor in the development of individual pride, morale, and self-respect, all essential to a military organization. Unfortunately, the Air Force environment in some instances leaves a little to be desired. There is a relation between morals and morale, just as there is a relation between fair and just treatment and morale, or cleanliness and morale. Organization commanders who are mindful of the religious and spiritual needs of their people will be able to make a strong appeal to the better instincts of all.

The Chaplain. Chaplains are charged with religious responsibility and a host of other duties. Although they conduct religious worship services and attend to baptisms, marriages, and funerals, their most important work may lie in the close, personal contacts they make throughout a command. Unless they receive the cooperation of commanders, their work cannot possibly achieve the utmost. The tasks of chaplains can be difficult ones. A word of suggestion to a chaplain as to a needed service for an individual will often result in the solution of a baffling problem. A word of encouragement to the chaplains to let them know their services are recognized and valued will stimulate further effort. Commanders who cooperate with the chaplains and seek to improve the spiritual, religious, and moral standards of their units will reap valuable dividends for their efforts.

Morale, Welfare, Recreation, and Services. The morale, welfare, recreation, and services officer leads the recreational services, including voluntary athletics. Close coordination and support should be developed between commanders and the services officer. The overall mission of the services officer is to provide an attractive, wholesome off-duty environment for personnel. Such a program should have a direct effect upon reenlistment rates, which are a matter of direct continual concern to commanders. Commanders of small units are their own services officers. They should be thoroughly familiar with facilities available for their use and make it possible for their people to make use of them to the fullest degree.

Athletic programs that encourage maximum participation by individuals constitute the heart of all recreational activities. The recreation center should be the hub around which many activities of interest to airmen revolve.

Commanders cannot take services programs for granted, especially during the current time of fiscal austerity; for example, the Air Force has closed many auto hobby shops.

The goal is to increase the degree of satisfaction experienced by all military personnel. The effect should be that airmen find interesting, constructive leisure activities on their bases, rather than seek every opportunity to visit nearby civilian communities.

Use of the Organization Fund. Through nonappropriated fund channels, commanders receive allotments of funds applicable to units on their bases for improving morale. Squadron commanders can apply for an allocation from this fund for specific morale-building activities of the squadron. A typical use of such a fund allocation would be to hold a squadron picnic or party. The commander can fund any worthwhile, enjoyable entertainment for squadron personnel in this manner. The squadron commander must make application for the allocation of funds, indicating the intended use.

Members of a unit are entitled to know the status of the fund at all times because, after all, it is *their* fund. Fund managers/commanders should inform members of the intent to make future purchases. A commander can lose the beneficial effect of announcing fund purchases if he or she delays in making those expenditures.

The American Red Cross and Morale. The American Red Cross acts as the means of communication between the military and the civilian community. This organization has chapters or representatives in all parts of the United States and its territories. At many bases, there is a Red Cross field director to serve the needs of the base. Although this nationwide organization always stands ready to perform a wide variety of worthy missions, its services are often useful in cases where airmen are troubled about conditions at home. In such instances, it is common practice to call upon the representative of the Red Cross, explain the problem fully, and ask for an investigation of the actual conditions. The situation can often be adjusted. In any event, officers will obtain reliable information that will enable many baffling human problems concerning the airmen of their organizations to be handled in a judicious manner based upon facts.

Air Force Aid Society. The work of the Air Force Aid Society is another valuable adjunct to the efforts of commanders to provide for the welfare and morale of their airmen. (See chapter 26, "Legal Documents and Assistance.")

Family Support Centers. Family Support Centers are a result of the Air Force's recognition that family issues have a direct effect on the morale and productivity of Air Force members and on decisions for making the Air Force a career. They serve as a focal point for responding to family issues that affect the Air Force mission. (See chapter 26, "Legal Documents and Assistance.")

Leave and Passes. The Department of the Air Force authorizes commanders to grant leaves so that people receive thirty days' leave a year. Leave is a privilege and not a right. However, except as a consequence of war or unpredictable contingencies, something is wrong in the management of a unit and its personnel if every member does not have the opportunity to take the full annual leave. Commanders should ensure that each airman plans, schedules, and takes annual leave. Commanders must keep themselves thoroughly informed on the procedures governing leaves prescribed by the department and local senior commanders. Commanders should study the program of the organization and determine periods most suitable for granting leaves and those periods when they should not grant leave, except for important emergency reasons. They must plan their leave policies and procedures. Air Force assignment policies direct supervisors to grant leave to personnel designated for reassignment overseas unless they have had a recent absence or military necessity prohibits a delay in departure. Military necessity must govern, and it will not always be possible to grant these absences. It is most unwise for commanders to announce leave policies in a manner that members could interpret as a promise. Broken promises are themselves a cause for some absences without leave. Commanders can inform unit personnel of the regulations, tell them of their plans and their intentions, inform them that circumstances at the time the leave is desired must determine their action, seek opportunities to send personnel on leave, and see to it that opportunities are equitably distributed to all personnel. These measures will replace ignorance with understanding and serve to reduce the causes for unauthorized absence.

Personal Problems of Servicemembers. Many servicemembers have left behind interests or problems that may require their attention or action while in military service. At home, they would turn for advice to parents, friends, clergy, lawyers, or other people in whom they have trust and confidence. In the service, they frequently turn to their commanders.

These occasions provide an opportunity for commanders to show true interest in the welfare of their troops. They should adopt an impersonal and kindly attitude in hearing these problems. Commanders must never improperly divulge personal, confidential matters. They should give the counsel they feel is correct, obtain the necessary information, or refer the airmen to authorities who can supply the information.

Good leaders must have a genuine understanding of human relations. Their tools are people, and therefore they must be able to deal with people. The necessary warmth of military leadership may be demonstrated when individuals carry their baffling personal problems to their commanders for advice or solution.

Complaints. The commander must be accessible to members of the unit who wish to make complaints. Some of the complaints may be petty or even deliberate attempts to injure the reputation of another with a charge that is without foundation. Others will be substantive; after all, even in the best organizations there can be genuine cause for dissatisfaction. This is information the commander must obtain so that the morale of the unit is not seriously impaired and the unit's mission is not jeopardized. Personnel must know that they may state a cause for complaint to their commander with the knowledge that the commander will give them a fair, impartial hearing and correct the grievance if convinced of its truth. They must believe that the commander will wish to remove causes for dissatisfaction. Commanders can request a climate assessment survey to help them determine what conditions of dissatisfaction might exist within the unit.

When ideas, suggestions, or reports are stated to the commander that affect the welfare, efficiency, or morale of the unit, or any individual, they must be heard sympathetically. If the commander determines the reported condition can and does deserve correction, then action should be taken at once.

Absence Without Leave. Commanders must face and solve the problem of unauthorized absences from duty. Particularly, commanders must analyze the causes and find solutions to the AWOL situation in their own units. It is not a new problem, and it exists during times of peace as well as in times of war. According to Article 86 of the Uniform Code of Military Justice, any member of the armed forces who, without authority "fails to go to his appointed place of duty at the time prescribed, goes from that place, or absents himself or remains absent from his unit, organization, or place of duty at which he is required to be at the time prescribed" is absent without leave and subject to court-martial. In time of war, the punishments authorized in Article 86 depend upon the circumstances of the absence, but in a crucial situation when in contact with the enemy, this is a most serious offense.

But the punitive approach is inadequate and will not provide the cure. Commanders who rely on punishment will fail to eliminate the cause of unauthorized absence. Officers must get acquainted with unit personnel. It is important for reasons of administration and leadership, but is especially necessary in connection with understanding the AWOL problem. Officers may facilitate this process through get-acquainted interviews. These should be preceded by an analysis of the servicemembers' records and related forms so that an officer will know in advance of the interviews each individual's age, education, aptitudes, length of service, training status, dependent situation, and conduct as shown by the disciplinary record. With that information in mind, commanders should proceed with an informal interview to get acquainted with the airmen and let the airmen get acquainted with them. Seek to find the views of the airmen as to family responsibilities and any worries they may have with respect to their families. By so doing, commanders may be able to correct oversights in dependents' benefits provided by the government and thus remove at once a cause for people absenting themselves without leave. Inquire of the servicemembers as to their career progress, and determine whether they are satisfied that they are contributing a maximum of talents. Encourage them to talk freely, and take the time to explain to the servicemembers those misunderstood things that may confuse or disappoint young people. Commanders should test each member's knowledge of leave regulations, for it is true that some personnel absent themselves without leave when they might have received an authorized absence simply by asking. Commanders should invite the servicemembers to bring problems to them when in need of help or advice so that they will feel they have someone to lean on when confused by personal problems.

The whole subject of eliminating unauthorized absences is of primary importance in building an effective Air Force. It is likewise of importance in developing pride in an organization. Success will identify the commanders who study causes of AWOL and remove them. Few people will absent themselves without leave from a well-commanded organization.

DISCIPLINE

Discipline Defined. In the military, *discipline* refers to intelligent, willing, and positive obedience to the will of the leader. Its basis rests upon the voluntary subordination of the individual to the welfare of the group. It is the cohesive force that binds the members of a unit, and its strict enforcement is a benefit for all. Its constraint must be felt not so much in the fear of punishment as in the moral obligation it imposes on the individual to heed the common interests of the group. Discipline establishes a state of mind that produces proper action and prompt cooperation under all circumstances, regardless of obstacles. It creates in the individual a desire and determination to undertake and accomplish any mission assigned by the leader.

Discipline is a controlling factor in the combat value of airmen. The military qualities of the leader and members and their "will to fight" determine the combat value of a unit. A point too often overlooked is the fact that poorly trained and poorly disciplined units reap the defeats and greatest losses. The greater the combat value of the organization, the more powerful will be the blow struck by the unit in a given combat environment.

People are and always will be the vital element in war. In spite of the advances in technology, the worth of the individuals is still decisive. Leaders must instill discipline and ensure their members have good morale.

In war, discipline is a matter of the gravest importance, affecting the questions of life and death of individuals. For example, commanders must brief their pilots to obey rules of engagement. Discipline, therefore, is the cement in the structure of the Air Force. Without it, the Air Force would be merely a mob. We *must* have a disciplined Air Force; otherwise, ultimately, we shall have none.

Relationship of Superiors toward Subordinates. The Air Force forbids superiors from injuring those under their authority by tyrannical or capricious conduct or by abusive language or sexual harassment. While maintaining discipline and the thorough and prompt performance of military duty, all officers, in dealing with airmen, must bear in mind the absolute necessity of preserving their self-respect. A grave duty rests on all officers and particularly upon organization commanders in this regard. Officers must impress upon the young airmen lessons of patriotism and loyalty and above all the necessity of obedience. These lessons must be repeated again and again. Leaders must carefully explain the difference in the status of airmen compared with that of civilians to make them understand that in becoming airmen they are subject to a new control and have assumed obligations they did not have as civilians. Officers must keep in as close touch as possible with the personnel under their command. They must take an interest in their unit's life, hear their complaints, endeavor on all occasions to remove the existence of those causes that make for dissatisfaction, and strive to build such confidence and sympathy that their people will seek out leaders for counsel and assistance, not only in military and organizational matters, but also in times of personal or family distress or perplexity. Leaders can and should establish these kinds of relationships and do so without relaxing the bonds of discipline. Commanders will find that fair treatment, equality of opportunity, and personal respect and protection are key to the health of their units.

Punishment. The maintenance of control requires instructions and policies for the guidance of members of the organization. These must include positive matters (things to do) and negative matters (things not to do). Good management requires that instructions and policies be few, entirely justified by conditions, easily understood, necessary for the accomplishment of unit objectives, and at least reasonably in harmony with those in use by neighboring organizations. Of course, all instructions and policies must meet the test of legality. There is little occasion for the adoption of additional restrictive orders that serve only to gratify the personal interests of the commander. The application of restrictive policies on an entire organization because of the transgressions of one or of a small number is a lazy and ineffective form of control. Mass punishment is poor leadership, as is the use of threats or naming a penalty in issuing an order. Such practices cause antagonism. The *Manual for Courts-Martial*, the instructions and policies of the Air Force, and the orders of higher authority prescribe the methods of control. Members should carefully study this material. An understanding of the requirements that must be enforced is an important part of the maintenance of control.

In any organization, there will be violations of standing orders and offenses committed that are punishable under the Uniform Code of Military Justice. In dealing with offenders against military law, a desire to serve the best interests of the Air Force should guide officer actions. Vengeance has no place in such a consideration. The object is not to punish for the sake of retribution, but to deter servicemembers from offenses, to exact recompense when government property has been lost, and to rehabilitate offenders when possible. It is usually wise to be lenient with first offenders, particularly when the subsequent attitude of the offender is commendable. It is equally wise to be rough on second offenders. Do not seek a reputation for mercy or one for ruthlessness. Rather, advance the reputation of the Air Force for levelheaded action in the interests of the national security.

The proper exercise of command requires leaders to fully inform personnel of what is required of them. The commander must be alert to prevent offenses, for very often a kind word of caution may prevent an offense. Offenses may be committed in ignorance, through carelessness, or with deliberate intent. The skilled commander can eliminate many offenses personnel might commit through ignorance or carelessness.

An immediate recognition and reward of the deserving does much to prevent the commission of offenses. A softly spoken "good work" may be more stimulating to pride than a flowery and lengthy speech. The award of extra privileges or mere recognition of merit has much to do with the development of both sound discipline and high morale.

When considering disciplinary action, commanders must consult the staff judge advocate for legal advice and guidance. The commander should prefer to take disciplinary action under Article 15 of the Uniform Code of Military Justice rather than submit charges that will result in a trial by court-martial. For first-time offenders or for petty offenses, this will usually suffice. Leadership must make careful investigation before any decision as to punishment is made. This investigation must be impersonal, fair, and just, and it must include an opportunity for the accused airman to refute the charge. The UCMJ is available online from a number of sources and can be found by searching its title.

Methods of maintaining discipline must stand the test of battle or the courtroom. Reliance upon trial by court-martial as the sole means of securing obedience to law will fail. When faced with a disciplinary problem, commanders should consider all the alternatives and choose that which best corrects the problem and prevents its recurrence. In any case, where serious action or punishment is considered, commanders should consult the staff judge advocate to ensure that the procedure is appropriate and is legally justified.

There is a distinction between *punitive* and *administrative* procedures. Punitive actions include nonjudicial punishment and trial by court-martial, and necessitate compliance with the *Manual for Courts-Martial*. In all cases, commanders should consult the staff judge advocate before taking punitive action. Neither the UCMJ nor the standards of criminal justice administration govern administrative procedures, yet they often require legal coordination and review. This is especially true in initiation of administrative discharge action or a demotion action.

In handling any disciplinary matter, commanders must be careful to remain objective. Haste and partiality can do much to harm commanders' images and respect in the eyes of their subordinates. It may also cement a bad attitude where airmen feel they cannot get a fair hearing or equitable treatment, thereby nullifying any rehabilitative effect that might otherwise result from the commander's action.

A common pitfall for some commanders and supervisors is failure to proceed through a graduated course of action employing the different levels of disciplinary tools. Generally speaking, a gradual increase in severity of action against a person with a disciplinary problem is the most effective method of getting the attention of those who can be rehabilitated. Too often, a supervisor will "forgive and forget"—that is, stay at the level of oral counseling—until some breaking point is reached, whereupon the supervisor wants the individual "hanged at sunrise" and discharged immediately thereafter. In this circumstance, some supervisors feel betrayed by the individual, who "has not appreciated all the chances I gave him." Since Air Force policies, instructions, and manuals are written in contemplation of a graduated response, there is often difficulty in meeting the requirements of these directives where there are erratic swings in the commander's response to a given discipline problem.

Disciplinary Tools. Commanders are responsible for maintaining good order and discipline within their commands. Military discipline refers to a person's self-control and ability to conform to the standard of conduct demanded by the service. The Air Force expects its commanders to set good examples, provide instructional guidance, and when necessary, impose disciplinary action upon personnel subject to their authority.

Commanders faced with problems of discipline, job performance, or maintenance of order have a number of administrative and disciplinary tools at their disposal. In connection with, but never in place of, disciplinary actions are counseling and other assistance with problems that underlie many discipline problems. For instance, valuable information, advice, and assistance is available from *The Military Commander and the Law* (found at www.afjag.af.mil/shared/media/document/AFD-120828-043.pdf), the chaplain, military equal opportunity, the hospital, the staff judge advocate, the area defense counsel, family services, and the personal financial management counselor. Commanders should be aware of the range of disciplinary tools and when the use of each is appropriate. These tools include the following:

- Oral counseling by the commander, first sergeant, or supervisor.
- Written counseling (AFI 36-2907)
- Admonitions and reprimands (AFI 36-2907)
- Control roster and unfavorable information files (UIF) (AFI 36-2907)
- Administrative demotion (AFI 36-2502)
- Administrative separation (AFI 36-3208)
- Nonjudicial punishment (AFI 51-202)
- Trial by court-martial (AFI 51-201)
- Discharge of commissioned officers (AFI 36-3206)

Note: Air Force Instructions can be found at www.e-publishing.af.mil.

Punishment under Article 15. Article 15 of the UCMJ provides authority to certain unit commanders to impose punishment of a degree less than that for which court-martial action is required. This authority, however, is qualified by the fact that any airman may demand trial by court-martial rather than accept punishment under Article 15. Nonetheless, when commanders have conducted a preliminary inquiry or are otherwise satisfied that court-martial action is not desirable, they should inform the offender in writing of the intent to impose punishment under Article 15. The offender must state, in writing, a willingness to accept Article 15 punishment or a demand for court-martial. If the offender demands court-martial, the appropriate authority prefers formal charges. If the offender certifies willingness to accept Article 15 punishment, the commander proceeds to impose the punishment. In this correspondence, the commander does not indicate what punishment is intended until after the offender has accepted punishment under Article 15.

Commanders may impose a wide variety of punishments under Article 15. Commanders in general officer grade may, under Article 15, punish officers under their command by imposing restriction for up to sixty days, arrest in quarters for thirty days, or forfeiture of half pay for sixty days. Colonels may impose on officers in their commands a reprimand and restriction for thirty days.

Commanders in the grade of major or above may adjudge punishment to airmen of their command as follows: not more than thirty days' correctional custody, forfeiture of half of their pay for two months, extra duty of forty-five days, restriction for two months, or reduction in grade (an E-4 or higher may not be reduced more than two grades).

Commanders below the grade of major may, under Article 15, punish airmen of their command by imposing not more than one week of correctional custody, forfeiture of one week's pay, extra duty for two weeks, restriction to limits for two weeks, detention of two weeks' pay, or reduction of one grade (provided the commander has the authority to promote to the grade from which the airman is to be demoted).

The commander should consult with the staff judge advocate if the punishment intended approaches the levels for which court-martial action is required. In general, when it is an appropriate procedure, the use of Article 15 is preferred by commanders, as opposed to court-martial. The court-martial procedure is costly to the government and consumes the time of valuable people. Commanders should employ Article 15 when the offender accepts it, when the punishments available under Article 15 are considered adequate, and when court-martial is not mandatory.

Administrative Discharges. The Air Force gives commanders the authority to eliminate the unfit and the undesirable from its ranks and to remove airmen who are mentally or psychologically unable to perform acceptably as airmen. Such people may well want to perform properly, but cannot. They should be discharged.

Air Force policy, instructions, and procedures provide for the separation of those who can be useful airmen but will not do so. These are the alcoholics, the drug users, the rebels, the repeating offenders, and/or the undisciplined. Commanders should remove them from the Air Force as quickly as possible. The Air Force also authorizes the separation of airmen who are sentenced by civil authorities to confinement for more than one year.

In preparing action to eliminate airmen, commanders must compile a record of offenses, instances, or other evidence of unsuitability. Usually, the process requires commanders to show that they made efforts to correct the situation, through counseling or other methods. The appropriate commander attaches this record to a letter to the discharge authority, asking senior command level to form a board of officers to review the case and determine disposition.

Officers dealing with cases of unsuitability should be guided entirely by the needs of the Air Force. An unfit airman stands in a space that might be filled by a productive airman. There is no room for the unfit or the undesirable. Each person in the total strength of the Air Force must be first class.

Military Courts-Martial. There are three kinds of courts-martial: the summary court, the special court, and the general court. Officers may serve as members of any court-martial. Enlisted personnel may serve on a general or a special court-martial for the trial of enlisted personnel when, before the convening of the court, the accused requests in writing that enlisted personnel be so detailed. When so requested, enlisted personnel must comprise at least one-third of the membership of the court.

Punishing power of the two inferior courts, summary and special, is limited by statute. The punishing power of the general court is usually, by the wording of the Uniform Code of Military Justice denouncing a particular offense, left to the discretion of the court. That power is not unlimited, however. In a few instances, the article itself prescribes the punishment for a particular offense. In all other cases, the president, under authority given him by an article of the UCMJ, has prescribed a table of maximum punishments. The punishment of nearly all offenses that are denounced by the civil common law and by nonmilitary codes has been similarly limited by the president. In the rare event that an offense is committed that is not covered by the president's limit of punishment order, the punishment may not exceed that fixed as a maximum for the offense by the U.S. Penal Code or the Criminal Code for the District of Columbia. The sentence of a court-martial has no validity until it has been approved by the officer appointing the court. The sentences of all general courts-martial are subject to a series of reviews and approvals or disapprovals in which higher levels of review examine the record of trial not only to determine its legal sufficiency, but also to ensure that the Service does not execute a sentence of unnecessary harshness.

Restraint. Any person in military service may sign and swear to charges that are an offense under military law. Usually, however, the person having knowledge of the alleged offense makes the information known to the immediate commander of the accused enlisted servicemember or officer. Ordinarily, this commander would be the squadron commander. The commander must then make an immediate decision as to whether to place the accused person under any degree of restraint, such as confinement to quarters. If restraint seems necessary, the commander should issue the appropriate orders at once.

Informal Inquiry. The commander (or a representative) must promptly make a preliminary inquiry of the accusations. This inquiry may be no more than a consideration of the charges and such evidence as is offered by the accuser. It may include a search of dormitories, quarters, or other pertinent areas. Collection of documentary evidence may be desirable, depending on the nature of the charge. Commanders or supervisors may question individuals informally. However, it is most important to remember that before questioning accused persons, the accused must be informed of the accusations made and warned that any statement they make may be used against them should a trial result (Article 31, UCMJ).

The commander must reach decisions as matters proceed. If the preliminary inquiry leads to a conclusion that court-martial action is not indicated, the commander may wish to adopt lesser punitive procedures or none at all. In many cases, the commander will find that accusations lack substance and may simply be dismissed.

Charges for Courts-Martial. If commanders believe that court-martial procedure is proper, they should have formal charges executed at once and so inform the accused. In carrying out this action, commanders must consult with the office of the staff judge advocate.

Area Defense Counsel. The Area Defense Counsel (ADC) is a certified judge advocate performing defense counsel duties for courts-martial, administrative actions, Article 15 actions, interrogations, and any other adverse actions in which counsel for an individual is required or authorized. Commanders or supervisors should refer active-duty servicemembers under any type of investigation to the ADC.

ADCs, who are outside any local chain of command, are responsible for vigorously representing their clients within the bounds of professional ethics. ADCs are advocates for their clients, not advisors for the command.

Commanders may talk to ADCs directly. ADCs can often fill in the "rest of the story," but they cannot reveal client confidences. Remember that ADCs are bound to represent their clients honestly and fairly and that your discussions will be on the record.

5

The Air Force of the Future

Each year, the secretary of the Air Force and the chief of staff of the Air Force issue a posture statement that is both a vision for the coming year and an overview of the Air Force's unique contributions to protecting the United States, deterring aggression, assuring our allies, and defeating our enemies. It details the characteristics of the future environment and the Air Force's mission and program priorities. This statement is part of a series of documents that guide the Department of Defense and the armed services in their support of national security objectives. Some of the key documents in this series include the president's National Security Strategy, the Secretary of Defense's (SECDEF's) National Defense Strategy, the Chairman of the Joint Chiefs of Staff's National Military Strategy, and service strategies like the Air Force Posture Statement. (All of these documents are available online; the AF posture statement is found at www.posturestatement.af.mil). DOD and the services also have guidance documents addressing strategy and planning efforts for specific missions like counterdrug operations, counterproliferation, and force management.

The Air Force officer will face many opportunities and challenges as the United States moves farther into the twenty-first century. Some challenges focus on the near-term, while others are long-term tasks. This chapter outlines the purpose and direction the Air Force has set for itself to leverage opportunity and meet future challenges.

AIR FORCE POSTURE STATEMENT

This section highlights three key ideas found in the 2013 Air Force Posture Statement. These concepts include the operational environments in which the Air Force sees itself operating, its core missions, and the development of its people to succeed in future challenges.

The Air Force is the world's preeminent aerospace force—part of an aerospace nation and a defense establishment that recognizes the continuing and growing importance of air, space, and cyberspace capabilities. The fact that each of the Air Force's sister services rely on aerospace power capabilities for unique applications in their operational domains is evidence of the importance of these capabilities to the nation.

The Air Force provides its unique capabilities to the nation and the joint team through its *Global Vigilance*, *Global Reach*, and *Global Power* and as part of its enduring core missions of air and space superiority; intelligence, surveillance, and reconnaissance (ISR); rapid global mobility; global strike; and command and control. By integrating its capabilities across these core missions, the Air Force believes it brings distinctive capabilities and options for deterring war and delivering rapid, lifesaving responses to threatened areas at anytime, anywhere on the planet.

Strategic Environment. Air Force strategists and planners use the new SECDEF defense strategic guidance (DSG), *Sustaining U.S. Global Leadership: Priorities for 21st Century Defense*. This document anticipates and describes the future security environment, prioritizes U.S. security concerns, and sets all these factors within the fiscal realities of the current sequestration challenges resulting from the 2011 Budget Control Act. The DSG anticipates a future environment summarized in one word—uncertainty. It foresees continuing and new challenges in the Asia-Pacific region, the Middle East, and Africa. In addition, problems like insurgency, terrorism, proliferation of weapons of mass destruction, and the international drug trade are part of the reality of future threats and challenges.

To meet these challenges, the nation requires an Air Force that combines the capability to meet future threats with concepts that guide effective and efficient operations in support of the joint team and national objectives. The future is uncertain, but the Air Force relies on the flexibility, versatility, agility, deployability, and network abilities of the force structure it has in order to plan for and to meet potential threats and challenges.

Fiscal Environment. The Budget Control Act of 2011 and the Consolidated and Further Continuing Appropriation Act of 2013 have resulted in a difficult fiscal environment for the U.S. government and especially DOD and the armed services. The Air Force has made adjustments in real time by meeting Fiscal Year (FY) 2013 funding cuts and is preparing for FY 2014 cuts in this same manner. It developed funding plans for FY 2015 in its Alternate-Program Objective Memorandum (A-POM—the planning and funding document of the Air Force). The first Air Force budget with sequestration effects incorporated in the Future Years Defense Plan (FYDP) will be the FY 2016 POM. These fiscal realities increase the leadership challenges facing the officer corps, as officers must balance operational requirements with future modernization and acquisition.

Air Force Core Missions. The Air Force is determined to remain a superb fighting force. It will invest in its five core missions, providing the best possible mix of forces and capabilities to the joint team and the nation. These core missions include:
- Air and space superiority
- Intelligence, surveillance, and reconnaissance (ISR)
- Rapid global mobility

- Global strike
- Command and control.

Each of these core missions has a central focus that guides the development of the concepts and capabilities the Air Force seeks as part of providing its unique contribution to national security. Air and space superiority means the Air Force will provide *freedom from attack* and the *freedom to attack*. Its ISR concepts and capabilities provide *eyes and ears on adversaries* anywhere, at any time. For its rapid global mobility, the Air Force looks to provide *delivery on demand*. Here again, the service plans to provide this capability on a global level. Another worldwide capability is that of global strike. The Air Force seeks the capacity to strike *any target, any time*. Finally, the Air Force will provide command-and-control capabilities that offer the nation and the joint team *total flexibility*. From the theater level to the individual, the Air Force plans for the ability to support command and control requirements across the spectrum of conflict.

Airman Readiness and Development. Despite facing a challenging security environment and tough fiscal constraints, the Air Force is determined to provide *Global Vigilance, Global Reach,* and *Global Power* to the nation and contribute its core missions to the joint team through ready and capable forces. Although the Air Force faces a high operations tempo and funding issues, it will make necessary adjustments to meet combatant command mission requirements for readiness and the continued development of its most valuable resource, its people. To meet future challenges, the Air Force is committed to Total Force Integration of its active-duty, Air National Guard, and Air Force Reserve units as a seamless entity.

PART II

Air Force Organization

6

The Departments of Defense and the Air Force

The U.S. Constitution establishes a basic principle that the armed forces be under civilian control. By giving the president the position of commander in chief, the Constitution provides the basic institutional framework for military organization. This chapter outlines the organization of the Air Force and its role in national defense.

THE COMMANDER IN CHIEF

Following World War II, an increasing need to integrate military policy with national policy compelled the president to assume a much more active role as commander in chief of the armed forces. As commander in chief, the president has the final word of command authority, but as head of the executive branch, he is subject to the checks-and-balances system of the legislative and judicial branches of government. The heavy demands of domestic and foreign duties require the president to delegate authority broadly and wisely. Responsibility for national defense matters is delegated to the Department of Defense (DOD).

THE DEPARTMENT OF DEFENSE

The basic purpose of the National Security Act of 1947, and its later amendments, was to establish the Department of Defense. This cabinet agency establishes policies and procedures for the government relating to national security. It includes the Office of the Secretary of Defense (OSD); the Joint Chiefs of Staff (JCS); the Departments of the Army, the Navy (which includes the Marine Corps), and the Air Force; unified, specified, and combined commands; defense agencies; and DOD field activities. As the civilian head of the DOD, the secretary of defense reports directly to the president.

Office of the Secretary of Defense. The president appoints the secretary of defense, with the advice and consent of the Senate. As the principal assistant to the president for military matters, the secretary has the authority to exercise direction and control over all elements of the DOD. The line of operational command flows from the secretary of defense *through* the JCS directly to the specified and unified commanders. The JCS is *not* in the chain of command.

Organization of the Department of Defense (DOD)

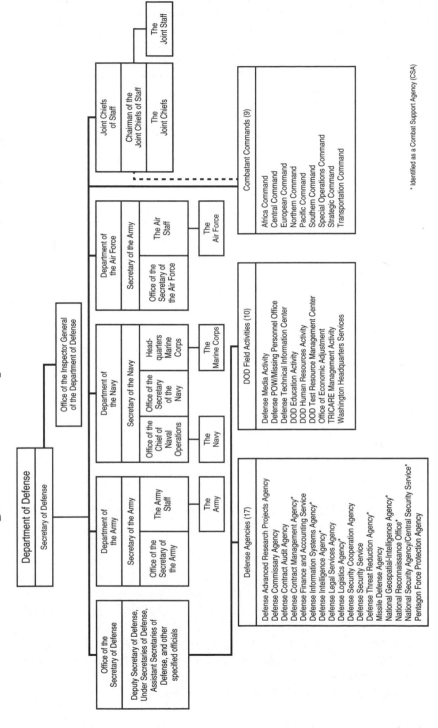

Department of Defense

Secretary of Defense

Office of the Secretary of Defense

Deputy Secretary of Defense, Under Secretaries of Defense, Assistant Secretaries of Defense, and other specified officials

Office of the Inspector General of the Department of Defense

Department of the Army

Secretary of the Army

Office of the Secretary of the Army

The Army Staff

The Army

Department of the Navy

Secretary of the Navy

Office of the Chief of Naval Operations

Office of the Secretary of the Navy

Head-quarters Marine Corps

The Navy

The Marine Corps

Department of the Air Force

Secretary of the Army

Office of the Secretary of the Air Force

The Air Staff

The Air Force

Joint Chiefs of Staff

Chairman of the Joint Chiefs of Staff

The Joint Chiefs

The Joint Staff

Defense Agencies (17)

Defense Advanced Research Projects Agency
Defense Commissary Agency
Defense Contract Audit Agency
Defense Contract Management Agency*
Defense Finance and Accounting Service
Defense Information Systems Agency*
Defense Intelligence Agency*
Defense Legal Services Agency
Defense Logistics Agency*
Defense Security Cooperation Agency
Defense Security Service
Defense Threat Reduction Agency*
Missile Defense Agency
National Geospatial-Intelligence Agency*
National Reconnaissance Office*
National Security Agency/Central Security Service*
Pentagon Force Protection Agency

DOD Field Activities (10)

Defense Media Activity
Defense POW/Missing Personnel Office
Defense Technical Information Center
DOD Education Activity
DOD Human Resources Activity
DOD Test Resource Management Center
Office of Economic Adjustment
TRICARE Management Activity
Washington Headquarters Services

Combatant Commands (9)

Africa Command
Central Command
European Command
Northern Command
Pacific Command
Southern Command
Special Operations Command
Strategic Command
Transportation Command

* Identified as a Combat Support Agency (CSA)

Chain of Command

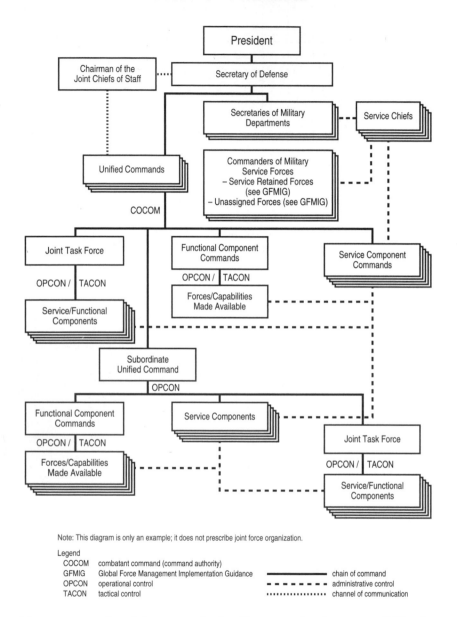

Note: This diagram is only an example; it does not prescribe joint force organization.

Legend

COCOM	combatant command (command authority)	
GFMIG	Global Force Management Implementation Guidance	——————— chain of command
OPCON	operational control	– – – – – administrative control
TACON	tactical control	·············· channel of communication

The secretary also delegates authority. For example, the responsibility for strategic and tactical planning is given to the JCS. The military departments have responsibility for training, administrative, and logistic support of the forces assigned to the unified and specified commands.

In the performance of his demanding duties, the secretary requires the help of many assistants, chief of whom is the deputy secretary of defense. When considering matters requiring a long-range view, and in formulating broad defense policy, a number of advisory bodies and individual advisors also assist the secretary of defense.

Joint Chiefs of Staff. The chairman of the Joint Chiefs of Staff is the principal military advisor to the president, the National Security Council, and the secretary of defense. Subject to the authority and direction of the president and the secretary of defense, members of the JCS serve as advisors and military staff to the unified and specified commanders. The JCS prepares strategic plans and provides for the strategic direction of the armed forces. It reviews the plans and programs of unified and specified commands, reviews major personnel and logistic requirements of the armed forces, and establishes unified doctrine. The JCS is also responsible for assigning logistic responsibilities to the military services, formulating policies for joint training, and coordinating military education.

The members of the JCS consist of the chairman; the chief of staff, U.S. Army; the chief of naval operations; the chief of staff, U.S. Air Force; and the commandant of the Marine Corps. The chairman of the JCS serves as a member of, and presides over, the JCS and furnishes the recommendations and views of the JCS to the president, the National Security Council, or the secretary of defense. Other members of the JCS may also provide advice to these bodies, when requested. If a member disagrees with an opinion of the chairman, the chairman presents that advice along with his own.

When the chairman is not present, the vice chairman of the JCS serves as chairman. The vice chairman may participate in all meetings of the JCS but may not vote on a matter before the JCS except when acting as chairman. JCS duties take precedence over all other duties; therefore, as the military heads of their respective services, JCS members delegate appropriate duties to their vice chiefs of staff, but retain responsibility.

The Joint Staff supports the JCS. The Defense Intelligence Agency provides intelligence support, over which the JCS has operational control. The Joint Staff is composed of officers in approximately equal numbers from all the services. The Joint Staff neither operates nor is organized as an overall armed forces general staff, and it has no executive authority. It performs such duties as the JCS prescribes. However, the Joint Staff is structured in such a way that it is responsible for many key agencies within the DOD. One of the agencies most vital to military success is the National Military Command System.

National Military Command and Control. The National Military Command System provides our command authorities with all the information they need to make decisions and the means to transmit those decisions to subordinate levels. At the peak of its communication system is the National Military Command Center (NMCC), which receives data from various command and control centers of the unified and specified commands. The NMCC also receives data from such defense agencies as the National Security Agency and the Defense Intelligence Agency. Members of the Joint Staff analyze and process this information and pass pertinent messages on through the State

Department Operations Center and the National Indications Center of the Central Intelligence Agency to the Situation Room in the White House. To ensure command and control survivability, the NMCC has an Alternate NMCC.

Unified, Specified, and Combined Commands. The president, with the advice and assistance of the chairman of the JCS, through the secretary of defense, establishes unified and specified commands for the performance of military missions.

A *unified command* has a broad, continuing mission and is under a single commander. The unified commands are the U.S. Strategic Command, U.S. Africa Command, U.S. European Command, U.S. Pacific Command, U.S. Southern Command, U.S. Central Command, U.S. Northern Command, U.S. Special Operations Command, and U.S. Transportation Command. Unified commands also consist of significant assigned components of two or more services and are normally organized on a geographical basis. A component consists of the component commander and those individuals, organizations, or installations under the military command that have been assigned to the unified command. Other individuals, organizations, or installations may operate directly under the component commander.

A *specified command* also has a broad continuing mission but normally consists of forces from only one service and is functionally oriented. It may include units and staff representation from other services. If the allocation of such staffs or units is to be major or of long duration, it will be established as a unified command. There are currently no specified commands designated.

The secretary of defense assigns the military mission to unified and specified commands. The commander of a unified or specified command deploys, directs, controls, and coordinates the action of the command's forces; conducts joint training exercises; and controls certain support functions. The unified or specified commander is responsible to both the secretary of defense and the president. The component commanders or the commanders of subordinate commands exercise operational command. After a force has been assigned to a unified command, it cannot be transferred except by authority of the secretary of defense or under special procedures of that office with the approval of the president. All units not assigned to a unified or specified command remain with their respective services.

Each military service furnishes administrative and logistic support for its forces assigned to a unified command. The individual services continue to issue assignment orders, logistic support orders, personnel change orders, and similar documents. DOD agencies, such as the Defense Logistics Agency and the Defense Communications Agency, perform certain logistic and administrative support functions. Even though the individual services furnish logistic support to their respective components of the unified command, a unified commander can exercise directive authority to ensure effectiveness and economy of operations.

The logistic authority of unified commands expands under wartime conditions and when critical situations make it necessary. Unified commanders have authorization to use the facilities and supplies of all forces assigned to their commands as necessary to accomplish their wartime missions. Achieving maximum effectiveness from our armed forces requires that the efforts of all the services be integrated closely. The authority of the president and the secretary of defense maintains unity of effort; the secretaries of the military departments and the JCS exercise this authority.

The capability of a unified commander can expand through the formation of either a *subordinate unified command* or a *joint task force* (JTF). Each is composed of joint forces under a single commander. The primary difference between the two lies in the scope of the operation. The subordinate unified command has a continuing mission and command arrangement. The JTF is limited by specific time, place, and mission.

Another structure within the DOD is the *combined command*, which consists of forces from more than one nation. For example, the U.S. European and U.S. Joint Forces Commands contribute forces to the NATO combined commands. Combined commands operate similarly to unified commands, except that command is much less structured in combined commands. Units from the member nations retain their national identities, and much negotiation between nations is necessary to make the command function effectively.

The Military Departments. Although operational command rests with the DOD, the military departments—the Army, the Navy (including the Marine Corps and, in wartime, the Coast Guard), and the Air Force—continue as separate agencies. Although service secretaries are not responsible for military operations, they assist the secretary of defense in managing the administrative, training, and logistic functions of the military departments. Except in operational matters, the secretary of defense issues orders to a service through its secretary. The service secretaries are responsible for the economy and efficiency with which their departments operate.

The traditional roles and mission of each branch of service are commonly referred to as "functions." In addition to specific combat roles, the branches furnish operational forces to unified and specified commands. The secretary of defense and the JCS established the functions of the armed forces in the 1948 Key West Agreement, which was revised through the 1953 National Security Act and again in 1958. The general functions of the armed forces are the following:
- Support and defend the Constitution of the United States against all enemies, foreign and domestic.
- Ensure, by timely and effective military action, the security of the United States, its possessions, and areas vital to its interests.
- Uphold and advance the national policies and interests of the United States.
- Safeguard the internal security of the United States.

In addition to the general functions, the military services also have some specific functions they share. These include the following:

- Preparing forces and establishing reserves of equipment and supplies for the effective prosecution of war, and planning for the expansion of peacetime components to meet the needs of war.
- Maintaining, in readiness, mobile reserve forces that are properly organized, trained, and equipped for employment in an emergency.
- Providing adequate, timely, and reliable department intelligence for use within the DOD.
- Organizing, training, and equipping interoperable forces for assignment to unified or specified commands.
- Providing, as directed, administrative and logistic support to the headquarters of unified and specified commands, including direct support of the development and acquisition of command and control systems for those headquarters.
- Preparing and submitting (to the secretary of defense) budgets for their respective departments, and justifying (before Congress) budget requests as approved by the secretary of defense.
- Administering the funds made available for maintaining, equipping, and training the forces of their respective departments, including those assigned to unified and specified commands.
- Conducting research; developing tactics, techniques, and organization; and developing and procuring weapons, equipment, and supplies.
- Developing, supplying, equipping, and maintaining bases and other installations, including lines of communication. Providing administrative and logistic support for all forces and bases.
- Assisting in training and equipping the military forces of foreign nations.
- Assisting each other in accomplishing their respective functions, including the provision of personnel, intelligence, training, facilities, equipment, supplies, and services.
- Preparing and submitting, in accordance with other military departments, mobilization information to the JCS.

Each service develops and trains its forces to perform the primary functions that support the efforts of the other services. Carrying out their primary functions helps to accomplish overall military objectives. The assignment of collateral functions may not be used as the basis for additional force requirements.

THE DEPARTMENT OF THE AIR FORCE

The Air Force is responsible for preparation of air forces necessary for the effective prosecution of war and military operations short of war, except as otherwise assigned. In accordance with integrated joint mobilization plans, the Air Force is also responsible for expansion of its peacetime components to meet the needs of war. The *primary functions* of the Air Force include the following:

Department of the Air Force—Secretariat and Field Operating Agencies

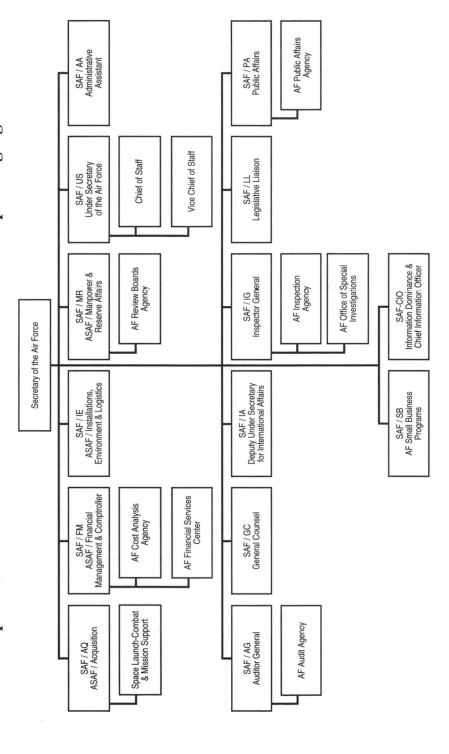

- To organize, train, equip, and provide forces for the conduct of prompt and sustained combat operations in the air—specifically, forces to defend the United States against air attack in accordance with doctrines established by the JCS; to gain and maintain general air supremacy; to defeat enemy air forces; to conduct space operations; to control vital air areas; and to establish local air superiority except as otherwise assigned herein.
- To organize, train, equip, and provide forces for appropriate air and missile defense and space control operations, including the provision of forces as required for strategic defense of the United States, in accordance with joint doctrines.
- To organize, train, equip, and provide forces for strategic air and missile warfare.
- To organize, train, equip, and provide forces for joint amphibious, space, and airborne operations, in coordination with other military services, in accordance with joint doctrines.
- To organize, train, equip, and provide forces or close air and air logistic support to the Army and other forces as directed, including airlift, air support, resupply of airborne operations, aerial photography, tactical air reconnaissance, and air interdiction of enemy land forces and communications.
- To organize, train, equip, and provide forces for air transport for the armed forces, except as otherwise assigned.
- To develop, in coordination with the other services, doctrines, procedures, and equipment for air defense from land areas, including the United States.
- To organize, train, equip, and provide forces to furnish aerial imagery for use by the Army and other agencies as directed, including aerial imagery for cartographic purposes.
- To develop, in coordination with the other services, tactics, techniques, and equipment of interest to the Air Force, and if not provided for elsewhere, for amphibious operations.
- To develop, in coordination with the other services, doctrines, procedures, and equipment employed by USAF forces in airborne operations.
- To provide launch and space support for the DOD, except as otherwise assigned.
- To develop, in coordination with the other services, doctrines, procedures, and equipment employed by USAF forces in the conduct of space operations.
- To organize, train, equip, and provide land-based tanker forces for in-flight refueling support of strategic operations and deployments of aircraft of armed forces and Air Force tactical operations, except as otherwise assigned.

Department of the Air Force—Air Staff and Field Operating Agencies

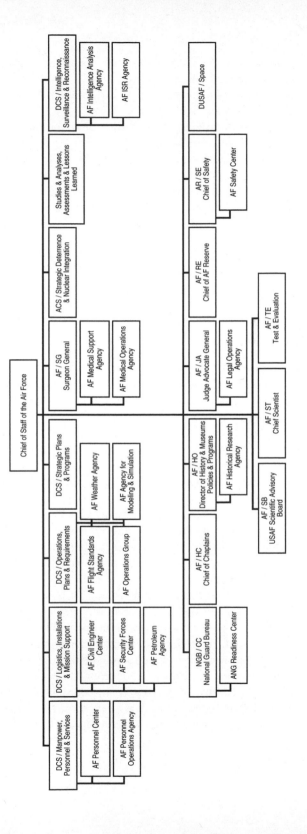

- To organize, train, equip, and provide forces, as directed, to operate air lines of communications.
- To organize, train, equip, and provide forces for the support and conduct of special operations.
- To organize, train, equip, and provide forces for the support and conduct of psychological operations.
- To provide equipment, forces, procedures, and doctrine necessary for the effective prosecution of electronic warfare operations and, as directed, support of other forces.

Collateral functions of the Air Force include the following:

- Surface sea surveillance and antisurface ship warfare through air operations.
- Antisubmarine and antiair warfare operations to protect sea lines of communications.
- Aerial minelaying operations.
- Air-to-air refueling in support of naval campaigns.

Air Force responsibilities *in support of space operations* include the following:

- Organizing, training, equipping, and providing forces to support space operations.
- Developing, in coordination with the other military services, tactics, techniques, and equipment employed by USAF forces for use in space operations.
- Conducting individual and unit training of Air Force space operations forces.
- Participating with the other services in joint space operations, training, and exercises as mutually agreed to by the services concerned, or as directed by competent authority.

Other responsibilities of the Air Force include the following:

- With respect to amphibious operations, the Air Force will develop, in coordination with the other services, tactics, techniques, and equipment of interest to the Air Force and not provided for by the Navy and the Marine Corps.
- With respect to airborne operations, the Air Force has specific responsibility to provide USAF forces for air movement of troops, supplies, and equipment in joint airborne operations, including parachute and aircraft landings; and to develop tactics and techniques employed by USAF forces in the air movement of troops, supplies, and equipment.
- With respect to close air support of ground forces, the Air Force has specific responsibility for developing, in coordination with the other services, doctrines and procedures, except as provided for in Navy responsibilities for amphibious operations and in responsibilities for the Marine Corps.

COMMON SERVICE FUNCTIONS

The Army, Navy, Air Force, and Marine Corps, under their respective secretaries, are responsible for the following functions:

- Determining service force requirements and making recommendations concerning those requirements to support national security objectives and strategy and meet operational requirements of unified and specified combatant commands.
- Planning for use of the intrinsic capabilities of the other services' resources that may be made available.
- Recommending to the JCS the assignment and deployment of forces to unified and specified combatant commands established by the president through the secretary of defense.
- Administering service forces.
- Providing logistic support for service forces, including procurement, distribution, supply, equipment, and maintenance, unless otherwise directed by the secretary of defense.
- Developing doctrines, procedures, tactics, and techniques employed by service forces.
- Conducting operational testing and evaluation.
- Providing for training for joint operations and exercises in support of unified and specified combatant command operational requirements, including the following:
  — Development of service training, doctrines, procedures, tactics, techniques, and methods of organization in accordance with policies and procedures established in service publications.
  — Development and preparation of service publications to support the conduct of joint training.
  — Determination of service requirements to enhance the effectiveness of joint training.
  — Support of joint training directed by commanders of the unified and specified combatant commands and conduct of such additional joint training as is mutually agreed upon by the services concerned.
  — Operating organic land vehicles, aircraft, and ships or craft.
  — Consulting and coordinating with the other services on all matters of joint concern.
  — Participating with the other services in the development of the doctrines, procedures, tactics, techniques, training, publications, and equipment for joint operations that are the primary responsibility of one of the services.

The forces developed and trained to perform the primary functions hereafter will be employed to support and supplement other military service forces in carrying out their primary functions, wherever and whenever such participation results in increased effectiveness and contributes to the accomplishment of overall military objectives. As for collateral functions, while the assignment of such functions may establish further justification for stated force requirements, such assignment will not be used as the sole basis for establishing additional force requirements.

AIR FORCE ORGANIZATION

The Department of the Air Force is made up of the Office of the Secretary of the Air Force, Air Staff, and USAF field units.

The U.S. Air Force is organized on a functional basis in the United States and on a geographic basis overseas by major commands (MAJCOMs), as well as a number of field operating agencies (FOAs) and direct reporting units (DRUs). There are ten MAJCOMs, twenty-four FOAs, and three DRUs.

MAJOR COMMANDS

Air Combat Command (ACC). Headquarters: Langley AFB, Virginia. ACC is the USAF's principal offensive war machine. ACC is the primary force provider of combat airpower to America's warfighting commands. To support the global implementation of national security strategy, ACC operates fighter, bomber, reconnaissance, battle-management, and electronic-combat aircraft. It also provides command, control, communications, and intelligence systems, and conducts global information operations. ACC units consist of twenty-two wings; the 1st, 9th, and 12th Air Forces; U.S. Air Forces Central Command; and the USAF Warfare Center.

Air Education and Training Command (AETC). Headquarters: Randolph AFB, Texas. AETC recruits, accesses, commissions, trains, and educates USAF enlisted and officer personnel, providing basic military training, technical training, and officer and flying training. AETC also provides professional military education and degree-granting professional education. AETC units include seventeen training wings and eight institutes/centers, the 2nd Air Force, the Air Force Recruiting Service, the 59th Medical Wing (a DRU), the Air Force Security Assistance Training Squadron, and the Air University.

Air Force Global Strike Command (AFGSC). Headquarters: Barksdale AFB, Louisiana. AFGSC is the Air Force's nuclear and global strike force charged with developing and providing combat-ready forces for nuclear deterrence and global strike operations. The command ensures the Air Force provides forces characterized by *safe, secure,* and *effective* support to the president of the United States and combatant commanders. AFGSC organizes, trains, equips, maintains, and provides ICBM forces and nuclear-capable bomber forces to combatant commanders. The command includes six wings, a flight test squadron, and a strategic operations squadron.

Air Force Materiel Command (AFMC). Headquarters: Wright-Patterson AFB, Ohio. AFMC manages the integrated research, development, test, acquisition, and sustainment of weapon systems; produces and acquires advanced systems; and operates major product centers, logistics and test centers, the Air Force Research Laboratory, and the National Museum of the USAF.

Emblems of Major Air Commands

Air Combat
Command

Air Mobility
Command

Air Force Space
Command

Pacific Air Forces

U.S. Air Forces
in Europe

Air Education and
Training Command

Air Force Material
Command

Air Force Special
Operations Command

Air Force Reserve
Command

Air Force Global Strike
Command

Air Force Space Command (AFSPC). Headquarters: Peterson AFB, Colorado. AFSPC operates to organize, train, equip, maintain, and provide space and cyberspace operations forces; develop, procure, and test space systems; and sustain national space launch facilities. It provides resilient and cost-effective space and cyberspace capabilities for the joint team and the nation. AFSPC is organized into the Space and Missile Systems Center, the Space Innovation and Development Center, AF Network Integration Center, AF Spectrum Management Office, and the 14th and 24th Air Forces.

Air Force Special Operations Command (AFSOC). Headquarters: Hurlburt Field, Florida. AFSOC is the Air Force component of the U.S. Special Operations Command, a unified command. As such, it provides forces for worldwide deployment and assignment in regional unified commands to conduct agile combat support, combat aviation advisory operations, information warfare, personnel recovery and rescue operations, precision aerospace fires, psychological operations, and specialized aerospace mobility and refueling. AFSOC is organized into three wings, four groups, an Air & Space Operations Center, and the USAF Special Operations School.

Air Mobility Command (AMC). Headquarters: Scott AFB, Illinois. AMC provides rapid global mobility and sustainment through tactical and strategic airlift and aerial refueling for U.S. armed forces. It is the USAF component of the U.S. Transportation Command, and in wartime provides forces to theater commands. AMC provides peacetime and wartime aeromedical evacuation, as well as global humanitarian support. AMC units include seventeen wings, three independent groups, the Tanker Airlift Control Center, the 18th Air Force, and the USAF Expeditionary Center.

Pacific Air Forces (PACAF). Headquarters: Hickam AFB, Hawaii. PACAF provides a full range of Air Force capabilities to U.S. Pacific Command, integrating expeditionary forces to defend the homeland, promote regional peace and stability, deter aggression, and swiftly defeat enemies. PACAF units include ten wings, five groups, and three operations centers organized under the 5th, 7th, and 11th Air Forces.

U.S. Air Forces in Europe—Air Forces Africa (USAFE–AFAFRICA). Headquarters: Ramstein AB, Germany. Serves as the air component for U.S. European Command and U.S. Africa Command. Directs air operations, including warfighting and humanitarian and peacekeeping actions, and maintains combat-ready forces for NATO responsibilities. USAFE-AFAFRICA has seven main operating bases along with 114 geographically separated locations. The main operating bases are RAF bases Lakenheath and Mildenhall in England; Ramstein and Spangdahlem air bases in Germany; Lajes Field, Azores; Incirlik AB, Turkey; and Aviano AB, Italy. The command is composed of nine wings, three groups, an operations center, and the 3rd Air Force.

Air Force Reserve Command (AFRC). Headquarters: Robins AFB, Georgia. AFRC comprises about 14 percent of the USAF's total force. Reservists support nuclear deterrence operations; air, space and cyberspace superiority; command and control; global integrated intelligence-surveillance-reconnaissance; global precision attack; special operations; rapid global mobility; and personnel recovery. They also perform space operations, aircraft flight testing, and aerial port operations, and provide civil engineering, security forces, military training, communications, mobility support, and transportation. The AFRC's 34 wings and 13 groups are organized under the 4th, 10th, and 22nd Air Forces and include the AFRC Recruiting Service, Air Reserve Personnel Center, Force Generation Center, and Readiness Management Group. (See chapter 7 for additional information on the Air Force Reserve Command, as well as on the Air National Guard.)

SUBCOMMANDS AND LOWER LEVELS OF COMMAND
Below the MAJCOMs are the following levels of command, in descending order: numbered air force, wing, group, squadron, and flight.

Numbered Air Force (NAF). There are sixteen NAFs, which are strictly tactical echelons with an operations orientation.

Wing. Under the "one base, one wing, one boss" concept, most Air Force bases have only one wing. All assets are combined under one commander, usually a brigadier general or senior colonel.

Group. Combat wings are composed of four groups—operations, maintenance, mission support, and medical—each of which is usually commanded by a colonel. The groups are broken down into functional squadrons.

Squadron. The squadron is the basic unit in the Air Force. It is used to designate the mission units in the operations groups. Squadrons are also used as the units for functional entities, such as civil engineering; services and security police in the support group; or supply, maintenance, and transportation. Regardless of the functional area that uses it, the squadron has a vital mission.

Flight. There are two types of flights. The Air Force uses numerically designated flights primarily where there is a need for small mission elements to be incorporated into an organized unit. This is the lowest unit level in the Air Force. Alphabetically designated flights are components of squadrons and consist of several elements with identical missions. These flights are not units and are equivalent to branches.

FIELD OPERATING AGENCIES
Field operating agencies (FOAs) are Air Force subdivisions that carry out field activities under operational control of Headquarters USAF functional managers, providing specialized services as their names indicate. Their missions are separate from major command missions. There are twenty-four FOAs.

Air Force Agency for Modeling and Simulation. Headquarters: Orlando, Florida. Oversees air, space, and cyberspace modeling and simulation requirements and joint interoperability.

Air Force Audit Agency. Headquarters: Washington, D.C. Conducts independent and quality internal audits.

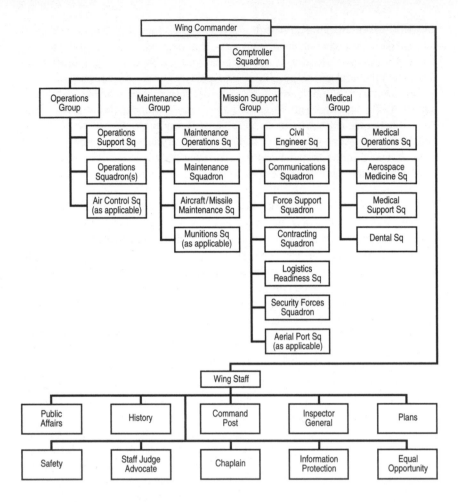

Objective Wing Organization

Air Force Civil Engineer Center. Headquarters: Joint Base San Antonio, Lackland, Texas. Delivers integrated engineering and environmental management and technical services. Activated with the merger of the Air Force Center for Engineering and the Environment, Air Force Real Property Agency, and the Air Force Civil Engineer Support Agency.

Air Force Cost Analysis Agency. Headquarters: Arlington, Virginia. Performs independent cost and risk analyses and provides special studies to aid long-range planning.

Air Force Financial Services Center. Headquarters: Ellsworth AFB, South Dakota. Processes travel transactions for active, guard, and reserve military personnel and Air Force civilians.

Air Force Flight Standards Agency. Headquarters: Oklahoma City, Oklahoma. Develops, standardizes, evaluates, and certifies policy, procedures, and equipment for flight operations and centrally manages air-traffic control and landing systems.

Air Force Historical Research Agency. Headquarters: Maxwell AFB, Alabama. Researches, records, and disseminates history; collects, preserves, and manages historical document collection and oral history program; determines unit lineage and honors; verifies aerial victory credits.

Air Force Inspection Agency. Headquarters: Kirtland AFB, New Mexico. Provides independent assessments of operations and activities; conducts nuclear surety inspection oversight, training, and certification; serves as primary action arm of SECAF inspection system.

Air Force Intelligence Analysis Agency. Headquarters: Pentagon. Provides intelligence, special security services, and imagery products; analyzes foreign air and air defense tactics and training; manages USAF national imagery collection and interagency civil air analysis; directs global tactics analysis reporting program for theater air components.

Air Force Intelligence, Surveillance, and Reconnaissance Agency. Headquarters: Joint Base San Antonio, Lackland, Texas. Organizes, trains, equips, and presents forces and capabilities to conduct intelligence, surveillance, and reconnaissance; oversees ISR capabilities expansion to meet current and future challenges.

Air Force Legal Operations Agency. Headquarters: Joint Base Anacostia-Bolling, District of Columbia. Administers military justice programs; provides legal research technology and trains legal professionals; supports the Department of Justice in civil or criminal litigation pertaining to the Air Force.

Air Force Medical Operations Agency. Headquarters: Joint Base San Antonio, Lackland, Texas. Oversees execution of surgeon general's policies; provides leadership for medical personnel and medical treatment facilities; promotes a cost-effective, modern, and prevention-based health care continuum.

Air Force Medical Support Agency. Headquarters: Joint Base Anacostia-Bolling, District of Columbia. Develops surgeon general's plans and programs; provides medical expeditionary capabilities; defines and executes health care policy.

Air Force Office of Special Investigations. Headquarters: Joint Base Andrews, Maryland. Provides investigative services to USAF commanders; identifies, exploits, and neutralizes criminal, terrorist, and intelligence threats; combats threats to information systems and technologies; defeats fraud affecting acquisitions and base-level capabilities.

Air Force Operations Group. Headquarters: Pentagon. Provides twenty-four-hour watch on current operations; trains and staffs Crisis Action Team; develops weather data for National Command Authority, JCS, National Military Command Center, Army Operations Center, and other federal agencies.

Air Force Personnel Center. Headquarters: Joint Base San Antonio, Randolph, Texas. Identifies proper grades, specialties, and skill levels for USAF mission; manages assignments; monitors professional development; plans and schedules expeditionary forces; oversees airmen and family readiness centers; assists casualty reporting and missing in action/prisoner of war actions. Formerly the Air Force Military Personnel Center and the Air Force Civilian Personnel Management Center. The Air Force Manpower Agency and Air Force Services formally merged with AFPC on 1 June 2012.

Air Force Personnel Operations Agency. Headquarters: Pentagon. Analyzes personnel life cycle; provides information technology applications; develops and operates officer, enlisted, and civilian models.

Air Force Petroleum Agency. Headquarters: Fort Belvoir, Virginia. Provides fuel-related technical, operational, and analytical support, planning, new technology development, and standards management.

Air Force Public Affairs Agency. Headquarters: Joint Base San Antonio, Lackland, Texas. Develops and sustains public affairs products; provides combat camera and graphics support; tests emerging technologies; manages PA personnel deployments.

Air Force Review Boards Agency. Headquarters: Joint Base Andrews, Maryland. Manages military and civilian appellate processes; serves as lead agent for DOD Physical Disability Board of Review.

Air Force Safety Center. Headquarters: Kirtland AFB, New Mexico. Manages mishap prevention, risk management, and nuclear surety programs; provides flight, ground, weapons, human factors, and space safety technical assistance; oversees major command mishap investigations and evaluates corrective actions for USAF-wide applicability and implementation; directs safety education programs.

Air Force Security Forces Center. Headquarters: Joint Base San Antonio, Lackland, Texas. Organizes, trains, and equips security forces; develops force protection doctrine, programs, and policies; identifies and delivers emerging force protection and force application solutions; manages corrections program and DOD military working dog activities.

Air Force Weather Agency. Headquarters: Offutt AFB, Nebraska. Provides air and space weather information to DOD, coalition, and national users; standardizes training and equipment for USAF weather forces.

ANG Readiness Center. Headquarters: Joint Base Andrews, Maryland. Ensures field units have resources to train and equip forces for state and federal missions; sustains airmen and helps shape leadership capability.

DIRECT REPORTING UNITS

Three direct-reporting units (DRUs) are directly subordinate to Headquarters USAF. DRUs have the same administrative and organizational responsibilities as the major commands, and are separate from the major commands and field operating agencies because of legal requirements or their unique missions.

Air Force District of Washington. Headquarters: Joint Base Andrews, Maryland. Orchestrates support for National Capital Region activities; trains, equips, and provides forces for contingency, homeland, and ceremonial support operations.

Air Force Operational Test and Evaluation Center. Headquarters: Kirtland AFB, New Mexico. Tests and evaluates new weapon systems. Provides effectiveness, suitability, and operational impact expertise in the battlefield environment.

U.S. Air Force Academy. Headquarters: Colorado Springs, Colorado. Develops and inspires young men and women to become USAF officers with knowledge, character, and discipline.

AIR AND SPACE EXPEDITIONARY FORCE

Since the end of the Cold War, personnel cuts have forced every branch of the U.S. armed services to reexamine its role as part of the national security puzzle. While the Cold War deployment plan had involved sending units to pre-designated bases with infrastructure already in place, the 1991 Gulf War demonstrated that the Air Force needed the ability to arrive at bare base sites and establish operational capability, often within hours of arrival. USAF airlift, long the "first in, last out" force, had to deliver air forces capable of providing air defense for follow-on forces. This "one-two-punch" became standard during the 1990s and early 2000s. In short, the Air Force evolved into an increasingly expeditionary force for the nation.

By definition, expeditionary means "sent on military service abroad." This entails the Air Force conducting global aerospace operations with forces based primarily in the United States that will deploy rapidly to begin operations as soon as they arrive at a forward operating location. As a key aspect of this new unit mobility, the Air Force developed air expeditionary capabilities for both its steady-state rotational requirements and crisis operations response. These air expeditionary forces, AEFs, included units sent to support missions such as Operation Southern Watch in Southwest Asia and Operation Northern Watch in Iraq. This attention to expeditionary forces, however, focused on aviation units and did little to help manage combat support capabilities. By the late 1990s, the tasking pressures on both aviation and combat support caused the Air Force to once again re-examine its expeditionary force structure.

The AEF rotational structure ushered into service in the late 1990s divided USAF forces into ten expeditionary components with two rotational emergency response wings. This ten-plus-two structure accounted for both aviation and combat support elements within the Air Force. Proof of its effectiveness came after Operation Allied Force as it showed the Joint Community the optimal way to recover the Air Force post-surge operations in the Balkans. The rotational structure allowed the Air Force to offer the Joint Chiefs options for recovering units to combat ready status using a combination of units from the Air Force and the other services, allowing the Air Force complete its recovery in the shortest timeframe. The Air Force used this concept when it ramped up operations after the September 9, 2001 (9/11), attacks on the United States.

After 9/11, the Air Force found its forces stretched thin supporting combat operations in Afghanistan and in near full surge mode once the second Gulf War against Iraq began in 2003. By the mid-2000s, the Air Force was fighting in two major contingencies and supporting ground forces in both with individual augmentees. In response, it modified the AEF structure into tempo bands in order to manage its forces by unit type codes (UTCs, or how the services express capabilities to Joint Force Commanders) rather than by units and individuals. The Air Force used the tempo bands to manage capabilities in high demand but short supply, minimizing the occurrence of consecutive tasking of the same units or individuals. This modification helped the Air Force manage its forces during surge operations. However, as it plans the return to rotational contingency tasking, the Air Force intends to re-establish its AEF construct using unit-based solutions.

As a result, the Air Force will return to an Air and Space Expeditionary Force (AEF) that is:

- Tailored to mission success with the right combination of capabilities and people to match the challenge.
- Rapidly deployable to any part of the world.
- Light and lean with the smallest possible footprint forward.
- Globally connected to reach back for worldwide information and support.
- Able to command and control the assigned forces in near real time.
- Led by a scheduled and seasoned air commander who can decisively apply the gamut of air and space capabilities across the spectrum of crisis.

Role of Airmen in the AEF. The AEF should provide stability and predictability in deployment schedules. When you arrive at a new duty station, inquire early on as to your new unit's AEF deployment status in order to prepare yourself and your family for this aspect of service. The expeditionary Air Force is a fact of life, not an exception in its support to our nation. AFPAM 10-100, the *Airman's Manual*, details what you need to meet the challenges of Air and Space Expeditionary Force requirements: basic war-fighting skills and knowledge, staying ready for deployment and dealing with field conditions, fighting, survival, and mission accomplishment in hostile situations.

SOURCES OF ADDITIONAL INFORMATION

AFI (Air Force Instruction) 38–101, *Air Force Organization*
AFPAM (Air Force Pamphlet) 10–100, *Airman's Manual*

7

The Reserve Component:
The Air Force Reserve and the
Air National Guard

The Total Air Force depends on personnel on active duty, in the Air Force Reserve, and in the Air National Guard, as well as civilians. The Air Reserve forces are the Air National Guard and the Air Force Reserve. All our reserve forces are placed in one of three categories: Active Reserve, Inactive Reserve, or Retired Reserve. The active Air Force alone is neither manned nor equipped to accomplish its missions without the full support of the Air Reserve forces. Downsizing of the active Air Force, combat tempo, number and geographic breadth of conflicts, and distribution of Air and Space capabilities have made the Total Air Force a reality, not merely a concept. The Air Force program for reserve forces puts into practice the concept of reliance on a "ready now" augmentation force.

THE ACTIVE RESERVE
Active Reserve means that portion of our reserve forces that can be ordered to active duty under conditions short of a congressional declaration of war or national emergency. The *Air National Guard* is composed entirely of units organized and trained to be used as Active Reserve units. The Active Reserve portion of the *Air Force Reserve* includes not only Active Reserve units but also individual active reservists assigned to specific mobilization positions with regular Air Force organizations and other individuals earmarked as attrition replacements.

In peacetime, the Air National Guard is commanded by the governors of the various states; it is supported by the Air Force through the National Guard Bureau, under Air Force policies and regulations. It is trained under the supervision of the gaining commands, who also have the inspection responsibility. Thirty states also have state guards as backup to their National Guard units.

Both components are governed by Air Force policies, instructions, and training directives, and both are responsive to training standards and performance requirements prescribed by the gaining command.

THE INACTIVE RESERVE

In addition to the Active Reserve, there is within the Air Force Reserve an Inactive Reserve, which can be ordered to active duty *only* when Congress declares war or a national emergency. The government ordered Inactive Reserve units to active duty for the Gulf War, and activated others for the wars in Afghanistan and Iraq. Some inactive reservists may not be available because of critical needs of the government or the civilian community as a whole. Although a number of inactive reservists participate in correspondence courses or train with Active Reserve units, the majority of them would need refresher training to function in their Air Force specialties.

WHY AIR RESERVE FORCES?

One reason we have reserve units is that the Constitution and the Congress say that we will. But another very good reason is that reserve units provide an economical way to maintain a surge expansion capability for the Air Force during peacetime.

The reserves—even the Inactive and Retired Reserves—provide the Air Force a strong base of grassroots community support. They are an effective influence in favor of Air Force recruiting as well. By talking about the Air Force, reservists help to interest young people in Air Force careers.

The primary reason for having reserves, however, is wartime support. Until a few years ago, the Air Force, like the other U.S. military services, traditionally relied on its reserve components to supply the extra manpower and capability needed for wartime expansion.

Under current concepts for their use, the "ready now" reserves are very much a part of our deterrent strength. Their readiness and usefulness are vital to the Air Force mission and, therefore, to the security of the nation. When the Air Force says its reserves are "ready now," it means that they can fight today. They can be and have been called up in a matter of hours. Call the roll: the Korean War, the 1961 Berlin Crisis, the 1962 Cuban Missile Crisis, the Vietnam War, Grenada, Panama, the Gulf War, the Balkans, and the wars in Afghanistan and Iraq.

The use of reserve forces to help keep the peace is sometimes thought to be a new concept. But it really isn't. The idea of the citizen-soldier was born as a "ready now" concept. As far back as 1607, the leaders of Virginia, following the practice in England, formed a local militia called the "train band." As rapidly as their populations could support them, train bands were formed in other nearby colonial settlements. The members of these organizations were not professional soldiers. They were farmers, craftsmen, and merchants. Their military obligation was a twenty-four-hour-a-day affair, and there was hardly a period from 1622 until after the American Revolution when some of the members of the train band were not serving as soldiers on a full-time basis. There was no active colonial military establishment; the citizen-soldiers were the sole defense of their individual communities. During certain periods, British regulars were responsible for the frontiers or were stationed in Atlantic seaboard cities. As the American economy and population grew, a standing military force became a necessity if only to prevent constant disruption of the increasingly complex national structure. With the oceans as effective barriers to sudden attack, our citizen-soldiers had time on their side and could become reserves, to be called upon only when the size and strength of the regular establishment had to be increased for war.

This, then, became the pattern for our military forces: an active-duty establishment strong enough to fend off the first attack, and a reserve that could be mobilized and quickly trained to expand the regular force to war-winning size.

But military weapons and concepts of war are constantly changing. Today, our Air National Guard and Air Force Reserve Command are much more than just a wartime mobilization force. They are, truly, an integral and vital part of our total aerospace power. Air Force missions and responsibilities are so broad in scope and of such variety that these missions can be accomplished only by a completely responsive, instantly reacting, and highly flexible force. Success is achieved only through the full use of all resources available to the Total Air Force, reserve as well as regular.

COMPOSITION OF AIR RESERVE FORCES

Air Reserve forces serve in many capabilities, from flying to medical units, engineers to cyber operators, and in training and education roles to combat operations. The National Defense Authorization Act and Budget Control Acts of recent years led to reductions of USAF force structure, including in its Reserve Forces. In the spring of 2013, the Department of Defense established the National Commission on the Structure of the Air Force to develop recommendations regarding the appropriate mix of active-duty and reserve component forces. This commission provides its recommendations to Congress in spring 2014. Officers can anticipate significant changes to force structure— changes that the active-duty and reserve components will implement over the course of the next several years.

AIR RESERVE FORCES TRAINING

Realistic training for wartime readiness is now par for the course for reserve units and personnel. Airlift units carry high-priority cargo while training their personnel in airlift skills. Fighter and reconnaissance units take the place of regular units to support joint Army–Air Force exercises. Air Defense units fly air alert intercept missions under active Air Force control.

Management has been improved to give Air Force combat commands responsibility for supervising and training and operational inspection of those reserve units that would be assigned to them in wartime. Standards of performance are identical for regular and reserve units. Each aircrew, regardless of component, is required to meet the same rigid requirements as regular Air Force crews before it can be designated combat ready.

The operations room of a reserve outfit is almost indistinguishable from that of a regular outfit—except perhaps on weekdays. Reserve combat crews receive the normal forty-eight inactive-duty training periods and fifteen days of active duty each year, plus thirty-six additional flying training periods for aviators and their support elements. Even this is not enough to meet all flying requirements, and so reserve personnel engage in training whenever they can get time off from their civilian jobs—these part-time airmen have to meet exactly the same training requirements that the full-time Air Force crews must meet. They pass their operational readiness inspections exactly like active-force units.

How is this possible with a part-time operation? A great deal of the reserve's success is due to the stability of personnel. It takes a while longer to train reservists, but the reserves do not have the problem of frequent turnover that challenges regular units.

Another asset, and an extremely important one, is the technician program. The air technicians of the Guard and the Air Reserve have a dual status: They are full-time employees in a civilian capacity, as well as being reservists who train with units on weekends and during annual active duty. In other words, they wear two hats. They provide a permanent, hardcore base of skill and experience, not only for the day-to-day maintenance and operating functions, but also for training younger personnel. This valuable resource of experience is augmented by a handful of active Air Force advisors who assist in training and assure standardization with the requirements of the gaining commands of the Regular Air Force.

CIVIL AIR PATROL
Although Civil Air Patrol (CAP) members are not a part of the armed forces, they belong to the auxiliary of the U.S. Air Force and deserve mention here. CAP was formed in December 1941, just days before Imperial Japan attacked Pearl Harbor. Its first mission was to aid in the defense of America's coastline, which it did under the jurisdiction of the Army Air Forces. In 1946 Congress chartered CAP as a nonprofit civilian corporation, and two years later it was made the auxiliary of the new U.S. Air Force and tasked with three primary missions: aviation education, cadet programs, and emergency services.

Today, CAP accomplishes its aerospace education mission by distributing an aerospace curricula for kindergarten through college, supporting college workshops, giving free aerospace training to America's teachers, and aiding in Air Force recruiting. The cadet program, which includes aviation education, orientation flights, and flight training, provides the U.S. military service academies with about 10 percent of each year's new cadets. CAP contributes aerial reconnaissance for homeland security, border patrol, and the war on drugs, and flies about 95 percent of all inland search-and-rescue sorties in the United States. CAP also provides disaster-relief in support of local, state, and national disaster relief organizations.

CAP members are either cadets aged twelve to twenty-one or senior members over age twenty-one. The members wear Air Force uniforms with distinctive CAP insignia and have a grade structure similar to the Air Force's. There are 1,500 units in 52 wings—representing each state, the District of Columbia, and the Commonwealth of Puerto Rico. CAP's 34,000 senior members and 22,000 cadets fly more than 120,000 hours each year in 530 CAP aircraft and more than 4,000 member aircraft.

CAP national headquarters is at Maxwell AFB, Alabama, and is supported by CAP-USAF, an active-duty cadre. For further information, visit www.gocivilairpatrol.com.

PART III

Career and Advancement

8

Officer Professional Development

Officer professional development is essential to fulfill the Air Force mission and to provide the professional growth that officers expect. The officer who is most effective at carrying out the mission is one who is professionally prepared to assume the responsibilities that go with a particular rank. The officer professional development program is designed to support Air Force requirements and maintain maximum combat effectiveness while developing a well-rounded, professionally competent officer corps. An officer's professional development must harmonize with long-term Air Force requirements. The virtual Military Personnel Flight (vMPF) on the Air Force Personnel Center website (www.afpc.af.mil) and the Career Field Education and Training Plan (CFETP) instructions found at the Air Force's e-Publishing website (www.e-publishing.af.mil) provide detailed information regarding establishment of career goals and insight into career path options by technical specialty. The information that follows is for all Air Force officers, regardless of technical specialty.

OBJECTIVES OF PROFESSIONAL DEVELOPMENT
Professional development includes actions and experiences that improve officers' ability to perform their technical specialties and increasingly contribute to the Air Force mission. Professional development starts with concentrating on expertise in a primary skill, broadens throughout one's career, and ends, one hopes, with the officer being a generalist (if not a general!) with both depth and breadth of expertise. Officers grow by combining their career specialties with ability to lead and to manage in peace and in war. The Air Force offers officers numerous ways to enhance their professional credentials.

CAREER PATHS
The purpose of the officer assignment system is to fill Air Force requirements. Although one may express preference, officers volunteer only one time—when they take the oath of office. Officers should not concern themselves with mapping out their careers in detail but instead concentrate on their current duty. The only assignment with which the officer should be concerned is the current one,

and when available for a new assignment, the one that immediately follows. Qualifications and professional development are the primary factors in making assignments, and commanders play a key role in the process. The assignment system is an integral part of officer professional development, but officers must realize that assignments are made to fill Air Force needs with the best-qualified officers.

There are some steps officers can take to enhance their careers. In addition to learning about career opportunities from the vMPF, CFETP, and their development team, officers should discuss their career aspirations, career plans, and assignment opportunities with their commanders. Mentors in the Career Broadening Program can also provide guidance on a wide variety of career and professional topics and share their knowledge of career development programs and initiatives.

PATH OF PROFESSIONAL DEVELOPMENT

The most important indicator of potential is the way an officer performs daily on the job and develops leadership abilities. This is certainly true for lieutenants, captains, and junior majors. A very limited number of captains will serve in lower-level staff assignments, and a larger number of majors will serve in staff jobs at all levels. Nevertheless, a staff job is not a prerequisite for promotion up through lieutenant colonel. A broader range of experience is more important for lieutenant colonels. In general, a demanding staff job as a senior major or lieutenant colonel will enhance the potential to perform as a colonel or above. Most colonel jobs require staff competence as well as skill in one's specialty and developed leadership talents.

Professional military education (PME) and graduate academic education should parallel and support job requirements. PME should build upon a solid foundation of officership laid during precommissioning programs. The uniqueness of the military profession and the particular values and culture of the officer corps are the bedrock on which all future professional development is based.

The focus for company-grade officers (lieutenants and captains) should be on developing the skills they need, especially leadership and communication skills. The emphasis for the field grades (majors and colonels) should shift to the effective management of people and resources, as well as skills needed for staff work. Lieutenant colonels and colonels must understand the elements of air and space force deployment and the policy considerations that drive them, so that is the role of the Air War College, the highest U.S. Air Force PME level.

Unique education opportunities exist to develop the officer corps. The Air Force Chief of Staff sponsors a Captains to Prestigious PhD program and the Academy, PME schools, and the Air Force Institute of Technology sponsor masters- and PhD-level degree programs. The School of Advanced Air and Space Studies (SAASS) educates strategists for the Air Force and the nation and provides the pathway for the Air University PhD.

THE OFFICER EVALUATION SYSTEM (OES)

The OES, an integral part of the officer professional development program, has three purposes: to furnish feedback to officers on how well they are doing and advise them on how to improve, to provide a long-term cumulative record of performance and potential, and to provide central selection boards with sound information to help them pick the best-qualified officers for promotion. The OES focuses on performance and is a tool that officers can use in their own professional development.

THE PROMOTION SYSTEM

Objectives of the officer promotion system are to select officers through a fair and competitive process that advances the best-qualified officers to positions of increased authority and responsibility and to provide the needed career incentive to attract and maintain an officer corps of high quality. Promotion boards are told that demonstrated leadership abilities and performance of primary duties are of overriding importance and far outweigh all other considerations. Therefore, officers should concentrate on duty performance in their current grade and not on "square-filling" maneuvering.

PROFESSIONALISM

The ultimate objective of career development is a quality called "professionalism," brought to its highest standard of excellence. All of us readily recognize the meaning of professionalism when we apply the term to a minister, a doctor, a lawyer, or a professor. What does it mean when applied to an Air Force officer? To assess this, it is first necessary to appreciate the unique scope of an Air Force officer's professionalism—the vast field of knowledge, experience, skills, and comprehension that is encompassed in an Air Force career. The armed forces of the United States constitute a significant effort of the American people. Approximately 17 percent of the federal budget is spent on our armed forces, and approximately 3.2 million active-duty, reserve, and civilian personnel maintain the armed forces of which about 573,200 serve in the Air Force. Currently, Air Force and Navy forces are declining, whereas Army and Marine Corps strength is increasing. The complicated, expensive tools of our military forces rest on the entire range of U.S. technology and industry, involving deeply other professional areas, such as medicine, engineering, law, education, and many scientific disciplines. Moreover, the armed forces are an integral, crucial part of U.S. diplomacy and international relations. "Peacetime" foreign policy cannot be separated from the existence and strength of U.S. armed forces. Finally, the armed forces exert, through their diverse requirements and activities, a major effect on the U.S. economy. Plainly, it is not enough that Air Force officers be expert in particular fields of Air Force operations; they are part of a vast complex that touches many aspects of American life and, therefore, must seek to achieve a professionalism that matches the multiple strands of responsibility and knowledge that uniquely characterize their profession.

Professionalism begins at less lofty levels than the ultimate responsibilities of the top officers of the Air Force. It begins with technical skill and knowledge relative to the particular task assigned to Air Force officers. It begins when Air Force officers know how to perform their own jobs at maximum efficiency, routinely, prudently, smoothly. The reliable sign of the true professional is the calm, seemingly easy performance of tasks under all circumstances, without noise or heroics, without unnecessary risk or extravagant use of resources.

Professionalism is expanded and exploited when Air Force officers know how to create professionalism in the enlisted force. This task means training, careful supervision, discipline, and morale. It is the mark of officer pros that they have working with them enlisted personnel who are also pros.

Because of the vast field of concerns, Air Force officers must steadily increase professional competence by taking every opportunity to upgrade basic educational levels, attend military schools, read widely, and volunteer for a variety of additional duties. In particular, Air Force professionals should come to understand the very serious business management aspects of the Air Force, because the net capabilities of the Air Force will always be an expression of the efficiency with which Air Force officers use the resources made available by the Congress. These resources are used in a thousand ways: as pay, for procurement of equipment and supplies, for construction, for maintenance and operations, and for research and development. The business end of this problem is not only the thousands of contracts with U.S. industry, but also the accurate determination of requirements, the formulation of realistic plans, and the efficient use of available resources. All Air Force officers participate in this vast business of the Air Force. The Air Force can obtain the most national security from its huge annual budget only when all Air Force officers obtain the most efficient results from their use of their part of total resources.

In their fields of career development, all Air Force officers should constantly seek to heighten and broaden their competence so that at each succeeding level of their careers, they will fully deserve the accolade "a professional."

9

USAF Training and Education

For the Air Force to accomplish its mission requires that the service be highly organized; thus it is also a large bureaucracy. It must be equipped efficiently, so a close working relationship with science and industry is essential. Its men and women must be prepared by training and education, the subjects of this chapter. There are three main components—precommissioning programs, specialty training, and professional military education (PME)—as well as other opportunities to help officers enhance their skills.

PRECOMMISSIONING PROGRAMS

The U.S. Air Force Academy. The Air Force Academy graduated its first class in 1958. Enrollment at the school, located in Colorado Springs, is about four thousand in a four-year college program leading to a bachelor of science degree. The academy commissions about one thousand second lieutenants each year, about a fifth of all newly commissioned second lieutenants. Beginning with the class of 1997, academy graduates have been commissioned as reserve, rather than regular, officers. Most AFA graduates incur a five-year active-duty service commitment. However, graduates entering pilot training incur a ten-year commitment after completing Specialized Undergraduate Pilot Training, and graduates entering navigator training incur a six-year commitment after completing Specialized Undergraduate Navigator Training. The minimum service obligation for the Air Battle Management career field is also six years. You can find additional information about the Academy at www.usafa.af.mil.

Air Force Reserve Officer Training Corps (AFROTC). Congress originally authorized ROTC on college campuses in 1916, just before the United States entered World War I. Thirty years later, after World War II, a separate Air Force ROTC came into being and is now overseen by Air University, Maxwell AFB, Alabama. There are two- and four-year programs, and in both, qualified applicants received AFROTC scholarships. There are over eleven hundred AFROTC "host" and "crosstown" programs. AFROTC usually commissions about 42 percent of the new second lieutenants each year. Most AFROTC graduates incur a four-year active-duty service commitment. Like Academy graduates entering pilot training, AFROTC graduates incur a ten-year commitment after completing Specialized Undergraduate Pilot Training, and graduates entering navigator training incur a six-year commitment after completing Specialized Undergraduate Navigator Training. The minimum service obligation for the Air Battle Management career field is also six years. You can find additional information about AFROTC at www.afrotc.com.

Officer Training School/Basic Officer Training (OTS/BOT). Located at Air University, Maxwell AFB, Alabama, OTS/BOT is a nine-week officer procurement program that recruits and trains non-AFROTC college graduates, including those from the Airman Education and Commissioning Program. Unlike the Air Force Academy and AFROTC, OTS/BOT has the capacity to quickly increase or decrease its output of second lieutenants to meet changing Air Force requirements. OTS/BOT commissioned nearly thirty-two hundred second lieutenants in 1985, but only 350 in 1991. OTS/BOT is now commissioning five hundred to seven hundred second lieutenants each year. OTS/BOT graduates' service commitments are the same as for AFROTC graduates. You can obtain additional information on OTS/BOT, OTS/Commissioned Officer Training, and the Academy of Military Science at www.holmcenter.com.

Officer Training School/Commissioned Officer Training (OTS/COT). Located at Air University, Maxwell AFB, Alabama, OTS/COT is a five-week course for chaplains, medical professionals, and judge advocates who have been given direct commissions. OTS/COT prepares these officers for service in the Air Force by providing training in leadership, professional military knowledge, defense studies, drill and ceremonies, and communication skills. OTS/COT is now graduating about eleven hundred officers each year.

Academy of Military Science (AMS). This academy is a detachment of the Air National Guard Readiness Center. It was relocated to Maxwell AFB, Alabama, in 2009. AMS commissions officers for the Air National Guard and the Air Force Reserve through an intensive six-week course. This Air National Guard institution opened in 1970 because the Air Force Academy, AFROTC, and OTS were unable to commission sufficient numbers of officers. Most current Guard and reserve officers, however, were commissioned by one of the three sources of active-duty officers and had prior active-duty service before joining the Guard or reserves. AMS has the capacity to produce up to five hundred new officers each year.

APPOINTMENT OF OFFICERS
Reserve and Regular Air Force Appointments. Reserve majors are eligible for regular commissions between an officer's ninth and twelfth years. The exception to this timetable is that some medical officers, who are frequently commissioned as captains or majors, must wait until they become lieutenant colonels before receiving regular commissions. The Air Force automatically considers eligible officers and neither requires nor accepts applications for regular status. See AFI 36-2610, *Appointing Regular Air Force Officers and Obtaining Conditional Reserve Status.*

THE
PRESIDENT
OF
THE UNITED STATES OF AMERICA

To all who shall see these presents, greeting:
Know Ye, that reposing special trust and confidence in the patriotism, valor,
fidelity and abilities of Lee R. Johnson *, I do*
appoint him Second Lieutenant *in the*

United States Air Force

to date *as such from the* First *day of* June *, two*
thousand and Fourteen *. This officer will therefore carefully*
and diligently discharge the duties of the office to which appointed by doing and
performing all manner of things thereunto belonging.
And I do strictly charge and require those officers and other personnel of lesser
rank to render such obedience as is due an officer of this grade and position. And,
this officer is to observe and follow such orders and directions, from time to time, as
may be given by the President of the United States of America or other superior
officers, acting in accordance with the laws of the United States of America.
This commission is to continue in force during the pleasure of the President of the
United States of America under the provisions of those public laws relating to
officers of the Armed Forces of the United States of America
and the component thereof in which this appointment is made.

Done at the city of Washington, this First *day of* July
in the year of our Lord two thousand and Fourteen *and of the*
Independence of the United States of America the Two Hundred and
Thirty-eight *By the President:*

Lieutenant General, USAF
Deputy Chief of Staff, Personnel

Secretary of the Air Force

SPECIALTY TRAINING

Whatever their source of commission, most newly commissioned USAF line officers will go to either flying training or technical training schools, except the few who will learn their skills in on-the-job training, or "OJT."

Air Force Flying Schools. All undergraduate flight training is conducted by the Air Education and Training Command (AETC). Pilot training is conducted at Air Force, Navy, or Army bases under the supervision of Headquarters, AETC, Randolph AFB, Texas. The Air Force conducts flight screening through the 1st Flying Training Squadron, located at the Air Force Academy in Colorado. Pilot training continues with an undergraduate pilot training program and ends with combat crew training in specific major weapons systems. Navigators train at NAS Pensacola, Florida, and conclude their training at NAS Pensacola or Randolph AFB.

Air Force Technical Schools. As the Air Force grows increasingly technical in its operations, the need for technically trained officers also increases. AETC operates a number of technical training schools to which officers may be assigned as students. Courses are designed to advance the officers' proficiency in their specialty fields, whether jet aircraft maintenance, electronics, missile maintenance and operation, intelligence, or scores of other technical and support field specialties. The main centers of such training are at Keesler AFB, Mississippi, and in Texas at Goodfellow AFB, Sheppard AFB, and Lackland AFB. Courses vary in length.

PROFESSIONAL MILITARY EDUCATION (PME)

Education in the discipline of the profession of arms is called professional military education, or PME, and is the systematic acquisition of theoretical and applied knowledge. In World War II, the United States surprised the German general staff with the ability of our armed forces to expand quickly from fewer than half a million men in 1940 to a well-organized and well-led force of more than 12 million in 1945. Three principal reasons that this rapid expansion was so successful were the Army and Navy PME systems between the two world wars, learning from our failures in industrial mobilization during World War I, and an available pool of about 74,000 reserve officers, 77 percent of them commissioned through ROTC.

The primary purpose of Air Force PME today is to educate officers in the application of aerospace forces and to provide the opportunity to participate in joint service operations. The USAF officer PME system consists of three levels of instruction conducted through resident and nonresident programs. In addition some officers will participate in programs of the National Defense University, the other U.S. armed services, the U.S. State Department, NATO, foreign countries, and civilian institutions.

Air Force PME is divided into three levels: Primary Developmental Education (PDE), conducted at the Squadron Officer College; Intermediate Developmental Education (IDE), conducted at the Air Command and Staff College;

and Senior Developmental Education (SDE), conducted at the Air War College. PME is a cumulative, coordinated process in which each level forms the foundation for the following level. All three levels are conducted by Air University at Maxwell AFB, Alabama, the center of Air Force PME programs.

Squadron Officers Course. The introduction to PME for newly accessioned officers, Squadrons Officers Course is taught at wing level and tailored to fit local requirements. It combines education in officership and leadership and the role of aerospace power with broad understanding of unit and installation operations and Air Force perspectives. This course of instruction is undergoing intense redesign to enable officers to blend their learning with a combination of home station and in-residence education. These changes will be implemented over time. You can find additional information about the Squadron Officer College at www.au.af.mil/au/soc.

Squadron Officer School (SOS). SOS is an eight-week temporary duty (TDY) course that is attended by almost all active-duty line officers during their fourth to seventh years of commissioned service. In addition, a number of National Guard and Air Force Reserve officers attend SOS during the summer. SOS is designed to increase junior officers' dedication to the profession of arms by stepping back from individual technical specialties and offering a broader look at the profession. SOS's objective is to develop dynamic young officers ready to serve air and space forces in an expeditionary warfighting environment. Consequently, SOS's curriculum focuses on the profession of arms, military and international studies, and leadership and communication skills. The school provides an interactive online version of the course as well as a Leadership Development Program.

Air Command and Staff College (ACSC). ACSC is the Air Force's intermediate service school (ISS). This ten-month course is attended by about six hundred U.S. and international officers whose performance clearly shows potential for further advancement. Active-duty line officers are chosen by Developmental Education Designation Boards (DEDBs) in a highly competitive selection process. Those eligible are majors with at least three years since their last PME education assignment, at least three years' retainability, and three years on station at projected departure date. Graduates incur a three-year active-duty service commitment upon completion of ACSC.

The college broadens the knowledge and increases the professional qualifications of future commanders and staff officers, emphasizing combat and combat support across the spectrum of service, joint, and combined operations. ACSC prepares officers to plan and execute warfare at the operational level; improves the communication, analytical, and problem-solving skills a staff officer needs; enhances command, leadership, and combat support skills; imparts an understanding of U.S. military power and our national interests; and fosters the understanding needed for joint duty assignments. For resident graduates, ACSC awards an academic degree of Master of Military Operational Art and Science. Each summer, ACSC conducts a Reserve Forces Course to update selected Air National Guard and Air Force Reserve majors on the USAF, its doctrine, and its weapon systems. Each academic year, selected Air Guard and reserve officers join the resident ACSC class for a week. All mid-level officers not selected for resident ACSC or other IDE should complete either the ACSC Distance Learning program (certificate awarded upon completion) or the Online Masters Program (OLMP, which leads to a master's degree and Joint PME Phase I credit). You can learn more about ACSC atwww.au.af.mil/au/acsc.

School for Advanced Air and Space Studies (SAASS). This Air University school graduated its first class at Maxwell AFB, Alabama, in 1992. The 11.5-month follow-on course for selected graduates of intermediate-level PME schools (or their equivalent) produces strategists—officers who have developed superior abilities to create strategies and evaluate and employ airpower—for the Air Force and the nation. The very demanding reading and seminar course focuses on theory, evidence, and application of air, space, and cyber power at the operational to strategic levels of war. A thesis and oral comprehensive examination are required. SAASS graduates are granted the academic degree of Master of Philosophy in Military Strategy. Qualified graduates are designated "all but dissertation" and enrolled into the Air University PhD program. Completion of an approved dissertation and defense leads to an accredited PhD in Military Strategy. You can find additional information at www.au.af.mil/au/saass.

Air War College (AWC). AWC is the Air Force's senior developmental education school. The student body is a carefully selected group of about 240 officers and U.S. government civilians brought together for a ten-month course of graduate-level study. They are joined by officers from the other U.S. services and a number of other nations. Active-duty line officers are chosen by annual Headquarters USAF DEDBs in a highly selective process. Students are colonels and lieutenant colonels and graduates incur a three-year active-duty service commitment upon graduation. AWC prepares senior military officers to lead at the operational and strategic levels in the employment of air and space forces in support of national security, including joint combined, coalition, and interagency operations. The AWC in-residence program offers an academic degree of Master of Strategic Studies and Joint PME Phase II credit. The AWC offers an online distance learning program for officers not selected for the in-residence course. For additional information on the college, please go to www.au.af.mil/au/awc.

Joint, Other Services, and Non-DOD PME Courses. The Goldwater-Nichols Defense Reorganization Act of 1986 established a requirement for the joint specialty officer (JSO). To meet JSO educational requirements, the chairman of the Joint Chiefs of Staff, with the services, began a two-phase Joint PME process whereby students receive Phase I Joint PME (JPME I) at IDE and JPME II at SDE. Initially, JPME credit accrued only at National Defense University (NDU) schools and colleges. Today, the NDU schools and the IDE and

SDE programs at each of the services' in-residence staff and war colleges provide the respective phase credit.

Joint Forces Staff College (JFSC). Located in Norfolk, Virginia, JFSC has the mission, prescribed by the JCS, of preparing selected officers of all services for joint and combined staff duty. The curriculum focuses on the strategic, doctrinal, and operational concerns of the JCS and the combatant commanders (COCOMs) of geographic and functional commands—the environment graduates will likely encounter.

Dwight D. Eisenhower School for National Security and Resource Strategy. Located at Fort McNair, District of Columbia, the Eisenhower School is a major component of the National Defense University and is a joint SDE college operating under JCS direction. It began after World War I as the Army Industrial College, with the mission to prevent future failures in military procurement. It became a joint service school after World War II and was renamed the Industrial College of the Armed Forces, with a focus on managing resources for national security. Its mission is to prepare selected officers from all services and senior career civilian governmental officials for positions of high trust in the federal government. Criteria for selection to the Eisenhower School are the same as for AWC and NWC; officers attend only one of the three Senior Service Schools.

National War College (NWC). Also at Fort McNair, NWC is an SDE college with a curriculum of study focused on national security policy preparation. It prepares selected personnel of the armed forces, State Department, and other U.S. government agencies for the planning and exercise of joint and combined high-level policy, command, and staff functions in support of national strategy. Criteria for attendance are the same as for AWC and ICAF; officers attend only one of the three Senior Service Schools.

Other Service Schools. A few Air Force officers may be selected to attend the other services' IDE schools—Army Command and General Staff College, the College of Naval Command and Staff, or the Marine Corps Command and Staff College—and their SDE schools, the Army War College or the College of Naval Warfare.

Non-DOD PME Courses. A few Air Force officers may be selected to attend international PME courses, such as the Western Hemisphere Institute for Security Cooperation (IDE) or the Inter-American Defense College or NATO Defense College (SDE). The USAF also participates in a large number of allied PME courses, such as the RAF Staff College or German Armed Forces Staff and Command College (IDE level), or the Royal College of Defence Studies, Canadian Forces College, or L'École de Guerre (War College) within the Joint Forces Defence College (SDE level).

Civilian PME Courses. These SDE equivalents for a chosen few are the U.S. State Department Seminar of National and International Affairs and the Harvard University Research Fellow Program.

OTHER TRAINING AND EDUCATION PROGRAMS

The Air Force sponsors a variety of training and educational opportunities for officers to develop their specialties and their military professionalism. Participation in some of the programs is selective; other programs are open to all officers. Each base's education services flight can provide general and location-specific information, including information on tuition assistance and veterans' benefits.

Air Force Institute of Technology (AFIT). An Air University organization located at Wright-Patterson AFB, Ohio, AFIT supports national defense through graduate and professional education and research programs. AFIT provides consulting and research services to Department of Defense agencies and conducts nondegree and degree programs; the latter include undergraduate through the doctoral level. The resident program includes the Graduate School of Engineering and Management and continuing education in the School of Systems and Logistics and the Civil Engineering and Services School.

AFIT's Civilian Institution Programs manage educational programs for students to meet specific Air Force requirements through civilian universities, research centers, hospitals, industrial and business organizations, and governmental agencies. Among these are the Graduate School Program for Air Force Academy graduates and the Education Delay Program for AFROTC graduates; both programs lead to graduate degrees, the former at Air Force expense and the latter at the expense of the individual officer. Civilian Institution Programs also encompass advanced degree programs in more than a dozen selected fields, legal and health-care education programs, research fellowship programs, education with industry programs, and professional continuing education programs in almost twenty fields.

The Ira C. Eaker Center for Professional Development. This Air University center located at Maxwell AFB, Alabama, provides consultation services and specialized research, as well as seven professional educational programs: AF Human Resource Management School, International Officer School, Professional Military Comptroller School, USAF Chaplain Service Institute, USAF First Sergeants Academy, USAF Historian Development School, and USAF Judge Advocate General School. The College for Professional Development also conducts courses for commanders of wings, support groups, maintenance groups, and operations squadrons.

CAREER-LONG PROFESSIONAL EDUCATION

Air Force officers have two career-long educational obligations: They must develop expertise both in their specialties and in the profession of arms. Junior officers, of course, must concentrate on acquiring expertise in their specialties. But even they cannot neglect their professional education obligations. Day-to-day duties in officers' specialties are usually so demanding of time and energy that officers can easily neglect their professional obligations. But, by themselves, the formal professional military education schools are inadequate for developing warfighting expertise. The profession of arms is so broad, and it requires knowledge in so many fields, and familiarity in even more, that career-long self-study programs are necessary for officers who aspire to real professionalism. Although officers may supplement their individual professional education programs with formal courses, such as correspondence courses or classes at local universities, the bulk of officers' self-education is achieved by reading.

Career-long professional education should be centered on warfighting. Junior officers should focus their study on how leadership and management, strategy and tactics, and doctrine relate to their individual specialties during wartime. More senior officers, after fully understanding how their specialties contribute to the Air Force's capabilities to wage war, should focus on how airpower contributes to joint warfighting capabilities.

Understanding how military force is used as a political tool is achieved by a critical study of military history and by analysis of contemporary politico-military events. The "Professional Reading Guide," appendix B of this book, is a place to begin. The books in this appendix are particularly useful in developing an understanding of military history; critical study of these books can enlighten the reader regarding employment of military forces today and in the future. But a historical understanding is not enough; contemporary politico-military events must also be followed and analyzed. All officers must keep abreast of a vast spectrum of domestic and international issues (religious, social, ethnographic, political, economic, scientific, technological, and so on) that bear on the profession of arms. This cannot be achieved by reading the local newspaper or watching the news on television. All officers should read at least one weekly newsmagazine; *The Economist* is particularly good. They should read general professional journals and journals concerned with their specialties. Officers should read *Defense Daily* (www.defensedaily.com), as well as scholarly journals such as *Foreign Affairs*, *Journal of International Affairs*, *Journal of Strategic Studies*, *Orbis*, and *Political Science Quarterly*.

The chairman of the Joint Chiefs of Staff, the chiefs of staff, and the Chief of Naval Operations produce reading lists that provide excellent direction for officers desiring to improve their knowledge of the profession of arms. All reading lists can be found via Internet search; the current CSAF reading list is available at static.dma.mil/usaf/csafreadinglist.

Two lists follow: one of selected professional journals and other periodicals, and a second of selected professional associations, each of which publishes a periodical for its members. Neither list is inclusive of all professional journals and associations that may be of interest to Air Force officers. Furthermore, all officers should identify those additional publications related to their specialties and keep abreast of them as well. All officers should also consider joining one or more of the associations listed below, as well as those societies devoted to their specialties. Please note that many of the journals and periodicals are available online free of charge, especially their current editions, and you will find many in hardcopy at your base library.

SELECTED PROFESSIONAL JOURNALS AND OTHER PERIODICALS

Ad Astra, National Space Society, www.nss.org/adastra

Air and Space Power Journal is an official Air Force quarterly with a focus on operational issues. The journal is online at www.airpower.maxwell. af.mil

Strategic Studies Quarterly is an official Air Force quarterly with a focus on strategic issues. The journal is online at www.au.af.mil/au/ssq

Air Force Times, www.airforcetimes.com

Air Forces Monthly, www.airforcesmonthly.com

Airman, airman.dodlive.mil

Armed Forces Journal, www.armedforcesjournal.com

Armed Forces and Society, afs.sagepub.com

Aviation Week and Space Technology, www.aviationweek.com/awst.aspx

Citizen Airman (official magazine of the Air Force Reserve), www.citamn. afrc.af.mil

Inside the Air Force, defensenewsstand.com.

Jane's Defence Weekly, www.janes-defence-weekly.com

Jane's International Defense Review, magazines.ihs.com/IDR

Joint Force Quarterly, http://www.dtic.mil/doctrine/jfq/jfq.htm

Marine Corps Gazette, www.mca-marines.org/gazette

Military Review, online at usacac.army.mil/cac2/militaryreview

Naval War College Review, www.usnwc.edu/Publications/Naval-War-College-Review.aspx

Parameters, www.strategicstudiesinstitute.army.mil/pubs/parameters

Surface Warfare, surfwarmag.ahf.nmci.navy.mil

SELECTED PROFESSIONAL ASSOCIATIONS

Air Force Association (membership fees include subscription to *Air Force Magazine*), 1501 Lee Highway, Arlington, VA 22209-1198; P.O. Box 790, Clinton, MD 20735-0790; www.afa.org.

Air Force Historical Foundation (membership fees include subscription to *Air Power History*), www.afhistoricalfoundation.com.

Military Officers Association of America (membership fees include subscription to *Military Officer*), 201 N. Washington St., Alexandria, VA 22314, www.moaa.org.

National Guard Association of the United States (membership fees include subscription to *National Guard*), One Massachusetts Ave. NW, Washington, DC 20001, www.ngaus.org.

Reserve Officers Association (membership fees include subscription to *The Officer*), One Constitutional Ave. NE, Washington, DC 20002-5618, www.roa.org.

Society for Military History (membership fees include subscription to *Journal of Military History*), George C. Marshall Library, Lexington, VA 24450-1600, www.smh-hq.org.

BASE LIBRARIES

Although individual officers may choose to subscribe to several professional or specialty publications, or to buy several books in the "Professional Reading Guide" (see appendix B), financial considerations will limit acquisition of a large professional library. Fortunately, most base libraries have adequate collections of professional books and subscribe to a wide variety of professional and specialty publications. Most base libraries will have the books of the CSAF's Reading List available for checkout.

Junior officers may be inclined to despair when confronted with professional education obligations in addition to day-to-day specialty obligations. But if professional reading is made a habit early in an officer's career, it will not be a burden, but something to enjoy, because it is at the heart of the officer's chosen profession. Moreover, professional self-study will inevitably relate to an officer's specialty, improving daily performance. The experiences of an ongoing Air Force career, and even the opportunities to broaden perspective afforded by foreign travel, will also contribute to developing professional military expertise.

PROFESSIONAL WRITING

All officers are frequently required to write and write effectively. As with expository and persuasive writing in the civil sector, writing in the Air Force should be well organized, clear, concise, and, of course, free of spelling, grammar, and punctuation errors. Avoid Air Force jargon, or militarese; rather, use plain, standard English. The Air Force has style rules and formats for a variety of written correspondence. Refer to AFMAN 33-326, *Preparing Official Correspondence*, and AFH 33-337, *The Tongue and Quill*. All officers need their own copies of *The Tongue and Quill*, which addresses military speaking and logic, as well as writing. Another popular practical guide is William McIntosh's *Guide to Effective Military Writing*, published by Stackpole Books.

10

Health and Fitness

The Air Force recognizes the direct link between physical fitness and job performance, health, and happiness. The importance of physical fitness can best be illustrated by the fact that supervisors record an officer's physical fitness test results on the new Officer Performance Report (AF Form 707). In addition, the Air Force Instruction governing fitness (AFI 36-2905, *Fitness Program*) begins with a Commander's Intent, just as do operational war plans, and states:

Commander's Intent:

It is every Airman's responsibility to maintain the standard set forth in this AFI 365 days a year. Being physically fit allows you to properly support the Air Force mission. The goal of the Fitness Program (FP) is to motivate all members to participate in a year-round physical conditioning program that emphasizes total fitness, to include proper aerobic conditioning, strength/flexibility training, and healthy eating. Health benefits from an active lifestyle will increase productivity, optimize health, and decrease absenteeism while maintaining a higher level of readiness. Commanders and supervisors must incorporate fitness into the AF culture establishing an environment for members to maintain physical fitness and health to meet expeditionary mission requirements. The Fitness Assessment (FA) provides commanders with a tool to assist in the determination of overall fitness of their military personnel. Commander-driven physical fitness training is the backbone of the AF physical fitness program and an integral part of mission requirements. The program promotes aerobic and muscular fitness, flexibility, and optimal body composition of each member in the unit.

AIR FORCE FITNESS PROGRAM

The Air Force has made fitness a part of its culture to ensure that every airman is personally fit for expeditionary mission requirements. In 2013, the Air Force instituted its new comprehensive fitness program (AFI 36-2905, *Fitness Program*). As indicated in the Commander's Intent, the program requires airmen to participate in a year-round physical conditioning program that emphasizes total fitness, including effective aerobic conditioning, strength and flexibility training, and healthy eating. The program requires each airman to follow a fit and healthy lifestyle. Units will have a Healthy Living Program to assist the member in making changes that support fitness and nutritional health. No longer will passing an annual fitness test suffice.

Physical Training. To establish and maintain a fitness environment, commanders are required to have unit-based physical training sessions at least three times each week, and each airman must participate in at least three weekly physical training sessions. Every airman is permitted to engage in ninety-minute exercise sessions, during duty hours, from three to five times a week. These physical training sessions aren't excuses for golf; rather, they must be effective cardiorespiratory and weight training exercise, specifically running and doing push-ups and crunches.

Healthy Eating. Aerobic and anaerobic physical training is one component of the Air Force Fitness Program. Healthy eating is another component; healthy eating includes what you eat, how much you eat, and when and how often you eat. Two-thirds of American adults are overweight, and about half of those are obese. We're naturally attracted to food that's unhealthy, and unlike our ancestors, we no longer engage in unrelenting physical activity and we're no longer threatened with starvation. In American society, it may seem that many factors work against healthy eating habits. Many fast-food options exist and most are happy to "supersize" the fried foods and sugar-infused drinks that often lead to obesity. The Air Force is determined to help you understand the benefits of good eating habits and the penalties of bad ones. This encourages healthy nutrition and a fit force. Your base's health and wellness center has a nutritionist on staff to advise you in making healthy eating choices. These nutrition experts are available to assist your dependents, too. See AFI 44-141, *Nutrition Standards and Education*, for additional information and program guidance.

Drugs. One of the most certain methods of destroying good health is through the use legal and illegal drugs. Alcohol, tobacco, and illegal drugs are frequently abused substances. The most frequently abused of these is alcohol, which can be legally consumed by Americans twenty-one years of age and older. Unfortunately, there's no pat answer as to what is excessive. Life would be far simpler for most people if there were pat answers—if it could be said that two drinks during an evening are not dangerous, but that three drinks are dangerous. Not so. It all depends on you; for those who are genetically programmed for alcoholism, one drink is too much. If you prefer, you need not drink at all. No one will think less of you. Even if they do, it's their problem, not yours.

The Department of Defense is making a concerted effort to discourage servicemembers from using tobacco products. Tobacco products not only damage active abusers, but tobacco smoke also puts passive smokers' health at risk. Today in the military, nonsmoking offices and workplaces are the rule. During off-duty hours, it's your choice to smoke or not, but if you smoke, you're responsible for being considerate of those who do not, because passive smoking is also dangerous—and irritating.

Just say no to illegal drugs. If you don't yet care about your health, at least consider the well-being of your family and your career. Mandatory urinalysis is deadly to an Air Force career, as is drug abuse to the individual. See AFI44-121, *Alcohol and Drug Abuse Prevention and Treatment Program*; AFI 40-102, *Tobacco Use in the Air Force*; and AFI44-120, *Military Drug Demand Reduction Program*.

Fitness Testing. The Air Force's fitness test has changed over the years; however, its focus remains on cardiorespiratory endurance, body composition, and muscular strength. The test consists of three components. The most heavily weighted component is the test for aerobic fitness, which consists of a 1.5-mile timed run, or for those who cannot run, a one-mile walk. The aerobic fitness portion of the test has a maximum point score of 60.

The second component is a measurement for body composition. This is scored by measuring the waist at the level of the upper hip bone, the abdominal circumference. The thinner that one is in the abdomen, the higher the component score, with the maximum component score being 20.

The last component tests muscular fitness through separately scored push-up and sit-up portions done in fixed-time repetitions. Each portion of the muscular fitness component carries a maximum score of 10, for a component total of 20.

The test's total overall maximum point score is 100. Tests are rated by use of charts calibrated to the airman's gender and age. Scoring tables for men and women by age are shown in appendix G.

Members must complete all the components unless medically exempted. Test components and maximum possible points are shown on this table:

Component	Possible Points
Cardiorespiratory Endurance	60
Body Composition-Abdominal Circumference	20
Muscle Fitness	
Push-ups	10
Crunches	10

Fitness levels are correlated to total scores as shown on this table:

Fitness Level	Total Score
Excellent	≥ 90
Satisfactory	$75 - 89.9$
Unsatisfactory	< 75

Airmen's scores determine how often they need to retest. Those scoring in the excellent category will retest after a year. Airmen scoring in the satisfactory category will retest every six months, and those scoring in the unsatisfactory category will retest after ninety days. In addition, airmen with unsatisfactory scores will receive additional help in order to meet standards, including programs like the healthy-living workshop that focuses on lifestyle behavior, time management, and fitness education.

MENTAL HEALTH

The Air Force Fitness Program focuses on physical fitness; however, the Air Force is equally concerned about mental fitness.

Duty. Combat operations tempo, especially, can produce tension and stress. Air Force officers lead lives characterized by long duty hours, steady pressure, sudden change, and tense occasions. Unless officers are more than usually careful of their health, the long years of tension may finally take their toll, perhaps grievously. Most doctors look on stress as the chief debilitating agent of modern times. Anxiety and worrying are probably the most expensive of all pastimes, because they not only prevent effective action to remove the cause of worry, but also degrade physical and mental strength, thus making those under stress less capable of taking action. Stress, however, is more a symptom than a disease. This thought brings us to the area of mental health. Mental health—serenity, happiness—is usually firm and stable when there's no cause for concern about health, family, career, or finances. An entire spectrum of special situations doesn't fall within these four categories, but a great deal of all unhappiness stems from these fatal four. Officers must take care of not only their own health, but also the health of others whose lives touch their own. In the Air Force, it is called being a good wingman.

Dependents' Health. You should not allow your official duties as an officer to prevent your taking proper steps to ensure the health of your loved ones. Personal duty may necessitate absenting yourself from your place of work for a few hours to take your child to the doctor for a needed checkup. Do so. Your commander will approve; but ask beforehand. Here is the point: If you fail to see that your spouse or child gets proper medical attention at the time it can do the most good, sooner or later your spouse or child may become seriously ill. If you become deeply disturbed as a result, the Air Force loses your most effective services, not for a few hours, but for weeks or months. Obviously, your duty may separate you from your family. This result is almost inevitable considering the missions that the Air Force faces today and the intensity of combat operations tempo. Minimize this possibility by keeping family health and your legal and financial matters in order. See chapter 26, "Legal Documents and Assistance," and chapter 27, "Financial Security for Your Family."

Family Problems. No person enjoys the best mental health when family relationships are abnormal. The foremost consideration in this area is the relationship between husband and wife. Air Force officers can't live a daily home life full of strain and turmoil and at the same time do a top-notch job at work. If trouble persists between husband and wife, the two should discuss their problem with a chaplain or a counselor. False pride in officers is poor justification for suppressing a situation that can wreck lives, careers, and the health, mental and physical, of all involved. Marital problems are the proper concern of the Air Force because these strains can and very often do result in poor health, poor efficiency, or both. Officers suffering from appendicitis do not hesitate to lay this problem before a doctor. They should as quickly seek competent advice on family problems because these can be, in the long run, more damaging than most bodily ailments.

Career Satisfaction. Concern about your career and duty conditions (such as TDY frequency and combat operations tempo) can become a source of worry, bitterness, or frustration amounting to a major menace to mental health. Perhaps you feel you've been forced into a career channel to which you're unsuited. Perhaps you believe you've been mistreated in the matter of promotion. These thoughts often lead to a state of mind incompatible with mental fitness, and can markedly degrade your job performance. If such a problem develops, talk it over with your commander in complete frankness. The commander may not agree with you but will at least know your state of mind. By sharing your problem with someone, you lighten it somewhat. Better still, the commander may be able to do something about it. If you don't feel comfortable talking to your commander, go see a chaplain or a lawyer or a community mental health professional. But do something—don't just keep it inside until you make yourself ill.

Finances. Finances are perhaps the greatest single source of worry among officers, and the greatest single source of career and marital troubles. All officers should spend ample time *thinking*—not worrying—about their finances. Trite as it may sound, there's no good substitute for a budget. A budget is simply a financial plan, a program for matching financial obligations and income. All officers can draw up a budget for themselves. The trick is to stick to it. If you do need assistance, then take advantage of one of the family advocacy programs available at most installations, whether for budgeting, taxes, or another reason.

Easy Credit. Foremost among the financial traps awaiting officers is easy credit. Officers are considered excellent credit risks because the services require them to meet their debts. Officers can buy on credit almost anything they are willing to sign for. There's a great temptation, therefore, to go for the high-priced car, the deluxe television set, a state-of-the-art personal computer, and the best-quality furniture. The best help in resisting these temptations is the cold logic of a personal budget. A budget will show you exactly what you can afford to buy with your income.

If, however, you slip into debt, the best action is to consult with Family Services. When you pay off your credit cards, however, make sure you don't simply run them up again.

Other than by foolhardy practices as spending too much money on liquor or gambling, the chief methods of encountering financial troubles are in connection with renting or buying a house, buying a car, and purchasing furniture or appliances.

Renting an Apartment or a House. Renting is an experience that Air Force officers often face, so consider these points. Begin at the base housing office, which will have leads regarding where to look, as well as where not to look—places that military personnel are forbidden to rent. A lease is binding on you as an Air Force officer unless you get permanent change of station (PCS) orders. Make sure your lease has a military clause. The Housing Office and the base Legal Office can assist you in this effort.

Be very clear as to what the rent covers. How about utilities? Water? Heat? Who pays for these? If the landlord requires an extra month's rent as a deposit in advance, exactly what are the conditions under which you will be able to get your deposit back? Is fair wear and tear chargeable? Before renting, ask to see a few utility bills for the winter and summer months. These are, in effect, additional rent. Consider such matters thoughtfully before you sign the lease.

Buying a House. Buying a house is probably the most momentous financial decision you will ever make. Thorough investigation of all angles is imperative, especially in these days of conventional, variable rate, and creative financing in addition to your eligibility for VA and FHA guaranteed loans. Current four-year tours often make buying a house *seem* like a reasonable investment. But before you buy, research the housing market in your area to assess your chances of being able to resell or rent your house when you PCS.

Buying Cars. The primary mistake of many young officers in buying an automobile is to sign up for a luxury car on an economy model budget. Any fully equipped automobile is a very expensive item, especially if it's also equipped with finance charges. Further, the higher the initial price, the higher the upkeep cost. When it comes to spare parts, another factor sets in with a vengeance. Compare the cost of a new muffler for a Porsche with the same item for a Honda. Generators, starters, water pumps, tires—you must replace these, too, when they wear out. In this area you find a significant differential. Whatever your final decision, at least take these matters into account.

Buying Furniture. An officer can easily go overboard in purchasing furniture and appliances. Repeated moves or storage can reduce furniture to shambles. Buy only the items of furniture you really must have. Stay away from very expensive, delicate items. Don't try to match the Joneses, who may not move every few years. Consider reliability, availability of service, and the size of your possible quarters—on base and off—in making your decision. Sometimes a very nice, smaller-sized product from a national chain with a reputation for service after the sale is a better choice than a one-of-a-kind item that can only be serviced in the location of purchase.

Bad Checks. Carefully monitor your checkbook balance and your entire credit rating. Impress upon your spouse the need for responsibility, and if you share a checking account, be sure that each party knows the extent to which the other may use it. Keep an amount in your account as a cushion above your monthly expenditures. If possible, either arrange with your bank to notify you if there is a slipup before bouncing a check, or authorize it to cover the amount by drawing against your savings account.

In April 2014, the Air Force introduced the Comprehensive Airman Fitness (CAF) program. The service designed this program as a holistic approach to the fitness and resilience of airmen—military members, civilians, and family members. CAF focuses on mental, physical, social, and spiritual aspects in a more comprehensive (rather than stand-alone) method and will implement a range of education, fitness training, activities, and other programs critical to "sustaining a fit, resilient, and ready force."

In summary, the Air Force depends on officers and enlisted personnel who are physically and mentally healthy and fit. Because of the demands made by the expeditionary mission, the Air Force is now taking a more active role to ensure that all airmen are capable of effectively accomplishing their duties. The fitness program addresses physical health and fitness. Although the fitness program does not directly address the issues of mental health, individual airmen are not left to deal with their problems by themselves. If you have a problem that threatens your mental health, seek competent advice, and seek it early. Remember that your health is a matter of proper and sincere concern to your superiors in the Air Force, your doctor, and your chaplain. Do not ignore the help they can and will gladly give if you ask. If troubles arise, do not just worry. Do something! In addition, be a good wingman to your unit members—one of them may need help and not know where to start to obtain assistance. Just your concern can be the difference in healthy change versus a worsening situation.

11

Promotion

The subject of promotion often comes up for discussion when officers gather. Such discussions are only natural because promotion is the avenue to increased responsibility and rank, as well as the pay that goes with increased responsibility. Promotion causes heated discussions, but often without full consideration of just what the promotion system is supposed to accomplish, the methods available, or the problems involved in the operation of a career promotion system. Understanding the promotion system—what it is, how it works, and some of the obstacles involved—requires a review of the laws and policies governing promotion. See AFPAM 36-2506, *You and Your Promotions: The Air Force Officer Promotion Program.*

DEFENSE OFFICER PERSONNEL MANAGEMENT ACT (DOPMA)

To an extent unparalleled by any other profession, U.S. law establishes the parameters of the careers of commissioned officers. These laws reflect the concern of the Congress and the nation in maintaining the high quality of our officer corps and the recognition that this quality is essential to national security. A landmark in the legislation governing officer personnel management was the enactment of the Defense Officer Personnel Management Act (DOPMA), which became effective on 15 September 1981.

DOPMA updated outmoded aspects of earlier law, introduced important new officer personnel management concepts, and completed the task begun with the Officer Personnel Act of 1947 of unifying and standardizing the law as it applies to officers of the armed services. Although DOPMA deals in comprehensive fashion with all aspects of officer personnel management, the bulk of the legislation concerns the dimensions and characteristics of the career system for officers and the specific rules governing promotion procedures. The changes from earlier systems and procedures were evolutionary, building on experience under previous laws to improve the overall quality of the officer corps.

DOPMA created a single system of permanent promotions for all officers on active duty. This system replaced a complex and sometimes confusing system of temporary and permanent promotions. With DOPMA, all active-duty officers are considered under the same rules governing promotion eligibility and consideration.

With DOPMA in force, the officer corps will continue to have a mix of regular and reserve officers on extended active duty, although all officers selected for promotion to major will be offered regular appointments. Most officers, who enter active service as reservists, will first be considered for a regular appointment before the eighth year of active service (approximately at the seventh year). The final consideration point is on selection for major.

PROMOTION SYSTEM OBJECTIVES
Air Force promotion plans have these objectives:
- To fill Air Force positions. The primary purpose of the active-duty promotion system is to select the best-qualified officers available to fill Air Force positions. Therefore, the system must be responsive to the needs of the Air Force. Promotion is not a reward for past service; it is based on demonstrated potential to serve in positions of greater responsibility.
- To provide reasonably stable, consistent, and visible career progression opportunities. The active-duty promotion system must also provide incentive to the officer. It must provide reasonable opportunity for promotion, including accelerated promotion from below the promotion zone for officers possessing exceptional potential. The active-duty promotion system should be relatively stable, so as to offer each year group of officers opportunity comparable with that of other year groups.
- To maintain force vitality. To carry out their role in support of national objectives, the armed forces have a unique requirement to maintain a young and dynamic officer corps that is capable of developing and managing a large combat-ready force and of assuming wartime leadership. The Air Force promotion system is designed to produce officers in sufficient quality and quantity while maintaining a well-balanced force in terms of age and experience.

The Air Force must continue to cultivate a promotion system that will select those who best meet the challenges for future leadership.

PROMOTION BOARDS
How does one officer get promoted and another not? No discussion of the subject is realistic that does not touch upon how officers get themselves promoted. Although cynics may say that the prerequisites are to be a general's offspring, in-law, or aide, you may reasonably doubt the truth of that point of view because there is too much evidence to the contrary. Others may subscribe to the philosophy that if they do a good job the system will take care of them, but this theory, too, is an insufficient explanation.

Discussing how a typical promotion board operates may help you understand better how the selection process—often shrouded in mystery and distorted by rumor—really works. First, to scotch some rumors, it does not help to have a friend on the board; job descriptions and word pictures *are* important, as are the blocks checked; and the process does not favor select groups.

A selection board uses the following officer records as instruments: all officer performance reports (OPRs) and training reports, citations or orders for approved U.S. decorations, the officer selection brief, letters pertaining to nonattendance at or ineligibility for professional military education, letters to the board from officers eligible in or above the promotion zone, and specified unfavorable information, such as court-martial orders and Air Force forms reflecting the imposition of nonjudicial punishment. The selection board also uses each officer's Promotion Recommendation Form that recommends "Definitely Promote," "Promote," or "Do Not Promote This Board."

All selection boards use the best-qualified method of selection. Because the board can recommend only a set maximum number, it must arrange those eligible in an order-of-merit listing (best to least qualified), apply the quota to this listing, and promote those officers above the line where the quota runs out. Boards evaluate officers using the whole-person concept. Board members carefully review each officer's selection folder, especially in the areas of job responsibility and performance, leadership, breadth of experience, professional competence, and academic and professional military education.

The board knows that records contain evaluations under several different assignments. The ratee's job, unit of assignment, and level of responsibility all play a part in evaluation. The new OPR reflects the tremendous importance now being put on the officer's physical fitness test. The selection folder reflects each officer's level of academic and professional military education, but the board judges to what extent these achievements improve performance and potential to assume greater responsibility. The board does not give mere completion of such courses disproportionate credit, but the board does weigh the completion/non-completion of advanced degrees or PME appropriate to the rank under consideration for promotion. Some officers, such as those assigned to engineering or scientific areas or to some particular rated specialty, may not receive an opportunity for career broadening, so boards do not penalize them for that reason.

Boards must promote the best officers they review for consideration, and the board members—highly qualified officers who have the experience and mature judgment to make accurate assessments of potential—must take an oath to perform their duties without prejudice or partiality, having in view the fitness of the officers considered and the efficiency of the USAF. The Air Force takes pains to ensure that board panels make selections on a uniform basis. Of course, in the last analysis, individuals' views of the promotion selection process may depend upon whether they are selected or not, but the Air Force makes strenuous and conscientious efforts to ensure that the selection basis is the best one possible.

HOW TO GET PROMOTED

This question has no perfect and unequivocal answer, but some observations based on experience may help. First, hit the ground running when you go on active duty. Whether you go first to flight or technical training or get on-the-job training, master your *job* quickly and thoroughly and give it 100 percent effort. Although your seniors, peers, and subordinates should give you aid and comfort, don't assume that anyone is going to help you learn the ropes. After this step, begin learning your *profession*, the profession of arms. Even in this age of specialization, just being a specialist—a pilot, a maintenance officer, or an intelligence officer—is usually not enough. Keep in mind, the higher up in rank you go, the greater the percentage of well-serving officers that will not be promoted by the board. You must distinguish yourself with your performance and your knowledge of the profession of arms. The military profession is an honorable profession. Learn it, understand it, and respect it.

Along the way, you may want to become an expert in some aspect of the military arts and sciences that few others know. If you are *the* expert, your expertise may lead you to some interesting experiences.

Strive for assignments at increasingly higher command and staff levels, including joint staff duties. When you can obtain advanced education and PME, go for it.

Because your fellow officer is at the same time your comrade, your peer, and your competitor for promotion, you must maintain a proper perspective about this business of promotion. Above all, keep a good sense of humor. Always be yourself, never forgetting Polonius's advice to Laertes in *Hamlet*: "This above all, to thine own self be true. Thou canst not then be false to any man." After your career has ended and if you have soldiered as a professional, not only will you cherish the worth of it all, having followed the path of duty, honor, country, but you will also cherish the camaraderie that was such an essential part of it.

12

Officer Evaluation System

The measurement of an officer's performance, with potentials, strengths, and weaknesses, is a matter of importance to the Air Force, as well as to the individual officer. Next to expertise in career specialty, performance reports constitute the most important single source of information for selection and assignment of people to do the work of the Air Force. They are the means by which all members may be placed where their work will be of greatest value. Here also will be recorded the information that will determine selection for promotion, for favored assignment, for the higher schools, or for actions leading possibly to termination of service.

Junior officers are not so much concerned with why performance reports are necessary, or even with the responsibility imposed upon the rating officers, as they are with how to obtain favorable performance reports. This chapter will therefore discuss the Officer Evaluation System (OES), how the rating system's forms work, and how you can get higher evaluations. A full explanation of the Officer Evaluation System can be found in AFI 36-2406, *Officer and Enlisted Evaluation Systems*, and AFPAM 36-2506, *You and Your Promotions: The Air Force Officer Promotion Program*.

Officers who study this information and apply it will improve their promotion opportunities. In addition, many officers will find themselves in the position of writing performance reports on other officers and enlisted personnel sooner than they may now think.

THE OES AND OFFICER PROFESSIONAL DEVELOPMENT
Because any appraisal system is an integral part of officer professional development, it is important to understand the Air Force concept of professional development. It has three basic objectives.

First, professional development must increase the officer's qualification and ability to perform duties, now and in the future. Formal training, education, and discussions with supervisors provide a foundation for building this competence. However, the most direct contributor is likely to be the officer's experiences in day-to-day duties.

Second, professional development involves preparing officers for future leadership challenges. Professional military education and most other education assist this effort. An officer should leverage the many "experiences" available through education to augment the individual experiences gained in the course of one's career.

The third objective of professional development is to ensure that the people who are best qualified are advanced in grade and responsibility. This objective point is where the Officer Evaluation System fits in.

What makes an officer "best qualified" for promotion? The right kind of experience, training, education, and, of course, job performance at the right time.

Lieutenants and captains become best qualified for promotion by concentrating on depth of experience in their fields of specialization. Staff assignments and other career-broadening experiences are not needed for promotion to major. Some captains will serve in staff jobs because their expertise is needed, but the OES strongly emphasizes performance in the assigned job for company grade officers, with neither credit nor penalty for staff jobs.

There is increased opportunity for field-grade officers to fill command and staff jobs, with more diverse job opportunities and accompanying broadened career opportunities. Field-grade officers who choose to forgo broader opportunities and remain in primary line duties should still have a reasonable prospect for promotion to lieutenant colonel, given a level of performance warranting promotion. The lieutenant colonel seeking promotion to colonel will generally need emphasis on broader considerations as well as job performance.

The point is that lieutenants and captains need not make a long-term career decision between a narrow focus on line jobs and broadening. Whatever their long-term goals, the right focus at the lieutenant and captain level is on their career specialty. The primary concern of all officers should be doing the very best possible job in their primary duties, day in and day out.

WHY AN OES?

The Air Force has a high-quality officer force, making competition for promotion inevitable. An evaluation system should not attempt to eliminate or even reduce the intensity of this competition. Rather, the OES must ensure that officers compete on the right basis by measuring the proper accomplishments and qualities.

The number of officers to be selected for promotion by any given board is limited because there is a ceiling imposed by law on the number of officers who can be serving in the field grades. Promotion opportunity and select rates to all grades remain relatively constant regardless of the evaluation system used. The purpose of an evaluation system is to ensure that promotion boards have the information to select, within these percentages, those officers who are the best qualified.

PERFORMANCE FEEDBACK

Performance feedback, for lieutenants to colonels, is an important element of the OES, and supervisors conduct these reviews during a private, formal meeting with the officer. It is designed to provide a realistic assessment of the officer's performance. An initial session requiring the supervisor to let an officer know what is expected establishes the basis for later feedback on how well the officer is meeting these expectations. The second feedback meeting will occur midway through the officer's reporting cycle to allow for corrections in deficient areas. Additional feedback meetings can be initiated by either the ratee or the rater.

The supervisor prepares a handwritten form (AF Form 724) that provides an assessment of the subordinate's performance, and the two discuss the comments on the form. At the conclusion of the session, the rater gives the form to the officer being provided the feedback. The feedback form does not become part of an officer's record, nor can the rater show the form to anyone other than the officer on whom the form has been prepared.

Supervisors provide feedback on duty performance, job knowledge, leadership skills, organizational skills, judgment and decisions, professional qualities, communication skills, and physical fitness using a scale that ranges from "does not meet" to "clearly exceeds." The rater includes written comments to expand on these ratings. The rater also addresses the ratee's strengths, goals, education, and future assignments.

OFFICER PERFORMANCE REPORT

The Officer Performance Report (OPR) is designed to build a continuing record of performance. For lieutenants through colonels, the rater is an officer's immediate supervisor, the same person who provides performance feedback, so the person being rated should not be surprised by the content of the report. Furthermore, the performance factors rated on AF Form 707, Officer Performance Report, are identical to those addressed during performance feedback. Annotation is provided only if the ratee does not meet standards. The OPR requires a brief job description and short overall assessment. The ratee signs the report to acknowledge all required feedback was accomplished during the reporting period. AF Form 707 allows for correction of factual errors before the report is forwarded.

The additional rater is the supervisor's boss. For officers below the grade of colonel, the additional rater must be at least one grade senior to the officer being rated. A senior officer, called the reviewer, will perform quality control on the report. The reviewer will not normally provide a rating and does not make comments about the officer unless there is disagreement with the rating of the rater or additional rater. For lieutenants through majors, the reviewer is the wing commander or equivalent staff officer. For lieutenant colonels and colonels, the reviewer is the first general officer in the rating chain. The reviewer will be in a position to have personal knowledge, or access to such knowledge, of the officer's job performance.

The emphasis of the performance report is on how well officers accomplish their primary duties. The raters will not consider or evaluate the probable

PERFORMANCE FEEDBACK WORKSHEET (Lt thru Col)

I. PERSONAL INFORMATION

NAME	GRADE	UNIT

II. TYPES OF	INITIAL	MID-TERM	RATEE REQUESTED	RATER DIRECTED

III. PRIMARY DUTIES

IV. PERFORMANCE FEEDBACK

1. Job Knowledge. Has knowledge required to perform duties effectively. Strives to improve knowledge. Applies knowledge to handle non-routine situations.

N/A Initial Feedback	Does Not Meet	Meets	Above Average	Clearly Exceeds

2. Leadership Skills. Sets and enforces standards. Works well with others. Fosters teamwork. Displays initiative. Self-sufficient. Motivates subordinates. Has respect and confidence of subordinates. Fair and consistent in evaluation of subordinates.

N/A Initial Feedback	Does Not Meet	Meets	Above Average	Clearly Exceeds

3. Professional Qualities. Exhibits loyalty, discipline, dedication, integrity, honesty, and officership. Adheres to Air Force standards. Accepts personal responsibility. Is fair and objective.

N/A Initial Feedback	Does Not Meet	Meets	Above Average	Clearly Exceeds

4. Organizational Skills. Plans, coordinates, schedules and uses resources effectively. Meets suspenses. Schedules work for self and others equitably and effectively. Anticipates and solves problems.

N/A Initial Feedback	Does Not Meet	Meets	Above Average	Clearly Exceeds

5. Judgment and Decisions. Makes timely and accurate decisions. Emphasizes logic in decision making. Retains composure in stressful situations. Recognizes opportunities. Adheres to safety and occupational health requirements. Acts to take advantage of opportunities.

N/A Initial Feedback	Does Not Meet	Meets	Above Average	Clearly Exceeds

6. Communication Skills. Listens, speaks, and writes effectively.

N/A Initial Feedback	Does Not Meet	Meets	Above Average	Clearly Exceeds

7. Physical Fitness. Maintains Air Force physical fitness standards.

Does Not Meet	Meets	Exempt

Performance Feedback Worksheet (front)

V. PROFESSIONAL DEVELOPMENT

STRENGTHS

SUGGESTED GOALS

ACADEMIC/PROFESSIONAL EDUCATION

DE (BDE, IDE, SDE RESIDENCE/SEMINAR/CORRESPONDENCE)

NEXT/FUTURE ASSIGNMENTS (BASE LEVEL, STAFF, JOINT, CONUS, OVERSEAS)

VI. ADDITIONAL COMMENTS

RATEE SIGNATURE	RATER SIGNATURE	DATE

AF FORM 724, 20070625   PREVIOUS EDITIONS ARE OBSOLETE (724A and 724B)

Performance Feedback Worksheet *(reverse)*

impact of professional military education, advanced degrees, or broadening assignments. This information is available elsewhere in an officer's record. The rater's task is to focus on performance and potential based on that performance.

Performance reports make up the cumulative record of an officer's performance. They will weigh heavily both in the promotion board's deliberations and in the senior rater's recommendation for promotion, which will be made on a separate form.

PROMOTION RECOMMENDATION

To assist promotion boards in selecting those officers best qualified for promotion, there is the Promotion Recommendation Form (PRF), which focuses strongly on duty performance for junior officers. It is completed sixty days before a promotion board on all officers eligible for promotion in or above the promotion zone and on a specific percentage of those officers eligible below the promotion zone. The individual completing the form is the officer's senior rater. For lieutenants, captains, and majors, this will be the wing commander or equivalent staff officer. For lieutenant colonels, it will be the first general officer in the rating chain. The senior rater is the same individual who acts as reviewer for the OPR. A different term has been chosen to reflect the different function on the PRF. The senior rater completes the PRF based on knowledge of the officer and on a review of the officer's overall record of performance.

The Promotion Recommendation Form consists of a brief description of the unit's mission, the officer's job description, narrative comments about the officer's promotion potential, and one of three possible recommendations: "Definitely Promote," "Promote," or "Do Not Promote This Board." A "Definitely Promote" recommendation tells the central promotion board that an officer's performance and performance-based potential alone warrant promotion, with minimal regard for broader considerations, such as variety of job experience, PME, and academic education. A "Promote" recommendation means that the officer is well qualified for promotion and should compete on the basis of performance, performance-based potential, and broader considerations.

The number of "Definitely Promote" recommendations for in- and above-the-promotion-zone officers is limited to a number smaller than the total number of officers that a board can select for advancement. These percentages will vary by grade. Experience suggests that when promotion boards are given a vehicle to assist them in differentiating among officers on the basis of performance, they will use it. Therefore, officers in and above the promotion zone who receive a "Definitely Promote" assessment will probably be promoted at a high rate. Even if all officers with a "Definitely Promote" are selected, a specified number of people who receive a "Promote" recommendation will also be promoted. The latter is a mathematical reality based on the fact that more officers will be promoted than will meet the board with a "Definitely Promote" recommendation.

OFFICER PERFORMANCE REPORT (Lt thru Col)

I. RATEE IDENTIFICATION DATA *(Read AFI 36-2406 carefully before filling in any item)*

1. NAME *(Last, First, Middle Initial)*	2. SSN	3. GRADE	4. DAFSC	5. REASON FOR REPORT	6. PAS CODE

7. ORGANIZATION. COMMAND. LOCATION. AND COMPONENT	8. PERIOD OF REPORT	9. NO. DAYS SUPV.
	THRU	

II. JOB DESCRIPTION *(Limit text to 4 lines)*
DUTY TITLE

10. SRID

III. PERFORMANCE FACTORS

	DOES NOT MEET STANDARDS	MEETS STANDARDS	FITNESS EXEMPTION
Job Knowledge, Leadership Skills, Professional Qualities, Organizational Skills, Judgment and Decisions, Communication Skills, and Physical Fitness *(see reverse if marked Does Not Meet Standards)*			

IV. RATER OVERALL ASSESSMENT *(Limit text to 6 lines)*

Last performance feedback was accomplished on: ¦(IAW AFI 36-2406) (If not accomplished, state the reason)

NAME. GRADE. BR OF SVC. ORGN. COMMAND & LOCATION	DUTY TITLE	DATE
	SSN SIGNATURE	

V. ADDITIONAL RATER OVERALL ASSESSMENT *(Limit text to 4 lines)* ☐ CONCUR ☐ NON-CONCUR

NAME. GRADE. BR OF SVC. ORGN. COMMAND & LOCATION	DUTY TITLE	DATE
	SSN SIGNATURE	

VI. REVIEWER *(If required, limit text to 4 lines)* ☐ CONCUR ☐ NON-CONCUR

NAME. GRADE. BR OF SVC. ORGN. COMMAND & LOCATION	DUTY TITLE	DATE
	SSN SIGNATURE	

VII. FUNCTIONAL EXAMINER/AIR FORCE ADVISOR
(Indicate applicable review by marking the appropriate box) ☐ FUNCTIONAL EXAMINER ☐ AIR FORCE ADVISOR

NAME. GRADE. BR OF SVC. ORGN. COMMAND & LOCATION	DUTY TITLE	DATE
	SSN SIGNATURE	

VIII. RATEE'S ACKNOWLEDGMENT

I understand my signature does not constitute agreement or disagreement. I acknowledge all required feedback was accomplished during the reporting period and upon receipt of this report.	Yes No ☐☐	SIGNATURE	DATE

AF FORM 707, 20080618   PREVIOUS EDITIONS ARE OBSOLETE (707A and 707B)   PRIVACY ACT INFORMATION: The information in this form is FOR OFFICIAL USE ONLY. Protect IAW the Privacy Act of 1974.

Company-Grade Officer Performance Report *(front)*

RATEE NAME:

IX. PERFORMANCE FACTORS (If Section III is marked Does Not Meet Standards, fill in applicable block[s])

DOES NOT MEET STANDARDS

1. Job Knowledge. Has knowledge required to perform duties effectively. Strives to improve knowledge. Applies knowledge to handle non-routine situations. ☐

2. Leadership Skills. Sets and enforces standards. Works well with others. Fosters teamwork. Displays initiative. Self-confident. Motivates subordinates. Has respect and confidence of subordinates. Fair and consistent in evaluation of subordinates. ☐

3. Professional Qualities. Exhibits loyalty, discipline, dedication, integrity, honesty, and officership. Adheres to Air Force standards. Accepts personal responsibility. Is fair and objective. ☐

4. Organizational Skills. Plans, coordinates, schedules and uses resources effectively. Meets suspenses. Schedules work for self and others equitably and effectively. Anticipates and solves problems. ☐

5. Judgment and Decisions. Makes timely and accurate decisions. Emphasizes logic in decision making. Retains composure in stressful situations. Recognizes opportunities. Adheres to safety and occupational health requirements. Acts to take advantage of opportunities. ☐

6. Communication Skills. Listens, speaks, and writes effectively. ☐

7. Physical Fitness. Maintains Air Force physical fitness standards. ☐

X. REMARKS (use this section to spell out acronyms from the front)

XI. REFERRAL REPORT (Complete only if report contains referral comments or the overall standards block is marked as does not meet standards)

I am referring this OPR to you according to AFI 36-2406, para 1.10. It contains comment(s)/rating(s) that make(s) the report a referral as defined in AFI 36-2406, para. 1.10. Specifically, _____

Acknowledge receipt by signing and dating below. Your signature merely acknowledges that a referral report has been rendered; it does not imply acceptance of or agreement with the ratings or comments on the report. Once signed, you are entitled to a copy of this memo. You may submit rebuttal comments. Send your written comments to:

not later than 3 duty days (30 for non-EAD members) from your date below. If you need additional time, you may request an extension from the individual named above. You may submit attachments (limit to 10 pages), but they must directly relate to the reason this report was referred. Pertinent attachments not maintained elsewhere will remain attached to the report for file in your personnel record. Copies of previous reports, etc. submitted as attachments will be removed from your rebuttal package prior to filing since these documents are already filed in your records. Your rebuttal comments/attachments may not contain any reflection on the character, conduct, integrity, or motives of the evaluator unless you can fully substantiate and document them. Contact the MPF career enhancement section, or the AF Contact Center if you require any assistance in preparing your reply to the referral report. It is important for you to be aware that receiving a referral report may affect your eligibility for other personnel related actions (e.g. assignments, promotions, etc.). You may consult your commander and/or MPF or Air Force Contact Center if you desire more information on this subject. If you believe this report is inaccurate, unjust, or unfairly prejudicial to your career, you may apply for a review of the report under AFI 36-2406, Chapter 10, once the report becomes a matter of record as defined in AFI 36-2406, Attachment 1.

NAME, GRADE, BR OF SVC OF REFERRING EVALUATOR	DUTY TITLE	DATE
	SIGNATURE	

SIGNATURE OF RATEE		DATE

INSTRUCTIONS

ALL: Recommendations must be based on performance and the potential based on that performance. Promotion recommendations are prohibited. Do not comment on completion of or enrollment in Developmental Education, advanced education, previous or anticipated promotion recommendations on AF Form 709, OPR endorsement levels, family activities, marital status, race, sex, ethnic origin, age, religion or sexual orientation. Evaluators enter only the last four numbers of SSN.

RATER: Focus your evaluation in Section IV on what the officer did, how well he or she did it, and how the officer contributed to mission accomplishment. Write in concise "bullet" format. Your comments in Section IV may include recommendations for assignment. Provide a copy of the report to the ratee prior to the report becoming a matter of record and provide follow-up feedback to let the ratee know how their performance resulted in this final product.

ADDITIONAL RATER: Carefully review the rater's evaluation to ensure it is accurate, unbiased and uninflated. If you disagree, you may ask the rater to review his or her evaluation. You may not direct a change in the evaluation. If you still disagree with the rater, mark "NON-CONCUR" and explain. You may include recommendations for assignment.

REVIEWER: Carefully review the rater's and additional rater's ratings and comments. If their evaluations are accurate, unbiased and uninflated, mark "CONCUR" and sign the form. If you disagree with previous evaluators, you may ask them to review their evaluations. You may not direct them to change their appraisals. If you still disagree with the additional rater, mark "NON-CONCUR" and explain in Section VI. Do not use "NON-CONCUR" simply to provide comments on the report.

RATEE: Your signature is merely an acknowledgement of receipt of this report. It does not constitute concurrence. If you disagree with the content, you may file an evaluation appeal through the Evaluation Reports Appeals Board IAW AFI 36-2406 Chapter 10, or through the Air Force Board for Correction of Military Records IAW AFI 36-2603 (Air Force Board for Correction of Military Records) and AFPAM 36-2607 (Applicant's Guide to the Air Force Board for Correction of Military Records Correction of Military Records (AFBCMR).

PRIVACY ACT STATEMENT

AUTHORITY: Title 10 United States Code, Section 8013 and Executive Order 9397, 22 November 1943.

PURPOSE: Information is needed for verification of the individual's name and Social Security Number (SSN) as captured on the form at the time of rating.

ROUTINE USES: May specifically be disclosed outside the DoD as a routine use pursuant to 5 U.S.C. 552a(b)(3).

DISCLOSURE: Disclosure is mandatory; SSN is used for positive identification.

AF FORM 707, 20080618   PREVIOUS EDITIONS ARE OBSOLETE (707A and 707B)   PRIVACY ACT INFORMATION: The information in this form is FOR OFFICIAL USE ONLY. Protect IAW the Privacy Act of 1974.

Company-Grade Officer Performance Report *(reverse)*

PROMOTION RECOMMENDATION

PRIVACY ACT STATEMENT

AUTHORITY: 10 United States Code, Section 8013, Secretary of the Air Force; Air Force Instruction 36-2110, Assignments, and Executive Order 9397 (SSN).
PURPOSE: Effectiveness/duty performance history, promotion, and other appropriate personnel actions.
ROUTINE USES: The "Blanket Routine Uses" published in the Air Force system of records notices apply to this system.
DISCLOSURE: May specifically be disclosed outside the DoD as a routine use pursuant to 5 U.S.C. 552s(b)(3)

I. RATEE IDENTIFICATION DATA   (Read AFI 36-2406, Officer and Enlisted Evaluation Systems, carefully before filling in any item)

1. NAME (Last, First, Middle Initial)	2. SSN	3. GRADE	4. DAFSC
5. ORGANIZATION. COMMAND. LOCATION			6. PAS CODE

II. UNIT MISSION DESCRIPTION

III. JOB DESCRIPTION
1. DUTY TITLE:

2. KEY DUTIES, TASKS, RESPONSIBILITIES:

IV. PROMOTION RECOMMENDATION

V. PROMOTION ZONE	VI. GROUP SIZE	VII. BOARD	VIII. SENIOR RATER ID
BPZ ☐ I/APZ ☐			

IX. OVERALL RECOMMENDATION	X. SENIOR RATER
	NAME, GRADE, BR OF SVC, ORGN, COMD & LOCATION
DEFINITELY PROMOTE ☐	
PROMOTE ☐	DUTY TITLE
DO NOT PROMOTE THIS BOARD ☐	SSN SIGNATURE

Instructions

Senior Rater:
Review previous OERs, OPRs, Education/Training Reports, and Supplemental Evaluation Sheets. May consider other reliable information that is not contained in the record of performance when completing the PRF. Evaluate the officer's performance and assess his or her potential. Write Promotion Recommendation (Section IV) in concise "bullet" format.
Provide an accurate unbiased assessment free from consideration of race, sex, ethnic origin, age, religion, or marital status.
Provide the officer a copy of this report approximately 30 days prior to the board for which this report is prepared.

Officer:
Review record of performance, Officer Pre-Selection Brief, and PRF for accuracy. Prior to your board convening date, you must contact your senior rater to discuss if your PRF is not accurate, omits pertinent information or has an error. If your senior rater concurs, there are procedures to correct prior to the board (reference 36-2406, chapter 8). Per DOD Directive 1320.11, Special Selection Boards, paragraph 4.3., a supplemental promotion board "shall not consider any officer who might, by maintaining reasonably careful records, have discovered and taken steps to correct that error or omission on which the original board based its decision against promotion."

AF FORM 709, 20090210   PREVIOUS EDITIONS ARE OBSOLETE.   FOR OFFICIAL USE ONLY (When filled in)

Promotion Recommendation Form

Senior raters also give a percentage of their below-the-promotion-zone (BPZ) candidates "Definitely Promote" recommendations. This amounts to a nomination for early promotion and means only that the officer's record will be reviewed by the selection board. Below-the-promotion-zone "Definitely Promote" recommendations are limited to a predetermined percentage of eligible officers for promotion to lieutenant colonel and colonel; this percentage is applied only to those officers eligible for BPZ consideration. PRFs on officers who are BPZ skip the evaluation board process discussed below and go directly to the central promotion board.

After the senior rater makes promotion recommendations on above- and in-the-promotion-zone candidates, the forms are sent to management-level review (MLR). This group, made up of senior raters, meets at major command or equivalent level. The MLR board performs a quality-control function and may, in certain circumstances, allocate a limited number of "Definitely Promote" recommendations. It cannot downgrade a recommendation given by a senior rater.

Allocation of additional "Definitely Promote" recommendations by MLR occurs in two cases. The first is when a subordinate unit is too small to earn an allocation of at least one "Definitely Promote." Units with fewer eligible officers are aggregated in order to produce a group size large enough for valid quality comparisons. This occurs at MLR.

The second case in which MLR allocates "Definitely Promote" recommendations is when additional "Definitely Promote" recommendations are available as a result of rounding down. When senior raters determine how many "Definitely Promotes" they can award, they must round down any fractions to the nearest whole number. For example, a senior rater who computes that 4.5 officers may receive "Definitely Promote" recommendations can give this rating to four people. Fractional remains accrue into whole number recommendations that are allocated by MLR based on job performance of officers whose records they have reviewed.

After MLR completes its tasks, it sends all the APZ and IPZ promotion recommendations to the selection board. By law, the central selection board is charged with selecting officers for promotion. Although a "Definitely Promote" recommendation will be a strong signal, it remains up to the selection board to determine which officers are selected for promotion.

Promotion recommendations for APZ and IPZ candidates are removed after the central promotion board has finished, whether or not the officer is selected for promotion.

QUESTIONS AND ANSWERS ABOUT THE PROMOTION RECOMMENDATION FORM

What types of comments are allowed in the "Promotion Recommendation" section of the PRF?

The senior rater is expected to make a decision on promotion potential based on the officer's performance. The rater first evaluates the cumulative record of job performance reflected in the file of performance reports and applies knowledge of the officer's most recent performance. The narrative section should explain why the senior rater feels the officer should be promoted. The narrative would most likely include a brief synopsis of the officer's cumulative record of performance, a statement linking that performance to advancement qualification, and an appropriate recommendation for promotion. The narrative would not address factors not related to performance, but rather should focus on performance. The rater may highlight any particular aspects of performance that set the officer apart from others and make the officer being rated best qualified for promotion.

How are senior rater positions and grades chosen?

These officers must be senior enough in grade to have the scope and breadth of experience to assess long-term performance based on the officer's record as reported on performance reports. At the same time, senior raters need to be close enough to the officers being rated to have reliable knowledge of their most recent performance or access to reliable knowledge and need to understand the significance of that performance as it relates to potential and promotion. The OPR reviewer and PRF senior rater are the same person. The terms are different to depict their different roles in the OES.

What is the significance of the three levels of recommendation the senior rater can make?

Definitely Promote. This recommendation indicates that the strength of the officer's performance and performance-based potential alone warrant promotion, with minimum regard for broader considerations.

Promote. This recommendation indicates that the officer is well qualified and should compete at the promotion board on the basis of performance, performance-based potential, and broader considerations. A "Promote" recommendation means exactly that—promote. The senior rater believes the officer should be promoted.

Do Not Promote This Board. This recommendation means that, based on the cumulative record of the performance and on personal knowledge of the most recent performance, the senior rater believes that the officer should not be promoted on the board for which the promotion recommendation is being prepared. As with all promotion recommendations prepared on IPZ and APZ officers, the "Do Not Promote This Board" recommendation is removed from the promotion file selection folder after the central promotion board reviews the record and makes final consideration. Thus, a "Do Not Promote This Board" does not become a permanent part of an officer's selection folder.

If an APZ or IPZ officer receives a "Definitely Promote" recommendation, does this mean promotion is virtually guaranteed?

"Definitely Promote" recommendations have a very powerful effect, and APZ and IPZ officers receiving such recommendations have a strong probability of promotion. However, by law, the promotion decision may be made only by the central promotion board. It is possible that an officer receiving a

"Definitely Promote" will not be promoted. However, there will, in all likelihood, be some indicator in the officer's selection folder of why, other than performance, this has occurred.

Why are all Promotion Recommendation Forms pulled from the record once an officer is promoted?

The promotion recommendation is intended to be a direct communication between a senior rater and a specific central selection board. This recommendation evaluates the officer's potential for advancement to a specific rank at a specific point in time based on a cumulative record of performance. Removing recommendations eliminates any potential stigma from having been selected for promotion with a "Promote" versus a "Definitely Promote" recommendation.

Why are there limits for "Definitely Promote" recommendations?

Limits are the result of two facts of life. First, the services cannot promote everyone. Public law limiting the number of officers who may serve in the field grade ranks forces choices. Second, without such limits, experience has shown that inflation is inevitable. Inflation tends to deny selection boards access to clear differentiation based on performance. To be assured their proper weight, "Definitely Promote" recommendations must be limited so that fewer officers meet the central board with a "Definitely Promote" than can be promoted. Said another way, value is associated with limited supply.

May I see my Promotion Recommendation Form?

Yes. You may have access to your Promotion Recommendation Form. Your senior rater will provide you with a copy of the form.

How are the number of "Definitely Promote" recommendations for my unit computed?

For the BPZ category, your senior rater multiplies the total number of BPZ-eligible officers in the wing or equivalent unit by the appropriate allocation percentage, rounding down. For the APZ and IPZ category, your senior rater multiplies only the number of in-the-promotion-zone eligible officers in the wing or equivalent unit by the appropriate percentage, again rounding down. If, for example, there are eight captains in your wing eligible for major IPZ and three eligible APZ, the number of "Definitely Promote" recommendations available to your senior rater is five (8 x .65). These five recommendations will go to the top performers among the eleven APZ and IPZ officers. Please note, the percentage factor can vary depending on year group size and number of promotions available on any given promotion board to any given rank.

ADDITIONAL INFORMATION ON OFFICER EVALUATIONS

Unfavorable Information Files (UIFs). UIFs provide commanders a repository of substantiated derogatory information concerning the member's personal conduct and duty performance that may form the basis for administrative, personnel, or judicial actions. These files are "For Official Use Only" and are closely controlled at all levels to preclude unauthorized disclosure. UIFs may include these items, among others: documentation concerning placement on the control roster, failure to discharge a just financial obligation, misconduct or substandard performance resulting from emotional instability, drug or alcohol abuse, or similar deviations from accepted norms of behavior. UIFs are maintained by the military personnel flight and contain only that unfavorable information that has been verified for file by the individual's commander or higher authority. In addition, a summary of UIFs on officers is maintained at MAJCOM level. Except for documentation concerning court-martial convictions, certain (specified) civil court convictions, drug abuse, records of certain (specified) Article 15 UCMJ actions mandatory for file, and control roster actions, the documentation must be referred to the member for comments. The notification of "intent to file" optional information in the UIF will be sent by the commander to the member for comments.

WHAT CONDUCT PRODUCES A MORE FAVORABLE RATING?

Of obvious importance if you seek to obtain good performance reports—and you should—are the factors your rating official weighs. First, read an OPR form. If, with objectivity, you cannot rate yourself highly, you'd better start a self-improvement regimen quickly.

An Aid to Receipt of Good Performance Reports. You must earn good performance reports that lead to selection for promotion and preferred assignments. *Forbes* magazine, a publication for business executives, included the following helpful principles as developed by management consulting firm Rogers & Slade. Observing these simple truths should help you not only in the execution of your responsibilities, but also in getting good performance reports.

In my relations with those who supervise me, I will—

- Accept my full share of responsibility.
- Make sure I know what is expected of me.
- Do what is requested in the best manner I know.
- Be agreeable when asked to do something difficult or unpleasant.
- Be honest—and not try to cover up my errors.
- Stand up for my decisions—but admit it promptly if they are shown to be wrong.
- Accept criticism in good spirit and not let a few rebukes get me down.
- Point to needed improvements but make sure my ideas are well thought out and clearly presented.

In my relations with those under my supervision, I will—

- Sell the job to be done, and not pull my rank.
- Be firm but reasonable.
- Treat those working under me as human beings—consider their feelings.
- Accept proffered suggestions—or explain why they should not be used.
- Give full job instructions and not pass the buck.
- Be friendly but not intimate—not play favorites.

- Set a good working example—not break rules I expect others to follow.
- Back up my people when they are right and give credit when and where due.

An Aid to Avoidance of Bad Performance Reports. Those who have had the opportunity of evaluating thousands of performance reports as they sat on selection boards for promotion or elimination have commented on the patterns that appear among officers whose records are below standard and have offered these tips for avoiding poor performance reports:

- Avoid unprofessional conduct, including intemperate use of liquor, questionable sexual practices, and obscenity or vulgarity.
- Avoid generating ill will among seniors, associates, or juniors.
- Avoid a reputation of mediocre or undependable performance of duty.
- Avoid a reputation of being a poor credit risk.

Summary. Officers may earn splendid reports that will lead to a successful career by establishing a reputation of always finding a legal and ethical way of getting things done; by winning the good will of those with whom they work, seniors and juniors alike; and by preparing themselves today and tonight for the discharge of the tasks of tomorrow or next week.

HOW TO WORK FOR AN "SOB"

In times past, readers have often asked for help in the delicate area of how to deal with the difficulties of working under certain officers. The editorial staff considered the matter and decided to attempt to offer something constructive. Surely, here was a field in which great good was possible. We invited an officer to write his views. Here is his answer:

Dear Editor:

You asked if I'd write a piece on how to work for an SOB. The mere thought raised wells of sympathy within me for those unfortunates who, as I did in times gone by, now suffer under a hair-shirt boss who is intolerable. How to live with the Grouchy, the Unreasonably Impatient, the Unfair, the Mean and Vicious— the summation of all the SOBs I've served under? My enthusiasm was quickened by the thought that I might be able to help those who had fallen on such evil times as to inherit an SOB as unit commander. Ah, the troubles I've known from SOBs!

Well, I began to cast about among the multitude of my SOB superiors to select the most horrendous one as my opening illustration, so as better to explain how I survived my painful ordeal while retaining my sanity. With elation upon discovering my perfect example, I began to describe old General Blank, the biggest SOB, surely, in all the world. As I wrote, however, I began to recall how, after I grew to know General Blank, I learned of his nerve-shattering war experiences, of his being finally relieved of his command and sent home more or less in physical collapse. These and other things about Blank occurred to me. On second thought, I decided he was not my candidate for Senior SOB.

When I remembered Major Dumguard, though, I knew I had my prize SOB. Dumguard's extreme impatience, his growled answers, his sudden violent anger over nothing, his indifference toward my problems—these and many other characteristics of a bonded 100-proof, aged-in-wood SOB came to mind. Yet, my resolve faded when I remembered Dumguard's young son hanging so long between life and oblivion with spinal meningitis; the deep shock of his wife's death; the fact that he lagged in promotion far behind his colleagues.

In fact, I must admit it, I can tell no one how to work for an SOB, because I've never worked for one. I have worked for people who were suffering from illnesses and who vented symptoms of these on me occasionally. I have worked for people who were bewildered, discouraged, tired, hurt, nervous, miserable, and afraid. These, too, made my life unpleasant. But I see now that these people were not true SOBs. They were human beings in some sort of trouble, people in pain, whether from real or fancied ills. Therefore, I must turn back to you unmarked pages on SOBs. I can't recall a one. Is it possible there aren't any?

Sincerely yours,

A LEGENDARY CLASSIFICATION SYSTEM

A distinguished military leader of the German army of a past era devised a classification of officers that applies even to the U.S. Air Force. According to this legend, officers fall into only four classes:

The brilliant and industrious. They make the best staff officers, for their talents provide maximum service to commanders.

The brilliant and lazy. They are the most valuable and constitute the commanders. Their tendency to avoid troublesome and time-consuming detail enables them to retain the perspective necessary in the art of making decisions. Their plans tend to the simple, the direct, and the most promising for easy success.

The stupid and lazy. Although this group will add little to military luster, they can be used on small tasks that are necessary to be accomplished. At least, they will do no great harm. They can be retained and used.

The stupid and industrious. Great damage may result from their actions. Attacking the ill-advised with zeal and energy, they may induce a disaster. They are the most dangerous. They must be eliminated!

PART IV

The Air Force Way

13

Military Courtesy

A very fine line distinguishes military courtesies from military customs. Both categories owe their existence to a common source: the respect for one another that is the proper attitude among military personnel. Military courtesies, however, are mandatory. Omission of them can bring disciplinary action. They are a part of an officer's duty; they are a strong strand in the mesh of discipline that holds a military organization together. Whoever ignores military customs will be privately censured. Whoever ignores military courtesies, however, will be officially disciplined.

Even though an officer has no choice about observing required military courtesies, a little thought would make this requirement no burden at all. Almost all the specifics of military courtesy reflect civilian etiquette. Such courtesies improve relations among people, ease the conduct of business affairs, and add smoothness to what otherwise could be awkward and undesirable situations. For example, common courtesy dictates one refer to their elders as "sir" or "ma'am/miss." One would greet such a person with "Good day, sir or ma'am/miss." Few, if any, people of younger age would say to such a man or woman, "Hey, you," or "Say, Mac . . ." Why? No discipline in civilian life requires it, only common courtesy, but people have learned through experience that to be respectful is better than not to be so. The Air Force and other military services have codified for you such lessons learned through long experience and made them mandatory so that you need not blunder along until experience teaches the proper reactions to all the many situations you may encounter. Consult AFMAN 36-2203, *Drill and Ceremonies*, for details. The Air Force expects courtesy to be "common" to all and practiced between its membership—officer, enlisted, and civilian.

CORRECT USE OF TITLES
Titles of Officers. Officially address lieutenants as "Lieutenant." Use the adjectives "First" and "Second" only in written communications. Address or refer to captains and majors by their titles. In conversation and in nonofficial correspondence, refer to and address lieutenant colonels and colonels as "Colonel" and brigadier generals, major generals, and lieutenant generals as "General."

Senior officers frequently address juniors by their first names, but this practice does not give juniors the privilege of addressing seniors in any way other than by their proper titles. If airmen are present, senior officers should address junior officers by their titles. Officers of the same grade, when among themselves, may address one another by their given names. Increasingly, servicemembers use first names. Junior officers, however, should always be conservative until they can sense what is appropriate. It is wiser to err by being too formal rather than too familiar.

Address chaplains as "Chaplain" regardless of their grades. Address Roman Catholic chaplains and Episcopal chaplains who prefer it as "Father," and address Jewish chaplains who prefer it as "Rabbi."

Titles of USAF Enlisted Personnel. In official communications, address enlisted personnel by their full titles. In conversation and in nonofficial correspondence, refer to and address enlisted personnel as follows:

Chief master sergeant	"Chief"
Senior master sergeant	"Sergeant"
Master sergeant	"Sergeant"
Technical sergeant	"Sergeant"
Staff sergeant	"Sergeant"
Senior airman	"Airman"
Airman first class	"Airman"
Airman	"Airman"
Airman basic	"Airman"

Identification and Titles of Officers of Other Services. You must also meticulously observe military courtesies with officers of the Army, Navy, Marine Corps, and Coast Guard in the same manner as for officers of the Air Force. The corresponding grades of commissioned officers in the Air Force, the Army, and the Navy are in the illustrations in chapter 14. The grades of commissioned officers in the Army and Marine Corps are the same as those of the Air Force. Coast Guard grades correspond to those of the Navy. Respective dates of commission determine relative rank within grades.

Titles of Cadets. Address cadets of the Air Force Academy and the Military Academy as "Cadet" officially and in written communications; informally, they are addressed as "Mister" or "Miss." Midshipmen of the Naval Academy are addressed as "Mister" or "Miss." In written communications, use the title "Midshipman."

MILITARY SALUTES

History of the Military Salute. For centuries, men of arms have used some form of the military salute as an exchange of greeting. Modern armed forces, which have inherited some of their military traditions from the Middle Ages, have preserved the military salute and continued its use. The method of giving the salute has varied through the ages, as it still varies in form among the armed forces of today.

Although the genesis of the military salute has been clouded by time, historians do have some idea of how it began. In the Middle Ages, for example, knights were mounted and wore armor that covered the body completely, including the head and the face. When two friendly knights met, their custom was for each to raise the visor and expose his face to the view of the other. They always raised the visor with the right hand and held the reins with the left. It was a significant gesture of friendship and confidence, because it exposed the features and also removed the right hand—the sword hand—from the vicinity of the weapon. Also, in ancient times, the freemen (soldiers) of Europe could carry arms; when two freemen met, both would raise their right hands and then shake hands to show that neither held a weapon in his hand. The knightly gesture of raising the hand to the visor came to be recognized as the proper greeting between soldiers. Its use continued even after modern firearms had made armor a thing of the past. The military salute is today, as it seems always to have been, a unique form of exchange of greeting between military people, between comrades in the profession of arms.

The Different Forms of the Salute. Although in this chapter, unless otherwise stated, *salute* means the hand salute, prescribed salutes can take several forms. All servicemembers use the hand salute. Besides the hand salute, other means of saluting include Present Arms, Eyes Right, Present Saber or Sword (in the three other services), Present Guidons, dipping unit colors, Ruffles and Flourishes (for flag-rank officers), the president's and vice president's marches, gun salutes, three rifle volleys at graveside, dipping airplane wings, and the ceremonial flyover.

When a salute is prescribed (except in formation), the military member either faces toward the person or flag saluted or turns the head so as to observe the person or flag saluted.

Covered or uncovered, military members exchange salutes in the same manner. People who are running come to a walk before saluting. The smartness with which officers and airmen give the salute indicates the degree of pride they have in their profession. A careless or half-hearted salute is discourteous.

In the Army and the Air Force, it is customary that newly commissioned officers give a dollar to the first enlisted member who salutes them.

Methods of Saluting Used by Officers. Officers salute by using the hand salute or, when in civilian clothes, by placing the right hand (and hat) over the left breast. The hand salute is the usual method. Although officers usually give the hand salute while standing or marching at attention, they may also give it while seated, such as when an officer seated at a desk acknowledges the salute of an officer or an airman who is making a report.

Officers in civilian clothes use the salute by placing the hat, held in the right hand, over the left breast under three conditions. At a military funeral, all military personnel dressed in civilian clothes use this form of the salute as a courtesy to the deceased. Members of the military service dressed in civilian clothes and wearing hats use the method to salute the national anthem or "To the Colors." While in the same dress, they also use this salute to pay respect to the national flag. Members in civilian clothing and without hats stand at attention, holding the right hand over the heart, as a courtesy to the national anthem or the national flag.

Execution of the Hand Salute. Salute within saluting distance, the distance within which recognition is easy. Begin the salute when you are about six paces from the person or the flag you are saluting or, if the approach is outside that distance, six paces from the point of nearest approach. Before the instant arrives to give the salute, stand or walk erectly, hold your head up, tuck in your chin, and pull in on your stomach muscles. Look squarely and frankly at the person to be saluted.

To execute the hand salute correctly, raise the right hand smartly, extending and joining the fingers and keeping the palm flat and facing the body. Tilt the hand slightly toward the face until the tip of the middle finger touches the right front corner of the hat, or the outside corner of the right eyebrow if uncovered or wearing a non-billed hat, or touch the front corner of glasses if you wear them. Hold the upper arm horizontal, slightly forward of the body, and parallel to the ground. To complete the salute, drop the arm to its normal position by the side in one motion, at the same time turning the head and eyes to the front if you turned your head to salute the senior officer.

If you are returning the salute of a servicemember junior to yourself, execute the two movements of the salute in the cadence of marching, ONE, TWO. If you are saluting a superior officer, execute the first movement and HOLD the position until the salute is acknowledged, and then complete your salute by dropping the hand smartly to your side.

Do these things correctly, and you will derive many rewards. Your airmen will be quick to notice your salute. Thus, you may set the example that may then extend to other matters. At the time of exchanging salutes, you should also say, "Good morning, (Sir/Ma'am)" or "Good afternoon, (Sir/Ma'am)."

Try to avoid making these frequently observed errors in saluting: failure to hold the position of the salute to a superior until it is returned, failure to look at the person or color saluted, failure to assume the position of attention while saluting, failure to have the thumb and finger extended and joined (a protruding thumb is especially objectionable), a bent wrist (the hand and wrist should be in the same plane), and failure to have the upper arm horizontal. By all means, avoid these gross errors: saluting with a cigarette in the right hand or in the mouth, saluting with the left hand in a pocket, or returning a salute in a casual or perfunctory manner.

Meaning of "Under Arms." The expression "under arms" means with arms in hand or having attached to the person a hand arm or the equipment pertaining directly to the arm, such as a cartridge belt, a pistol holster, or a rifle belt.

Uncovering. As a general rule, officers and airmen under arms do not uncover (remove their hats). They do uncover, however, in these circumstances:

- When they are seated as members of or in attendance at courts or boards.
- When they enter places of divine worship. (Honor guards, however, remain covered.)
- When they are indoors not on duty and want to remain informal.
- When they attend official receptions.

Members in uniform may salute civilians when appropriate, but they do not raise the uniform hat as a form of salutation.

Interpretation of "Outdoors" and "Indoors." In the application of military courtesies, the military considers as "outdoors" buildings such as hangars, gymnasiums, and other roofed structures when used for drill or exercise of troops. "Indoors" means offices, hallways, dining halls, orderly rooms, recreation rooms, libraries, and quarters.

COURTESIES AIRMEN GIVE TO OFFICERS

Occasions. Uniformed airmen give the hand salute outdoors both on and off military installations, except when the salute would be obviously inappropriate or impractical. Although it is appropriate to salute in civilian clothing, this practice has fallen into disuse. Airmen must also give the hand salute in all official greetings in the line of duty, for ceremonial occasions, and when the national anthem is played or the colors pass by.

Those entitled to the salute are commissioned officers of the Air Force, Army, Navy, Marine Corps, and Coast Guard. Saluting officers of friendly foreign countries, such as officers of the armed forces of NATO, when they are in uniform is also customary.

The Air Force urges its members to be meticulous in giving salutes to and returning salutes from personnel of the sister services. Such courtesy increases the feeling of respect that all members should feel toward comrades in arms.

Covered or uncovered, military members exchange salutes in the same manner.

Members salute only once if the senior remains in the immediate vicinity and no conversation takes place.

Among a group of airmen on a military base and not in formation, the first person noticing the approach of an officer calls the group to attention. If the group of airmen is in formation, the one in charge calls the group to attention and salutes. If outdoors and not in formation, they all salute. If indoors they come to attention.

Officers driving vehicles return the salutes of gate guards on military installations.

Uniformed servicemembers on foot salute senior officers whose automobiles have rank plates on their bumpers. The senior officer will return the salute.

Courtesies Exchanged When an Officer Addresses an Airman. In general, when a conversation takes place between an officer and an airman, the following procedure is correct: They exchange salutes; they complete the conversation; they exchange salutes again. *Exceptions:* An airman in ranks comes to attention and does not salute. Indoors, they do not exchange salutes except when an airman reports to an officer.

When NOT to Salute. The following cases require no salutes:

An airman in ranks and not at attention comes to attention when addressed by an officer but does not salute.

Details or individuals at work do not salute. The officer or noncommissioned officer in charge, if not actively engaged at the time, salutes or acknowledges salutes for the entire detail.

When actively engaged in athletic games, such as baseball, tennis, or golf, one does not salute.

When in churches, theaters, or other public places or when using public transportation, military members do not exchange salutes.

When carrying articles with both hands, or when otherwise so occupied as to make saluting impracticable, a military member does not salute. A nod and a greeting are, however, always courteous.

A member of the guard who is engaged in the performance of a specific duty, the proper execution of which would prevent saluting, does not salute.

Reporting to Officers in Their Offices. When reporting to officers in their offices, airmen (unless under arms) uncover, knock, and enter when told to do so. Upon entering, they march to within about two paces of the officer's desk, halt, salute, and report in this manner: "Sir, Airman Jones reports to Captain Smith" or "Ma'am, Airman Jones reports to the squadron commander." When the business is complete, the airman salutes, executes an about face, and withdraws. An airman uncovers (unless under arms) on entering a room where an officer is present.

Procedure When an Officer Enters a Dining Hall. When an officer enters the dining hall, airmen seated at meals remain seated at ease and continue eating unless the officer directs otherwise. *Exception:* An airman addressed stops eating and sits at attention until the conversation is completed.

Procedure When an Officer Enters a Dormitory. In a dormitory, airmen rise, uncover (if unarmed), and stand at attention when an officer enters. If more than one person is present, the first to perceive the officer calls, "Attention." On suitable occasions, officers command, "Rest" or "At Ease," when they expect to remain in the room and do not want the airmen to remain at attention. It is not strictly correct to call officers to attention when the commander enters a room. Instead, the person nearest the door should warn of the commander's approach by calling, "Ladies and gentlemen, the commander!" Officers will then come to attention.

Personal Courtesies. When accompanying a senior, a junior walks or rides on the left.

Entering Automobiles, Small Aircraft, and Small Boats. Military persons enter automobiles, small aircraft, and small boats in inverse order of rank; that is, the senior enters last and leaves first. Juniors, although entering first, take their appropriate seats. The senior is always on the right. Officers sit in the backseat of passenger cars driven by airmen unless the car is full.

COURTESIES AN OFFICER GIVES TO A SENIOR OFFICER

General. The courtesies exchanged between officers are prescribed in AFMAN 36-2203 and also include those observed through the force of custom, as discussed in chapter 14, "Customs of the Service." Of course, officers should return the salutes of airmen and junior officers.

Many of the courtesies airmen must extend to officers apply with equal force and in identical manner to junior officers in relations with senior officers. The junior individual salutes first. In making reports at formations, however, the person making the report salutes first regardless of rank. A squadron commander, for example, salutes first when reporting to the adjutant at a ceremony.

Several courtesies airmen extend to officers are not required between officers. The prescribed formalities airmen must observe in a dining hall while at meals, for example, do not apply to officers. Also, in an officer's quarters, courtesies prescribed when an officer enters a dormitory occupied by one or more airmen are not necessary.

Specific Courtesies Observed Between Officers. An individual officer outdoors must salute when meeting a person entitled to the salute or when addressed by a senior entitled to the salute.

When reporting in an office to an officer senior in rank, the junior follows the same procedure as described for airmen.

An officer who is outdoors in uniform and sees an occupied staff car with a senior officer's rank displayed either on a bumper plate or on a flag located on the right side of the fender, should salute. Hold the salute until the car has passed or the officer inside the car has returned the salute.

An officer (or a noncommissioned officer) in charge of a detail riding in a vehicle salutes for the entire detail.

Organization or detachment commanders salute officers of higher grades by bringing the organization or detachment to attention before saluting.

The officer (or the noncommissioned officer) in charge of a detail at work, if not actively engaged at the time, salutes for the entire detail.

The officer uncovers (unless under arms) on entering a room where a senior is present.

HONORS AND CEREMONIES ACCORDED DISTINGUISHED VISITORS (DVs)

Honors and ceremonies are often designed for greeting distinguished visitors on arrival and are accorded to some on departure. The intent of honors is to extend a mark of courtesy to a distinguished visitor. The military accords honors to individuals rather than to groups and honors committees and delegations in the person of the senior or ranking member. Commanders with the advice and assistance of protocol officers arrange the specific honors afforded visiting DVs.

COURTESIES TO THE NATIONAL FLAG AND NATIONAL ANTHEM

The Flag of the United States. The term *flag* applies regardless of size, relative proportions, or manner of display. The national flag, in its various sizes and uses, is the base flag, the all-purpose flag, the ceremonial flag, and the interment flag.

Air Force bases fly the following flags from a staff:

- U.S. base flag: a nylon bunting flag 8' hoist by 17' fly; used in pleasant weather.
- U.S. all-purpose flag: 5' hoist by 9'6" fly; used in stormy and windy weather and as prescribed by the commander.

A military unit carries these flags:

- Ceremonial flag: 4'4" hoist by 5'6" fly; carried when the Air Force ceremonial flag is appropriate and trimmed with 2"-wide fringe on three sides.
- Organizational flag: 3' hoist by 4' fly; not a national but a unit flag; carried when the organizational flag is appropriate.

The interment flag used to cover a casket at a funeral has the same dimensions as the all-purpose flag.

Special-Purpose Flags. A guidon is a swallow-tailed organizational flag carried by smaller units, such as squadrons. Other special-purpose flags include Air Force Recruiting Service, chapel, chaplain, and Geneva Convention flags.

Flag Appurtenances. A silver spearhead tops the pike or staff of Air Force flags. Other flag appurtenances may include unit streamers and silver bands, cords and tassels, and flag slings.

Respect. Members of the armed forces meticulously observe the courtesies that the national flag or the national anthem require. Colors or standards of organizations receive the same courtesy as the national flag flown from a flagstaff. The trumpet call "To the Colors" receives the same courtesy as the national anthem.

When the national anthem sounds indoors, officers and airmen stand at attention and face the music or the flag if one is present. They do not salute unless under arms.

Officers and airmen show the same marks of respect to the national anthem of any other country played upon official occasions.

Courtesies at Retreat and Escort of the Colors. Retreat is a daily ceremony at bases during which all personnel must pay respect to the flag. The ceremony may include a retreat parade; if units on parade carry organization colors or standards, participants in the ceremony or spectators at the ceremony usually pay respect to those colors or standards. The ceremony of retreat includes a trumpeter sounding the trumpet call "Retreat" and then, if present, the band playing the national anthem; in the absence of the band, recorded music sounds the trumpet call "To the Colors." Personnel lower the flag slowly, as if reluctantly, whereas in the morning at colors, they raise it smartly, as if eagerly. After they lower the flag, they fold it into a triangular shape, supposedly commemorative of the Revolutionary War soldier's cocked hat.

At the first note of the national anthem, or its counterpart in field music, all officers and airmen present, but not in formation, face the colors or flag and give the prescribed salute. They hold the salute until the last note of the music sounds. For all officers and airmen not in formation, the prescribed salute is the hand salute. The prescribed salute for military personnel dressed in civilian clothes and wearing a hat is to stand at attention, remove the hat with the right hand, and hold it over the left breast.

Vehicles in motion halt, and occupants remain seated in the vehicle until completion of the playing of the national anthem.

Salute to Passing Colors. When passing or being passed by an uncased national colors, personnel give honors in the same manner as described above. For purposes of protection, the colors may be furled and then covered with a special case. When so carried, they do not require honors.

Courtesies to the National Anthem. Whenever or wherever the national anthem or "To the Colors" sounds, at the first note, officers and airmen present, but not in formation, face the music, stand at attention, and give the prescribed salute. *Exception:* At the ceremony of retreat or escort of the colors, they face the colors or flag. They hold the position of salute until the last note of the music sounds. The prescribed salute is the same, in all cases, as those described for the ceremonies of retreat and escort of the colors.

Remembering this obvious rule can help prevent embarrassment: If you are paying respect to the flag, face the flag and salute; if you are paying respect to the national anthem or "To the Colors" played by field music, face the source of the music and salute.

Dipping the Flag or Colors. Do not dip the national flag by way of salute or compliment. Dip the organization colors as a salute when the reviewing officer has the rank of a general officer. Lower the pike (as the staff of a colors is called) to the front so that it makes a 45-degree angle with the ground.

The organization flag salutes in all military ceremonies while the national anthem or "To the Colors" sounds and when honoring its commander or a person of higher rank, but in no other case.

When not in use, the unit flag is usually on display in the commander's office.

Display and Use of the Flag. International usage forbids the display of the flag of one nation above the flag of another in time of peace. When the flags of two or more nations are on display, they should fly from separate staffs or from separate halyards of equal size and on the same level.

The national flag, when not flown from a staff or mast, should always hang flat, whether indoors or out, neither festooned over doorways or arches nor tied

HOW TO DISPLAY THE FLAG

1. When displayed over the middle of the street, the flag should hang vertically with the union to the north in an east-and-west street or to the east in a north-and-south street.

2. When displayed with another flag from crossed staffs, the U.S. flag should be on the right (the flag's own right), and its staff should be in front of the staff of the other flag.

3. When flying the flag at half-staff, the flag detail should first hoist the flag to the peak and then lower it to the half-staff position, but before lowering the flag for the day, they should again raise it to the peak.

4. When flags of states or cities or pennants of societies fly on the same halyard with the U.S. flag, the U.S. flag should always be at the peak.

5. When the flag hangs over a sidewalk from a rope extending from house to pole at the edge of the sidewalk, the flag should go out from the building, toward the pole, union first.

6. When the flag is on display from a staff projecting horizontally or at any angle from the windowsill, balcony, or front of a building, the union of the flag should go to the peak of the staff (unless the flag is to be at half-staff).

7. When the flag covers a casket, the union should be at the head and over the left shoulder of the deceased. The flag should not be lowered into the grave or allowed to touch the ground.

8. When the flag is on display other than by flying from a staff, it should be flat whether indoors or out. When displayed either horizontally or vertically against a wall, the union should be uppermost and to the flag's own right—that is, to the observer's left. When displayed in a window, it should appear the same way—that is, with the union or blue field to the left of the observer in the street.

9. When carried in a procession with another flag or flags, the U.S. flag should be either on the marching right or, when there is a line of other flags, in front of the center of that line.

10. When a number of flags of states or cities or pennants of societies are grouped on display from staffs with our national flag, the U.S. flag should be at the center or at the highest point of the group.

11. When the flags of two or more nations are on display, they should fly from separate staffs of the same height, and the flags should be of about equal size. International usage forbids displaying the flag of one nation above that of another nation in time of peace.

in a bow knot or fashioned into a rosette. When used on a rostrum, it should be above and behind the speaker's desk. It should never cover the speaker's desk or drape over the front platform; bunting of the national colors, arranged with the blue above, the white in the middle, and the red below, serves such purposes well. Under no circumstances should anyone drape the flag over chairs or benches, place any object or emblem of any kind above or on it, or hang it where something could easily contaminate or soil it. No lettering of any kind should ever appear on the flag. When metal or cloth replicas of the national flag are decorations for civilian clothing (such as costume jewelry) or an identifying symbol, the positioning and treatment should be with the greatest possible respect. When carried with other flags, the national flag should always be in front or on the right as color bearers are facing. When a number of flags are grouped on display from staffs, the national flag should always be in the center or at the highest point of the group. Strictly speaking, no one should ever degrade the national flag for advertising purposes. Today, however, the flag is everywhere, not just at military headquarters, post offices, and schools. Because it is everywhere, it has lost a great deal of its reverence, and the public no longer considers it disrespectful to use it for commercial purposes.

DISPLAY OF UNITED NATIONS FLAG
When the United States flag and the United Nations flag are on display together, the United States flag is on the right, best identified as "the marching right." The United States flag will be equal in size or larger, in the position of honor on the right (observer's left), and/or above the United Nations flag. Troops will carry the United Nations flag only on occasions honoring the United Nations or its high dignitaries. When so carried, the United Nations flag will be on the marching left and below the United States flag.

COURTESIES TO THE MILITARY DEAD
General. Military dead receive a dignified and ceremonial funeral service in keeping with military tradition, with the flag at half-staff and prescribed salutes to the deceased. At a military funeral, one salutes the caisson or hearse as it passes and the casket as it is carried. One also salutes during firing of volleys and playing of taps. If a unit or detail passes a burial procession or coffin, the officer or NCO in charge will give the command "Eyes Right (or Left)" and salute. When an officer dies, the commander details another officer from the unit to escort the remains to the place of burial.

Funerals. The national flag covers the casket at the military funeral of members of the military service. The flag is lengthwise on the casket with the union at the head and over the left shoulder of the deceased. Personnel do not lower the flag into the grave and do not allow it to touch the ground.

Occasions for the Flag at Half-Staff. On Memorial Day at all Air Force installations, the national flag flies at half-staff from reveille to retreat.

On the death of an officer at a base, the flag flies at half-staff and remains so between reveille and retreat or until completion of the burial service, after which the flag detail hoists it to the top. If the burial service is not at the base, the flag flies at half-staff until the remains depart the base.

Whenever instructions prescribe or proper authority orders military mourning for the death of any person entitled to personal honors, all flags are at half-staff.

The Flag at Half-Staff. When displaying the national flag at half-staff, the flag detail first hoists it to the top of the staff and then lowers it to the half-staff position. Before lowering the flag, they again raise it to the top of the staff. A flag in any position below the top of the staff is technically in the half-staff position. For an unguyed flagstaff of one piece, the middle point of the hoist of the flag should be midway between the top of the staff and its base.

14

Customs of the Service

A custom is an established usage. Customs include both positive actions (things to do) and taboos (things to avoid doing). Customs are those reasonable, consistent, widely accepted practices that make for a more pleasant life or more orderly procedures. Continued without interruption for a long time, they become compulsory. Some customs may even have the force of law.

AIR FORCE CUSTOMS

The Air Force has its own customs, some older than others. For instance, the dining-in, explained in chapter 17, "Social Life in the Air Force," is a relatively new American military custom. Those customs that persist stand on their own merits and are unwritten in the sense that they do not appear in official instructions or policy directives. Many Air Force customs complement procedures required by military courtesy. The breach of some customs merely brands the offender as uninformed or careless, but the violation of others brings official censure or disciplinary action.

Unquestionably, most Air Force customs derive from Army customs. Because the Air Force descended from the Army, most Air Force customs are almost identical to Army customs. The personalities of several early Air Force leaders directly influenced the behavior of all officers. The simplicity, cordiality, and human warmth, combined with personal dignity, displayed on all occasions and with all people by such leaders as Arnold, Doolittle, and Vandenberg have served as a broad pattern to emulate.

Sanctity of Official Statements. Ordinarily, people accept an officer's official word or statement without question. The knowledge that a false official statement not only is illegal but also is contrary to the ethics of the military profession has placed personal and official responsibility for an official statement on a high level.

The Officer-Enlisted Relationship. Good officers strive to develop their organizations to their maximum efficiency while providing for their people effective leadership, impartial justice, and wise and fair attitudes in every way. Good officers also strive to avoid things that work against this efficiency. Because undue familiarity breeds contempt, officers and enlisted personnel do not generally associate together in social activities outside of official unit functions. No officers can violate this custom with one or two people of their command and convince the others of their unswerving impartiality.

Civilians and the inexperienced cannot really understand the officer-enlisted relationship, nor can they realize that it often develops into something very deep and valuable. Only those officers and enlisted personnel who have endured together the hardships of service or the ordeals of battle can understand. Those conditions often develop a mutual trust and complete confidence between officer and airman that carries each forward to acts of sacrifice, courage, and leadership. This deep tie is a force that helps win wars.

Provide for the Needs of Enlisted Personnel. Officers must always provide for the needs and requirements of enlisted personnel. Officers in command of or responsible for airmen must provide for the airmen's housing, food, and comfort before taking care of their own personal needs.

Public Breaches of Discipline and Misconduct of Enlisted Personnel. Officers are responsible for making proper corrections and taking the necessary actions whenever and wherever they see airmen conducting themselves in an improper fashion. Officers must not fail to take the necessary preventive or corrective steps because the offenders are not from the same organization or because they are off duty. Officers are never off duty. Generally, it is a matter of protecting the airmen from their own indiscretions, to save them from more serious trouble.

Approach the delinquent offenders in a quiet, dignified, unobtrusive manner. Talk in an impersonal, officerlike way. Use a tone of voice no louder than necessary to be heard. Avoid threats. Do not scold or argue. Tell enlisted personnel that the things they have done bring discredit upon the uniform they are wearing. If possible get their names and organizations. Generally, a contact of this sort will be sufficient. Whatever action you take, you must follow up, or the deterring effect will likely vanish as soon as you are out of sight. No officers worthy of their positions of trust will fail or avoid their responsibilities, however unpleasant they may seem at the time. But do not get involved in an undignified shouting match or resort to physical measures. If your action may discredit the uniform or degrade the officer corps, back off.

Drunkenness, foul language and cursing, and other acts that discredit the uniform are things to avoid. For the most part, the standards of airmen are high, and they will give their loyal support to the necessary measures. Officers must distinguish clearly between acts that are merely unwise or on the boisterous side and those that are actually offensive. You should ignore the former. A word of caution should suffice for the borderline cases. You must handle the others with judgment.

RANK HAS ITS PRIVILEGES (RHIP)
The military system is a hierarchy. Leaders placed in charge of units in the military structure exercise control. These leaders are officers and noncommissioned officers. All must display disciplined obedience combined with loyalty,

in accordance with law and policy. From the highest to the lowest, subordinates must extend an unfailing respect to the authority that issues their orders. Personal admiration is a voluntary tribute to another that the military service does not demand. But the service does demand respect for authority by unfailing courtesy to people who exercise it.

The privileges of rank do not include the privilege of abuse of position. The needs of the organization as a whole come first. Officers who use official transportation for personal use are abusing the position. Officers who divert equipment to their own use do likewise. In general, officers who take the stand that they are above the policies that guide others, especially their own subordinates, are abusing their positions, and other people will condemn their acts.

The privileges of rank and position are privileges indeed, well worth striving for and attaining. They may mean more in the Air Force than in many civil professions because, in most instances, civilian leaders receive far greater pay or other monetary benefits.

"I Wish" and "I Desire." When the commander states, "I wish," or "I desire," rather than, "I order you to do so-and-so," this wish or desire has all the force of a direct order.

The Place of Honor. The place of honor is on the right. Accordingly, when juniors walk, ride, or sit with seniors, they take the position abreast and to the left of the seniors. The deference young officers should pay to civilian elders pertains to this relationship. The junior should walk in step with a senior, step back and allow the senior to be the first to enter a door, and show similar acts of consideration and courtesy. Usually, in the relations between seniors and juniors, the senior will never think of the difference in rank; the junior should never forget it.

Addressing a Senior. In military conversation, junior officers address senior officers and all enlisted personnel address officers as either "Sir" or "Ma'am." The "Sir" or "Ma'am" precedes a report and a query; it follows the answer of a question. For example: "Sir, do you wish to see Sergeant Brown?" "Sergeant Brown, Ma'am." "Thank you, Sir." Address a general officer, however, as "General."

Departing after the Commander. Officers should remain at a reception or social gathering until after the commander has departed. The corollary: thoughtful commanders leave early.

Reception of a Newly Joined Officer. Customarily, newly joined officers receive a cordial welcome, and most units extend courtesy to officers and families to make their arrival more pleasant and convenient. People assume that newly joined officers know their professional duties and that they have every intention of performing them ably.

Wing commanders or unit commanders customarily send letters of welcome to officers under orders to join, informing them of local conditions that may be important or interesting for them to know before arrival. The commander will inquire as to the date and hour of arrival and the number of persons accompanying. The commander will detail sponsor officers to assist newly joined officers.

Sponsors should take steps to provide temporary accommodations at the BOQ or temporary lodging facility. Sponsors usually introduce newly joined officers to the commander and to the other officers of their units. Sponsors should also inform the newcomers about local procedures they will need to know at once. Maps of the base are especially useful to strangers.

IMPORTANT PERSONAL EVENTS

Military Weddings. Military weddings follow the same procedures as any other formal wedding except for additional customs that add to their color and tone. At military weddings, all officers should wear the prescribed uniform for the occasion. Officers may wear their medals or ribbons. Whether the wedding is held in the morning, afternoon, or evening has no bearing on the selection of appropriate uniforms. For the wedding party, the thoughtful servicemember should express a preference as to the uniform.

Birth of a Child. When a child is born to the family of an officer, the officer's commander sends a personal letter of congratulations to the parents on behalf of the command. The same procedure is appropriate for a child born to the family of an airman, except that the organization commander writes the letter of congratulations, and the gift, if any, is from the airman's unit.

Death of an Officer or a Member of an Officer's Family. When an officer dies, the commander immediately designates an officer to give every possible assistance to the bereaved family. The officer's commander writes a letter of condolence on behalf of the organization.

Death of an Airman. When an airman dies, the immediate commander of the deceased writes a letter of condolence to the airman's nearest relative. Flowers sent in the name of the members of the deceased's unit accompany the body. All officers and members of the deceased airman's unit, the commander, and other members who so desire and whose duties permit attend the funeral and/or memorial service if that is the wish of the airman's family.

SUPPORT OF BASE AND ORGANIZATION ACTIVITIES

Your commander expects you to support the activities of your unit, such as wing, group, squadron, or flight, as well as the activities of the entire base. Your unit is a closely knit group around which official duties and athletic and social activities revolve for the benefit of all. You are a member of an official family. Your assignment must mean more than the place where you perform required and official duties, important as they are. Your commander expects you to support and assist, at least by your presence, many events that form a part of military life. A proper interest and pride in activities of your unit and base stimulate morale. An officer should be a good military citizen, sharing with other good citizens responsibility for the unofficial life and activities of the base.

Officers' Club. An officers' club (officers' open mess) is a membership association of commissioned officers established to provide food and beverage services, entertainment, and social and recreation programs for its members and their families and guests. Installations extend membership to retired officers of all armed services of the United States, officers of the National Guard and reserve components, and authorized Department of Defense civilian employees working on the installation, as determined by the installation commander. Because all officers are eligible for voluntary membership, they cannot use the officers' club unless they become members. In this sense, the officers' club resembles a private civilian club because the members themselves generate funds from sales and dues to support the services and programs. Historically, the officers' club has been the social center of Air Force community life for officers and their families. As such, it is customary, but not mandatory, for every officer to join the officers' club on the base of assignment. Officers who decline membership may be authorized limited club use.

The scope of activities and programs offered by the officers' club vary from base to base. Membership in your installation's officers' club, as verified by your United States Air Force Clubs credit card, assures you of reciprocal privileges in all other officers' clubs. Usually, the benefits and services offered include dining and beverage services, private party catering, special events, check cashing, charge privileges, and perhaps swimming and tennis.

For financial reasons, the dining rooms of officers' clubs are increasingly open for enlisted personnel and their families and even for civilians. This sharing of facilities does not include bars. No officer should ever drink with enlisted personnel; the potential for awkward or unpleasant situations arising is just too great.

Attendance at Athletic Events. As a matter of policy, to demonstrate an interest in base affairs, as well as for personal enjoyment, officers should attend athletic events in which their units' teams participate.

Attendance at Chapel. Similarly, officers should show their support of base religious activities by periodic attendance at services at the base chapel, to the extent that individual religious preferences permit.

Armed Forces Day. The third Saturday in May is usually designated Armed Forces Day. Many bases host special celebrations on this day. This day unifies all the former service days and is symbolic of the unity of action and purpose of all our armed services.

Combined Federal Campaign (CFC). This annual fund drive, similar to the civilian United Way campaign, enables servicemembers to make tax-deductible contributions to numerous charitable and nonprofit institutions. Participation, through cash donation or military pay allotment, is voluntary. Officers, however, should seriously consider participation in this worthy program.

FAREWELL TO A DEPARTING OFFICER

Before an officer departs from his unit or station on change of assignment or upon retirement, the officers and spouses usually give a suitable function in honor of the departing officer and family. Customarily, the unit gives an inexpensive memento to the one departing.

RETIREMENT CEREMONY
Retirement of a servicemember is an occasion that merits special commemoration. It is a just reward for honorable service. For most individuals, it is also a day of serious reflection on the value of military friendships accompanied by heart tugs of regret that these fine associations will change. A suitable ceremony should mark the occasion.

Retirement of an Officer. The officer's unit should arrange for a final ceremony in the officer's honor with a reception for the officer and family. The ceremony includes the reading of retirement orders, presentation of awards, remarks by a senior officer and by the officer retiring, and recognition of the support of the officer's family. Friends and family of the retiring officer may also wish to hold informal retirement parties.

TABOOS
Do Not Defame the Uniform. Officers must not disgrace their uniforms or their official positions. Conduct unbecoming an officer is punishable under the Uniform Code of Military Justice. The confidence of the nation in the integrity and high standards of conduct of officers is an asset that the military may permit no one to lower.

Do Not Criticize Members of Other Services. Never belittle members of the Army, the Navy, or the Marines. They are part of our team. For that matter, don't downgrade your own service.

Appointment with the Commander Only through the Aide or the Executive. Customarily, officers ask the commander's aide or executive officer for an appointment with the commander. Often, you may do so informally by asking when the commander can see you.

Give No Excuses. Never volunteer excuses or explain a shortcoming unless someone requires an explanation. Giving unsought excuses does more damage than good.

Scorn Servility. Servility, "bootlicking," and deliberate courting of favor are beneath the standard of conduct expected of officers, and any who practice such things earn the scorn of their associates.

Say Things like "Old Man" with Care. Some commanders acquire the accolade "the old man" by virtue of their position and without regard to their age. Although the term, which is used infrequently today, usually implies approbation and admiration, using it in the presence of the commander is disrespectful.

Avoid "Going over an Officer's Head." Jumping an echelon of command is called "going over an officer's head." For example, a squadron commander may make a request of the wing commander concerning a matter that should first have gone through the group commander. The act is contrary to military procedure and decidedly disrespectful.

Avoid Harsh Remarks. Gossip, slander, harsh criticism, and faultfinding are unofficerlike practices. In casual conversation, follow this guide: "All fellow officers are valiant and virtuous." Don't criticize or correct fellow officers in front of airmen.

Avoid Vulgarity and Profanity. Although you certainly will hear profanity in the military, foul language is repulsive to most self-respecting people, and to them its use by officers is reprehensible. Officers should avoid vulgarity if they are to gain respect, and officers cannot lead others without their respect.

Avoid Excessive Indebtedness. Few offenses injure the standing of an officer more than earning the reputation of being a poor credit risk. Officers are people, and they are subject to the same temptations and the same hazards of life as any other adult. Sometimes you may find that assuming debt is unavoidable and necessary, but you must, of course, repay all debts. When circumstances prevent payment, you and the creditor must make a mutually satisfactory arrangement. You should make some payment, however small, at the time a payment is due; this practice protects the legal standing of the obligation and shows your intention to pay. Permitting bills to accumulate, with no attempt to pay or to arrange a method of payment, is reprehensible and subject to official military censure.

Officers enjoy an exceptional individual and group credit standing earned and deserved because of the scrupulous care officers have taken through the years to meet obligations when due. An officer who violates this custom brings discredit upon the entire officer corps.

Never Lean on a Senior Officer's Desk. Avoid leaning against a senior officer's desk. Most officers resent such unmilitary familiarity. Stand erect unless invited to be seated. Don't lean.

Never Keep Anyone Waiting. Report on time when notified to do so. Never keep anyone waiting unnecessarily. Being on time, whether as the junior or senior officer, is one of the easiest ways to let people know how much you value them and their time.

Avoid Having People Guess Your Name. Do not assume that someone whom you have neither seen nor heard from for a considerable period will remember your name when you renew contact. Say at once who you are, and then renew the acquaintance. If this act of courtesy is unnecessary, the other person will view it only as an act of thoughtfulness; if it happens to be necessary, you will save the other person and perhaps yourself embarrassment. At official receptions, always announce your name to the aide.

Don't Trade on Your Commission. Officers may not use or permit others to use their military titles in connection with commercial enterprises of any kind.

Stay Out of Politics. Don't become embroiled in politics. Political activity is contrary to American military tradition. As a citizen, you have a right to your opinions and a duty to vote, but keep your opinions to yourself, within your home, or within your own circle of friends. You can do this without being an intellectual eunuch. Also remember that criticism of the president is particularly improper because the president is, after all, the commander in chief of the armed forces. Article 88 of the Uniform Code of Military Justice makes it a punitive offense for an officer to use "contemptuous words" against the president and certain high-ranking government officials.

What Not to Discuss. Avoid talking shop at social occasions, and of course, never discuss classified matters, no matter how obliquely. Use great discretion in discussing politics and religion.

Look Smart in Public. Avoid smoking or chewing gum when on the street in uniform. Keep your hands out of your pockets, your uniform coat (blouse) buttoned, your tie tight, and your cap squared away properly.

CUSTOMS CONCERNING AIRCRAFT

A representative of Base Operations meets all transient aircraft and determines crew and passenger transportation requirements. If possible, the installation commander usually meets general officers.

Pilots of aircraft carrying classified material are responsible for safeguarding such material unless they can remove it from the aircraft and store it in an adequately guarded area.

Regardless of grade, aircraft commanders are the final authority on operation of their aircraft. If they decide to alter their flight plans, passengers of whatever grade or service will not question their decisions.

Aircraft passengers must be prompt, obey safety regulations, and avoid moving around unnecessarily.

The pilot is the last to leave an abandoned aircraft.

Parades and other ceremonies honoring dignitaries often use aircraft flyovers.

When airplanes participate in the funeral of an aviator, they fly in tactical formation, less one aircraft, over the graveside service, but not so low as to drown out the service with noise.

CUSTOMS OF SISTER SERVICES

Although there are similarities regarding the customs of the separate armed services, there are significant differences as well. Before visiting an installation of a sister service or before participating in a formal ceremony, ascertain what behavior is expected of you. Ask your host for guidance, and be observant during your visit. Take your cues from your hosts.

ORIGINS OF SOME MILITARY CUSTOMS

Military customs are more meaningful if you understand how the customs began. Although some of the stories may be apocryphal, they are of interest.

The dress parade was originally supposed to impress visiting emissaries with the strength of the monarch's troops, rather than to honor the visitor.

Inspecting the guard of honor began with the restoration of Charles II to the throne of England. When one of Oliver Cromwell's regiments offered its allegiance, the king carefully scrutinized the face of each soldier in ranks looking for signs of treachery. Convinced of their sincerity, he accepted the escort.

The "Sound Off," in which the band plays the "Three Cheers" and marches down the front of assembled troops, stems from the crusades. Those selected as crusaders were at the right of the line of troops, and the band marched past them in dedication while the populace gave three cheers. "The right of the line" was the critical side in ancient battle formations and is the unit place of honor in ceremonies.

The saber salute, still employed on occasion of ceremony in the other services, demonstrated the officer's dedication to Christ in his bringing the hilt (symbolic of the cross) to his lips, while dipping the saber tip signified submission to the liege lord commanding him.

Age generally determines precedence; the order of precedence of U.S. military services is based on the date founded—Army, Marine Corps, Navy, Air Force, and Coast Guard.

Raising the right hand in taking an oath stems from ancient days when the taker called upon God as his witness to the truth and pledged with his sword hand. If gloved, people taking the oath removed the right glove, supposedly because criminals were once branded on the right palm, and courts could thus determine whether the witness was reputable.

Wearing decorations and medals on the left breast also goes back to the crusaders, who wore their order's badge of honor over their hearts and protected by their shields, which they carried on the left arm.

The origin of the aiguillette and the fourragère is open to debate. One story has it that squires used to carry metal-tipped thongs (*aiguillette* is French for "little spike" or "lace-tag") in a roll over their shoulders to lace their knights into their armor, and it thus became the badge of an aide-de-camp. Another story concerns the fourragère, which states that the Duke of Marlborough's foragers carried fodder sacks for their mounts attached to their shoulders by a looped-up cord hooked to the jacket.

The white flag of truce may derive from the Truce of God arranged on certain days by Pope Urban V in 1095 between warring medieval barons.

The use of the arch of sabers in military weddings recalls the days when the groomsmen pledged to protect the wedded couple, particularly elopers.

The term *chaplain* supposedly derives from Saint Martin of Tours, who gave half his military cloak, or "cappa," to a beggar. The kings of France made it a relic and war talisman guarded by special clerical custodians, who celebrated services in the field.

Saluting a ship's quarterdeck apparently derives from ancient times when the ship's stern carried a pagan altar to propitiate the gods. Later, it carried the Christian crucifix, and it is still the seat of authority.

At a military funeral, the national flag is on the coffin to indicate that the dead died in service of the country, which acknowledges its responsibility.

The firing of three volleys over the grave may derive from the Romans, who honored their dead by casting earth thrice on the grave, calling the name of the dead, and saying "Vale" (farewell) three times.

A military funeral plays taps to mark the beginning of the servicemember's last sleep and to express hope in the ultimate reveille.

15

Uniforms and Insignia

The Air Force requires all members to maintain a high standard of dress and personal appearance. Pride in each member's personal appearance and uniform greatly strengthens the esprit de corps essential to an effective military force. Today's uniform choices and the options given individuals have resulted in extremely detailed directions about what is and is not authorized; consequently, consult AFI 36-2903, *Dress and Personal Appearance of Air Force Personnel*, for details.

The Air Force is currently making major changes to the uniform—something that long-serving airmen have come to expect. The most visible changes involve the airman battle uniform (ABU). Minor changes involve ABU boots, the flight suit, sweaters, berets, physical training gear, and instructions for completing AF Form 4428, *Air Force Tattoo/Brand/Body Marking Screening/Verification Form* (in attachment 7 of the AFI).

WEARING THE UNIFORM
When to Wear the Uniform. Air Force personnel must wear the prescribed service uniform at all places of duty during duty hours, except as specifically authorized by AFI 36-2903. The installation commander designates the appropriate uniform combinations in accordance with local climate and mission requirements. Special occasions require wearing the service dress uniform.

Standards of Dress and Appearance. Although all Air Force personnel must maintain a high standard of dress and appearance, officers in particular—whose manner of dress and personal appearance provide a visual example for enlisted personnel—must wear the uniform in a manner that emphasizes pride and must keep their personal appearance above reproach.

The elements of the Air Force standard are neatness, cleanliness, safety, uniformity, and military image. The first four are absolute, objective criteria. The last standard, military image, is subjective in that the American public draws certain conclusions based on the image presented by Air Force members. The military image, therefore, must instill public confidence and leave no doubt that Air Force members live by a common standard and respond to military order and discipline. There are no "fads" in this military image.

Appearance in uniform is an important part of the military image. Because judgment as to what constitutes the proper image differs in and out of the military, the Air Force must spell out what is and what is not acceptable. For example, when in uniform, servicemembers will not put their hands in their pockets. The image of disciplined and reliable servicemembers excludes the extreme, the unusual, or the faddish.

Uniform Standards. Keep your uniforms clean, neat, correct in design and specification, properly fitted, pressed, and in good condition—not frayed, worn-out, torn, faded, or stained. Keep uniform items, including pockets, buttoned, snapped, or zipped as appropriate. Keep your shoes shined and in good repair. Keep your badges, insignia, belt buckle, and other metallic devices clean and free from scratches. Keep your ribbons clean, and replace them when they begin to look frayed. Keep the gig line—shirt placket, belt buckle, and trouser fly—in alignment. Standard creases are required for shirt sleeves and trouser legs, but "military creases" are forbidden for shirts.

Of course, you may wear wristwatches and identification bracelets, but they should be of conservative design (black, brown, silver, or gold) and not jewel encrusted or with brightly colored straps. Do not wear watchbands exceeding 1 inch in width. You must conceal necklaces under the collar or undershirt. You may wear a conservatively designed gold or silver bracelet; however, it must be no wider than $1/2$ inch and must not present a safety hazard. You may also wear rings, but only a total of three rings on both hands at any one time (wedding rings count as one ring if worn as a set). Wear rings at the base of the finger, never on the thumb.

Women may wear one pair of small (not to exceed 6 mm in diameter), matching, conservative gold, diamond, white pearl, or black spherical earrings. When worn, earrings must fit flat against the ear and must not extend below the earlobe unless the extending piece is the connecting piece of clip-on earrings. Do not wear earrings when safety considerations dictate. Women who choose to wear nail polish may use a single conservative color, in good taste and not containing any ornamentation.

Eyeglasses must be conservative in shape and style; frames and lenses are only authorized to have conservative ornamentation. Minor ornamentation on sunglasses as well as conservative, wrap-around sunglasses are authorized. Never wear sunglasses in formation unless prescribed by medical authority and authorized by the commander.

Except in the special pocket on the airman battle uniform (ABU) shirt, pens and pencils must be concealed. Headphones and earphones are prohibited unless required to perform duties. One small, black, nondescript pager or cellular phone can be worn on the uniform belt, clipped to a handbag, or carried in the left hand.

Commanders may restrict wear of visible and nonvisible body ornaments when they interfere with the performance of a servicemember's military duties. Factors to be considered include, but are not limited to, ornaments that impair the safe and effective operation of weapons, military equipment, or machinery; pose a health or safety hazard to the wearer or others; or interfere with the proper wear of special or protective clothing or equipment, such as helmets, flak jackets, flight suits, ABUs, gas masks, wet suits, and crash rescue equipment.

PERSONAL APPEARANCE AND GROOMING STANDARDS

One of the most important elements of your personal appearance as an officer is your hair. Keep your hair clean, well groomed, and neat. Avoid extreme or faddish hairstyles. If you dye or treat your hair, it must look natural. When groomed, your hair must not touch your eyebrows. Your hair style must never interfere with professional and/or safety headgear.

Men. Hair, which must have a tapered appearance on sides and back, must not touch the ears. Only the closely shaved hair on the back of the neck may touch the collar. The bulk of a man's hair may not exceed $1\frac{1}{4}$ inches in depth, regardless of length. Hair must not protrude in front below the band of a properly worn hat. Sideburns must be neatly trimmed and tapered, straight, not flared, and end with a horizontal line. They can be no longer than the lowest part of the exterior ear opening. The Air Force permits cleanly shaven heads, military high-and-tight, or flattop cuts; however, it prohibits cuts as the Mohawk, mullet, cornrows, dreadlocks or etched design. Men who choose to wear mustaches must ensure that they do not extend downward beyond the lipline of the upper lip, or extend sideways beyond a vertical line drawn upward from the corners of the mouth. Wigs or hairpieces are authorized only to cover baldness or disfiguration, and then only when documented in medical records. The Air Force does not allow its members to wear beards or handlebar mustaches. On the advice of a medical officer, however, the commander may authorize a beard, but it must not exceed $\frac{1}{4}$ inch in length.

Women. Hair must not extend in length on all sides below an invisible line drawn parallel to the ground at the bottom edge of the shirt collar at the back of the neck. Hair may be visible in front of a woman's flight cap. Keep your hair length/bulk between a minimum of 1 inch and a maximum of 3 inches. Hair ornamentation is not permitted. To keep hair in place, women may wear conservative black hairpins, combs, headbands, elastic bands, or barrettes with all-natural female hair colors. Although dreadlocks are not authorized, conservative braids, micro-braids, and cornrows are authorized in solid colors similar to the individual's hair color. The AFI contains additional guidance on styling standards.

Tatoos/Brands. In the recent past, body mutilation was considered incompatible with service in the Air Force. Members who failed to remove or alter unauthorized tattoos in a timely manner (or remove or alter inappropriate, excessive tattoos/brands) and/or who attached, affixed, or displayed objects, articles, jewelry, or ornamentation to or through the ear, nose, tongue, or any exposed body parts were subject to disciplinary action or involuntary separation. This prohibition of body mutilation also extended to alteration or modification to achieve a visible, physical effect that disfigured, deformed, or otherwise detracted from a professional military image, such as tongue splitting or forking, tooth filing, and acquiring visible, disfiguring skin implants. Failure to observe these mandatory provisions and prohibitions by active-duty Air Force members, USAFR members on active duty or on inactive duty for training, and Air National Guard members in federal service was a violation of Article 92, Uniform Code of Military Justice.

The previous prohibition of body mutilation has been relaxed. Nevertheless, tattoos/brands anywhere on the body that are obscene or that advocate sexual, racial, ethnic, or religious discrimination are prohibited in and out of uniform. Tattoos/brands that are prejudicial to good order and discipline or of a nature that tends to bring discredit on the Air Force are also prohibited in and out of uniform. Members obtaining unauthorized tattoos will be required to remove them at their own expense. Using uniform items to cover unauthorized tattoos is not an option. In addition to these prohibited tattoos/brands, excessive tattoos and brands that are inappropriate for military image will not be exposed or visible (including visible through the uniform) while in uniform.

"Excessive" is defined as any tattoo/brand that exceeds one-fourth of the exposed body part and those above the collarbone and readily visible when wearing an open-collar uniform. Air Force members are not allowed to display excessive tattoos that detract from an appropriate professional image while in uniform. Air Force members with existing tattoos not meeting an acceptable military image are required to maintain complete coverage of the tattoos/brands using current uniform items (long-sleeved shirt/blouse, pants/trousers, dark hosiery) or remove their tattoos. Depending on the circumstances, commanders may seek Air Force medical support for voluntary tattoo removal. Upon notification by their commanders, servicemembers who receive tattoos/brands not meeting standards will be required to have them removed at their own expense; they may not use Air Force medical centers for removal.

Body Piercing/Ornamentation or Body Alteration/Modification. Air Force servicemembers remain prohibited from attaching, affixing, or displaying objects, articles, jewelry, or ornamentation to or through the ear, nose, tongue, or any exposed body part, including those visible through the uniform. (Women's conservative, matching earrings are excepted from this prohibition; although women may pierce their earlobes, piercing must not be extreme or excessive.) This prohibition is total: it applies in and out of uniform, on and off duty, on and off military installations.

Installation or higher commanders may impose more restrictive standards for tattoos and body ornaments, on or off duty, in those locations where the Air Force–wide standards are inadequate to address cultural sensitivities (such as overseas) or mission requirements.

Members not complying with these requirements will be subject to disciplinary action for failure to comply with Air Force standards and may be involuntarily separated.

CLASSIFICATION OF UNIFORMS

Uniforms worn by USAF personnel fall into three categories: service uniforms, mess dress uniforms, and utility uniforms.

Service Uniforms. Wear service uniforms during regular duty hours. You may wear all service uniform combinations year-round, but the installation commander may prescribe when members will wear certain combinations. If the commander does not prescribe specific combinations, use good judgment based on weather conditions and duties when selecting the particular service uniform combination to wear.

Mess Dress Uniforms. The mess dress is for year-round wear for semiformal and formal occasions. As this uniform is the equivalent of civilian "black tie," it should be reserved for evening wear. Members may, however, choose to wear the mess dress for weddings at any time of day.

Utility Uniforms. Wear the flight duty uniform (FDU) or the airman battle uniform (ABU) whenever mission requirements make the service uniform inappropriate. These uniforms should not be worn off base, except to go to and from your residence. However, you can wear FDUs and ABUs at gas stations, convenience stores, or drive-through fast-food establishments. You can wear these utility uniforms for short convenience stops, including malls, and into fast-food establishments, or even restaurants, if customers are wearing comparable (work/utility) civilian attire. Do not wear these uniforms to restaurants where customers are wearing business attire, or to establishments that primarily serve alcohol. When flying on a commercial flight, you can wear any authorized uniform combination except the FDU. When flying overseas, consult the *Foreign Clearance Guide* for specific uniform guidance. When wearing any uniform off base, you must present the proper standards of cleanliness, neatness, and military image.

SERVICE UNIFORMS

There are several service uniform combinations: the service dress uniform for men and women, long- and short-sleeved shirts with trousers for men, and long- and short-sleeved blouses with skirts or slacks for women. The cardigan and pullover sweaters are for indoor or outdoor wear; if worn outdoors, all of the cardigan's buttons must be buttoned.

Service Dress Uniform. The polyester/wool blend, serge weave, semi-drape, single-breasted coat has three buttons, one welt pocket on the upper left side, and two lower pocket flaps. The breast pocket is used to align ribbons and specialty badges (see chapter 16). The metallic name tag is worn on the right side of the service dress jacket with the bottom of the name tag level with the bottom of the ribbons. Colonels and below wear regular-size metal grade insignia $5/8$ inch from the end of the epaulets, and $1/2$ inch of sleeve braid 3 inches from the end of the sleeve. With the exception of the satin-finished Hap Arnold (wing and star) buttons, the lapel U.S. and epaulet grade insignia and specialty badges are highly polished. With arms hanging naturally, coat sleeves

Men's Service Dress Uniform
(Eventually, this coat will be replaced by
the four-button, belted "heritage" coat.)

Women's Service Dress Uniform
(Eventually, this coat will be replaced by
the four-button, belted "heritage" coat.)

Men's Long-Sleeved and Short-Sleeved Shirts

Women's Long-Sleeved and Short-Sleeved Shirts

should end approximately $^1/_4$ inch from the heel of the thumb, and the bottom edge of the coat should extend 3 to $3^1/_2$ inches below the top of the thigh. The tie or inverted-V tie tab is worn with either the long- or short-sleeved light blue shirt or blouse with epaulets. Coat and trousers or skirt must match in shade and material. The front of the trouser legs rests on the front of the shoe, with a slight break in the crease; the back of the trouser legs will be approximately $^7/_8$ inch longer than the front.

Other Service Uniforms. In addition to the service dress uniform, there are numerous combinations of shirts or blouses and trousers, slacks, or skirts. Name tags are worn on the shirts or blouses, except for the service dress coat. Aeronautical and chaplain specialty badges are required; see chapter 16 for wear of ribbons and other specialty badges. Both men and women may wear the pullover sweater with or without tie or tab, unless specified by the installation commander; if the shirt or blouse collar is open, it may be in or out of the sweater's V-neck. A blue cardigan sweater worn with or without tie or tab is for indoor and outdoor wear. If worn outdoors, all buttons must be buttoned. Men can wear the long-sleeved shirt with tie or the short-sleeve shirt with or without tie. The tie should end approximately in the middle of the belt buckle, and the tie tack or clasp (Air Force coat of arms, grade insignia, wing and star, or new Air Force symbol) should be placed halfway between the bottom of the knot and the tip of the tie. Women have more uniform combinations than men because there are several types of long- and short-sleeved blouses, slacks, and skirts, as well as maternity uniforms.

Footwear. Footwear for service uniforms must be black and made of smooth or scotch-grained leather or man-made material, of either high-gloss or patent finish. They must always be clean and polished; worn-down heels should be replaced. Shoe heels must not exceed one inch in height. Men may wear low-quarter shoes or dress boots; socks must be black, although white socks can be worn with ABUs/boots if they are not visible. Women may wear pumps, oxfords, or oxfords with low-wedge heels. Dress boots are authorized for wear with pants but not with skirts.

Headgear. Men wear the flight cap with all service uniform combinations. The flight cap is worn slightly to the wearer's right, with the vertical crease of the cap in line with the center of the forehead, in a straight line with the nose; the cap extends approximately 1 inch from the eyebrow in front. Indoors, the flight cap may be tucked under the belt above the officer's right thigh; the cap should be flush with the top of the belt or protrude only slightly so as not to fold over. Male field-grade officers (major through colonel) are required to have the service cap (wheel hat) with clouds and darts ("scrambled eggs") on the visor. The service cap, with plain visor, is optional for company-grade officers (lieutenants and captains). The U.S. coat-of-arms service cap insignia is satin-finished to match the buttons of the service dress uniform. The service cap is worn squarely on the head, with no hair protruding. Any type of religious head coverings must be approved by the individual's commander on a

Men's Service Cap

Majors and Above

General Officers

Women's Service Cap

Unit Baseball Cap

Officer   Enlisted

Beret

Men's Flight Cap

1½"

Women's Flight Cap

1½"

ABU Cap

Men's and Women's Headgear

case-by-case basis in accordance with DOD Dir. 1300.17 and AFI 36-2903. (Basically, the servicemember requests permission of the installation commander after obtaining an endorsement from the installation chaplain.) Women wear a blue service cap or the female version of the flight cap. (Women in rated career fields may wear the men's flight cap with the flight suit.) Eight USAF career fields are authorized to wear colored berets along with the crest of that particular field: combat control team, special tactics team, pararescue and combat rescue officer, security forces, survival evasion, tactical air control party, tactical liaison officers, and weather parachutist.

MESS DRESS UNIFORMS

Men's Mess Dress. *Required items:* Blue mess jacket with officers' silver sleeve braid, blue shoulder boards with grade insignia, miniature badges and decorations; blue trousers with striping; plain white pleat-fronted shirt; blue bow tie; blue cummerbund with open edge of pleats facing up (hence "crumb-catcher"), silver studs and cuff links, and chain buttons; suspenders; plain black socks and low-quarter shoes. *Optional items:* Blue topcoat, black gloves, and scarf.

Women's Mess Dress. *Required items:* Blue mess jacket with officers' silver sleeve braid, blue shoulder boards with grade insignia, miniature badges and decorations; blue ankle-length skirt; plain white pleat-fronted shirt with blue tie tab, blue cummerbund, with pleats facing down. Cufflinks and studs are optional; if worn, they will be wing-and-star design, oval, or plain with satin finish. *Optional items:* Blue topcoat, black gloves, and black vinyl, leather, or suede clutch handbag.

UTILITY UNIFORMS

Officers generally wear either the flight duty uniform (FDU) or airman battle uniform (ABU) as utility uniforms. The flight suit, which was originally worn as overalls to protect the service uniform worn underneath, is increasingly worn for nonflight duties. Nevertheless, the flight suit must not be worn off base for dining, shopping, or socializing (except as noted earlier). Off-base wear of the ABU is less restrictive.

Airman Battle Uniforms. The ABU replaces both the temperate- and hot-weather battle dress uniforms (BDU) and the desert camouflage uniform. You wear this uniform with the desert sand-colored (tan) T-shirt. If a unit emblazons the T-shirt with a unit logo, the logo must not be visible when you wear the ABU coat (shirt). MAJCOM commanders may approve long-sleeved turtlenecks, dickies, or thermal undershirts with the FDU as weather conditions warrant. Thermal undergarments for the ABU/FDU may be desert tan, white, or cream colored. You must keep all pockets buttoned with no items visible in the pocket, other than in the pen pocket. The ABU trousers can be bloused (at boot-top level) or tucked (into boot tops); however, make sure they appear bloused around the boot. This uniform requires sewn-on rank (on the collar),

Men's Mess Dress Uniform

Women's Mess Dress Uniform
(This jacket will eventually be replaced by a looser-fitting one.)

Men's and Women's Airman Battle Uniform

nametape, and U.S. Air Force tape. When you roll up ABU sleeves, ensure the sleeve shows at all times and the cuff is within 1 inch of the forearm when the elbow is bent 90 degrees. (This requires that the shirt be off in order to roll up the sleeves.) You wear the ABU cap with this uniform.

ADDITIONAL UNIFORM ITEMS

Outergarments. Besides the pullover and cardigan sweaters, there are several kinds of outerwear for men and women: the lightweight blue jacket with knit cuffs and waist; the lightweight blue jacket with knit cuffs (for women only); the double-breasted, belted all-weather coat; and the double-breasted, belted topcoat. The lightweight blue jacket must be zipped at least halfway up, preferably higher. When worn over a sweater or with a liner, the sweater or liner must not be visible.

Women have the option of wearing the men's lightweight blue jacket but also have one of their own, which does not have a knit waistband. Regular-size metal grade insignia are worn on all outergarments $^5/_8$ inch from the end of the epaulet. The pullover sweater requires cloth shoulder marker grade insignia.

The lightweight blue jacket, pullover, and cardigan are the only outerwear garments authorized for indoor wear.

Leather Flight Jacket. The brown Army Air Forces' World War II–type leather flying jacket is authorized for aircrew members only. It is worn without grade insignia but with an embossed leather name patch showing the wearer's grade. The jacket must be zipped up at least halfway, preferably higher. Brown leather flying gloves are authorized for wear with the A-2 leather jacket.

Gloves. Sage-green or black gloves are authorized for wear with the ABU and FDU and all authorized outerwear for these uniforms. Only black gloves may be worn with the service dress uniform and all approved outergarments worn with the blue service and service dress uniforms.

Distinctive Badges and Specialty Badges. See chapter 16, as well as AFI 36-2803, AFI 36-2903, and AFI 36-2923 for distinctive badges and specialty insignia authorized for wear on the uniform.

Name Tags. A $3^3/_{16}$-inch by $^5/_8$-inch ultramarine blue plastic name tag with the servicemember's last name in $^1/_4$-inch block white letters is worn on long- and short-sleeved shirts. The Air Force recently adopted a metallic name tag for wear on pullover sweaters and the service dress uniform coat.

Identification Tags. All Air Force personnel must wear identification tags (dog tags) when engaged in flying or field training or when outside the continental limits of the United States when engaged in combat or contingency operations.

Aiguillettes. Aides and attachés wear aiguillettes of silver-colored rayon or metallic cord with service uniforms and with the mess dress uniform. Presidential and White House aides wear their aiguillettes on the right shoulder, while other aides and attachés use the left. The aiguillette is secured to the underside of the epaulet about midway between the epaulet button and the shoulder seam.

Men's and Women's Lightweight Blue Jackets
Men's and Women's All-Weather/Topcoat

OFFICER INSIGNIA OF GRADE

AIR FORCE	ARMY	MARINES	NAVY
General of the Air Force	General of the Army	(None)	Fleet Admiral
General	General	General	Admiral
Lieutenant General	Lieutenant General	Lieutenant General	Vice Admiral
Major General	Major General	Major General	Rear Admiral (Upper Half)
Brigadier General	Brigadier General	Brigadier General	Rear Admiral (Lower Half)
Colonel	Colonel	Colonel	Captain
Lieutenant Colonel	Lieutenant Colonel	Lieutenant Colonel	Commander
Major	Major	Major	Lieutenant Commander

OFFICER INSIGNIA OF GRADE

AIR FORCE	ARMY	MARINES	NAVY
Captain	Captain	Captain	Lieutenant
First Lieutenant	First Lieutenant	First Lieutenant	Lieutenant Junior Grade
Second Lieutenant	Second Lieutenant	Second Lieutenant	Ensign

(None)	SILVER AND BLACK	SCARLET AND SILVER	
	W-5 W-4 W-3	W-5 W-4 W-3	W-4 W-3
	Chief Warrant Officer Chief Warrant Officer Chief Warrant Officer	Chief Warrant Officer Chief Warrant Officer Chief Warrant Officer	Chief Warrant Officer Chief Warrant Officer
	SILVER AND BLACK	SCARLET AND GOLD	
	W-2 W-1	W-2 W-1	W-2 W-1
	Chief Warrant Officer Warrant Officer	Chief Warrant Officer Warrant Officer	Chief Warrant Officer Warrant Officer

COAST GUARD

Coast Guard officers use the same rank insignia as Navy officers. Coast Guard enlisted rating badges are the same as the Navy's for grades E-1 through E-9, but they have silver specialty marks, eagles and stars, and gold chevrons. The badge of the Master Chief Petty Officer of the Coast Guard has a gold chevron and specialty mark, a silver eagle, and gold stars. For all ranks, the gold Coast Guard shield on the uniform sleeve replaces the Navy star.

ENLISTED INSIGNIA OF GRADE

AIR FORCE	ARMY	MARINES	NAVY
Chief Master Sergeant of the Air Force (CMSAF)	Sergeant Major of the Army (SMA)	Sergeant Major of the Marine Corps (SgtMajMC)	Master Chief Petty Officer of the Navy (MCPON)
Chief Master Sergeant (CMSgt) / Command Chief Master Sergeant	Command Sergeant Major (CSM) / Sergeant Major (SGM)	Sergeant Major (SgtMaj) / Master Gunnery Sergeant (MGySgt)	Fleet/Command Master Chief Petty Officer / Master Chief Petty Officer (MCPO)
Senior Master Sergeant (SMSgt) / First Sergeant (E-8)	First Sergeant (1SG) / Master Sergeant (MSG)	First Sergeant (1stSgt) / Master Sergeant (MSgt)	Senior Chief Petty Officer (SCPO)
Master Sergeant (MSgt) / First Sergeant (E-7)	Platoon Sergeant (PSG) or Sergeant First Class (SFC)	Gunnery Sergeant (GySgt)	Chief Petty Officer (CPO)
Technical Sergeant (TSgt)	Staff Sergeant (SSG)	Staff Sergeant (SSgt)	Petty Officer First Class (PO1)
Staff Sergeant (SSgt)	Sergeant (SGT)	Sergeant (Sgt)	Petty Officer Second Class (PO2)
Senior Airman (SrA)	Corporal (CPL) / Specialist (SPC)	Corporal (Cpl)	Petty Officer Third Class (PO3)
Airman First Class (A1C)	Private First Class (PFC)	Lance Corporal (LCpl)	Seaman (Seaman)
Airman (Amn)	Private E-2 (PV2)	Private First Class (PFC)	Seaman Apprentice (SA)
Airman Basic (AB) (no insignia)	Private E-1 (PV1) (no insignia)	Private (Pvt) (no insignia)	Seaman Recruit (SR)

OPTIONAL ITEMS

Umbrellas. A solid black umbrella with unobtrusive handle is authorized. Carry it in your left hand so that your right hand is free for saluting.

Women's Handbags. An Air Force–approved vinyl handbag, leather handbag, or clutch-style purse is authorized. Handbags may have up to two adjustable shoulder straps with or without buckles on the straps and will not exceed 13 (W) x 9 (H) x 4.5 inches in bulk. One can carry a clutch-style purse with all uniform combinations. The clutch may be of plain black smooth or scotch-grain leather, patent leather, or high-gloss man-made material. With formal attire, the purse may be of fabric, suede, or patent leather. Do not carry a patent leather–styled purse when wearing semiformal attire. This purse style will not exceed 6 (H) x 11 (W) inches or be smaller than 5 (H) x 9 (W) inches. Carry the handbag in your left hand so that your right hand is free for saluting.

Scarves. The scarf, which is worn only with the overcoat, should not be more than 10 inches wide, black wool or cotton, with or without napped surface. The scarf is worn folded flat and tucked in.

Earmuffs. You may wear commercially designed earmuffs of any material, of plain design in black. The earmuffs may wrap around over or behind the head.

Cuff Links. Men and women may wear cuff links with long-sleeved light blue shirts or blouses. The design may be plain, the Air Force coat of arms, or wing and star.

Physical Training Uniforms. Both Air Force uniform shorts/T-shirt and sweat suit physical training uniforms are available. Installation commanders set rules for wear of uniforms at sporting events.

Attachés, Gym Bags, and Backpacks. You can carry an attaché in the left hand. The case must be solid black in color and have a small black logo. In addition, you can carry black backpacks or dark-blue or black gym bags (small logos authorized) with any uniform. You can carry ABU-patterned, olive drab, or Air Force sage-green backpacks or gym bags when wearing utility uniforms. Wear backpacks and gym bags with a strap over the left shoulder or over both shoulders, or carry in the left hand in order to keep the right hand free for saluting. Use both backpack straps when on crutches or riding a two-wheeled vehicle.

Lanyards/Access Passes/Identification Badges/Common Access Cards (CAC). You must wear plain, solid black or dark blue, conservative small silver link chains, or clear plastic lanyards (you may wear a green lanyard with the utility uniform). The Air Force allows DOD or USAF logos on lanyards. Only wear the lanyard with badge in authorized locations and always on the front of the body below the neck and above the waist. Never wear a lanyard in a manner that could constitute a safety hazard.

UNIFORM WEAR POLICIES

Active Servicemembers. Air Force members may not wear the uniform, or any part of the uniform, in situations that are counter to the interests of the United States or the U.S. Air Force, including the following:

- A meeting of, or sponsored by, an organization, association, movement, or group that the Attorney General of the United States has named as totalitarian, fascist, communist, or subversive; that advocates acts of force or violence to deny others their rights under the Constitution; or that seeks to change the U.S. government by unconstitutional means.
- Activities such as public speeches, interviews, picket lines, marches, rallies, or any public demonstration not approved by the Air Force. To do so could imply the Air Force's sanction of the cause for which the demonstration or activity is conducted.
- When furthering private employment or commercial interests, if official sponsorship might be inferred.
- When engaged in off-duty civilian employment.
- When doing so would discredit the armed forces or if discharged under other than honorable conditions.
- Any public meeting, demonstration, march, rally, or interview if the purpose may be to advocate, express, or approve opposition to the U.S. armed forces.

Air Force members are also prohibited from wearing combinations of uniforms not prescribed in AFI 36-2903 and from wearing or mixing distinctive uniform items (grade insignia, cap devices, badges, insignia, and so forth) with civilian clothing.

Reserve Servicemembers. Except as otherwise prescribed, a reserve officer on active duty will wear the uniform, including insignia, prescribed for officers of the Regular Air Force.

Reserve officers not on active duty, when within the limits of the United States or its possessions, may wear the uniform when participating in inactive-duty training, on occasions of military ceremony, at social functions and informal gatherings of a military character, when engaged in military instruction, or when responsible for the military discipline at an educational institution.

Reserve officers will wear the uniform when participating in an inactive-duty training period, when performing equivalent or appropriate duties, or when engaged in equivalent training or instruction, when such duty, training, or instruction is within the confines of a military installation.

Reserve officers will wear the appropriate uniform when engaged in military flying activities.

Reserve officers not on active duty and residing outside the United States or its possessions, except when granted authority by the secretary of the Air Force, will *not* wear the uniform. These officers, on occasions of military ceremony or other military functions, upon reporting to the nearest military attaché and having their status accredited, may receive authority to appear in uniform. In a country without a military attaché, these officers should obtain authority to wear the uniform for a specific occasion from the proper civil or military authorities of the country concerned.

Special Occasions. The proper uniform for special occasions, such as ceremonies, weddings, funerals, and White House social functions and similar duties, depends on the circumstances in each case. Such occasions may also require white silk, cotton, or nylon gloves or gray suede or double-weave cotton gloves.

In Foreign Countries. Air Force personnel departing for foreign countries in official capacities will be responsible for getting information regarding uniform matters before they leave the United States. The U.S. air attaché or the defense attaché can answer questions regarding uniforms that arise in a foreign country.

Members of the Air Force, active or retired, visiting or residing in a foreign country in an unofficial capacity will **not** wear the uniform except when attending, by formal invitation, ceremonies or social functions that, by the terms of the invitation or by the regulation or customs of the service, require wearing the uniform.

Retired Officers. The uniform of retired officers will be, at their option, either that for officers of corresponding grade at date of retirement or that for officers on the active list, but not a mixture of the two uniforms.

Retired officers not on active duty are prohibited from wearing the uniform in connection with nonmilitary, civilian, or personal enterprises or business activities.

Retirees and honorably discharged veterans may on ceremonial occasions wear either full-size or miniature decorations and service medals on appropriate civilian clothing, such as "black tie" or "white tie" evening wear or equivalents.

Former Members of the Armed Forces. All persons honorably separated from the armed services of the United States may wear on ceremonial occasions the uniform of the highest grade held during that service. The uniform may be either that authorized at the time of separation or that authorized by current regulations. Ceremonial occasions means those with military significance. Persons honorably discharged from the service may wear their uniforms from the place of discharge to their homes, provided such wear is within three months of the date of discharge.

Illegal Wearing. Any person within the jurisdiction of the United States who wears a uniform or a distinctive part of a uniform of the armed services without authority is subject to the penalties prescribed by Title 18 U.S. Code 702. This policy is frequently violated, especially by veterans. Nevertheless, officers should scrupulously adhere to policy.

Illegal Manufacture, Sale, and Possession. The protection of law extends to wearing, manufacture, sale, possession, and reproduction in regular size of any U.S. decoration, medal, badge, or insignia that requires the approval of the secretary of the Air Force.

16

Awards, Decorations, and Badges

Decorations awarded to members of the armed services are an acknowledgment by the government for a job well done. They consist of awards for heroism, the highest of which is the Medal of Honor, and awards for meritorious achievement and meritorious service, the highest of which is the Distinguished Service Medal. Just as the degree of heroism or achievement above and beyond the call of duty varies, so too does the importance or rank of the several awards given for these three purposes. The Air Force Personnel Center (AFPC) provides fact sheets on the following awards and decorations at www.afpc.af.mil/library/factsheets. You can find the specific fact sheet for each award by using the site's search function.

HISTORY OF MILITARY AWARDS
The granting of awards dates at least as far back in history as classical times. The Greeks crowned citizens who were outstanding in war, athletics, literature, and oratory with the laurel wreath. Roman rulers also adopted the laurel wreath. (Today the laurel wreath forms a part of America's highest award for valor.) In the Middle Ages, a system of rewards emerged in the form of titles of nobility and membership in knightly orders, which often included a special badge.

Before the Napoleonic period, such military rewards were given mostly to the aristocracy, who were the principal military leaders. Rewards given to drafted fighting men were infrequent. Napoleon started the modern concept of military awards. He originated a decoration that could be worn by anyone, regardless of rank or social background—the *Légion d'Honneur*. It was the spearhead of the system he used to instill loyalty in the nation he led—because anybody could be awarded it. The French Legion of Honor was followed by the Russian Order of Saint George, the German Iron Cross, and the British Victoria Cross. They were products of the era of nationalism, created to reward courage and loyalty.

In the United States, the custom of awarding military decorations dates from the American Revolution. A resolution of the Continental Congress approved on 25 March 1776 gave the first medal to General George Washington. General

Horatio Gates received the second on 25 November 1777, for the defeat of the British at Saratoga. The third went to General Henry Lee, "Light Horse Harry," who won his nickname on 24 September 1779 in recognition of his successful attack on the British at Paulus Hook, New Jersey, during which he captured 160 of the enemy without loss to his own forces. John Paulding, Isaac van Wart, and David Williams received the fourth, fifth, and sixth of what were known as "André" medals. These three American militiamen captured the British intelligence officer Major John André while he was en route to New York from West Point, after having plotted with Benedict Arnold to betray the American cause.

The Purple Heart was the first military decoration established in the United States. It was authorized by General Washington in 1782 as the Badge of Military Merit, a decoration for unusual gallantry or extraordinary fidelity. Three men received it in 1783. In 1932, the United States reestablished the Purple Heart on a permanent basis.

In the first winter of the Civil War, a feeling developed that a way must be found to recognize and honor the heroism and valor of American soldiers who had distinguished themselves on the battlefield. A Navy and Marine Corps medal was approved by President Abraham Lincoln on 21 December 1861, and on 12 July 1862, a Medal of Honor was provided for award to enlisted men of the Army "who shall most distinguish themselves by their gallantry in action, and other soldier-like qualities." It was amended by an act approved 3 March 1863, which extended its provisions to include officers as well.

The Medal of Honor, the first American military decoration since General Washington's Badge of Military Merit, is the highest military decoration awarded by the United States. Some thirty-four hundred have been awarded since 1861. There are now more than fifty other military awards and decorations.

PRINCIPLES GOVERNING THE AWARD OF DECORATIONS

The award of decorations is a powerful stimulus to pride of service and to encourage heroism or achievement. But if the greatest benefit is to be obtained, the process of making awards must be most carefully administered.

Awards must be made only to those who have truly earned them. The giving of unmerited awards is cheapening and destructive of the purpose for which the awards were authorized. But to fail to recognize true valor or merit promptly and make the awards also defeats the purpose. Both a proper evaluation of facts plus promptness in making awards are required.

This requirement presents a serious problem of decision to commanders of combat organizations. Evidence is often sketchy. The witnesses may be dead as a consequence of combat. The weighing of facts as to which of the several awards is most appropriate is also a delicate choice. To justify any award, the act must be above and beyond the call of duty. Final consideration of the facts before decision by a senior commander will rest with a board of officers who can establish a reasonable yardstick against which to measure and compare these events. Individual commanders, especially junior commanders, must recognize or identify those acts that are truly above and beyond the call of duty, make prompt recommendation for the awards they consider most appropriate, and document those awards with the statements of witnesses, so that the reviewers may arrive at an independent and accurate decision. Unless a careful process is followed by all, there will be many serious errors, anomalies, and variations among organizations, which may greatly reduce or even nullify the powerful stimulus to pride of individual service that may be attained through awards. AFI 36-2803, *The Air Force Awards and Decorations Program*, describes the policy on when and how to award decorations.

Decorations, Service Medals, and Achievement Awards. *Decorations* are awarded in recognition of extraordinary, unusual, or outstanding acts or services. They are the visible evidence of such acts or services. Properly used, they are incentives to greater effort and instrumental in building and maintaining morale. Decorations are awarded for heroism, achievement, and meritorious service. Although most decorations are awarded for one of these distinct purposes, the Distinguished Flying Cross and the Bronze Star Medal may be awarded for either heroism or achievement.

Service medals are awarded to members of the active military service of the United States for performance of specified duty, usually during periods of war or national emergency.

Achievement awards are presented to recognize specific types of achievements for individuals serving on active duty in the Air Force or as members of the Air Reserve Forces.

Oak Leaf Clusters. The oak leaf cluster is awarded in place of a second award of the same decoration. It consists of a bronze twig with four oak leaves and three acorns on the stem. It is affixed to the ribbon. One silver oak leaf cluster is worn in place of five bronze ones.

Award by Foreign Governments. No one holding any office under the United States will, without the consent of Congress, accept any present, emolument, or title of any kind from any foreign government.

In this connection, special authority was granted by Congress with respect to foreign decorations awarded during World War II, the Berlin Airlift, the Korean War, the Vietnam War, and the Gulf War. Officers to whom such awards may be tendered are advised to obtain the advice of their headquarters personnel division or judge advocate. Awards from foreign governments can be accepted only for active combat service or outstanding or unusually meritorious performance, not for peacetime support of an ally.

Penalty for Unauthorized Wearing of Decorations, Service Medals, or Badges. A federal statute provides for a fine or imprisonment for individuals convicted of unauthorized wearing of any decoration, service medal, ribbon or rosette, or badge, or of wearing the uniform or decorations of a foreign nation for the purpose of deception.

USAF DECORATIONS FOR HEROISM

Medal of Honor (MH). The Medal of Honor is awarded for conspicuous gallantry and intrepidity at the risk of life above and beyond the call of duty while a member of the Air Force was engaged in action against an enemy of the United States, while engaged in military operations involving conflict with an opposing foreign force, or while serving with friendly foreign forces engaged in an armed conflict against an opposing armed force in which the United States is not a belligerent party. The Medal of Honor is a gold star with the head of the Statue of Liberty centered upon it and surrounded with green enamel laurel leaves suspended by rings from a trophy consisting of a bar inscribed with the word "Valor" above an adaptation of the thunderbolt from the U.S. Air Force coat of arms.

Air Force Cross (AFC). Congress established the Air Force Cross on 6 July 1960 as a parallel to the U.S. Army Distinguished Service Cross and the U.S. Navy Cross. Earlier, the Air Force had awarded the Distinguished Service Cross.

The Air Force Cross (and its sister service counterparts) is our nation's second-highest military decoration and is awarded to U.S. Air Force airmen for extraordinary heroism in an action against an enemy of the United States, while engaged in military operations involving conflict with an opposing foreign force, or while serving with friendly foreign forces engaged in an armed conflict against an opposing armed force in which the United States is not a belligerent party. The Air Force Cross may be awarded to members of foreign military forces and to American and foreign civilians serving with the armed forces of the United States. The Air Force Cross is a bronze cross with green wreath on which is centered a gold-plated American bald eagle with wings spread against a cloud formation.

Silver Star (SS). The Silver Star was instituted by Congress in 1918. It is granted to persons serving in any capacity with the Air Force cited for gallantry in action that does not warrant the award of a Medal of Honor or the Air Force Cross. The Silver Star is a bronze star on which is centered a wreath within which is inset a silver star.

Distinguished Flying Cross (DFC). *For Heroism.* The Distinguished Flying Cross has been awarded to airmen since 1917 for heroism or extraordinary achievement while participating in aerial flight. It is the United States' oldest military aviation award. The heroism must be evidenced by voluntary action in the face of great danger and beyond the line of duty. The Distinguished Flying Cross is a bronze cross with rays on which is displayed a propeller. The DFC for heroism includes the "V" device.

Airman's Medal (AmnM). The Airman's Medal is awarded for heroism involving voluntary risk of life under conditions other than those of actual conflict with an enemy. The Airman's Medal is a bronze metal disk bearing a representation of Hermes, son of Zeus, releasing an American bald eagle.

Bronze Star Medal (BSM). *For Valor.* The Bronze Star Medal is awarded for heroism or meritorious achievement or service not involving participation in aerial flight while engaged in military action against an enemy of the United States. The award for valor includes the "V" device.

Purple Heart (PH). The Purple Heart is our nation's oldest medal. It was first established by General George Washington on 7 August 1782. The Purple Heart is awarded for wounds received or death after being wounded in action against an enemy of the United States or as a direct result of an act of such enemy. The Purple Heart bears a gold replica of the head of General George Washington and the Washington coat of arms.

USAF DECORATIONS FOR ACHIEVEMENT

Distinguished Service Medal (DSM). The Distinguished Service Medal is awarded to members of the armed forces, military and civilian, who distinguish themselves by exceptionally meritorious service to the government in a duty of great responsibility.

The term "duty of great responsibility" means duty of such a character that exceptionally meritorious service therein has contributed in high degree to the success of a major command, installation, or project. The performance of the duty must be such as to merit recognition of the service as clearly exceptional. A superior performance of the normal duties of the position will not alone justify the award. The accomplishment of the duty for which the award is recommended should have been completed, or it should have progressed to an exceptional degree if the person rendering the service has been transferred to other duties before its full accomplishment.

The Air Force Distinguished Service Medal features a blue stone representing the firmament at the center of a sunburst of thirteen gold rays separated by thirteen white enamel stars. The center motif represents the vault of the heavens; the stars symbolize the thirteen original colonies. The stylized wings on the ribbon bar are symbolic of the USAF.

Legion of Merit (LM). The Legion of Merit, without reference to degree, is awarded to members of the armed forces of the United States who, while serving in any capacity, distinguish themselves by exceptionally meritorious conduct in the performance of outstanding services. In peacetime, awards by the Air Force are generally limited to recognizing services of marked national or international significance—those services that aided the United States in furthering national policy or national security.

This decoration, like the Purple Heart, stems from the Badge for Military Merit, America's oldest decoration, established by George Washington in 1782. As was the case with the Badge for Military Merit, it is awarded for "extraordinary fidelity and essential service." It constitutes a reward for service in a position of responsibility, honorably and well performed. The design of the Legion of Merit has been developed from the Great Seal of the United States, also approved by Congress in 1782.

Distinguished Flying Cross (DFC). *For Achievement.* The Distinguished Flying Cross is awarded to members of the armed forces who, while serving in any capacity with the Air Force, distinguish themselves by heroism or extraordinary achievement while participating in aerial flight. To warrant an award of the Distinguished Flying Cross for extraordinary achievement while participating in aerial flight, the results accomplished must be so exceptional and outstanding as to clearly set the individual apart from comrades who have not been so recognized. The DFC for achievement does not include the "V" device.

Bronze Star Medal (BSM). *For Achievement.* The Bronze Star Medal is awarded to members of the armed forces who, while serving in any capacity, distinguish themselves by meritorious achievement or meritorious service not involving participation in aerial flight in connection with military operations against an enemy of the United States. The required meritorious achievement or meritorious service for award of the Bronze Star Medal is less than that required for award of the Legion of Merit, but must nevertheless be accomplished with distinction. The Bronze Star Medal may be awarded to recognize meritorious service or single acts of merit. The award for achievement does not include the "V" device.

Meritorious Service Medal (MSM). The Meritorious Service Medal is awarded for outstanding noncombat meritorious achievement or service to the United States. Normally, the acts or services rendered must be comparable to those required for the Legion of Merit, but in a duty of lesser though considerable responsibility. It must, nevertheless, be accomplished with distinction and be above and beyond that for the award of the Air Force Commendation Medal.

Air Medal (AM). *For heroism or meritorious achievement.* Authorized by executive order of President Franklin Roosevelt in 1942, the Air Medal is awarded to military or civilian persons who, while serving in any capacity with the armed forces of the United States subsequent to 8 September 1939, distinguish themselves by heroic or meritorious achievement while participating in an aerial flight. This decoration is awarded in those cases where the act of meritorious service does not warrant the award of the Distinguished Flying Cross.

Aerial Achievement Medal (AAM). The Aerial Achievement Medal may be awarded to military or civilian persons for sustained meritorious achievement while participating in aerial flight. The achievement must be accomplished with distinction above and beyond that normally expected of professional airmen.

Air Force Commendation Medal (AFCM). The Air Force Commendation Medal may be awarded to military persons for outstanding achievement or meritorious service rendered specifically on behalf of the Air Force, for acts of courage that do not meet the requirements for award of the Airman's Medal or the Bronze Star Medal, or for sustained meritorious performance by crew members. The medal is a bronze hexagon medallion bearing the eagle, shield, and arrows from the Air Force seal. It is awarded to those below the grade of brigadier general.

Air Force Achievement Medal (AFAM). Awarded for outstanding achievement or meritorious service, this award is intended for outstanding airmen below the grade of colonel. The pendant is a silver-colored nebular disk bearing the winged thunderbolt from the USAF seal.

DOD DECORATIONS FOR ACHIEVEMENT

In addition to the USAF decorations listed above, the Department of Defense awards five military decorations corresponding to their service counterparts; however, they are worn before the USAF decorations on the uniform.

Defense Distinguished Service Medal (DDSM). This medal is usually awarded to high-ranking military officers for exceptionally meritorious service in a position of unique and great responsibility. Only the secretary of defense can initiate and award this decoration.

Defense Superior Service Medal (DSSM). This medal may be awarded to U.S. military personnel who render superior meritorious service in a position of significant responsibility within the Office of the Secretary of Defense, on a joint staff, or in a joint activity. The pendant design is that of the DDSM, except that it is in silver.

Defense Meritorious Service Medal (DMSM). This medal may be awarded to U.S. military personnel who distinguish themselves by noncombat meritorious achievement or meritorious service within the Office of the Secretary of Defense, on a joint staff, or in a joint activity.

Joint Service Commendation Medal (JSCM). This medal is awarded to personnel on duty in the Office of the Secretary of Defense, the Joint Staff, the Defense Supply Agency, the National Security Agency, other joint agencies reporting to the Joint Chiefs of Staff, joint task forces, or NATO organizations for meritorious achievement or service. It precedes the AFCM when worn on the uniform. A bronze "V" is authorized for a combat award after 25 June 1963.

Joint Service Achievement Medal (JSAM). Worn before the AFAM, this medal may be awarded to any members of the U.S. armed forces below the rank of colonel who distinguish themselves by meritorious achievement or service while serving in specified joint activities after 3 August 1983.

UNIT AWARDS

The following types of unit awards are authorized as recognition of certain types of service and as a means of promoting esprit de corps:

- Unit decorations
- War service streamers
- Campaign and expeditionary streamers

U.S. Unit Decorations. The following U.S. unit decorations have been established to recognize outstanding heroism or exceptionally meritorious conduct in the performance of outstanding services:

- Presidential Unit Citation
- Joint Meritorious Unit Award
- Air Force Gallant Unit Citation
- Air Force Meritorious Unit Award
- Air Force Outstanding Unit Award
- Air Force Organizational Excellence Award

Presidential Unit Citation (PUC). The Presidential Unit Citation (formerly the Distinguished Unit Citation) is awarded to any identified units of the armed forces of the United States and cobelligerent nations for extraordinary heroism in action against an armed enemy. The unit must display such gallantry, determination, and esprit de corps in accomplishing its mission under extremely difficult and hazardous conditions as to set it apart and above other units participating in the same campaign. The degree of heroism required is the same as that which would warrant award of an Air Force Cross to an individual. Extended periods of combat duty or participation in a large number of operational missions, either ground or air, is not sufficient.

Air Force Gallant Unit Citation (GUC). Established in 2004, this citation is awarded to Air Force active-duty, Reserve, and Guard units for extraordinary heroism in action against an armed enemy of the United States while engaged in military operations involving conflict with an opposing foreign force on or after 11 September 2001. The GUC requires a lesser degree of gallantry, determination, and esprit de corps than required for the Presidential Unit Citation. Nevertheless, the unit must have performed with marked distinction under difficult and hazardous conditions in accomplishing its mission so as to set it apart from and above other units participating in the same conflict. The degree of heroism required is the same as that which would warrant award of the Silver Star, which is awarded for gallantry and heroism of high degrees, including risk of life in action. The GUC will normally be earned by units that have participated in single or successive actions covering relatively brief time spans. Only on rare occasions will a unit larger than a group quality for the GUC. Extended periods of combat duty or participation in a large number of operational missions, either air or ground, is not sufficient.

Air Force Meritorious Unit Award (MUA). Also established in 2004, the MUA is awarded to Air Force active-duty, reserve, and Guard units for exceptionally meritorious conduct in the performance of outstanding achievement or service in direct support of combat operations for at least ninety continuous days during the period of military operations against an armed enemy of the United States on or after 11 September 2001. The unit must display such outstanding devotion and superior performance of exceptionally difficult tasks as to set it apart and above other units with similar missions. The degree of achievement required is the same as that which would warrant award of the Legion of Merit. Superior performance of normal mission will not alone justify award of the MUA. Service in a combat zone is not required, but service must be directly related to the combat effort. Squadrons, groups, and wings may be recommended for this award. The MUA is not awarded to any unit or unit component previously awarded the Air Force Outstanding Unit Award, the Air Force Organizational Excellence Award, or unit awards from other service components for the same act, achievement, or service.

Joint Meritorious Unit Award (JMUA). This ribbon is awarded in the name of the secretary of defense to joint activities of the Department of

Defense for meritorious achievement or service, superior to that normally expected, during combat with an armed enemy of the United States, during a declared national emergency, or under extraordinary circumstances that involve the national interest.

Air Force Outstanding Unit Award (AFOUA). Established in 1954, this award recognizes units that distinguish themselves by exceptionally meritorious service or outstanding achievement that clearly sets the units above and apart from similar units. This award consists of a predominantly blue streamer with a narrow red band center bordered by white lines and red bands. Theater or area of operations is embroidered in white on the streamer. The individual emblem is a ribbon of the streamer color. It is awarded to units not larger than a wing for meritorious achievement or service in support of military operations or of great significance in accomplishment not involving combat operations. A bronze "V" device is worn on the ribbon to denote award for combat or direct combat support.

Air Force Organizational Excellence Award (AFOEA). Established in August 1969, this decoration is awarded to Air Force internal organizations that are organizational entities within larger organizations in recognition of achievements and accomplishments of units that did not meet eligibility requirements of the AFOUA. The organizations are unique, unnumbered organizations or activities that perform staff functions and functions normally performed by numbered wings, groups, squadrons, and so on. A bronze "V" device is worn on the ribbon to denote award for combat or direct combat support.

ACHIEVEMENT AWARDS

Air Force achievement awards recognize specific types of achievement by members serving on active duty in the Air Force or in the Air Reserve Forces.

Prisoner of War Medal (POWM). This award is authorized for all U.S. military personnel who were taken prisoner of war during an armed conflict and who served honorably during the period of captivity. An American eagle is surrounded by a border of barbed wire.

Combat Readiness Medal (CRM). This medal is authorized for members of combat crews of manned weapons delivery systems for sustained individual combat or mission readiness or preparedness for direct weapon system employment. The medal is a circle marked with arrowheads and the points of overlapping triangles to indicate the hours of round-the-clock duty and performance.

Air Force Good Conduct Medal (AFGCM). This medal is awarded only to enlisted persons in recognition of exemplary conduct during a three-year period. An oak leaf cluster is awarded for each successive period of service that meets the requirements for award.

Air Reserve Forces Meritorious Service Medal (ARFMSM). This award, equivalent to the Air Force Good Conduct Medal, is for issuance to Air Reserve personnel who demonstrate exemplary behavior, efficiency, and fidelity for four continuous years.

Outstanding Airman of the Year Ribbon (OAYR). This ribbon is awarded to airmen nominated by major air commands and field operating agencies for competition in the 12 Outstanding Airmen of the Year Program.

Air Force Recognition Ribbon (AFRR). This ribbon is awarded to named individual Air Force recipients of special trophies and awards, except for the Outstanding Airman of the Year award.

Air Force Overseas Ribbon (AFOSR). This ribbon is awarded for completion of an overseas tour of duty. There are short- and long-tour versions of this ribbon, with precedence given to the short-tour ribbon.

Air Force Expeditionary Service Ribbon (AFESR). Established in 2003, the AFESR is awarded to Air Force active-duty, reserve, and Guard personnel who complete a contingency deployment after 1 October 1999. Deployed status is defined as either deployment on contingency, exercise, deployment orders, or members sourced in direct in- or out-theater support of expeditionary operations with an overnight away from home station. Individuals must have deployed for forty-five consecutive days or spent ninety nonconsecutive days on a deployed status. The time criteria can be waived for actual combat against an enemy of the United States. Any contingency (overseas or stateside) deployment qualifies regardless of the duty, destination, or location of the TDY. There is no time limit to accumulate the ninety nonconsecutive days. Permanent party overseas personnel are not eligible for the AFESR unless they are forward deployed on a contingency deployment. Members on an overseas short tour may receive both the AFESR and the Overseas Short Tour Ribbon, provided they meet the requirements of both. To receive both, the number of days forward deployed must be subtracted from the number of short-tour days credited and still meet the minimum requirement for short-tour credit. A gold border worn on the AFESR represents participation in combat operations. It is authorized for wear by individuals who were engaged in conducting or supporting combat operations in a designated combat zone or in a hazardous duty area. Combat action is defined as when a member is subject to hostile fire, explosion, or is engaged in employing lethal weapons. To receive the gold border, the individual must have been assigned to an Air Expeditionary Force or have been on Contingency Exercise Deployment orders.

Air Force Longevity Service Award (AFLSA). All members of the Air Force on active duty and all reservists not on active duty are eligible for this award. Requirements for the basic award are four years of honorable active federal military service with any branch of the U.S. armed forces. A bronze oak leaf cluster is worn on the ribbon for each additional four years of service. A silver oak leaf cluster is worn in lieu of five bronze clusters. No medal is authorized.

USAF Basic Military Training Instructor Ribbon. This ribbon is awarded to Air Education and Training Command personnel staffing basic military training upon graduation from the instructor school.

Air Force Recruiter Ribbon. This ribbon is worn by active-duty, Guard, and reserve personnel on completing recruiting training and while serving as a recruiter, and on a permanent basis after serving for thirty-six months as a recruiter.

NCO Professional Military Education Graduate Ribbon (NCOP-MEGR). This ribbon is awarded to graduates of certified Noncommissioned Officer Professional Military Education Schools.

USAF Basic Military Training Honor Graduate Ribbon (BMTHGR). This ribbon is awarded to honor graduates of BMT who, after 29 July 1976, have demonstrated excellence in all phases of academic and military training. Award is limited to the top 10 percent of the training flight.

Small Arms Expert Marksmanship Ribbon (SAEMR). Awarded after 1 January 1963 to persons qualifying as "expert" in small-arms marksmanship with either the M-16 rifle or issue handgun. Qualification as "expert" in both after 22 June 1972, is denoted by a bronze service star worn on the service ribbon.

Air Force Training Ribbon (AFTR). Awarded to Air Force members on completion of initial military accession training (BMT, OTS, ROTC, academy, medical services, judge advocate, chaplain orientation, and so on).

SERVICE MEDALS

Service medals are awarded to members of the armed forces of the United States to denote the honorable performance of duty. Most service medals pertain to federal duty in a time of war or national emergency. A person's entire service during the period for which the award is made must be honorable.

Service Medals Authorized through the Vietnam War. Service medals that pertain only to wars or campaigns through the war in Vietnam are not included, since there are few airmen still on active duty who might wear such items. See AFI 36-2803 for details on these awards.

National Defense Service Medal (NDSM). This medal has been authorized for honorable active service for any period between 27 June 1950 and 27 July 1954. Persons on active duty for purposes other than extended active duty are not eligible for this award. The NDSM was also authorized for Cold War service from 1 January 1961 to 14 August 1974, and again for service during Operations Desert Shield and Desert Storm from 2 August 1990 to 30 November 1995. The NDSM is also authorized for honorable service from 11 September 2001 to a date to be determined. Servicemembers on active duty, members of the Selected Reserve in good standing, and members of other than the Selected Reserve who were called to active duty, including USAF Academy cadets, are eligible. Ineligible are members called to active duty for physical examinations, training only, or to serve on boards, courts, or commissions. A bronze service star is authorized for persons who have served during more than one such period.

Antarctica Service Medal (ASM). This medal is awarded to members of any of the armed forces who, as members of a U.S. expedition, participated in scientific, direct support, or exploratory operations in the Antarctic or who participated in fifteen missions to and from Antarctica in support of such operations. The medal includes a "Wintered Over" clasp for those who stayed in

Antarctica during winter months. There is a corresponding circular device for wear on the ribbon bar, depicting the map of the Antarctic continent.

Armed Forces Expeditionary Medal (AFEM). This medal was established on 4 Dec 1961 and is awarded to members of the United States Armed Forces who, after 1 July 1958, have participated in a United States military operation and encountered foreign-armed opposition, or were in danger of hostile action by foreign armed forces. The medal may be awarded for three categories of U.S. military operations: expeditionary operations, actions in direct support of the United Nations, and operations of assistance to friendly foreign nations.

Refer to DOD 1348.33-M for operations that qualify for this award. Also, a listing of Department of Defense–recognized military campaigns associated with eligibility for the Armed Forces Expeditionary Medal is provided at the AFPC Department of Defense Awards Database. The Department of the Army's Institute of Heraldry also provides a listing of qualifying operations at its website, www.tioh.hqda.pentagon.mil.

No servicemember may be awarded more than one of these four medals for service in the same approved expedition or operation to combat terrorism: the Global War on Terrorism Expeditionary Medal, the Global War on Terrorism Service Medal, the Armed Forces Expeditionary Medal, and the Armed Forces Service Medal.

Southwest Asia Service Medal (SWASM). This medal has been authorized to servicemembers who served in the Persian Gulf area in Operations Desert Shield and Desert Storm from 2 August 1990 through 30 November 1995. Those who served in Egypt, Israel, Jordan, Syria, and Turkey, including airspace, directly supporting combat operations between 17 January 1991 and 30 November 1995 are also eligible. Servicemembers who earned the SWASM on their initial tour in Southwest Asia and who later become eligible for the Armed Forces Expeditionary Medal are entitled to wear both awards, but not for a single tour in Southwest Asia.

Kosovo Campaign Medal. This medal is awarded for participation in NATO operations related to Kosovo from 24 March 1999 to a date to be determined. The award is for thirty days continuous or accumulated service on land, at sea, or in the airspace of Kosovo, or other territories of Serbia, Montenegro, Croatia, Bosnia and Herzegovina, Slovenia, Albania, Macedonia, and the Adriatic and Ionian Seas. Award is also for aircrews participating in Operation Allied Force, 24 March 1999 through 10 June 1999, with fifteen sorties into Kosovo of the Federal Republic of Yugoslavia; and ninety days continuous or accumulated service in Italy, Greece, or Hungary in direct support of NATO operations conducted in the area of eligibility.

Afghanistan Campaign Medal. Servicemembers authorized the AFGM must have served in direct support of Operation Enduring Freedom on or after 24 October 2001 to a date to be determined. The area of eligibility encompasses all land areas of the country of Afghanistan and all air spaces above the land. Service members must have been assigned, attached, or mobilized to units operating in this area for thirty consecutive days or for sixty nonconsecutive days and meet one of the following criteria: engaged in combat during an armed engagement regardless of time in the area of eligibility, been wounded or injured and required medical evacuation from Afghanistan, or while participating as a regularly assigned air crewmember flying sorties into, out of, within, or over the area of eligibility in direct support of the military operations (each day of operations counts as one day of eligibility).

Servicemembers qualified for the Global War on Terrorism Expeditionary Medal (GWOT-E) for service between 24 October 2001 and 30 April 2005, in the area for which the AFGM was subsequently authorized, shall remain qualified for that medal. On application, any such servicemember may be awarded the AFGM in place of the GWOT-E for such service. No service member shall be entitled to both medals for the same action, achievement, or period of service. Servicemembers serving in the qualifying area of eligibility for which the AFGM was subsequently authorized are no longer qualified to receive the GWOT-E after 30 April 2005.

Iraq Campaign Medal. The ICM is authorized for servicemembers directly supporting Operation Iraqi Freedom on or after 19 March 2003 to a date to be determined. The area of eligibility encompasses all land area of the country of Iraq as well as the contiguous water area out to 12 nautical miles and all air spaces above the land area of Iraq and above the contiguous waters out to 12 nautical miles. Service members must have been assigned, attached, or mobilized to units operating in this area for thirty consecutive days or for sixty nonconsecutive days and meet one of the following criteria: engaged in combat during an armed engagement regardless of time in the area of eligibility, been wounded or injured and required medical evacuation from Afghanistan, or while participating as a regularly assigned air crewmember flying sorties into, out of, within, or over the area of eligibility in direct support of the military operations (each day of operations counts as one day of eligibility).

Servicemembers qualified for the Global War on Terrorism Expeditionary Medal (GWOT-E) for service between 19 March 2003 and 30 April 2005, in the area for which the ICM was subsequently authorized, shall remain qualified for that medal. On application, any such servicemember may be awarded the ICM in place of the GWOT-E for such service. Servicemembers serving in the qualifying area of eligibility for which the ICM was subsequently authorized are no longer qualified to receive the GWOT-E after 30 April 2005.

Global War on Terrorism Expeditionary Medal. The GWOT-E is awarded to active-duty, reserve, and Guard servicemembers who have deployed abroad in service of Operations Enduring Freedom or Iraqi Freedom. Participants must have been assigned or attached to a unit in OEF/OIF and served thirty consecutive days or sixty nonconsecutive days (on or after 11 September 2001) in one of a large number of geographic areas, primarily in the Middle East, but also in the Balkans, northeast Africa, and the Philippines, as well as offshore areas. Also eligible are those who have engaged in actual combat against the enemy under circumstances involving grave damage or death or serious bodily harm from enemy action, regardless of time served in OEF/OIF. Service as a crewmember flying sorties into, out of, within, or over the areas of eligibility in direct support of Operations Enduring Freedom or Iraqi Freedom are eligible, accruing one day's credit for the thirty- or sixty-day requirement for each day that one or more sorties is flown. The government made additional locations eligible effective 13 February 2004. For the location listing, see www.afpc.af.mil/library/factsheets/factsheet.asp?id=7812.

Note the restriction regarding the GWOT-E and the AFGM and ICM immediately above.

Global War on Terrorism Service Medal. While the GWOT Expeditionary Medal recognizes servicemembers who participated in an expedition to combat terrorism on or after 11 September 2001, the GWOT Service Medal recognizes service in DOD-designated operations to combat terrorism on or after 11 September 2001, from outside the area of eligibility designated for the GWOT Expeditionary Medal. Servicemembers must have been assigned or attached to a unit participating in or serving in support of designated operations for thirty consecutive days or sixty nonconsecutive days. Also eligible are those who have engaged in actual combat against the enemy under circumstances involving grave damage or death or serious bodily harm from enemy action, regardless of time served. Service as a crewmember flying sorties into, out of, within, or over the areas of eligibility in direct support of Operations Enduring Freedom or Iraqi Freedom are eligible, accruing one day's credit for the thirty- or sixty-day requirement for each day that one or more sorties is flown.

No servicemember is entitled to more than one award of the Global War on Terrorism Expeditionary Medal or the Global War on Terrorism Service Medal, and no servicemember may be awarded more than one of these four medals for service in the same approved expedition or operation to combat terrorism: the Global War on Terrorism Expeditionary Medal, the Armed Forces Expeditionary Medal, and the Armed Forces Service Medal.

Korean Defense Service Medal (KDSM). Established in 2004, this medal is awarded to servicemembers who have been assigned, attached, or mobilized to units operating or serving all the land area of the Republic of Korea and the contiguous waters and airspace for thirty consecutive or sixty nonconsecutive days, or who were actually engaged in combat during an armed engagement or who were killed, wounded, or injured in the line of duty and required medical evacuation from the area of eligibility. Service is between 28 July 1954 and a date to be determined.

Armed Forces Service Medal (AFSM). This medal is awarded to servicemembers who, after 1 June 1992, participated in military operations deemed to be a significant activity by the Joint Chiefs of Staff and who encountered no foreign armed opposition or imminent threat of hostile action. The

AFPC factsheet contains detailed qualification criteria and is found at www.afpc.af.mil/library/factsheets/factsheet.asp?id=7815.

No servicemember may be awarded more than one of these four medals for service in the same approved expedition or operation to combat terrorism: the Global War on Terrorism Expeditionary Medal, the Armed Forces Expeditionary Medal, and the Armed Forces Service Medal.

Air Force Combat Action Medal (AFCAM). The AFCAM recognizes Air Force members below the general officer grades who actively participated in ground or air combat. The principal eligibility criterion is that the individual must have been under direct, hostile fire while operating in an unsecured space (outside a defended perimeter) or physically engaging hostile forces with direct, lethal fire. The AFCAM is awarded for qualifying service from 11 September 2001 to a date to be determined.

Humanitarian Service Medal (HSM). This medal is awarded to those who distinguished themselves by meritorious direct participation in significant military acts or operations of a humanitarian nature or who have rendered a service to mankind. Specifically excluded from eligibility are servicemembers remaining at a geographically separated location and who did not make a direct contribution to influence the action.

Military Outstanding Volunteer Service Medal (MOVSM). This medal is awarded to members of the armed forces of the United States who, subsequent to 31 December 1992, performed outstanding volunteer community service of a sustained, direct, and consequential nature. To be eligible, an individual's service must be to the civilian community, including the military family community, and be significant in nature and produce tangible results, and reflect favorably on the military service and the Department of Defense. The MOVSM is intended to recognize exceptional community support over time, and not a single act or achievement, and to honor direct support of community activities.

Air and Space Campaign Medal (ASCM). This medal, authorized by the secretary of the Air Force and awarded to members of the United States Air Force who, after March 24, 1999, participated in or directly supported a significant U.S. military operation designated by the chief of staff of the Air Force. The medal is awarded only to personnel who provided direct support of combat operations from outside a geographic area determined by the Joint Chiefs of Staff.

Servicemembers must be assigned or attached to a unit engaged in the operation. Personnel must be engaged in direct support for at least thirty consecutive days or for sixty nonconsecutive days. For this medal, direct support is defined as: (1) deploying in support of an operation, or (2) if at home station, performing functions or missions that historically were deployed forward, or entirely new and future missions, which due to technological advances, are no longer constrained by geographic location. This includes, but is not limited to, sortie generation, intelligence, surveillance, targeting, and computer network attack operations.

The Chief of Staff of the Air Force designates the military operations that qualify for the ASCM. The Commander, Air Force Forces, will designate those organizations that provided direct qualifying support. The AFPC website lists the approved military operations for this award at www.afpc.af.mil/library/fact-sheets/factsheet_print.asp?fsID=7818&page=1.

Armed Forces Reserve Medal (AFRM). Required for this award is honorable and satisfactory service in one or more of the reserve components of the armed forces for a period of ten years, not necessarily consecutive, provided such service was performed within a period of twelve consecutive years. Periods of service as a member of a regular component are excluded from consideration.

NON-U.S. SERVICE MEDALS

United Nations Medal (UNM). This medal is awarded by the United States to specific individuals for service with United Nations Forces. Each UN mission or action for which a UNM is awarded is commemorated by a suspension and service ribbon of unique colors and design. The ribbon and medallion combination takes on the name of the specific operation for which the combination was created; for example, the operation in the former Republic of Yugoslavia is the United Nations Protection Force (UNPROFOR), yielding the UNPROFOR Medal. U.S. servicemembers who meet the criteria may accept and wear the first UNM with the unique suspension and service ribbon for which they qualify. To recognize subsequent awards (if approved by the secretary of defense) for service in a different UN mission or action, the servicemember will affix a bronze service star to the first UN suspension and service ribbon awarded.

NATO Medal. Approved for U.S. military personnel who served under NATO command or operational control in direct support of NATO operations in the former Republic of Yugoslavia and in Kosovo, or as designated by the Supreme Allied Commander Europe (SACEUR), beginning July 1992. Only one NATO service medal/ribbon is authorized for wear. Recipients should wear the one awarded first with a bronze service star for each subsequent award. Currently, two NATO Medals are authorized: NATO Medal–Former Republic of Yugoslavia and NATO Medal–Kosovo Operations.

Multinational Force and Observers Medal. This medal may be awarded to those who served with multinational forces and observers for at least ninety cumulative days after 3 August 1981. Subsequent awards are designated by numeral appurtenances.

Kuwait Liberation Medal, Kingdom of Saudi Arabia (KLM). Awarded to U.S. military personnel who served in the theater of operations of the Gulf War between 17 January and 28 February 1991.

Kuwaiti Liberation Medal, Kuwait. (KLM) Awarded to U.S. military personnel who served in the theater of operations of the Gulf War between 2 August 1990 and 31 August 1993.

BADGES

Badges are appurtenances of the uniform. In the eyes of their wearers, several badges have significance equal to or greater than all but the highest decorations. Although there is no established precedence among badges, aerospace badges are worn above any others, with the exception of the chaplain insignia. New specialty badges for all USAF personnel were authorized in 1994, but only one may be worn at a time.

Two categories of badges and specialty insignia are currently approved for wear. The first category consists of duty badges and insignia, while the second category encompasses occupational badges. See AFI 36-2903, and its directed AFIs, for eligibility requirements for wearing these badges and insignia. Those granted aeronautical ratings no longer current are authorized to wear the aerospace badge that was in effect when the rating was granted.

Duty Badges and Insignia. These include the presidential service, vice-presidential service, Office of the Secretary of Defense, Joint Chiefs of Staff, and permanent professor at the Air Force Academy badges. In addition, these include the combat crewmember, security police, AETC instructor, Air Force recruiting service, fire protection, Junior AFROTC instructor, Air Force Reserve recruiting service, and Defense Language Institute instructor badges.

Occupational Badges. This category includes aeronautical (pilot, navigator/observer, enlisted aircrew member, astronaut, flight surgeon, flight nurse, officer aircrew member, missileer, and air battle manager), space, cyberspace, chaplain, dental corps, nurse corps, enlisted medical, medical corps, medical service corps, biomedical science corps, judge advocate, air traffic control, acquisition and financial management, information management, operations support, band, intelligence, paralegal, chaplain service support, civil engineer, force protection, public affairs, command and control, logistics, services, communications and information management, space/missile, explosive ordnance disposal, manpower and personnel, supply/fuels, historian, meteorologist, transportation, and weapons director badges.

Other Badges. These include distinguished international shooter, USAF distinguished rifleman, USAF bronze excellence-in-competition rifleman, USAF distinguished pistol shot, USAF distinguished-in-competition pistol shot, and USAF bronze excellence-in-competition pistol shot badges.

DEVICES

Service Ribbons. The service ribbon is a strip of ribbon identical to that from which the service medal is suspended. (Not all ribbons reflect the award of a medal, such as service longevity ribbons.) Service ribbons will not be worn with protective coverings.

Bronze Oak Leaf Cluster. Represents second and subsequent entitlements of awards.

Silver Oak Leaf Cluster. Represents the sixth, eleventh, etc., entitlements or is worn in lieu of five bronze OLCs.

Service Stars. The service star is a bronze or silver five-pointed star that represents participation in campaigns or operations, multiple qualifications, or an additional award to any of the various ribbons on which it is authorized. A silver service star is worn in lieu of five bronze ones.

Wearing on Service Ribbons. Service stars are authorized to be worn on the service ribbons of some pre-Vietnam medals and the following medals only:

- National Defense Service Medal to represent a second award.
- Small Arms Expert Marksmanship Ribbon to represent qualification with M-16 rifle and with handgun.

Letter "V" Device. The bronze letter "V" device indicates an award for valor in combat.

Miniature Decorations, Service Medals, and Appurtenances. Miniature decorations, service medals, and appurtenances are replicas of the corresponding decorations and service medals on the scale of one half. The Medal of Honor is not worn in miniature. Its rosette is authorized for civilian wear.

Miniature Service Ribbons. Miniature service ribbons are replicas of corresponding service ribbons on a scale of about one half.

Lapel Buttons. *For All Decorations and Service Medals.* The lapel button is $2^1/_{32}$ inch long and $^1/_8$ inch wide, in colored enamel, being a reproduction of the service ribbon. Miniature appurtenances may be placed on lapel buttons.

Air Force Lapel Button. This is a small metal replica of the Air Force star and wings. It is authorized for wear by all active-duty and reserve personnel, including AFROTC cadets.

Air Force Retired Lapel Button. This button is presented to each retiree.

Supply of Appurtenances. Only the following appurtenances will be supplied by the Department of the Air Force:

- Service ribbons
- Clasps
- Service stars
- Letter "V" device
- Arrowheads
- Lapel buttons for U.S. military decorations (except Medal of Honor)
- Air Force lapel button
- Air Force retired lapel button

An initial issue of the above appurtenances will be made with the corresponding service medals. Replacements for military personnel on active duty will be supplied to commanders on requisition in the usual manner. Replacements for retirees and veterans should be requested through Air Force Reference Branch, National Personnel Records Center, 9700 Page Ave., St. Louis, MO 63132-5100.

Presidential
Service Badge

Vice-Presidential
Service Badge

Office of the Secretary
of Defense Badge

Joint Chiefs of Staff
Badge

Headquarters Air Force
Badge

Command Insignia

Permanent Professor

Special Service Identification Badges

PILOT

ENLISTED AIRCREW

ASTRONAUT

NAVIGATOR

FLIGHT SURGEON

FLIGHT NURSE

OFFICER AIRCREW

AIR BATTLE MANAGER

SENSOR OPERATOR

UNMANNED AIRCRAFT
SYSTEMS

MISSILE OPERATIONS

DECORATIONS, AWARDS, AND SERVICE MEDALS

USAF AND DEPARTMENT OF DEFENSE
MILITARY DECORATIONS

**Medal of Honor
(Air Force)**

Air Force Cross

**Defense
Distinguished Service
Medal**

**Distinguished Service
Medal
(Air Force)**

Silver Star

**Defense Superior Service
Medal**

Legion of Merit

Distinguished Flying Cross

Airman's Medal

Bronze Star Medal

Purple Heart

Defense Meritorious Service Medal

Meritorious Service Medal

Air Medal

Aerial Achievement Medal

Joint Service Commendation Medal

**Air Force
Commendation
Medal**

**Joint Service
Achievement
Medal**

**Air Force
Achievement
Medal**

USAF AND DEPARTMENT OF DEFENSE UNIT AWARDS

**Air Force
Combat Action
Ribbon**

**Presidential
Unit Citation
(Air Force)**

**Joint Meritorious
Unit Award**

**Air Force
Gallant Unit Award**

**Valorous Unit
Award**

**Air Force
Meritorious Unit
Award**

**AF Outstanding
Unit Award**

**AF Organizational
Excellence Award**

MILITARY SERVICE AWARDS

**Prisoner of War
Medal**

**Combat Readiness
Medal**

**Good Conduct Medal
(Air Force)**

**Air Reserve Forces
Meritorious Service
Medal**

**National
Defense Service
Medal**

**Antarctica Service
Medal**

**Armed Forces
Expeditionary
Medal**

**Vietnam Service
Medal**

**Outstanding
Airman of the Year
Ribbon**

**Air Force
Recognition
Ribbon**

**Air Force
Overseas Ribbon
(short tour)**

**Air Force
Overseas Ribbon
(long tour)**

**Air Force
Expeditionary
Service Ribbon**

**Air Force
Longevity Service
Award Ribbon**

**USAF Basic Military
Training Instructor
Ribbon**

**Air Force
Recruiter
Ribbon**

**NCO Professional
Military Education
Graduate Ribbon**

**USAF Basic Military
Training Honor
Graduate Ribbon**

**Small Arms Expert
Marksmanship
Ribbon**

**Air Force
Training
Ribbon**

**Southwest Asia Service
Medal**

**Kosovo Campaign
Medal**

**Afghanistan Campaign
Medal**

Iraq Campaign Medal

Global War on Terrorism Expeditionary Medal

Global War on Terrorism Service Medal

Korean Defense Service Medal

Armed Forces Service Medal

Humanitarian Service Medal

Military Outstanding Volunteer Service Medal

Air and Space Campaign Medal

Armed Forces Reserve Medal

NON-U.S. SERVICE MEDALS

United Nations Medal

NATO Medal

Multinational Force and Observers Medal

Republic of Vietnam Campaign Medal

Kuwait Liberation Medal (Kingdom of Saudi Arabia)

Kuwait Liberation Medal (Government of Kuwait)

ACQUISITION & FINANCIAL
MANAGEMENT

AIR TRAFFIC CONTROL

BAND

CHAPLAIN SERVICE
SUPPORT

CIVIL ENGINEER

COMMAND & CONTROL

COMMUNICATIONS &
INFORMATION

CYBERSPACE
OPERATOR

CYBERSPACE
SUPPORT

EMERGENCY
MANAGEMENT

EXPLOSIVE ORDNANCE
DISPOSAL

FORCE PROTECTION

FORCE SUPPORT

HISTORIAN

INTELLIGENCE

JUDGE ADVOCATE

LOGISTICS PLANS

LOGISTICS READINESS
OFFICER

MAINTENANCE

MANPOWER & PERSONNEL

METEOROLOGIST

OPERATION SUPPORT

PARACHUTIST

PARALEGAL

PUBLIC AFFAIRS

SERVICES

SPACE

SPACE & MISSILE

SUPPLY & FUELS

TRANSPORTATION

WEAPONS DIRECTOR

BIOMEDICAL SERVICE
CORPS

DENTAL CORPS

ENLISTED MEDICAL

MEDICAL CORPS

MEDICAL SERVICE
CORPS

NURSE CORPS

BUDDHIST
CHAPLAIN

CHRISTIAN
CHAPLAIN

JEWISH
CHAPLAIN

MUSLIM
CHAPLAIN

Manufacture, Sale, and Illegal Possession. There are restrictions on manufacture and sale of service medals and appurtenances by civilians and penalties for illegal possession and wearing of service medals and appurtenances.

GUIDE FOR WEARING AWARDS

Individuals entitled to wear decorations, service medals, ribbons, and badges should be certain that they place them on the uniform in the prescribed location and in the prescribed order. Ribbons are arranged symmetrically in rows of three, with the exception of wear on the service dress coat. When the coat lapel covers the usual symmetrical arrangement of three ribbons in a row, they can be staggered to the wearer's left and arranged in rows of four. This asymmetrical arrangement is authorized only for the service dress coat. For detailed information, see AFI 36-2903.

U.S. Military Service Medals. U.S. military and naval service medals are awarded by the Department of Defense and by the departments of the Air Force, Army, and Navy.

Occasions for Wearing. Commanders may prescribe the wearing of decorations and service medals on the following occasions:

- Parades, reviews, inspections, and funerals
- Ceremonies and formal occasions

The servicemember has the option of wearing decorations and service medals on the following occasions:

- Holidays when not on duty with troops
- Social occasions of a private nature ("black tie" or "white tie")

U.S. Nonmilitary Decorations. The following nonmilitary decorations may be worn only if military decorations or service medals are worn: the Medal for Merit, the National Security Medal, the Presidential Medal for Freedom, and decorations awarded by NASA, the Treasury Department, Public Health, and Maritime Services. Nonmilitary service awards may not be worn on the Air Force uniform. State decorations and service awards may be worn only by Air National Guardsmen in nonactive-duty status.

Foreign Service Medals. In general, the acceptance or wearing of foreign decorations and service medals for service performed while a member of the armed forces of the United States is prohibited. See AFI 36-2903.

Decorations and service medals awarded by the national government of a friendly country may be worn, provided such service medals were earned during service as a bona fide member of the armed forces of that friendly foreign nation. At least one U.S. decoration or service medal must be worn at the same time that a foreign service medal is worn.

The wearing of foreign service medals (except those indicated above), including civilian service medals awarded by a foreign national government and all service medals awarded by an inferior foreign jurisdiction, is prohibited.

Wear of Decorations and Service Medals. Decorations and service medals are worn on the service coat. The Medal of Honor is worn as a pendant

Women's Open Collar

Men's Shirt   **Women's Blouse**

Wear of Ribbons on Service Uniform Combinations

Men's Mess Dress   **Women's Mess Dress**

Wear of Miniature Medals on the Mess Dress Uniforms

from the cravat (ribbon placed around the neck) outside the shirt collar and inside the coat collar, with the medal proper hanging over the necktie near the collar. Other decorations and service medals are worn in order of precedence from right to left of the wearer immediately above the pocket on the left breast in one or more lines, which are overlapped. The top line consists of those decorations and service medals highest in the order of precedence, which is as follows: decorations (in order listed at the end of this chapter); U.S. unit citations; achievement awards; service medals, in order earned; foreign decorations; USN service awards; and foreign service awards.

A *bronze oak leaf cluster* is authorized for wear for each additional Presidential Unit Citation received by a unit. A *silver oak leaf cluster* is authorized for wear in lieu of five bronze oak leaf clusters.

Wear of Decorations and Service Medals on Civilian Clothing. The wearing of decorations, service medals, or miniatures on civilian clothes should be limited to ceremonial occasions—and then only when strictly appropriate to the occasion.

When permitted by the employing agency, employees of federal, state, and city government who served honorably in active service and whose duties require that they wear special uniforms to denote their authority may wear U.S. service ribbons.

Wear of Unit Awards. An individual assigned to, or permanently attached to, and present for duty with a unit in the action for which a unit award was given may wear the award as a permanent part of the uniform.

The framed awards (the Presidential Unit Citation and the Joint Meritorious Unit Award) are worn with the laurel leaves pointing up. The unit award emblems may be worn with service ribbons or full-size medals but are not worn with miniature medals.

Wear of Badges. Only one U.S. aerospace badge may be worn at a time. Medical Corps and Nurse Corps officers may wear both the aviation medical badge and authorized medical insignia. For placement of badges, see the accompanying illustrations of placement of accouterments in AFI 36-2903.

BRASSARDS
A brassard is a cloth band worn around the upper arm to designate its wearer as a member of a special group or service and usually bearing an identifying mark, such as the Red Cross. Special duty brassards are worn centered on the left sleeve of the outergarment—overcoat, raincoat, coat, jacket, or shirt when worn as an outergarment—halfway between the elbow and the sleeve shoulder seam.

ORDER OF PRECEDENCE OF DECORATIONS AND AWARDS
There is a definite ranking among decorations and awards. Consult this listing and your base's military personnel flight before you assemble authorized

decorations and awards on your uniform to be sure you have them in the proper sequence. Air Force personnel wear U.S. military decorations of the Air Force, Army, Navy, and Coast Guard in the following order:

Medal of Honor
Air Force Cross
Distinguished Service Cross
Navy Cross
Defense Distinguished Service Medal
Distinguished Service Medal (Air Force, Army, Navy, Coast Guard)
Silver Star
Defense Superior Service Medal
Legion of Merit
Distinguished Flying Cross
Airman's Medal
Soldier's Medal
Navy–Marine Corps Medal
Coast Guard Medal
Bronze Star
Purple Heart
Defense Meritorious Service Medal
Meritorious Service Medal
Air Medal
Aerial Achievement Medal
Joint Service Commendation Medal
Air Force Commendation Medal
Army Commendation Medal
Navy Commendation Medal
Coast Guard Commendation Medal
Joint Service Achievement Medal
Air Force Achievement Medal
Army Achievement Medal
Navy Achievement Medal
Air Force Combat Action Medal
Presidential Unit Citation
Navy Presidential Unit Citation
Joint Meritorious Unit Award
Air Force Gallant Unit Citation
Air Force Meritorious Unit Award
Air Force Outstanding Unit Award
Air Force Organizational Excellence Award
Prisoner of War Medal
Valorous Unit Award
Navy Unit Commendation

Coast Guard Unit Commendation
Meritorious Unit Commendation (Army, Navy, Coast Guard)
Navy "E" Ribbon
U.S. nonmilitary decorations (see AFI 36-2803)
Combat Readiness Medal
Air Force Good Conduct Medal
Army Good Conduct Medal
Navy Good Conduct Medal
Marine Corps Good Conduct Medal
Coast Guard Good Conduct Medal
Air Reserve Forces Meritorious Service Medal
Army Reserve Component Achievement Medal
Navy Reserve Meritorious Service Medal
Selected Marine Corps Reserve Medal
Coast Guard Reserve Good Conduct Medal
Outstanding Airman of the Year Ribbon
Air Force Recognition Ribbon
American Defense Service Medal
American Campaign Medal
Asiatic-Pacific Campaign Medal
Euro-African Middle Eastern Campaign
World War II Victory Medal
Army of Occupation Medal
Medal for Humane Action
National Defense Service Medal
Korean Service Medal
Antarctica Service Medal
Armed Forces Expeditionary Medal
Vietnam Service Medal
Southwest Asia Service Medal
Kosovo Campaign Medal
Afghanistan Campaign Medal
Iraq Campaign Medal
Global War on Terrorism Expeditionary Medal
Global War on Terrorism Service Medal
Korean Defense Service Medal
Armed Forces Service Medal
Humanitarian Service Medal
Military Outstanding Volunteer Service Medal
Air and Space Campaign Medal
Air Force Overseas Ribbon (short)
Air Force Overseas Ribbon (long)
Army Overseas Ribbon
Sea Service Deployment Ribbon (Navy, Marine)

Coast Guard Special Operation Service Ribbon
Coast Guard Sea Service Ribbon
Air Force Expeditionary Service Ribbon
Air Force Longevity Service Award Ribbon
USAF Basic Military Training Instructor Ribbon
Air Force Recruiter Ribbon
Armed Forces Reserve Medal
USAF NCO PME Graduate Ribbon
Army NCO Professional Development Ribbon
USAF Basic Military Training Honor Graduate Ribbon
Coast Guard Reserve Honor Graduate Ribbon
Small Arms Expert Marksmanship Ribbon
Navy Pistol Shot Medal
Air Force Training Ribbon
Army Service Ribbon
Foreign decorations (see AFI 36-2803)
Foreign unit citations (see AFI 36-2803)
United Nations Medal
NATO Meritorious Service Medal
NATO Medal (Yugoslavia)
NATO Medal (Kosovo)
Multinational Force and Observers Medal
Republic of Vietnam Campaign Medal
Kuwait Liberation Medal (Saudi Arabia)
Kuwait Liberation Medal (Kuwait)
Republic of Korea Korean War Service Medal
Foreign service medals (see AFI 36-2803)

17

Social Life in the Air Force

Air Force social life helps bind individuals into units and individual families into the larger Air Force family. It is an outward sign that service in the Air Force is more than a job, that the Air Force is a way of life.

Air Force social life, coupled with interaction among officers in the workplace, especially under conditions of shared adversity, binds individuals in life-long friendships. Invariably, officers cite these friendships as being among the most rewarding aspects of their Air Force service.

Social activities and relationships in the Air Force are similar to those of society in civilian communities. Although officers and their spouses will find little need for adjustment from their civilian habits with respect to social activities while on duty in the Air Force, there are a few differences. Many air bases are in themselves small communities in which everyone knows almost everyone else. This makes for tight-knit social relations and close scrutiny by all of each family's activities. In this sense, officers and their families live in goldfish bowls. Bear this carefully in mind at all times.

SOCIAL LIFE ON THE BASE

How to Be a Good Citizen of the Air Base. The following tips can make the officer and spouse a helpful unit in air base social life. Strive to be on good terms, if not good friends, with all. Choose your close associates with great care. Do not openly express your personal dislike of individuals. Do not become a member of a clique. Keep your dinner guests, your running partners, and your tennis matches open to a broad sweep of the families on your base. Do not attempt to live beyond your means. In repaying your social obligations, do so within your means. Call on newly arrived families, and offer them your assistance. Don't merely sit there for fifteen minutes making conversation. See what you can do to help when members of officers' families are ill. Take appropriate part in the community activities on base.

The Geography of Military Social Life. As soon as the officer and family arrive at a base, they will observe that people fall into one of two categories: those that live on base in government quarters and those that live off base. As the Air Force has reduced its number of bases, on-base housing comprises an increasingly smaller percentage of housing such that more people live off base, changing the on-base community dynamic. Regardless of which category your family may fall into, you may find that the officers' club is the center of your social activity. At the officers' club, you can find a program of entertainment. Traditionally, military social life consisted of either visiting the homes of friends on or off base or attending some kind of entertainment at the officers' club. Today this is more likely to be the case for unmarried junior officers and for married senior officers. Many midgrade officers and their spouses no longer participate in evening and weekend activities at officers' clubs. The base gymnasium or sports center has also become a social center for many officers and their spouses.

SOCIAL LIFE IN THE CIVILIAN COMMUNITY

Because many married Air Force officers live in civilian communities rather than on base, a substantial amount of their social life pertains to their civilian neighbors. In such circumstances, officers are well advised to become active participants in the social activities of their communities. The idea that an officer on duty in a foreign country is an ambassador of the United States is well advertised. Less emphasized, but just as important, is the fact that officers living in civilian communities are ambassadors of the Air Force to the American public. Accordingly, Air Force officers should constantly seek to create a good impression with their civilian neighbors. In the main, this good impression is accomplished through conduct of the officer and family that is above reproach. It is also helpful, however, if officers become members of the churches, societies, and clubs of the civilian community and participate in the civic activities and with the schools and youth activities of their children. Of course, on-base gymnasiums, sports centers, golf courses, rod and gun clubs, aeroclubs, bowling alleys, hobby shops, youth centers, and chapel programs, where available, also play roles in Air Force social life. It is perhaps more important that Air Force officers discharge their social obligations to their civilian neighbors in ways that reflect credit on the Air Force than it is that they meet these criteria in respect to other Air Force personnel. In a sense, all social niceties can be summed up in the phrase "Be a good neighbor." This notion certainly applies to your civilian friends as well as to your Air Force associates.

TIPS ON ETIQUETTE

Manners matter; courtesy counts. Etiquette is merely an aspect of good manners, the essence of which is helping create an atmosphere in which everyone is comfortable, an atmosphere of mutual respect. Before commissioning, every officer candidate learns that officers always return salutes, that junior officers initiate an exchange of the greetings and/or salutes with their superiors (civilian or military), that juniors walk to the left of their superiors, that they stand in the presence of their superiors, that when riding in the backseat of an automobile the senior civilian or officer sits on the right. Knowing these customs makes everyone comfortable. Social etiquette is the same; it is not a way to separate those in the know from the uninformed or the in-group from outsiders. It is not to embarrass anyone, although ignorance of customs and courtesies, manners and etiquette does make individuals uncomfortable. If you do not know the rules of social etiquette—standard table manners, introductions, social correspondence such as thank-you notes, telephone manners, responsibilities of hosts and guests, and other social practices—the remedy is to expand your comfort zone by learning the rules.

In addition to AFI 34-1201, *Protocol*, and AFPAM 34-1202, *Guide to Protocol*, the following references are very helpful. Both reflect common practice. Consult them in your base library, and you will probably decide that you want your own copies.

> Mary Jane McCaffree, Pauline Innis, and Richard M. Sand, Esquire, *Protocol: The Complete Handbook of Diplomatic, Official and Social Usage*.
> Cherlynn Conetsco and Anna Hart, *Service Etiquette*.

There are several general rules about etiquette:

- Follow the Golden Rule: Do unto others as you would have them do unto you.
- Do not do or say anything that would embarrass anyone or make someone uncomfortable.
- Be gracious; take second place.
- Do not act superior; to do so puts another in a place of inferiority.
- If you do not know, ask; try to find out what is expected beforehand.
- If you do not know, observe; follow the lead of those who do know.
- Junior officers defer to senior civilians and officers; youth to age; hosts to guests; gentlemen to ladies—even today.
- Be conservative, not avant-garde.
- Always express your thanks, either in word or a thank you note. You can never say "thank you" too often.

Some practices occur so often, and are so often flubbed, that they need special mention.

Reaction to Invitations. You must respond to an invitation promptly and in the manner specified by the host within the invitation. **Promptly** means within twenty-four hours. If the invitation is received orally, respond orally. If received in an informal note, respond by informal note. If the invitation is received in the form of a formal note or card, respond fully, in writing, on formal note paper, and in the third person: "Lieutenant Jones is happy to accept the kind invitation of Colonel and Mrs. Smith to dinner on 3 June 2002, at seven o'clock." RSVP or R.S.V.P. (*Répondez s'il vous plaît*, which literally translates "Respond if it pleases you") means that *you must respond whether or not you will attend*. Your host deserves the courtesy; not to do so is extremely rude. If the invitation says "Regrets" or "Regrets only," you are expected to respond only if you will not attend. Even in this case, a short note expressing your appreciation of the invitation is acceptable but, of course, is not required.

Always explain a regret to an informal invitation; normally, you do not give reason in regretting a formal written invitation. *Do not* regret an invitation issued by your commander unless official duties or family emergency unavoidably prevent your attendance.

If the invitation is informal, ask if there is anything that you can bring. If not, a bottle of wine or flowers that can easily be put in a vase are appropriate symbols of your appreciation for the invitation.

If invited to dinner and you are a bachelor, inquire of your hosts whether they wish you to escort anyone to the function. After attending a private social function, it is essential to write a note to your hostess (or make a telephone call) thanking her for the entertainment.

Remember to return the courtesy extended to you. It is not necessary that this be in exactly the same form as the courtesy you received.

Introductions. Introducing your wife to any man (except chiefs of state and very high church dignitaries): "Mary, this is Colonel Brown."

Introducing your husband to another man: "Colonel Brown, may I introduce my husband, Jack," or "Jack, this is Lieutenant Black." The correct order is to introduce the junior to the senior or the younger to the older.

Introducing one lady to another: "Mrs. Jones, may I present Mrs. Green," or "Mary, this is Mrs. Green."

Introducing one officer to another: "Major Smith, this is Captain Brown."

Introducing yourself to an officer senior to you: "Sir, may I introduce myself? I am Captain Jones." (Wait for the other to extend a hand.)

Introducing yourself to an officer of equal or lesser rank: "I'm Captain Margaret Jones." (Extend your hand.)

Introducing children or teenagers to adults: "Lieutenant Jones, this is Mary Smith."

Gentlemen are introduced to ladies, not the reverse. This holds even though the gentleman may be very distinguished and the lady very young. Exceptions: the president of the United States, a royal personage, a high church dignitary.

The most common way to make introductions, always in good taste, is to state the names in proper sequence, the lady, the senior, more distinguished, or more elderly first. "General Smith—Captain Jones." "Miss Youthful—Colonel Adams." "Mrs. Elderly Lady—General Cole." Use a rising inflection for the first name pronounced. The more formal method: "General Smith, may I introduce Captain Jones?"

Acknowledgment of an introduction by saying, "How do you do?" is always appropriate.

When men are introduced, they shake hands, standing without reaching across another person, if possible. They may say nothing, just look pleasant or smile, or say a courteous "It is nice to meet you" or "How do you do?"

When women are introduced to each other, with one sitting, one standing, the seated one rises to greet her hostess, or a very distinguished lady, as an act of respect. This would apply, for example, to the wife of a very senior officer. In the usual case, the seated lady does not rise. The reply to an introduction may be a simple "How do you do?"

When a gentleman is introduced to a lady, he does not offer his hand unless the lady offers hers. In Europe, gentlemen are taught to take the initiative in shaking hands. A lady does not refuse an extended hand.

A lady or gentleman, introducing husband or wife to another, may say, "This is my husband," or "May I introduce my wife?"

At a social occasion, host and hostess should shake hands with guests in greeting and upon their departure.

Using titles with names:

Major General Black	"General Black"
Brigadier General White	"General White"
Colonel Smith	"Colonel Smith"
Lieutenant Colonel Jones	"Colonel Jones"
First Lieutenant Brown	"Lieutenant Brown"
Second Lieutenant Green	"Lieutenant Green"

Social Functions. Receptions, dinners, dances, and other such social functions are conducted in the Air Force in essentially the same manner as in civilian society.

It is a courtesy to your host or hostess to accept or regret invitations as soon as you possibly can, preferably within twenty-four hours of receiving the invitation. *You must fulfill this obligation without fail.* If regretting an informal invitation, be sure to state clearly a sound reason why you cannot accept it, such as illness in the family, a previously accepted engagement, or military duty.

Often a reception includes a receiving line. The line is based upon the position taken by the senior officer or honored visitor. Other members of the receiving line form on the left of the senior or honored person in order of rank of the officers, with their spouses on their left. An aide or an officer acting in that capacity usually greets the guests and introduces them to the first person in the receiving line. In Air Force receiving lines, the officer precedes the spouse in passing through the line. To avoid embarrassment and confusion, be certain to announce your name very clearly to the aide, who may then present you accurately to the receiving line. Greet each person in the receiving line before proceeding into the main area of the reception. In greeting the members of the receiving line whom you do not already know, repeat their names, as for example, "Colonel Smith, I am very happy to meet you, sir."

At dinner dances, guests should invite their dinner partners, their hostesses, guests of honor, and houseguests to dance, regardless of dancing ability.

At cocktail parties, circulate as much as possible, conversing with as many people as you can. Do not retire to a corner to tell jokes, discuss flying, or talk shop.

Upon leaving a social function, bid your host and hostess farewell, expressing thanks for the hospitality you have received. Do not leave the function before the senior officer present leaves (unless duty or a family emergency make an early departure a necessity). Thank your host and hostess when departing a social function by saying, "Thank you for a delightful evening." If you *must* leave a function noticeably early, say, "Mrs. (Hostess), I'm sorry I must leave early." (Then give your reason, and make it good!)

It is customary to reciprocate an invitation received, regardless of whether you accepted or regretted the invitation. Furthermore, you extend to house-guests of officers invitations to social gatherings to which their host has been invited.

Social Behavior and Foreigners. Although etiquette and manners are based on making everyone comfortable because they know what is expected of them and what to expect of others, etiquette and manners are not the same the world over. Military officers and their families often come into contact with foreigners. First recognize that the practices of one culture or nationality, such as those of the United States, are not right, logical, reasonable, and civilized while the practices of another are wrong, illogical, irrational, and barbarous. The customs are merely different. Try to learn the customs of your foreign guests and hosts. Do not assume that things are what they appear to be; always be attentive and observant. You and your family represent not just yourselves, but also the Air Force and the United States.

DINING-IN AND DINING-OUT

Certain ceremonies and traditions are part of the Air Force way of life. One of these is the dining-in, a formal, ceremonial dinner *only* for members of an organization. The dining-out is a similar function for servicemembers and their spouses and guests. The dining-out, a relatively new function, has largely replaced the dining-in.

The material here was prepared at Air University, Maxwell Air Force Base, to assist officers who desire to hold a dining-in or dining-out for their units, or whose commanders have assigned them the duty of making preparations for such a function.

Background. The custom of dining-in is a very old tradition in England, but it is not exclusively military. Dining-in probably began as a custom to welcome new members in monasteries; it was adopted by early colleges, and later spread to military units of the country when the officers' mess was established. AFPAM 34-1202, *Guide to Protocol*, provides specific guidance to the various types of dinings-in/out of the Air Force, as well as guidelines for proper dress.

General Hap Arnold is considered to have started the dining-in within the Army Air Forces when he used to hold his famous "wing-dings." The contacts of U.S. Army Air Forces personnel with the British and their dinings-in during World War II gave additional impetus for the growth of this custom in the USAF. Dinings-in provided situations where ceremony, tradition, and good fellowship played an important part in the life of military organizations.

The dining-in provides an occasion for officers to meet socially at a formal military function. Further, it provides an opportunity to recognize individual and unit achievements. All of these are very useful in building high morale and esprit de corps.

Planning. Preparation for a dining-in or dining-out should begin well in advance. Date, location, and speaker should be selected, and reservations made. Details for the various arrangements should be allocated to individuals and their specific duties outlined. An order of events, or agenda, should be prepared.

Attendance. Traditionally, attendance at a dining-in was mandatory, and many commanders still consider this function a mandatory requirement, similar to a commander's call. Other commanders feel that since a goal of the dining-in or dining-out is to bring members closer together, attendance should be voluntary to avoid having persons who feel that they were forced to attend dampen the spirit and enthusiasm of the others. The decision whether a dining-in is voluntary or mandatory rests with the commander.

Dinings-out are attended by officers assigned to the unit holding the dining-out. They are the "members of the mess." Officers not assigned to the unit or of similar units, as well as spouses, invited to participate by the commander are not members of the mess, and may attend only if invited as guests. Most dinings-out are held at the officers' club.

There are two types of guests: official and personal. Official guests are honored guests of the mess. The guest speaker is an official guest. All official guests are seated at the head table, and their expenses are shared by the members of the mess. Because of the costs and limited space at the head table, the number of official guests should be limited. Personal guests may be either military officers or civilians. They are not seated at the head table, and their expenses are paid by the sponsoring member.

Senior officers from other units and organizations and civic leaders from the local community should be considered when inviting guests. It is a good way to enhance relations among base units and with civilian neighbors. Usually, these guests pay for their way unless part of the official party.

Guest Speaker and Other Guests. The guest speaker should be a military member or a civilian who can be expected to address the mess in an interesting manner on an appropriate subject. The guest speaker should be invited well in advance and advised of what is expected of a dining-out guest speaker. Arrangements should be made for the guest speaker and for other invited guests as protocol and custom dictate.

Dress. The dress for the dining-out should be the mess dress uniform. Civilian guests usually wear semiformal wear (dinner jackets or tuxedos), but business attire may be acceptable. The proper dress for civilians should be clearly stated in the invitation. Retired officers may wear the mess dress or civilian attire. One recent addition to the dining-in tradition is the "combat dining-in." For this form of dining-in, the attire would be ABUs or FDUs.

PROPER DRESS

Event	Civilian	Air Force	Army	Navy	Marines
Formal:* official formal evening, state occasions (white tie)	Men: tails and white tie Women: long dress	Mess dress	Blue mess	Formal dress	Evening dress "A" or blue dress "A"
Semiformal: social function of general or official nature (black tie)	Men: tuxedo/dinner jacket Women: long dress or cocktail dress	Mess dress	Blue mess or Army blue with bow tie	Dinner dress, blue jacket, or dinner dress, white jacket	Evening dress "B," blue dress "B," or white dress "B"
Informal:** receptions, daytime/early evening occasions	Men: dark suit Women: tea-length, short dress or suit	Service dress	Army blue, with four-in-hand tie	Dinner dress, blue, or dinner dress, white	Blue dress "B" or white dress "B"
Informal:** ceremonies, military parades, reviews, official visits of civilian dignitaries, change of command	Men: business suit/coat and tie Women: short dress or suit	Service dress	Class A	Full dress, blue, or full dress, white, or service dress, blue, or service dress, white	Blue dress "A" or "B" or white dress "A" or "B," or service uniform "A"
	Men: open collar/sport shirt Women: short dress	Short-sleeved shirt, with or without tie	Class B	Short-sleeved shirt, without tie (uniform of day)	Blue dress "D"
Casual:** barbecues, picnics, parade spectator	Men: sport shirt/open collar (with jacket or sweater, as needed) Women: blouse and skirt	Short-sleeved shirt, without tie	Class B	Short-sleeved shirt, without tie	Blue dress "D"

*Because formal (white tie/tails) is unusual today, semiformal (black tie/tuxedo) is occasionally referred to as "formal." Invitations specifying formal are likely to mean semiformal, so confirm exactly what the host means.

**Be specific about what you expect your guests to wear if you host an event. If attending an event, ensure that you know exactly what your host expects you to wear.

The Formal Dinner. All members of the mess should arrive within ten minutes after the opening time. When the signal is given for dinner, the members should enter the dining room and stand behind their chairs. Members, unless properly excused, should not leave the mess before the guest of honor and the president have departed.

The guest of honor and the president of the mess are the last to join the head table. The president formally opens the mess and continues according to the agenda. The president remains standing while speaking but seats the other members of the mess after the last formal toast.

Toasting. The custom of toasting is universal. It is believed that this custom came into wide acceptance after the effects of poison were discovered. When two persons, who might be antagonists, drank from the same source at the same instant and suffered no ill effects, a degree of mutual trust and rapport could be established. With this foundation laid, discussions could continue on a more cordial basis. Today, toasting is a simple courtesy to the person being honored.

It is not proper to drain the glass at the completion of each toast. A mere touch of the glass to the lips satisfies the ceremonial requirements. Toasts, which are drunk standing, not seated, should be proposed in sequence and at intervals during the program of the evening.

The president proposes the first toast. If a toast to the colors is done, it is always the first toast, to which the members of the mess respond, "To the colors."

The second toast, in order of precedence, is to the heads of state of the allied nations represented. The toasts are made in the order determined by the seniority of foreign officers present. Remember that Commonwealth nations toast the British sovereign (head of state), not an elected official (head of government). Consult the installation protocol office or the individual foreign officers for the proper terminology to be used in toasting their heads of state.

After the president of the mess has toasted the head of each allied nation represented, the senior foreign officer then proposes a toast to the president of the United States. The response is "To the president." If no allied nations are represented, the president proposes the toast to the commander in chief, rather than to the president of the United States. The response is "To the president."

Following the president's or senior allied officer's toasts, Mister or Madam Vice proposes a toast to the chief of staff, Air Force. The response is "To the chief of staff." If officers of other services are present at the mess, toasts to their chiefs of staff would precede the toast to the chief of staff, United States Air Force: A toast to the chief of staff of the Army, chief of Naval Operations, and commandant of the Marine Corps is appropriate. The senior-ranking officer representing a sister service would then propose a toast to the chief of staff, United States Air Force.

Excessive toasting can make for a long evening. Although other toasts may be appropriate, too many toasts can cause the evening to run behind schedule and dampen the enthusiasm of the members of the mess. At some locations, there may be a large number of foreign officers present. In this case, it is appropriate to collectively propose a toast to the heads of state of all allied nations represented. The absolute last of the formal toasts is the prisoner of war (POW) toast, which is customarily drunk with water, rather than wine.

Following the formal toasts, the president seats the mess with one rap of the gavel.

President's Opening Remarks. Besides setting the tone for the evening, the president's remarks provide the opportunity to officially welcome guests. After the head table is introduced, the president should either personally introduce the remaining guests or poll the host officers. When all guests have been recognized, Mister or Madam Vice proposes a toast to the guests. Members of the mess stand, guests remain seated. The response to this and all future toasts is "Hear, Hear!"

The president then seats the mess and invites the members to eat.

Informal toasts are also an important part of the occasion. They should be humorous, but in good taste. It may be advisable to "plant" some impromptu toasts to set the tone of the evening.

Dinner. The first course may be placed on the table while the mess assembles in a nearby room. However, salad should not be wilted. Consider the capabilities of the club.

Courses are always served to the head table first. Mister or Madam Vice should be served immediately after the head table. Toasts requested by the mess during dinner and related activities will take up so much of the vice's time that he or she simply will not have a chance to eat unless served early. The president always has the option to limit toasts to keep the evening on schedule or to permit members to eat uninterrupted.

Before serving the main course, the president may wish to add some humor to the meal by asking Mister or Madam Vice to sample the meal to make sure it is fit for consumption by members of the mess. The vice may compose a short poem to the meal. There are numerous variations that are best left to the imagination of the planning committee and the dictates of the president. But if these are not really witty, inoffensive, and well done, they should be omitted.

The Grog Bowl. Although a "grog bowl" has been used by many organizations, it is not required. If there is no grog bowl, however, some other means of punishment for infractions should be considered.

The contents of the grog bowl are best left to the imagination of the planning committee, but the contents must be nonalcoholic so as not to dampen the spirits and participation of those individuals who do not consume alcoholic beverages. Some units plan ahead and have two grog bowls, allowing the participant to choose his or her punishment drink. Some organizations have successfully used a "grog-mixing ceremony," in which the individual contents of the grog are combined along with a humorous narrative by Mister or Madam Vice.

At various points during the evening, a member may be sent to the grog bowl as punishment for violating the rules of the mess, such as the following:

- Arriving late at the cocktail lounge.
- Carrying drinks into the dining room.
- Wearing the cummerbund inverted (the pleats should face up for men and down for women), or other uniform wear infraction (colored suspenders and spirit cuff links are frequent infractions).
- Wearing an ill-fitting or discolored mess jacket.
- Toasting with an uncharged glass.
- Starting a course before the president.
- Applauding a particularly witty, sarcastic, or succinct toast (unless following the example of the president).
- Discussing business, referred to as "opening the hangar doors."
- Talking while another person has the floor.

Certain members of the mess seem to be frequent violators, such as Mister or Madam Vice. It is not uncommon for the president and the guest speaker to be charged with at least one violation. If the president must leave his or her position at the head table, he or she must appoint another individual to assume the position.

Infractions warranting a trip to the grog bowl may be noted at any time by the president, vice, or any member of the mess. Members bring infractions to the attention of the president by raising a "point of order." If the validity of the charge is questioned, members vote by tapping their spoons on the table.

When the president directs a violator to the grog bowl, the individual proceeds to the bowl promptly. The bowl is usually located on Mister or Madam Vice's table.

Upon arriving at the grog bowl, the violator does the following:

- Does an about-face and salutes the president.
- Turns to the bowl and fills the cup.
- Does another about-face and toasts the mess, with "To the Mess."
- Drains the contents of the cup without removing it from the lips.
- In some messes, the officer turns the cup upside down on the head.
- Replaces the cup, again salutes the president, and returns to his or her seat. With the exception of the toast, the violator is not permitted to speak during this process.

Recess. At the time scheduled for recess, the president raps the gavel three times to gain attention. When the mess is silent, the president raps twice and announces a short recess so the dishes may be cleared and dessert served. Members stand by their places until the head table departs. Everyone then proceeds to the cocktail lounge, where the bars have reopened.

Reconvening the Mess. At the end of the recess, Mister or Madam Vice sounds the chime and directs everyone to return to the dining room. Traditionally, drinks should not be brought into the dining room following the recess.

When members reach their places, they stand directly behind their chairs. The president then leads the head table party into the dining room. The president then seats the mess with one rap of the gavel. Coffee is immediately served, and dessert is eaten.

Recognition and Awards. If individual and unit achievements are to be recognized, an appropriate time would be after the dessert. Individual recognition may be those officers selected for promotion or an award such as Junior Officer of the Year. A toast to those recognized may also be appropriate. Following the formal toasts at the beginning of the dinner, all others may be made either in a serious vein or through the use of a humorous poem.

Guest Speaker's Address. After recognition and awards, and any scheduled entertainment, the president introduces the guest speaker. The speaker's address typically lasts fifteen to twenty minutes and should be of a patriotic or entertaining nature. After thanking the speaker for his or her time and thoughts, the president presents a gift to the speaker. The president then asks the vice to propose an appropriate toast to the guest speaker.

Closing the Mess. After the toast to the guest speaker, the president can have the color guard post the colors before adjourning the mess.

Rules of the Mess. The following is a list of the original "thou shalt" rules under which the mess will be conducted. They are designed to conform to tradition and promote levity. Violators of these rules are subject to the wrath and mischievousness of Mister or Madam Vice. All assigned penalties will be carried out before the membership.

- Thou shalt arrive within ten minutes of the appointed hour.
- Thou shalt make every effort to meet all guests. (The number of guests and members of the mess may make this impractical and burdensome to the guests. Before introducing yourself, ascertain if the members of the mess, especially junior officers, are actually introducing themselves. As always, be observant.)
- Thou shalt move to the mess when you hear the chimes and remain standing until seated by the president.
- Thou shalt not bring drinks into the mess.
- Thou shalt not leave the mess while it is convened. Military protocol overrides all calls of nature; plan ahead.
- Thou shalt participate in all toasts unless you or your group is honored with a toast.
- Thou shalt ensure that thy glass is always charged when toasting.
- Thou shalt keep toasts and comments within the limits of good taste and mutual respect. Degrading or insulting remarks will be frowned upon by the membership. However, good-natured needling is encouraged.
- Thou shalt not murder the Queen's English.
- Thou shalt not open the hangar doors (talk business).
- Thou shalt always use the proper toasting procedure.

- Thou shalt fall into disrepute with thy peers if the pleats of thy cummerbund are not properly faced (up for men, down for women).
- Thou shalt also be painfully regarded if thy clip-on bow tie rides at an obvious list. Thou shalt be forgiven, however, if you also ride at a comparative list.
- Thou shalt consume thy meal in a manner becoming a gentleman or lady.

PART V

Benefits and Restrictions

18

The U.S. Air Force as a Career

The relative attractiveness of a military career is the subject of continuing national debate. It should be. The officer corps of the U.S. armed forces plays a central role, and a crucial one, in the security of the country. For this reason, the officer corps must be of the highest quality. Only you know whether you might improve that quality. Furthermore, only you know whether a military career appeals to you. If you are undecided, perhaps the following considerations will help you reach a decision.

Whatever careers people may choose, certain criteria seem to apply to their choices:

- Pay
- Security
- Advancement possibilities and use of one's talents and/or education opportunities
- Living conditions
- Prestige of the career
- Challenge of the career
- Associations
- Retirement benefits

Rarely do young people deliberately choose a career in which, in their minds, most of the above criteria seem unfavorable. Yet, few career fields offer positive favors in all of the criteria cited. Each career emphasizes some and slights others of these criteria. This chapter takes an objective look at a military career in light of the above criteria.

PAY AND BENEFITS

Military officers receive comparatively good pay and benefits.

- Medical expenses are normally a minor item to most active-duty officers and their families. The Air Force provides medical attention for officers and their families, thus almost eliminating the financial hazard of serious illness. Though officers may suffer extended illnesses, their pay continues in full, except for flight pay.
- Insurance costs are lower because of the availability of government term life insurance and certain survivor benefits.

- Commissaries and base exchanges offer food and merchandise at costs lower than those in a typical civilian establishment.
- Travel and transportation expenses usually match government allowances, although the average officer can suffer a net loss in this regard, especially if the officer's spouse is employed.
- Leave with pay is available to each officer, thirty days a year.
- Travel to foreign countries and in the United States is an experience that officers take as a matter of course, but one that would cost a shocking amount of money if undertaken privately. Civilians spend many hard-earned dollars traveling for work and pleasure.

SECURITY

Officers enjoy a relatively high degree of job security. They cannot be separated from the service except by due process of applicable laws. Although physical disability incurred in the first eight years of service results in separation without retirement benefits, important VA benefits accrue. After eight years of service, the officer who becomes physically disabled receives retirement status and pay depending on the degree of disability. For all practical purposes, a regular officer has job security, barring only serious misconduct and/or incompetence.

Security may seem an insignificant quality to a young person contemplating a vigorous career. Yet, with the addition of a family, even the young must give due concern to the certainty of their income. Officers never grow rich on their military pay, but they can enjoy the peace of mind that comes from an assured income for themselves and their families. As an officer, you can plan a stable future with confidence. Realistically considering not only the merits of security in your present job but also the needs of retirement and even security for your yet unborn children may convince you that security is a career criterion of high value.

ADVANCEMENT

For the career officer, advancement in rank is available at stipulated periods, and the opportunity to advance more rapidly challenges the most competitive. You do not need to seek help through special influence. Merit alone will take you upward. Of course, the competition is keen and grows sharper as you reach higher grades. Nevertheless, you may aspire to any military position to which your capabilities can carry you.

On the other hand, not every officer can be a general; mathematics points this fact out inexorably. Most officers end even full careers as lieutenant colonels. Therefore, if you assess yourself as no better than average, you cannot reasonably expect to wear stars. The stars are there, however, waiting for officers with the ability and the will to earn them.

Advancement in the Air Force is more than a matter of promotion; it also includes advancement in responsibility. Whereas in some professions

advancement takes the form of a steadily increasing income, often these monetary increases are not associated with increased responsibility or authority. In
some careers, men and women may labor at essentially the same level of
responsibility for their entire careers, doing work that grows dull and burdensome. Not so in the Air Force.

LIVING CONDITIONS
The living conditions of Air Force officers and their families range across a
wide spectrum. Not all married officers can expect to have quarters on base
because not that many lodgings exist. Consequently, officers may find themselves occupying housing in civilian communities near air bases.

Although housed off base, many officers and their families find the base
the center of their activities. The various facilities of the base, the exchange, the
officers' club, athletic/sports facilities, child development centers, and social
gatherings may appeal to you and your family.

Depending on local enrollment rules, your children may attend schools on
base. More likely, they will enroll in schools of the civilian community. Your
children's schooling may include numerous shifts among schools in various
parts of the world.

Perhaps the most notable "living condition" of an Air Force career is the
frequent changes of station. These moves often mean temporary (and not so
temporary) separation of the family.

Hazard is also part of Air Force life. As a member of the Air Force, each
officer is subject to being dispatched suddenly into danger. Indeed, hazard is a
greater factor in an Air Force career than it is in almost any civilian vocation.

PRESTIGE OF THE CAREER
Officers of the Air Force generally hold a place of high respect in the minds of
Americans. The career officer is a member of an honorable profession, the
importance of which is beyond question. The officer is accepted in any social
group, is considered an excellent credit risk, and is assumed to be an intelligent
and responsible citizen. These are the basic attributes of prestige in its actual
application. Public opinion polls continue to reflect the public's high rating of
the military officer in the United States.

CHALLENGE OF THE CAREER
Few, if any, career fields offer greater challenges to the individual than does the
Air Force. Never before in the history of mankind has so much power been
assembled in organized fashion as by the U.S. Air Force. Making ready, or
employing if need be, this almost incredible power is a job of endless ramifica-
tions. The task fully embraces the fields of engineering, law, medicine, political
science, personnel management, industrial production, research, science, and

even advertising. Nearly every element of American resources is reflected in the operation of the Air Force. At the same time, the Air Force does not have a single solution for every situation, because nothing is static. Events and the progress of technology do not permit or tolerate stereotyped procedures. The problems are many, difficult, and urgently in need of solution. If you seek a challenge to your own abilities, you need look no further than an Air Force career.

CAREER ASSOCIATIONS

Probably the most satisfying aspect of an Air Force career lies in the associations it offers with a company of fine men and women. They are honorable people who adhere to a high code of conduct. They are loyal people who serve the nation without stint. They are able people who meet the great tasks of the Air Force and the realities of Air Force life with sure competence. They are interesting people who contribute to the knowledge and the culture of the nation from their worldwide experiences. They are, on the whole, good people whom it is good to know. Comradeship of the Air Force is truly a great attraction.

Not only does a career offer fine associations with the people of the Air Force, but also it affords a matchless opportunity to meet and know men and women of many backgrounds, talents, and interests. Few civilian Americans compare with the average Air Force officer in the cosmopolitan nature of friendships. Almost any Air Force officer of twenty years' service can name personal friends in many states and in several foreign countries.

RETIREMENT BENEFITS

Officers of the Air Force enjoy excellent retirement prospects. Subject to the approval of the Department of the Air Force, an officer may retire after twenty years' service. Retired officers receive a substantial percentage of their active-duty base pay and retain privileges of access to clubs, commissaries, exchanges, and athletic and some medical facilities. Taken together with a reasonable investment and insurance program, these provisions permit a retired officer to live comfortably, though not luxuriously.

Medical benefits, however, are in flux. Funding for TRICARE appears to be increasingly problematic, so retirees, if not active-duty servicemembers, may need to consider medical insurance, as well as long-term care insurance.

As an Air Force officer, you may retire after twenty years' service at about forty-two years of age and can look forward to retirement early enough to permit you to embark on another career. Your spouse must select (or decline) the Survivor's Benefit Plan (SBP) annuity upon your retirement if that spouse desires to have a portion (up to 55 percent of retirement pay) as part of their retirement planning option. Make sure you and your spouse understand this decision before signing the paperwork as part of your retirement process.

19

Rights, Privileges, and Restrictions

When citizens enter military service, their legal status changes. Some civilian rights are restricted or modified. They take on additional hazards and obligations that are balanced by additional benefits not enjoyed by civilians. To a lesser degree, officers in inactive status and retired officers enjoy benefits and are also subject to restrictions. Some former members of the armed forces whose separation was honorable enjoy important benefits administered by the Department of Veterans Affairs.

JUSTIFICATION FOR BENEFITS

Strong reasons justify granting military rights and privileges called benefits. Those citizens who are members of the Army, the Navy, the Marines, or the Air Force have the primary mission of protecting and preserving the United States, including our institutions and way of life, the prosecution of wars with the incidental hazard, and the service of the federal government wherever duty is directed. They give up many freedoms of choice that civilians take for granted.

The active-duty armed forces consist of the officers and enlisted members who are volunteers. They are backed up by the several categories of reserves, also volunteers. Volunteers will not be obtained in the number required or the quality necessary unless the conditions of their lives are acceptable. Because of international tensions and recurrent wars, our country needs the armed forces to protect itself. These armed forces must be strong enough, courageous enough, and proud enough to do their job.

As long as the nation has need of the best military leadership of all grades and ages, it will be wise to recognize that all officers are volunteers by granting appropriate benefits, first to attract good people to service and then to hold them.

There is an inescapable difference between the individual in civilian employment and the member of the armed services. The civilian may quit or refuse a task with no greater penalty than loss of employment, then being free to choose another job. But members of the armed forces can do so only at the peril of punishment by action of court-martial. In addition, few in civilian employ routinely put their lives in harm's way; for the military member, that reality is an expectation.

JUSTIFICATION FOR RESTRICTIONS

There is a sufficient case also for imposing restrictions upon military people, especially commissioned officers, that civilians do not bear. The government must have a clearly defined rationale to deploy its forces and require individuals to perform specific missions, however unpleasant or hazardous such duties or locations may be. The government must insist upon full service of its officers and thus is justified in defining and prohibiting improper outside activities of individuals.

Since procurement officers and others in the business end of the armed forces have many prerogatives related to the letting of contracts, the government requires high standards of ethics as well as clearly codified methods of conducting these affairs.

To ensure fair treatment for all and to prevent abuses in the exercise of federal power, limitations must be placed on authority, especially in the field of punishments, sentences of courts-martial, and the like.

RIGHTS

Although there are many obligations of service, there are not many actual rights. A right is a benefit established for military people by federal law. Unless a benefit is established by law, in contrast to a departmental policy that is subject to administrative change or withdrawal, it is something less than a right.

Acquisition of Military Rights. A citizen who has subscribed to the oath of office as an officer becomes entitled at once to certain rights of military service, such as the right to wear the uniform. Other rights accrue only by completing specified requirements, such as the right to retire after completing a stipulated period of service.

The Right to Wear the Uniform. Members of the military service have the right to wear the uniform of their service. That the department may require the wearing of the uniform is beside the point. First of all, it is a right.

Members of the reserve components on inactive status, retired personnel, and former members of the service who have been honorably separated have the right to wear the uniform only at stipulated times or circumstances, and unless these conditions exist, the right is denied.

The Right of Officers to Command. In the commission granted an officer by the president are these words: "And I do strictly charge and require those officers and other personnel of lesser rank to render such obedience as is due." The commission itself may be regarded as the basic document that gives military officers the right to exercise command and to exact obedience to proper orders.

The Right to Draw Pay and Allowances. Pay scales for grade and length of service are established by law (see chapter 20, "Pay and Personal

Allowances"). The rights as to pay and allowances may be suspended, in part, by action of a court-martial or forfeited in part by absence without leave.

The Right to Receive Medical Attention. Members of the armed services and, with restrictions, their families are entitled to receive appropriate medical and dental care for the treatment of wounds, injuries, disease, or illness. In fact, refusal to accept treatment ruled to be necessary may be punishable by court-martial. For rights of dependents to receive medical care, see chapter 22, "Medical Care."

The Right to Individual Protection under the Uniform Code of Military Justice (UCMJ). All members of the military service are under the jurisdiction established by the Articles of the Uniform Code of Military Justice. Many persons regard the *Manual for Courts-Martial,* which contains this code, merely as the authorization of courts-martial and the implementation of their procedures as a means of maintaining discipline or awarding punishment for crime. This view is incomplete. Except for the punitive articles, the Uniform Code of Military Justice pertains in considerable measure to the protection of individual rights, such as these:

- No people may be compelled to incriminate themselves before a military court.
- No people shall without their consent be tried a second time for the same offense.
- Cruel and unusual punishments of every kind are prohibited.
- Although the punishment for a crime or offense is left to the discretion of the court, it shall not exceed such limits as the president may prescribe.

The Soldiers' and Sailors' Civil Relief Act. The Soldiers' and Sailors' Civil Relief Act, passed in 1940 and still in effect, has as its purpose the relief of draftees, enlistees, and reservists on active duty of some of the pressure of heavy financial obligations they may have assumed in civil life.

Redress of Wrong. Each of the armed services provides a procedure by which any members of the armed services may seek redress of wrong. Officers may have occasion to register official objections or complaints with respect to their own treatment, although such occasions should be rare because most officers complete their entire service without finding it necessary to use this right. But officers should certainly know that their juniors also enjoy this right and that if they take action that is grossly injurious to an individual or action that is so considered, they may be obliged to endure the process as the injuring party.

There may come a time in the service of all people when they feel that they have been wronged by a superior, such as in these situations: an unfavorable ruling regarding pay or allowances, unsatisfactory living conditions, undeserved stigma, or treatment by a superior that is directly contrary to military laws or policies. Any person contemplating registering an official complaint should first get the facts straight and be quite certain of sustaining them. It is contrary to policy to punish anyone for filing a complaint. But a person can be

COMPARISON WITH CITIZENS' DUTIES

As a Civilian	As a Servicemember
1. Support and defend the Constitution.	1. Same.
2. Stay informed of the issues affecting your community.	2. Same.
3. Participate in the democratic process.	3. Duty & right to vote; may express private opinions informally.
4. Respect and obey federal, state, and local laws.	4. Same.
5. Respect the rights, beliefs, and opinions of others.	5. Includes responsibility to protect as well as respect.
6. Participate in your local community.	6. Same.
7. Pay income and other taxes honestly, and on time, to federal, state, and local authorities.	7. Modified—may be exempted by law from certain taxes of state where stationed; USG may exempt tax during time deployed to a combat zone.
8. Serve on a jury when called upon.	8. Modified—may be exempted from jury duty; may be appointed to serve on a court-martial.
9. Defend the country if the need should arise.	9. Same.

COMPARISON WITH CITIZENS' RIGHTS

As a Civilian	As a Servicemember
1. Freedom to express yourself.	1. Modified by duty to maintain respect toward the president, vice president, & other officials.
2. Freedom to worship as you wish.	2. Same.
3. Right to a prompt, fair trial by jury.	3. Same in civil courts; by court-marital in military court.
4. Right to vote in elections for public officials.	4. Same. Military facilitates absentee voting.
5. Right to apply for federal employment requiring U.S. citizenship.	5. Usually not an issue; non-citizens may join military as one path to citizenship.
6. Right to run for elected office.	6. Requires service secretary permission; serving in elected office may have restrictions.
7. Freedom to pursue "life, liberty, and the pursuit of happiness."	7. Modified by requirements of military service.

Source: Citizenship Rights and Responsibilities, U.S. Citizenship and Immigration Services. Additional information found available at http://www.uscis.gov/citizenship/learners/citizenship-rights-and-responsibilities. Also see DOD Directive 1344-10, "Political Activities by Members of the Armed Forces."

punished for knowingly making statements that are unfounded, untruthful, or unjustly harmful to another person's good name. No person should fear the effects of filing an honest complaint or stating a genuine grievance. But the basis of the grievances must be factual and subject to proof.

After getting the facts straight, the person should normally state the entire situation to the commander and seek advice. In most instances, this step will end the matter because, if the grievances are real, the commander should correct the situation.

If the conference with the commander is unsatisfactory or for some sufficient reason is not held, the person may bring the problem to the attention of the inspector general who serves the organization. More than likely, the inspector general will require a written statement. This officer will advise the complainant of the final action taken on the complaint or grievance. Nor need this be all. The officer or airman may write directly to the inspector general of the major command or to the inspector general of the Air Force.

Right to Request Correction of Military Records. Military records serve as the basis for recording the fact, nature or character, and duration of military service. Accordingly, the military records that pertain to each individual are of inestimable value. Therefore, when any individual military record contains an error, means have been made available to petition for correction. Each service secretary, acting through boards of civilian officers or employees of his or her service, is authorized to correct any military record where such action is necessary to correct an error or remove an injustice. In the Air Force, this board is known as the Air Force Board for Correction of Military Records.

Application for correction should be submitted by the person requesting corrective action or by other persons as authorized by the board when the person concerned is unable to submit application. In general, a statute of limitations of three years applies to applications. There must be a showing of exhaustion of normal administrative remedies. Hearing on an application may be denied if a sufficient basis for review has not been established or if effective relief cannot be granted. When an application has been found to be within the jurisdiction of the board, and sufficient evidence has been presented indicating probable error or injustice, the applicant will be entitled to a hearing before the board either in person or by counsel or in person with counsel.

The Right to Vote. Air Force personnel are encouraged to exercise the privilege of voting in federal, state, and primary elections. To encourage and assist eligible servicemembers to vote, the Department of Defense maintains liaison with the various state election authorities to obtain current voting information, which, through Air Force channels, is disseminated to all Air Force installations for the information of all personnel. Voting officers are available at squadron level to answer pertinent questions concerning forthcoming elections in the servicemember's state of domicile and to provide printed postcard applications for state absentee ballots, which are transmitted, postage free, to the appropriate state. Every effort is made to ensure that all personnel are protected against coercion of any sort in making their political choices and to maintain the integrity and secrecy of the ballots cast.

Although the Air Force provides information and assistance concerning elections and voting procedures, the actual decision to vote rests with the individual servicemember. Voting must be entirely voluntary; no servicemember will be required or ordered to participate in political elections.

The determination of eligibility and the specification of requirements for voting are completely governed by the appropriate state. To vote, all servicemembers must meet such requirements and must be declared eligible to vote by the state in which they desire to exercise their voting privilege.

The Right to Retire. After satisfying specific requirements of honorable service or having endured physical disability beyond a fixed degree, commissioned officers of the armed forces have the right to retire. See chapter 24, "Retirement."

The GI Bill of Rights. Former members of the armed forces and retired personnel may obtain benefits under the GI Bill of Rights. VA benefits for *eligible* veterans, their dependents, and beneficiaries include these:

- Servicemembers' Group Life Insurance
- Educational aid
- Guarantee of loans for the purchase or construction of homes, farms, or business property
- Readjustment allowances for veterans who are unemployed
- Disability compensation
- Vocational rehabilitation
- Physical examinations, hospital care, and outpatient medical and dental treatment
- Domiciliary care and guardianship service
- Pensions
- Death benefits to survivors

Social Security Benefits of Retired Personnel. Retired officers, including those who are employed or self-employed, qualify for Social Security benefits in the same manner as other citizens. See chapter 24, "Retirement."

The Right to Be Buried in a National Cemetery. The rights of a deceased servicemember to be buried in a national military cemetery are discussed in chapter 25, "Benefits after Separation."

PRIVILEGES

The Privileges of Rank and Position. That "rank has its privileges" is a concept as old as the armed forces. It is similar to the deference in all walks of life to one's elders or seniors. It is no more or less pronounced, although it may be more codified, than among faculty members, in a business establishment, in legislative bodies, or among doctors, lawyers, and ministers.

Leave. Under current laws and regulations, military people become entitled to accumulate leave and to take it when their duties permit (see chapter 21,

"Leave"). But people in uniform must apply for permission to take leave, regardless of how much leave they have accumulated. Their applications may be denied. The training or tactical situation will govern the decision. If they absent themselves without permission, they are subject to forfeiture of pay and to disciplinary action. Hence, it is a privilege, rather than a right.

Election to Public Office. Members of the Air Force other than the Regular Air Force, while on active duty, may become candidates for election to public office without resigning and may file such evidence of their candidacy as required by local laws. Their candidacy must not interfere with duty. If elected, the officers must not, while in active-duty status, act in their official capacity as the holders of the offices or perform any of the duties. Members of the Regular Air Force on the active list do not enjoy this privilege. DOD Directive 1344-10 provides guidance on this issue.

Because this particular privilege has been questioned several times in recent years, servicemembers considering becoming candidates for office should consult local military authority, or risk losing their commissions.

Membership in Officers' Clubs. Officers have the privilege of club membership, if clubs are provided. They must follow the rules of the club as to payment of dues, bills, and other matters, and unless they do so, this privilege may be curtailed or denied.

The Privilege of Writing for Publication. Traditionally, active-duty officers have been permitted to write for publication, as long as it was done on their own time and was not part of their official duties. One need only remember William J. Hardee, West Point commandant of cadets before the Civil War, whose *Rifle and Light Infantry Tactics* became the officer's manual for both Union and Confederate armies; General John J. Pershing's World War I and Dwight D. Eisenhower's World War II memoirs; and Colonel John A. Warden's *The Air Campaign: Planning for Combat*. Major General A. J. Kinney, the first author of this *Guide*, revised it for more than twenty years while on active duty.

In 1992, in an effort to clean its own house, the U.S. Congress passed a law prohibiting federal officials and employees from accepting honoraria for public appearances, speeches, or articles. Enforced throughout the U.S. government, the law proved unworkable and was challenged as a violation of the First Amendment. The U.S. Court of Appeals did find the law unconstitutional. Today, Air Force officers can again accept remuneration for their writing.

Publishing Articles on Military Subjects Is Authorized. Subject to restrictions stated below, any member of the armed services may publish articles on military subjects that contain nothing prejudicial to military discipline. If publication is not objectionable, such permission will be granted, but no reference to approval by the Department of the Air Force will appear in the publication. The inclusion of classified military information (Top Secret, Secret, or Confidential) in any article published by a member of the Air Force is prohibited.

If the author offers the work to the Department of the Air Force and it is accepted and published by the Department of the Air Force in original form, proper recognition will be given to the individual.

Manner of Obtaining Clearance on Proposed Addresses and Military Publications. The Office of Public Affairs, Department of Defense, is responsible for reviewing for security and coordination with existing policies of the Department of Defense and its components information disseminated to the public on a national scale by individuals or agencies of the Departments of the Army, Navy, and Air Force.

The agency is charged with reviewing manuscripts, speeches, advertising material, radio scripts, and films submitted for clearance by individuals and agencies of the Department of Defense and its components.

Active-Duty Personnel. All material containing information about the Air Force prepared by officers or airmen on active federal service will be submitted to the appropriate public affairs authority for security and policy review before publication.

Attention is called to a long-standing policy prohibiting military and civilian personnel assigned to public affairs divisions from accepting direct remuneration from civilian agencies for any type of public affairs activity without approval. Exceptions may be granted in cases where the subject matter is in no way related to the official duties of the personnel.

Inactive Personnel. Inactive Air Force Reserve and National Guard personnel assume civilian status upon completion of terminal leave and are not required to submit for review material that they have prepared. This, of course, does not relieve them of the responsibility to protect sensitive or classified information.

Retired Personnel. Retired military personnel are responsible for the security and propriety of material that they have prepared.

Inventions and Rights to Profit Therefrom. Another way active-duty personnel may seek to add to their income is through an invention. It is likely that many good ideas are unexploited because of lack of information on how to proceed. An officer who makes an invention has the same right as any other citizen to profit if it does not refer to and is not evolved in the line of duty. However, if it was created or evolved in the line of duty, the Air Force has certain ownership rights. Contact your staff judge advocate for information.

A free pamphlet on the subject is issued by the Commissioner of Patents, Washington, D.C. Novice inventors should obtain it before disclosing anything about their projects.

Defense Department Exchange Privileges. The following are entitled to all exchange privileges:

- Uniformed personnel on active duty more than seventy-two hours and their families.
- Officers and airmen of foreign nations when on duty with U.S. armed services under competent orders issued by one of the armed services.
- Widows and widowers of servicemembers of the following categories who have not remarried: members of the uniformed services who at the time of death were on active military duty for a period exceeding seventy-two hours, members of the reserve components of the armed forces who died in line of duty while on active duty, and retired personnel.

Retired personnel entitled to the privilege include these people:

- Personnel carried on the official retired lists of the armed services.
- Uniformed personnel of the Red Cross assigned to duty within an activity of the armed services.

Patrons Entitled to Limited Privileges. The following are entitled to make limited purchases at exchanges:

- Honorably discharged veterans who are receiving medical treatment at a facility where exchanges are operated.
- Exchange employees.

Snack bar privileges may be extended to the following when civilian facilities are not conveniently available: civilian employees, Red Cross nonuniformed personnel working in offices within an activity of the armed forces, visitors, and reserve component members on duty for periods less than seventy-two hours.

Members of reserve components not on active duty are entitled at all times to purchase such necessary articles of uniform clothing, accouterments, and equipment as would be required immediately when called to active duty.

Unlimited exchange privileges are authorized for reserve component personnel who participate in regularly scheduled inactive-duty training. This training must be appropriately documented by the individual's commander.

Identification. All patrons must identify themselves as entitled to full or restricted privileges at the time purchase is made. Family members and nonuniformed people are required to obtain an official identification card. Widows and widowers and retired personnel will be obliged to establish their right to purchase by the same card. Uniformed people should be prepared to display their official identification cards or official orders before sales are made.

Private Practice by Medical and Dental Officers. Private practice by medical and dental officers is strictly regulated by the Air Force. Established application procedures must be followed. Approval is not ordinarily granted unless there is demonstrated community need, including a letter to support the need from the local medical or dental society. In no case may such practice be in conflict with military requirements, and the establishment of an office for the purpose of engaging in civilian practice is prohibited. Medical officers engaging in private practice must be licensed in that state and must provide their own professional liability insurance. The same provisions govern private practice for dental officers.

Concessions and Scholarships at Civilian Educational Institutions. Several civilian educational institutions offer concessions to service children and grant scholarships to discharged airmen whose records and educational qualifications justify the action. Any person in the military service who desires information relating to scholarships should apply directly to the sponsoring activity or, at base level, go through the personal affairs office or the education office.

Privileges Extended by Civilian Organizations. In many localities, civilian professional, civic, golf, or social clubs may extend the privilege of membership to officers stationed at a nearby military establishment. This custom, which is by no means universal, is of great importance to officers. In some instances it enables officers to obtain membership without the costly entrance fees. Before accepting the offered privileges, officers are morally obligated to ascertain that these organizations have no discriminatory practices, such as restricting membership because of race, gender, religion, etc. The base legal office can assist with such determinations.

Abuse of Privilege. The evil that has been practiced by a few and that has discredited many of the officer corps is *abuse of privilege*. It consists of taking advantage of position or rank to secure pleasures or facilities to which one is not entitled by law, policy, or custom. It is "getting away with something." This chapter is an attempt to clarify what is meant by proper benefits so that officers may observe and evaluate alleged rights and privileges before practicing them. The selfish and grasping may not be deterred. But officers who might offend innocently may be helped on a correct course.

Here is a simple way to determine whether an alleged benefit or privilege is genuine or spurious. Find the answers to these two questions:

- Can you establish authorization in any current departmental or major command document?
- Observe the five or ten best officers of experience known to you whom you observe frequently. They must have high standing as good officers among their colleagues. Is the questioned privilege used or practiced by them?

RESTRICTIONS

There are many *Thou shalt nots* in the military life. They consist for the most part of restrictions or standards of conduct inapplicable to civilians. Some are in federal laws. Others are in departmental policies. A few are in observed customs. They need not be regarded as onerous. They have come about through experience and necessity. In any event, they are well balanced by military benefits. Because their violation would be regarded as a serious matter, at the worst resulting in trial by a court-martial, officers should know of them.

Conduct Unbecoming an Officer. Article 133 of the Uniform Code of Military Justice reads as follows: "Any officer, cadet, or midshipman who is convicted of conduct unbecoming an officer and a gentleman shall be punished as a court-martial may direct" (*Manual for Courts-Martial, United States*, 1951).

There are certain moral attributes common to the ideal officer, a lack of which is indicated by acts of dishonesty or unfair dealing; of immorality, indecency, or indecorum, or of lawlessness, injustice, or cruelty. Not everyone is or can be expected to meet ideal standards or to possess the attributes in the exact degree demanded by the standards of the time, but there is a limit of tolerance below which individual standards of officers or cadets cannot fall without their being morally unfit to be officers or cadets. This UCMJ article contemplates such conduct by officers or cadets that, taking all the circumstances into consideration, satisfactorily shows moral unfitness.

This article includes acts made punishable by any other article of the code, provided such acts amount to conduct unbecoming an officer; thus, an officer who embezzles military property violates both this and the article dealing with embezzlement. Instances of violation of this article include knowingly making a false official statement, dishonorable neglect to pay debts, opening and reading another's letters without authority, giving a check on a bank where one knows or reasonably should know there are no funds to meet it and without intending that there should be, using insulting or defamatory language to other officers in their presence or about them to other military persons, being grossly drunk and conspicuously disorderly in a public place, public association with prostitutes, cruel treatment of airmen, committing or attempting to commit a crime involving moral turpitude, and failing without good cause to support one's family.

Racial Discrimination. Racial prejudice and discrimination still exist in American society. The armed forces, however, have made great strides since the late 1940s, and today they are positive examples to the nation as a whole of the harmony that can exist in a multiracial and multiethnic society that is based on equal opportunity for all. Although the Air Force cannot control what personal opinions individual servicemembers may have, the institution itself does not practice racial discrimination, nor does it tolerate any form of racially discriminatory behavior among servicemembers.

Sexual Harassment. Sexual harassment is a form of sex discrimination that involves unwelcome sexual advances, requests for sexual favors, and other verbal or physical conduct of a sexual nature when submission to such conduct is made either explicitly or implicitly a term or condition of a person's job, pay, or career; submission or rejection of such conduct by a person is used as a basis for career or employment decisions affecting that person; or such conduct has the purpose or effect of unreasonably interfering with an individual's work performance or creates an intimidating, hostile, or offensive working environment.

It is rather easy to recognize sexual harassment of the type of "submit to my sexual requests or you will be (fired, demoted, intimidated, denied a promotion, and so on)." To recognize hostile environment sexual harassment is more complicated. Such a hostile environment can be created by discussing sexual activities, unnecessary touching, commenting on physical attributes, displaying sexually suggestive pictures, using demeaning or inappropriate terms, using unseemly gestures, members of one gender ostracizing workers of the other gender, granting job favors to those who participate in consensual sexual activity, and using crude and offensive language. The particular facts of each situation determine whether offensive conduct has crossed the line to unlawful gender discrimination.

Servicemembers should avoid all sexually offensive conduct or any behavior that is in any way demeaning to others. All complaints, regardless of whether they meet the legal test of hostile environment sexual harassment, must be quickly investigated and appropriate action taken to stop offensive conduct.

Sexual Misconduct. Congress has directed a program to deal with unacceptable sexual conduct. The program includes education on prevention and how to respond to complaints, as well as how complaints are to be investigated, medical care for victims, confidential reporting of incidents, and provision of advocates to victims. The program also addresses the use of alcohol to diminish the victim's ability to resist sexual assault (rape).

Fraternization and Unprofessional Relationships. Fraternization is a personal relationship between officers and enlisted members in violation of acceptable behavior in the Air Force that prejudices good order and discipline or discredits the armed services. If good professional judgment and common sense indicate that a relationship is causing, or may reasonably result in, damage to morale, good order, discipline, unit cohesion, or mission accomplishment, corrective action will be taken. Criminal charges can be brought under Article 134, Uniform Code of Military Justice.

Unprofessional relationships encompass all relationships between military members (officer-officer, officer-enlisted, enlisted-enlisted, or certain military-civilian relationships) that result in inappropriate familiarity or create the appearance of favoritism, preferential treatment, or impropriety. These relationships create the appearance that personal friendships and preferences are more important than individual job performance and contribution to the mission. They are, therefore, matters of official concern because unprofessional relationships erode morale, discipline, and the unit's ability to perform its mission. Unprofessional relationships can occur whether or not the members are in the same chain of command, unit, or closely related units. Officers may not gamble with, lend money to, borrow from, date, engage in sexual relations with, or enter into business enterprises with enlisted members. Additional guidance can be gotten from a staff judge advocate and AFI 36-2909, *Professional and Unprofessional Relationships*.

Sexual Orientation. In September 2011, per the direction of the president, the "Don't Ask Don't Tell" policy ended and sexual orientation ceased to be a criterion for service. Today, gay and lesbian servicemembers may openly serve in the armed forces, receiving the same rights, benefits, and protections as would any other serving officer or enlisted person.

Searches and Seizures. Servicemembers are subject to searches and seizures when legally authorized. These are usually authorized by installation commanders only after they have consulted with the staff judge advocate.

Searches are examinations of an individual, property, or premises with the purpose of finding criminal evidence, including contraband or stolen property. Searches may be consensual—that is, with the written or oral consent of the individual whose person, property, or premises are to be searched. Searches without consent can be made with or without probable cause. Without-probable-cause searches are those of government property, within jails, incident to a lawful stop or apprehension, or an entry or exit from military installations, aircraft, or vessels. Probable-cause searches exist when there is reasonable belief that the person, property, or evidence is currently located in a particular place or on a particular individual. Drug dogs can be used at any time in common areas where there is no reasonable expectation of privacy, and they may be used during inspections anywhere within the scope of the inspection, including dormitory rooms, whether the occupant is present or not.

Seizures are the meaningful interference with an individual's possessory interest in property. Individuals, property, and evidence associated or believed to be associated with a crime can be seized.

Urinalysis Program. This program is to detect and deter drug use by servicemembers. There are several categories of urinalysis testing: inspection urinalysis, in which individual members are not singled out for inspection and the entire unit or part of it is tested by random selection; command-directed urinalysis for servicemembers who have displayed aberrant, bizarre, or unlawful behavior or are suspected by their commanders of such behavior; probable-cause urinalysis, in which there is reasonable belief that illegal drugs will be present in the individual's urine; consent urinalysis testing, in which the individuals are told that they do not have to give their consent; and medical urinalysis, in which urine collected for medical reasons is subject to drug testing. Positive urinalysis tests can be the basis for administrative and Uniform Code of Military Justice action.

Smoking. Department of Defense and Air Force policy is to promote a healthy work environment and healthy and fit servicemembers. Smoking-cessation programs are offered to help smokers quit. Educational programs are aimed at discouraging smoking; tobacco products cannot be advertised in Air Force publications. Nonsmokers are protected from passive smoking by the prohibition of smoking in almost all facilities, including Air Force vehicles. Smokers and nonsmokers will not be billeted together, and if they must be, smoking is prohibited in the billet. During normal duty hours, smoking is also prohibited to students at the Air Force Academy, basic military training, Officer Training School, Undergraduate Pilot Training, and professional military education courses. Flagrant violations of these policies occasionally occur.

Religious Accommodation. The Air Force recognizes the importance of worship, spiritual health, and religious growth of servicemembers. The Air Force promotes the whole-person concept, which recognizes that individuals reach their full potential when they have developed the emotional, intellectual, physical, and spiritual aspects of their nature.

Commanders attempt to accommodate servicemembers' religious practices, such as holidays and dietary restrictions. Still, respect for religious beliefs should not infringe on military readiness, unit cohesion, standards, or discipline. When accommodation is not possible, the individual must conform to military requirements or face disciplinary action, administrative separation, or reassignment or reclassification.

Religious apparel that is part of the religious faith practiced by a service-member may be worn if it is not visible and if it does not interfere with the proper wear of the uniform. Visible items of religious apparel must be authorized individually.

Liability Regarding Classified Documents. By the very nature of their duties, most officers are required to have access to and use classified documents. Officers must be mindful of the restrictions placed upon such documents and the punitive actions that may be taken against them for improper handling or use.

The inclusion of classified military information in any article, speech, or discussion by a member of the Air Force is prohibited unless specifically authorized:

> Whoever, being entrusted with or having lawful possession or control of any document, writing, code book, signal book, sketch, photograph, photographic negative, blueprint, plan, map, model, note, or information, relating to the national defense, through gross negligence permits the same to be removed from its proper place of custody or delivered to anyone in violation of his trust, or to be lost, stolen, abstracted, or destroyed, shall be punished by imprisonment and may, in the discretion of the court, be fined.

Effect of Disrespectful Language Concerning Certain Government Officials. The 88th Article of the Uniform Code of Military Justice reads as follows:

> Any officer who uses contemptuous words against the President, Vice President, Congress, Secretary of Defense, or a Secretary of a Department, a Governor or a legislature of any State, Territory, or other possession of the United States in which he is on duty or present shall be punished as a court-martial may direct.

Restrictions on Outside Activities. Officers will not engage in or permit their names to be connected with any activity in which participation is incompatible with the status of an officer.

There are limitations on officers and other personnel subject to military law relating to the activities outside of their military duties in which they may properly engage and upon the outside interests they may have without impropriety. Some outside activities and interests are specifically prohibited by statute or policy or both; there are many others from which certain military personnel are barred by the high standards of conduct required of persons in the armed services. The general principle underlying the limitations mentioned above is that every member of the military establishment, when subject to military law, is bound to refrain from all business and professional activities and interests not directly connected with military duties in which participation would tend to interfere with or hamper in any degree full and proper discharge of such duties or would normally give rise to a suspicion that such participation would have that effect. Any substantial departure from this underlying principle would constitute conduct punishable under the articles of the Uniform Code of Military Justice.

It is impossible to enumerate all the various outside activities to which this restriction applies. The following examples are typical: (1) acceptance by an officer or, with the approval of the officer, by a member of the officer's immediate family of a substantial loan or gift from a person or firm with whom it is the officer's duty as an agent of the government to carry on negotiations, or (2) acquisition or possession by an officer of a financial interest in any concern whose business includes the manufacture and sale of articles that it is the duty of the officer to purchase for the government.

An officer who is engaged or who contemplates engaging in outside professional or business activities should learn pertinent laws, policies, and standards of the service to determine whether such activities or interests might be considered in any way incompatible with the proper performance of official duties or in any sense adverse to the interests of the government. If after such investigation there is any doubt, the individual concerned should report all pertinent facts to the Department of the Air Force and request instructions. An officer who has certain outside interests that have no bearing upon the performance of military duties at the time of acquiring such interests, and who is later assigned to duties in the performance of which the possession of such interests might normally be suspected of having an influence adverse to the interests of the government, will immediately dispose of such outside interests and report the facts to superior military authority or without disposing of such interests will report all pertinent facts and circumstances to superior authority with a view to change assignments or such other action as may be deemed appropriate.

Acting as Consultant for Private Enterprise Prohibited. No member of the military establishment on active duty or a civilian employee of the Department of the Air Force shall act as a consultant for a private enterprise with regard to any matter in which the government has an interest.

Assistance to Persons Preparing for Civil Service Examinations Prohibited. No officer or employee of the government will, directly or indirectly, instruct or be concerned in any manner in the instruction of any person with a view to his or her special preparation for the examination of the U.S. Civil Service Commission or of the boards of examiners for the diplomatic and consular services. *The fact that any officer or employee is found so engaged will be considered sufficient cause for removal from the service.*

Solicitation for Contributions for Gifts. Servicemembers are prohibited by law from soliciting contributions from government employees, including fellow servicemembers, for gifts to be presented to those in a superior official position. Very restricted exceptions are made to this policy: Government employees may voluntarily contribute nominal amounts to purchase a superior an inexpensive memento. These mementos are customarily given to superiors, especially commanders, on their departure or retirement. Expensive gifts and involuntary contributions are absolutely forbidden.

Acceptance of Gifts from Subordinates. Superiors do not solicit or accept gifts from subordinates. Not only is pressure, favoritism, or bribery forbidden, but so too is the appearance of illegal behavior. Under restricted circumstances, such as a PCS move or retirement, a superior can accept a nominal gift from subordinates. These customary gifts must have little monetary value; they are merely mementos of service, command, and camaraderie.

Receiving Gifts from Civilian Sources in Recognition of Services Prohibited. The practice of receiving presents from persons not in the military establishment or in the employ of the government in recognition of services or from firms or their representatives with whom the officer has negotiated as an agent of the government is prohibited. Furthermore, officers should ensure that members of their immediate families do not receive or accept contributions or gifts from such persons or firms.

Effect of Refusal of Medical Treatment. A servicemember may be brought to trial by court-martial for refusing to submit to a surgical or dental operation or to medical or dental treatment at the hands of the military authorities if it is designed to restore or increase fitness for service and is without risk of life.

Communication with Members of Congress. Communication with members of Congress by personnel of the Air Force on matters of personal interest is slightly restricted: "No person may restrict any member of an armed force in communicating with a member of Congress, unless the communication is unlawful or violates a regulation necessary to the security of the United States." All members of the Air Force, however, are advised that all legislative matters affecting the Department of the Air Force program shall be conducted through the Office of the Secretary of the Air Force or as authorized by that office. See AFI 90-401, *Air Force Relations with Congress.*

Action on Attempts to Secure Personal Favor. Except when properly made by the officers themselves, requests for personal favor or consideration for any officers will be referred to the officers in question for statement whether they directly or indirectly procured the requests to be made and whether they avow or disavow the request as one on their behalf.

Writing Checks with Insufficient Funds and Payment of Debts. When servicemembers write checks against accounts with insufficient funds or fail to clear their personal accounts before departing for a permanent change of station, they are contributing to a reputation that adversely affects other servicemembers. Such irresponsible financial dealings are intolerable for officers. Creditors can attach a servicemember's bank account or personal property in pursuit of bad debts. Furthermore, up to 25 percent of a servicemember's paycheck (excluding subsistence and housing allowances) can be attached by private creditors to pay overdue debts. To involuntarily garnish a servicemember's pay to satisfy a debt, a creditor must have a court judgment and pay all processing expenses. Base exchanges can garnish up to 67 percent of a servicemember's paycheck. Needless to say, this situation must be avoided; it is morally wrong to incur debts that cannot be paid on time, and to do so negatively reflects on an officer's ability to manage personal affairs.

Restrictions on Using Franked Envelopes and Letterheads. All Department of the Air Force letterheads, envelopes, and other stationery are for OFFICIAL USE ONLY and may not be used as personal stationery.

STANDARDS OF ETHICAL CONDUCT

It is fundamental Air Force policy that personnel will not engage in any personal business or professional activity that places them in a position of conflict between their private interests and the public interest of the United States. To preserve the public confidence in the Air Force, even the appearance of a conflict of interest must be avoided. Air Force personnel shall not use inside information to further a private gain for themselves or others if that information is not generally available to the public and was obtained by reason of their Air Force position.

- Active-duty members may not make personal commercial solicitations or solicited sales to DOD personnel junior in rank at any time (on or off duty, in or out of uniform), specifically for insurance, stocks, mutual funds, real estate, or any other commodities, goods, or services.
- Accepting any gift, entertainment, or thing of value from any person or company that is engaged in procurement activities or business with any agency of the DOD is prohibited. Because interpretation of this paragraph is sometimes difficult, do not hesitate to consult the staff judge advocate.
- Solicitation of contributions for gifts to an official superior (except voluntary gifts or contributions of nominal value on special occasions like marriage, illness, transfer, or retirement) is prohibited.
- Active-duty military or civilian personnel may not use their grades, titles, or positions in connection with any commercial enterprise or for endorsing a commercial product.
- Outside or off-duty employment, if it interferes with or is not compatible with the performance of government duties, or if it might discredit the government, is prohibited. Squadron commanders are normally the approving authority for requests for off-duty employment.
- Air Force personnel, on base or while on duty, may not participate in any unauthorized gambling activity, including football pools. Although this prohibition is widely ignored, especially regarding football pools, the best policy is always to follow established Air Force standards.

20

Pay and Personal Allowances

The most current source for pay and allowance information is Defense Finance and Accounting Services' (DFAS) myPay website at mypay.dfas.mil. To access this site for your personal pay and allowances you will need your Login ID and Password or you can use your military ID card (common access card) with your personal identification number (PIN). If you need customer support for a new password or other pay issue, the DFAS lists contact instructions at www.dfas.mil/customerservice.html. You may be able to resolve many questions simply using the online help functions at either the DFAS home page or the myPay website.

MYPAY PROGRAM
MyPay is a flexible and reliable program; participation is mandatory. It is the primary means for you to view and print your Leave and Earnings Statement, as well as conduct online financial transactions. MyPay allows you to make these online transactions: view and print tax statements, change federal and state tax withholdings, update bank account and electronic fund transfer information, manage allotments, make address changes, purchase U.S. Savings Bonds, view and print travel vouchers, control Thrift Savings Plan enrollment, view and print retiree account statements, view and print annuitant account statements, and update certificate of annuitant eligibility.

FUNDAMENTAL ELEMENTS
An officer's pay and allowances consist of four fundamental elements:
- Basic pay
- Basic allowance for subsistence (BAS)
- Basic allowance for housing (BAH)
- Incentive and special pay

Basic Pay. Basic pay is set by grade and longevity, or years in service. Because of inflation, military pay has increased annually since 1964 to reflect the increased cost of living. This trend seems likely to continue, so consider the accompanying pay table as merely a guide, a reflection of 2014 military pay. On the other hand, as federal budget constraints increase, cost-of-living allowance (COLA) increases could decrease or end. Military pay tables, past

and current, are found at www.dfas.mil/militarymembers/payentitlements/
militarypaytables.html.

Basic Allowances. The basic allowance for subsistence (BAS) is the same
for all officers of all grades, with or without dependents. This pay stems from a
military tradition where pay included room and board. BAS offsets the member's food costs, but is not intended to pay this expense for dependents. Additional information is provided at militarypay.defense.gov/pay/bas/index.html.

Basic allowance for housing (BAH) is for officers authorized but not occupying government quarters. The BAH rate is based on the member's rank, marital status, dependency status, and where the member and his or her dependents reside. The tax-free monthly housing allowance follows either of two schedules, with dependents and without dependents. The dependents' schedule is the same regardless of the number of dependents. A "partial rate" BAH is paid to officers living in government bachelor quarters. "BAH differential" is paid to officers assigned to single-type quarters and authorized a BAH in order to pay court-ordered child support. Additional BAH information is available at www.defensetravel.dod.mil/site/bah.cfm.

Incentive and Special Pay. *Flight pay*, or *aviation career incentive pay*, for aircrew officers ranges from a minimum of $125 a month to a maximum of $840 after fourteen years on flying status and at twenty-two years' service decreases to $585, falling gradually to $250 after twenty-five years' service. *Hazardous duty incentive pay* is $150–$250 per month for officers. A variety of other hardship, incentive, and special pay is offered to nonrated flying personnel, medical and dental officers, veterinarians, pharmacists, nurses, lawyers, some officers with critical nuclear skills and foreign language proficiency, and so on.

INTERMITTENT AND NONRECURRING ELEMENTS OF PAY AND ALLOWANCES

Uniform Allowance. On commissioning, all officers are entitled to a one-time payment to purchase required uniforms and insignia.

Advance Pay. If authorized by a servicemember's commander, a servicemember may draw permanent-change-of-station (PCS) advance pay of not more than three months' basic pay minus standard deductions (FICA, etc.).

Travel Allowance. A daily allowance (per diem) for each member, as well as a standard mileage reimbursement for the official distance is authorized for servicemembers moving under PCS orders by private vehicle. Per diem rate for dependents is based on age (under twelve, 50 percent of member's rate; over twelve, 75 percent of member's rate). Two vehicles are authorized for CONUS travel. You can find travel regulations and allowances information at the DoD website at www.defensetravel.dod.mil.

Dislocation Allowance. This allowance is to partially reimburse servicemembers for the expense incurred in relocating households from one permanent change of station to the next. Officers' allowances depend on grade and

MONTHLY BASIC PAY TABLE (EFFECTIVE JANUARY 1, 2014)

Years of Service

Pay Grade	<2	2	3	4	6	8	10	12	14	16	18	20	22	24	26
Commissioned officers															
O-10[1]												16,072.20	16,150.50	16,486.80	17,071.50
O-9[1]												14,056.80	14,259.90	14,552.10	15,062.40
O-8[1]	9,946.20	10,272.00	10,488.30	10,548.60	10,818.60	11,269.20	11,373.90	11,802.00	11,924.70	12,293.40	12,827.10	13,319.10	13,647.30	13,647.30	13,647.30
O-7[1]	8,264.40	8,648.40	8,826.00	8,967.30	9,222.90	9,475.80	9,767.70	10,059.00	10,351.20	11,269.20	12,043.80	12,043.80	12,043.80	12,043.80	12,105.60
O-6[2]	6,125.40	6,729.60	7,171.20	7,171.20	7,198.50	7,507.20	7,547.70	7,547.70	7,975.70	8,735.10	9,180.30	9,625.20	9,878.40	10,134.60	10,632.00
O-5	5,106.60	5,752.50	6,150.60	6,225.60	6,474.30	6,622.80	6,949.50	7,189.50	7,499.70	7,974.00	8,199.30	8,422.20	8,675.70	8,675.70	8,675.70
O-4	4,405.80	5,100.30	5,440.80	5,516.40	5,832.30	6,171.00	6,593.10	6,921.30	7,149.60	7,280.70	7,356.60	7,356.60	7,356.60	7,356.60	7,356.60
O-3	3,873.90	4,391.40	4,739.70	5,167.80	5,415.40	5,687.10	5,862.60	6,151.50	6,302.40	6,302.40	6,302.40	6,302.40	6,302.40	6,302.40	6,302.40
O-2	3,347.10	3,812.10	4,390.50	4,538.70	4,632.30	4,632.30	4,632.30	4,632.30	4,632.30	4,632.30	4,632.30	4,632.30	4,632.30	4,632.30	4,632.30
O-1	2,905.20	3,024.00	3,655.50	3,655.50	3,655.50	3,655.50	3,655.50	3,655.50	3,655.50	3,655.50	3,655.50	3,655.50	3,655.50	3,655.50	3,655.50
Commissioned officers with over 4 years active duty service as an enlisted member or warrant officer															
O-3[3]				5,167.80	5,415.30	5,687.10	5,862.60	6,151.50	6,395.40	6,535.50	6,726.00	6,726.00	6,726.00	6,726.00	6,726.00
O-2[3]				4,538.70	4,632.30	4,779.90	5,028.60	5,220.90	5,364.30	5,364.30	5,364.30	5,364.30	5,364.30	5,364.30	5,364.30
O-1[3]				3,655.50	3,903.30	4,047.90	4,195.20	4,340.10	4,538.70	4,538.70	4,538.70	4,538.70	4,538.70	4,538.70	4,538.70
Warrant officers															
W-5												7,118.40	7,479.60	7,748.40	8,046.30
W-4	4,003.50	4,306.50	4,429.80	4,551.60	4,761.00	4,968.30	5,178.00	5,493.90	5,770.50	6,033.90	6,249.30	6,459.30	6,768.00	7,021.80	7,311.00
W-3	3,655.80	3,808.20	3,964.50	4,015.80	4,179.60	4,501.80	4,837.20	4,995.00	5,177.70	5,366.10	5,704.50	5,933.10	6,069.90	6,215.40	6,413.10
W-2	3,234.90	3,540.90	3,635.40	3,699.90	3,909.90	4,236.00	4,397.40	4,556.40	4,751.10	4,902.90	5,040.60	5,205.30	5,313.60	5,399.70	5,399.70
W-1	2,839.80	3,145.20	3,227.40	3,401.10	3,606.60	3,909.30	4,050.60	4,247.70	4,442.40	4,595.40	4,735.80	4,906.80	4,906.80	4,906.80	4,906.80
Enlisted members															
E-9[4]							4,836.90	4,946.40	5,034.70	5,246.70	5,411.10	5,673.60	5,895.60	6,129.30	6,486.90
E-8						3,959.40	4,134.30	4,242.90	4,372.80	4,513.80	4,767.60	4,896.30	5,115.30	5,236.80	5,535.90
E-7	2,752.50	3,004.20	3,119.10	3,271.50	3,390.60	3,594.90	3,709.80	3,914.40	4,084.20	4,200.30	4,323.90	4,371.60	4,532.40	4,618.50	4,946.70
E-6	2,380.80	2,619.60	2,735.10	2,847.60	2,964.90	3,228.60	3,331.50	3,530.40	3,591.30	3,635.70	3,687.30	3,687.30	3,687.30	3,687.30	3,687.30
E-5	2,181.00	2,327.40	2,440.20	2,555.10	2,734.50	2,922.30	3,076.20	3,094.80	3,094.80	3,094.80	3,094.80	3,094.80	3,094.80	3,094.80	3,094.80
E-4	1,999.50	2,101.80	2,215.80	2,328.00	2,427.30	2,427.30	2,427.30	2,427.30	2,427.30	2,427.30	2,427.30	2,427.30	2,427.30	2,427.30	2,427.30
E-3	1,805.40	1,918.80	2,034.90	2,034.90	2,034.90	2,034.90	2,034.90	2,034.90	2,034.90	2,034.90	2,034.90	2,034.90	2,034.90	2,034.90	2,034.90
E-2	1,716.90	1,716.90	1,716.90	1,716.90	1,716.90	1,716.90	1,716.90	1,716.90	1,716.90	1,716.90	1,716.90	1,716.90	1,716.90	1,716.90	1,716.90
E-1[5]	1,531.50	1,716.90	1,716.90	1,716.90	1,716.90	1,716.90	1,716.90	1,716.90	1,716.90	1,716.90	1,716.90	1,716.90	1,716.90	1,716.90	1,716.90

NOTES:
1. Basic pay for an O-7 to O-10 is limited by Level II of the Executive Schedule which is $15,125.10. Basic pay for O-6 and below is limited by Level V of the Executive Schedule which is $12,266.70.
2. While serving as Chairman, Joint Chief of Staff/Vice Chairman, Joint Chief of Staff, Chief of Staff, Chief of Navy Operations, Commandant of the Marine Corps, Army/Air Force Chief of Staff, Commander of a unified or specified combatant command, basic pay is $21,147.70. (See note 1 above).
3. Applicable to O-1 to O-3 with at least 4 years and 1 day of active duty or more than 1460 points as a warrant and/or enlisted member. See Department of Defense Financial Management Regulations for more detailed explanation on who is eligible for this special basic pay rate.
4. For the Master Chief Petty Officer of the Navy, Chief Master Sergeant of the AF, Sergeant Major of the Army or Marine Corps or Senior Enlisted Advisor of the JCS, basic pay is $7,816.20. Combat Zone Tax Exclusion for O-1 and above is based on this basic pay rate plus Hostile Fire Pay/Imminent Danger Pay which is $225.00.
5. Applicable to E-1 with 4 months or more of active duty. Basic pay for an E-1 with less than 4 months of active duty is $1,017.00.
6. Basic pay rate for Academy Cadets/Midshipmen and ROTC members/applicants is $1,017.00.

BASIC ALLOWANCES FOR HOUSING RC/TRANSIENT
(JANUARY 1, 2014)

Grade	Partial	Without Dependents	With Dependents	Differential
Officer Personnel				
0-10 to 0-7	$50.70	$1,555.80	$1,913.70	$333.30
0-6	$39.60	$1,426.50	$1,722.60	$276.30
0-5	$33.00	$1,373.70	$1,660.80	$267.00
0-4	$26.70	$1,272.60	$1,463.70	$177.60
0-3	$22.20	$1,020.60	$1,211.10	$177.60
0-2	$17.70	$808.80	$1,033.50	$209.40
0-1	$13.20	$693.90	$925.20	$226.20
03E	$22.20	$1,101.60	$1,302.00	$186.00
02E	$17.70	$936.60	$1,174.50	$222.30
OlE	$13.20	$814.50	$1,085.70	$261.00
W-5	$25.20	$1,293.30	$1,413.60	$111.00
W-4	$25.20	$1,148.10	$1,295.70	$136.80
W-3	$20.70	$965.70	$1,188.00	$206.40
W-2	$15.90	$856.80	$1,091.40	$218.10
W-1	$13.80	$718.50	$944.70	$211.20
E-9	$18.60	$942.90	$1,243.20	$278.70
E-8	$15.30	$866.40	$1,146.90	$261.30
E-7	$12.00	$798.60	$1,064.40	$302.40
E-6	$9.90	$738.00	$983.40	$292.20
E-5	$8.70	$663.60	$884.70	$248.70
E-4	$8.10	$577.20	$768.90	$215.10
E-3	$7.80	$536.70	$715.20	$176.10
E-2	$7.20	$511.50	$681.60	$235.50
E-1	$6.90	$511.50	$681.60	$278.70

dependent status. A dislocation allowance is paid only once in connection to any one PCS and only when dependents have completed travel in connection with a PCS that authorizes transportation of dependents or travel allowances. Dislocation is not paid for the move from home of record to first duty station or from last duty station to retirement home.

Temporary Lodging (Stateside). Servicemembers on PCS orders with families can draw advance payment of temporary lodging expenses.

Temporary Lodging (Overseas, Including Alaska and Hawaii). Servicemembers on PCS orders with families can draw advanced payment of temporary lodging allowance.

Advanced Housing Allowance. If authorized by a servicemember's commander, this allowance is paid if money is needed for rental housing in the United States. In the United States, the amount can be as great as three months' basic allowance for housing. Overseas, advance housing allowance can be up to twelve months of the overseas housing allowance. Your commander's approval is required on AF Form 1039.

CONUS COLA. This cost-of-living allowance is paid to those living in selected high-cost areas in the United States.

Overseas COLA. Servicemembers stationed in a number of foreign countries, as well as Alaska and Hawaii, may receive an allowance to equalize the overseas cost of living and housing with that in the United States if the overseas cost is greater.

Family Separation Allowance. This allowance is payable only to servicemembers with dependents. It is paid to servicemembers assigned to locations where the Air Force will not move their families or whose military orders separate them from their military spouses. The family separation allowance is a partial reimbursement for daily expenses incurred during the servicemember's separation from family. The family separation allowance is tax free.

Hardship Duty Pay/Hostile Fire Pay. When serving in an officially declared "imminent danger area," at several overseas locations, hardship duty pay varies by location, whereas hostile fire pay is a set amount for all servicemembers. To qualify for the entitlement for the entire month, a member need only be assigned or on TDY to a designated area for at least one day a calendar month.

DEPENDENTS

Definition. The term "dependents" includes the lawful spouse, and unmarried children and wards of court under twenty-one years of age, of any member of the uniformed services, and the father or mother of the member, provided he or she is in fact dependent on the member for more than half of his or her support. It also includes unmarried children over twenty-one years of age who are incapable of self-support because they are mentally or physically incapacitated and who are in fact dependent on the member for more than half of their support. The term *children* includes stepchildren, adopted children, and wards of the court dependent upon the member. The term *father* or *mother* includes a stepparent or parent by adoption and any other person, including a former stepparent, who has stood *in loco parentis* to the person concerned at any time for a continuous period of not less than five years during the minority of the member.

Credit for Dependent Parents. An officer will receive credit for basic allowance for quarters because of a dependent parent only when the dependent parent actually is residing in the household of the officer claiming the increased allowance.

DEDUCTIONS

Social Security Tax. The law requires the Air Force to deduct Social Security taxes (FICA and Medicare) from individual basic pay.

Federal Income Tax. Members of the armed services are subject to the federal law providing for payroll deductions for income tax. Taxable income includes all pay (basic, flight, hazardous duty, incentive, and so on), but does not include subsistence, housing, or family separation allowances.

In special situations, limited federal income-tax relief is granted for servicemembers on duty in designated war zones. For example, officers can exempt an amount not to exceed the amount paid to the highest-paid enlisted member. Officers serving in designated income-tax exclusion combat zones should carefully examine Box 1 of their W-2 forms. If their taxable incomes appear too high, they should consult their finance officers or the myPay website.

State Income Tax. Members of the armed services are subject to the laws of their state of legal residence providing for payroll deductions for state income taxes.

INCOME TAX EXEMPTION

Combat Zone Tax Exemption (CZTE). Members are entitled to CZTE for any month in which they are either in a designated combat zone or assigned to a unit, either permanently or on TDY, in direct support of operations conducted in a combat zone. Servicemembers not entitled to Hazardous Duty Pay or Hostile Fire Pay (due to leave, TDY, etc.) are not entitled to CZTE for that period. For officers, there is a monetary limit for CZTE. Social Security and Medicare withholdings are not impacted by CZTE benefits.

Taxation of Pay for Retired Service Personnel. Members of the armed services who are retired for length of service or age pay the same federal income taxes as other citizens. The same tax withholdings as for active-duty officers are made.

Members retired for physical disability receive an important exemption in the computation of federal income tax. The amount of the exemption depends upon the degree of disability and applies to their active-duty base pay at the time of retirement. However, the Internal Revenue Service does allow for retroactive Veterans Administration disability determinations.

ALLOTMENTS AND STOPPAGES

Allotments. Air Force regulations permit you to make allotments from your pay for various purposes; in fact, they are the preferred method to pay your bills and save money. The word *allotment* means a definite portion of your pay that you authorize the Air Force to pay a financial institution by electronic funds transfer. Of course, you must provide the routing number, account number, and type of account when you complete the allotment paperwork. The *allotter* is the person who makes the allotment, in this case you. The *allottee* is the person or institution to whom you make the allotment. The allottee will receive the full amount of the allotment on the first of the month, although your pay will have been deducted at mid-month and at the end of the month. Generally, you can make an allotment for an indefinite time. Allotments are made on the myPay website.

Allotments can make life simpler for you, as you may have to go anywhere in the world at any time for temporary duty or permanent change of station. With allotments, although you still have control of your money, you do not have to write out the checks and mail them every month. You may want to consider making allotments for the following purposes:

- Buying U.S. Savings Bonds
- Donating to charity, including the Combined Federal Campaign
- Supporting dependents
- Repaying home loans
- Paying commercial life insurance premiums
- Adding to savings accounts or investments

While Prisoner of War or Reported Missing. Any officer who is interned, taken prisoner of war, or reported missing and who has made an allotment of pay for the support of dependents or for the payment of insurance premiums is entitled to have such allotments or insurance deductions continued for a period of twelve months from the date of commencement of absence. Allotments of officers under any of the above conditions may not continue beyond twelve months following the officially reported date of commencement of absence, except that when that twelve months is about to expire and the Air Force has received no official report of death or of being a prisoner of war or of being interned; the Air Force can then fully review the case. Following such review, and when the twelve months' absence has expired, or following any subsequent review of the case, the Air Force may direct the continuance of the officer's missing status if it can be reasonably presumed that the officer is still alive. Such missing officers continue to be entitled to have pay and allowances credited and payment of allotments as authorized to be continued, increased, or initiated.

In the absence of an allotment, or when the allotment is not sufficient for reasonable support of a dependent and for the payment of insurance premiums, the Air Force may direct payment of an appropriate allotment, not to exceed the total basic pay of the person concerned.

Authorized Stoppages. The Air Force may withhold the pay of officers on account of an indebtedness to the United States admitted or shown by the judgment of a court, but not otherwise unless specifically ordered by the secretary of the Air Force.

CREDITABLE SERVICE FOR BASIC PAY

The Department of Defense Financial Management Regulation (DODFMR) establishes the rules for counting the various conditions of active duty in computing cumulative years of service for credit toward basic pay.

Active-duty. You will receive full-time credit for all periods of active duty served in any reserve or regular component of any uniformed service in any military status, commissioned or enlisted.

Retired Status. You will receive additional credit for any period of time you are on any retired list. This provision does *not* increase retired pay, but if you return to active duty from a retired list, you benefit from inclusion of your time on the retired list in computing basic pay.

Academies. Service as a cadet or midshipman in the service academies or ROTC is *not* creditable.

Fraudulent Enlistment. You may receive credit for service in a fraudulent enlistment not voided by the government.

Beginning Dates of Service. Service as an officer begins from the date of acceptance of appointment; as an enlisted member, from the date of enlistment.

REIMBURSEMENT FOR OFFICIAL TRAVEL EXPENSES

The DOD manages all travel, from orders to vouchers, using the Defense Travel System (DTS). DTS is a fully integrated, automated, end-to-end travel management system, enabling travelers to create authorizations (TDY travel orders), prepare reservations (air/ground travel and lodging), receive approvals, generate travel vouchers, upload receipts, and receive a split reimbursement between the Government Travel Charge Card (GTCC) vendor and the traveler's bank account. DTS operates at more than ninety-five hundred sites worldwide. You access DTS at www.defensetravel.osd.mil. Online training in the use of DTS is available and your unit training manager can help you make arrangements for completing the DTS training course.

Government Travel Charge Card (GTCC). The GTCC is used by all U.S. government personnel to pay for costs incident to TDY and PCS official business travel. Fees for the use of this charge card are reimbursable on completion of your settlement vouchers. Your unit will have a program coordinator who will assist you in card issuance and instruct you on how to use the card.

Per Diem. The per diem allowance, the "Lodging-Plus" system, within the United States and overseas varies according to locality. Rates are updated frequently. Per diem covers the cost of lodging and meals plus incidental expenses. Within the United States, members using commercial air are granted one travel day. Authorized automobile travel days are determined by the number of official miles traveled divided by 350.

Reimbursable Travel Expenses. When traveling under orders, keep a detailed record of all expenses, however minor. Many are reimbursable. Note the following list of reimbursable items:

Lodging. In instances requiring certificates of availability of government quarters and messing facilities, you must adhere to the provisions of the Joint Federal Travel Regulations (JFTR) if you wish to receive proper per diem reimbursement. For PCS moves, Temporary Lodging Expense (TLE) allowance is authorized for a total of ten days in connection with PCS moves within the United States. Overseas' TLEs differ. If government quarters are not available, commercial lodging must be in the vicinity of the old and/or new PCS station. If you stay with a relative or friend, you will not receive the TLE allowance.

Taxi Fares. You may receive reimbursement for taxi fares between home or business and stations, airports, other carrier terminals or local terminuses of the mode of transportation used, between carrier terminals, while en route when free transfer is not included in the price of the ticket or when necessitated by change in mode of travel, and from carrier terminals to lodgings and return in connection with unavoidable delays en route incident to the mode of travel. Itemization is required.

Allowed Tips. You may receive reimbursement for tips incident to transportation expenses as follows: tips of 15 percent to taxi drivers and tips to baggage porters, not to exceed customary local rates, but not including tips for baggage handling at hotels. Itemization is required, including the number of pieces of baggage handled.

Excess Baggage. When excess baggage is authorized in the orders, actual costs for such excess baggage in addition to that carried free by the carrier are reimbursable.

Telephone and Other Electronic Communication. Cost of official telephone and similar communication services is reimbursable when incident to the official duty or in connection with items of transportation. Such services when solely in connection with reserving a hotel room and so on are not, however, considered official. Copies of messages sent are required for all electronic transmissions unless the message is classified, in which case a full explanation and a receipt will suffice. Local official calls are allowable when itemized. Long-distance calls require full explanations and certification by the orders-issuing official.

Local Public Carrier Fares. Expenses incident to travel by bus, subway/metro, or other usual means of transportation may be reimbursable in lieu of taxi fares under certain conditions and limitations. Itemization is required.

Tolls. Ferry fares and road, bridge, and tunnel tolls may be reimbursable. Itemization is required.

Local Transportation. Reimbursement is sometimes authorized on orders for transportation obtained at personal expense in the conduct of official business within and around either the permanent or temporary duty station.

Nonreimbursable Travel Expenses. The government cannot reimburse you for the following travel expenses:

- Travel under permissive orders to travel, in contrast to orders directing travel.
- Travel under orders but not on public business, such as travel as a participant in an athletic contest. Unit or command welfare funds, which come from such sources as operation of exchanges and movie theaters, may reimburse you for such travel, but appropriated funds cannot.
- Return from leave to duty abroad. Unless government transportation is available, such as space on a transport, you must pay your own return expenses from leave in the United States.
- Attendance at public ceremonies or demonstrations paid for by the sponsoring agency.

Certificates of Nonavailability. When government quarters are available, the government will reduce the per diem allowance. If government quarters are not available, you must get certificates or a contact number from the billeting officer of an installation at which you perform temporary duty if you want reimbursement for nongovernment lodging and meals.

Amount of Overseas Travel Allowances. The allowances for TDY travel costs overseas vary. You may expect allowances for necessary expenses provided you use reasonable care. Before undertaking travel outside the United States, you should consult local transportation or financial services officers to determine the exact amount of the expected allowances, which appear in the Joint Federal Travel Regulations.

Preparation of Vouchers for Payment. You will prepare your voucher using the Defense Travel System. This system is challenging for the new user, so contact your unit DTS expert for assistance with the system. The DTS website also offers online training programs.

WEIGHT ALLOWANCES FOR CHANGE OF STATION

The weight allowances for change of station include those for unaccompanied baggage and household goods. The Air Force allows up to 800 pounds of unaccompanied baggage for shipment to overseas locations, depending on your rank and the change of station location. Your move advisor will determine the weight allowance during the initial briefing to prepare you for your move. The following table shows weight allowances authorized for shipment of household goods at government expense for both temporary and permanent change of station.

PCS & NTS WEIGHT ALLOWANCES
(POUNDS)

Grade	With Dependents	Without Dependents
Officer Personnel		
0-10 to 0-6	18,000	18,000
0-5/W-5	17,500	16,000
0-4/W-4	17,000	14,000
0-3/W-3	14,500	13,000
0-2/W-2	13,500	12,500
0-1/W-1/Service Academy Graduates	12,000	10,000
Enlisted Personnel		
E-9	15,000	13,000
E-8	14,000	12,000
E-7	13,000	11,000
E-6	11,000	8,000
E-5	9,000	7,000
E-4	8,000	7,000
E-3 to E-1	8,000	5,000
Aviation Cadets	8,000	7,000
Service Academy Cadets/Midshipmen		350

21

Leave

The privilege of taking leave is a valuable benefit of military service, and the Air Force encourages its members to take leave. Leave should be used as you earn it and not hoarded to build up large cash payments for unused leave upon discharge or retirement. Periods of cessation from routine work for the purpose of travel, healthful recreation, and diversion are essential to the efficiency of people in the military service. Arrange duties so that both you and your subordinates can take all leave earned. Particularly encourage any members who are exhibiting signs of physical or mental stress to take leave to help lessen the effects of job stress leading to burnout.

Conversely, if you are reluctant to take leave because you are afraid your unit cannot get along without you for two weeks or a month, consider these thoughts: Your unit survived before you arrived; your unit will survive after you leave; if you die today of a heart attack at your duty station, your unit will survive and find time to do the paperwork for your death, attend your funeral, request a replacement, and do your work in the meantime. It is your responsibility to organize your work so that both your seniors and your subordinates can function well in your absence; sometimes, it is good to let them miss you for a while.

AIR FORCE POLICIES

Commanders will ensure that members of their commands have an opportunity and the encouragement to take leave. Commanders at all levels should encourage people in their commands to avail themselves frequently of accrued leave, and subject only to military necessity, all commanders will approve such requests of leave.

Commanders should bear in mind that the persistence of conditions within their commands in time of peace that preclude granting leave to their officers is an indication of poor organization, administration, and/or leadership. No military organization should rest on seemingly indispensable people. Moreover, commanders who grumble that they are so short of officers that they "can't afford" to permit their officers to take leave are admitting that they have no workable plan to meet the occurrence of sickness, accident, or death among their officers.

TYPES OF LEAVE

Ordinary Leave. Leave the Air Force grants upon your request at any time during a fiscal year to the extent of the leave that you may earn during that fiscal year, plus your leave credit from previous years.

Sick or Convalescent Leave. Leave the Air Force grants for absence because of illness or convalescence upon recommendation of the surgeon. It is not chargeable as leave. Usually the doctor will provide an order for non-duty illness restrictions to quarters or for convalescent leave.

Advance Leave. The Air Force may grant advance leave in anticipation of the future accrual of leave. In the case of officers, such leave would typically apply in case of emergency leave and pre-embarkation leave.

Emergency Leave. Leave the Air Force may grant upon assurance that an immediate family emergency exists and that granting of such leave will contribute to the alleviation of the emergency. The total leave advanced, including emergency leave, may not exceed sixty days, unless approved by HQ AFPC. AFI 36-3003, *Military Leave Program*, provides detailed guidelines for this type of leave. Emergency leave does not affect granting future leave, but the Air Force does charge it against present or future accrued leave.

Excess Leave. Leave the Air Force grants that is in excess of the amount you have accrued, except for such advance or ordinary leave as specifically authorized. It is taken without pay and allowances, and you may take it only under exceptional circumstances upon authority of commanders up to sixty days and HQ AFPC for more than sixty days. Of course, this leave is chargeable.

Convalescent Leave Due to Pregnancy. Women who become pregnant while on active duty continue to perform normal duties until delivery or as determined by medical authorities. Post-delivery for a normal pregnancy, the service allows forty-two days of convalescence leave to allow the member to recover physically. Medical authorities can extend this time, as required for the medical condition.

Delays En Route in Executing Travel. Typically one uses this type leave during permanent change of station moves. The Air Force counts and charges as leave authorized delays stated in travel orders.

COMPUTATION OF LEAVE CREDITS

The Air Force credits leave on a fiscal year basis. In any case in which the Air Force considers only a part of the fiscal year, it will prorate earned leave at the rate of $2^1/2$ days for each month of active (honorable) service.

Leave may not accumulate in excess of sixty days (except that personnel in a combat zone may accumulate ninety days). Members of USAF Reserve Forces ordered to active duty for periods of thirty days or more will receive leave in accordance with these computations. Those ordered to active duty for periods of less than thirty days will not receive leave.

COMPENSATION WHILE ON LEAVE
Personnel in the following circumstances shall receive the same pay and allowances while on leave that they would receive if on duty status: when absent on sick or convalescent leave; absent with leave not exceeding the aggregate number of days of leave standing to their credit or authorized to be advanced to their credit; and absent awaiting orders on disability retirement proceedings in excess of the number of days of leave accrued or authorized.

Personnel granted excess leave shall receive no pay or allowances while absent from duty. The Air Force may, however, grant advance leave with pay and allowances, but if the member is separated before accruing sufficient leave to cover the advance leave, the Air Force will consider the unaccrued portion excess leave without pay and allowances.

APPLICATION FOR LEAVE
Airmen throughout the Air Force use an automated online leave system called *LeaveWeb*, which allows airmen to submit leave requests, coordinate leave with supervisors and orderly rooms, receive approvals, and notify the finance office electronically, thus saving time and improving customer service.

LEAVE TO VISIT OUTSIDE THE UNITED STATES
Air Force officers may visit foreign countries on leave, either from the United States or from their overseas stations. Such leaves are chargeable as ordinary leave.

WARNINGS
As an officer, you are responsible to report to your duty station, not just any Air Force base, at the expiration of your leave. You may use military air transport on a space-available basis during leave, but a delay in securing a flight is no excuse for failing to return from leave on time.

HOLIDAYS
The following days in each year are public holidays established by law. The Air Force observes them except when military reasons prevent:

New Year's Day—January 1
Birthday of Martin Luther King Jr.—third Monday in January
Washington's Birthday—third Monday in February
Memorial Day—last Monday in May
Independence Day—July 4
Labor Day—first Monday in September
Columbus Day—second Monday in October
Veterans Day—November 11
Thanksgiving Day—fourth Thursday in November
Christmas Day—December 25

When a holiday falls on a Sunday, the following day is a holiday. When a holiday falls on Saturday, the preceding day is a holiday.

Above all, use your leave and holidays as time for relaxation and rejuvenation. Have fun, but take it easy.

22

Medical Care

The health of airmen and their families is mission-essential to the Air Force. Servicemembers cannot function at peak performance if they are not fit and in good health. Individuals who are distracted by sickness or health problems of family members are also incapable of full concentration on the mission. Consequently, the Air Force provides medical and dental care to servicemembers and their families. Many consider medical and dental care as primary benefits of their service in the Air Force.

Medical and dental care for servicemembers is free of charge. If the required specialists are unavailable at your duty station, you will be medevaced to a regional military hospital or referred to local civilian physicians or hospitals.

As the Air Force is concerned with preventive medicine, periodic medical and dental examinations are required of servicemembers. Frequency varies depending on job specialty; flying personnel, for example, are given annual flight physicals. Fitness and weight programs, as well as antitobacco campaigns and emphasis on the use of alcohol in moderation, are also efforts to maintain the health and fitness of servicemembers.

Medical and dental care for families of active-duty servicemembers and for retirees and their families has been provided on base on an as-available basis. In most cases, a dental insurance plan covers dental care for dependents and retirees. The Defense Department has introduced TRICARE as its overarching health management program in an effort to balance healthcare needs and costs.

TRICARE
TRICARE is DOD's health-care program for active-duty and retired military personnel, their families, and their survivors. The program's objectives are to improve beneficiary access to health care, assure affordable and high-quality care, provide choice, and contain costs to both beneficiaries and the DOD. TRICARE is the primary healthcare plan until the member and/or dependents reach the age for Medicare eligibility, at which time Medicare becomes the primary system and TRICARE for Life becomes a supplemental plan, if desired. For the most up-to-date information on TRICARE, see www.tricare.mil.

TRICARE's Health Service Regions, each with a lead agent, coordinate regional health-care delivery between military treatment facilities (MTFs) and civilian health-care providers. The regional lead agents oversee contracts with civilian managed-care companies that establish civilian health-care networks for beneficiaries to use when care is not available in the MTFs. TRICARE service centers are established at or near each military installation to assist beneficiaries in obtaining care and services.

Beneficiaries have options for seeking care as the program provides fifteen different TRICARE plan options, including a U.S. Family Health Plan. Most active-duty officers, single or married, will use a Prime or Standard option (or overseas/remote variations). As your assignment locations change during your career, you may find you need to change your plan (or at the very least update your address) to meet your family healthcare needs. Once you retire and reach the age for Medicare eligibility, programs like TRICARE for Life provide supplemental coverage for payments or care not covered by Medicare. Options have different cost-sharing features and degrees of freedom for using civilian providers. All options require that participants (members and dependents) be listed as eligible in the Defense Enrollment Eligibility Reporting System (DEERS); registration may be accomplished at the nearest Uniformed Services Personnel Office (military personnel flight). You can find additional information regarding DEERS requirements for TRICARE at www.tricare.mil/Welcome/Eligibility/DEERS.aspx. Your selection of a plan option can be complicated, so before selecting an option, you should study the informational materials available from the health benefits advisor at the nearest military medical facility, the beneficiary counseling and assistance coordinator at your TRICARE region's lead agent office, the regional TRICARE contractor's local TRICARE service center, and from information available at www.tricare.mil. Consider the two examples provided below.

TRICARE Standard and Extra has no annual enrollment fee. This option offers the most freedom to choose a provider, but costs will be higher than with TRICARE Prime options. Beneficiaries can use non-network civilian providers of their choice, but must pay a deductible and cost share when doing so. Standard is especially useful to beneficiaries who do not live within a TRICARE Prime service area, which DOD defines as within forty miles of a military clinic or hospital (a 2013 change). You may have to file your own claim forms and perhaps pay up to 15 percent more for allowable charges if your selected provider does not participate in TRICARE Standard. Providers that do participate accept the TRICARE Standard allowable charges as the full fee for care provided and will file the claims. TRICARE Standard beneficiaries must meet an annual outpatient deductible.

TRICARE Prime options are the only ones that require enrollment, and most TRICARE participants select Prime. Active-duty members and their families do not pay an annual enrollment fee or annual deductibles, and they do not pay co-pays or cost shares when using a military medical treatment facility.

Retirees under the Medicare eligibility age and their families selecting TRICARE Prime options require annual enrollment and payment of the enrollment fee, but they do not pay annual deductibles, unless using point-of-service facilities.

Prime is similar to a civilian health maintenance organization (HMO). TRICARE Prime beneficiaries either choose or are assigned a primary care manager (PCM), who will provide routine health care. The PCM will manage all aspects of the beneficiary's care, including referrals to specialists before care can be given. Except in emergency situations, if care is received before approval, there is an annual deductible, and after the deductible is met, the TRICARE Prime beneficiary must meet 50 percent of the TRICARE allowable charge. In addition to the services covered by TRICARE Standard, TRICARE Prime offers preventive and primary care services.

Before TRICARE Prime was an option, it was wise for servicemembers to carry supplemental insurance to cover family medical expenses that would not be reimbursed by the Air Force. Retirees and their families also were wise to carry supplemental insurance. Theoretically, this is no longer so critical for those selecting TRICARE Prime, but those selecting TRICARE Standard or Extra may want to continue carrying supplemental insurance through military-associated insurance companies and service associations that offer such services to their members.

TRICARE for Life serves as a Medicare supplemental coverage and is available worldwide for Medicare-eligible uniformed services beneficiaries, their eligible family members, and survivors. Participation requires annual purchase of Medicare Part B coverage. In most cases, Medicare pays first and TRICARE for Life pays its share of the remaining expenses second.

TRICARE ACTIVE-DUTY FAMILY MEMBER DENTAL PLAN
Dental care is provided to all servicemembers. At overseas locations, dental care for the families of active-duty servicemembers is provided on a very limited, space-available basis. On-base MTF dental care is essentially nonexistent for retirees and their families.

The TRICARE Active-Duty Family Member Dental Plan is available for the families of active-duty servicemembers for a monthly premium for the servicemember's spouse only or for spouse and children. Premiums change from time to time, so check options at www.tricare.mil/Dental.aspx. What dental services are covered, the limits of co-payments for specific services, and so forth are rather complicated. A pamphlet is available at your base medical facility. The monthly premium is so reasonable—it is supplemented by the government—that you should decline participation only in the most unusual circumstances. The TRICARE Retiree Dental Plan offers coverage and retirees can find options at www.trdp.org.

23

Voluntary and Involuntary Separations

There are voluntary and involuntary separations from the Air Force, as well as retirement.

From time to time, active-duty service commitments for some specialties are reduced or waived in order to reduce Air Force end strength to conform to service end strength goals or to meet Congressional manpower authorizations. These programs include the Palace Chase and the Limited Active Duty Service Commitment Waiver Programs. Officers interested in these programs should consult their military personnel flights or the vMPF (available through the Air Force Portal).

INVOLUNTARY SEPARATION

Under the provisions of pertinent sections of Title 10, U.S. Code, the Air Force may discharge officers for moral or professional dereliction, in interests of national security, or for substandard performance of duty (also see AFI 36-3207, *Separating Commissioned Officers*). Commanders may recommend initiation of action when they determine that action is appropriate. Reasons for initiating action to determine whether a regular or reserve officer should be retained in the Air Force include:

- Reserve officers who reach the age limit
- Officers who aren't selected for promotion
- Second lieutenants found not qualified for promotion
- Officers who aren't continuing on active duty
- Officers who lose their ecclesiastical endorsement
- Officers who have reached their maximum years of commissioned service or service in grade
- Officers who don't complete medical education or training programs
- Officers who fail the National Council Licensure Examination for Registered Nurses
- Officers who don't complete the USAF Nurse Transition Program
- Probationary officers who do not complete initial skills training

- Probationary reserve officers who can't exercise unrestricted clinical privileges
- Officers who do not have or fail to obtain required licenses as part of their commissioning requirements
- Administrative discharge for cause (for example: drug violations, performance)
- Substituting administrative discharge for dismissal
- Secretarial-directed release
- Reserve officers who don't qualify for permanent change of station
- Officers with disapproved requests for extension of active-duty tours
- Strength adjustments
- Officers eligible for retirement
- Officers serving with the Selective Service System
- Officers not selected for the Regular Air Force
- Incompatible status such as reserve accepting Regular Air Force officer appointments; accepting civil office, or appointments in diplomatic or consular service; or officers who do not accept Senate-confirmed Regular Air Force appointments

Officers against whom separation action is initiated may submit written statements or other documentary evidence they feel should be considered in evaluating their cases, may tender their resignations, or may apply for retirement, if eligible.

If an officer does not tender resignation or apply for voluntary retirement, and if the major commander determines that further action is warranted, the case is referred to a selection board. If the selection board determines that the officer should be required to show cause for retention in the Air Force, the major commander convenes a board of inquiry. The board of inquiry examines witnesses and documentary evidence and then recommends that the officer be retained or removed from active duty. The major commander sends the board of inquiry report to Headquarters USAF, where the case is reviewed by a board of review and final action is taken by the secretary of the Air Force.

Rights of Officers Required to Show Cause for Retention. The recorder invites witnesses, both for the officer and for the government, to appear if the legal advisor judges that they are reasonably available and that their testimony can contribute materially to the case.

Officers may tender their resignations or apply for voluntary retirement, if eligible, before the secretary of the Air Force makes a final decision.

SELECTIVE CONTINUATION PROGRAM

Captains and Majors. Officers with the regular grade of captain or major who are subject to discharge or retirement because they were not selected for promotion may, subject to the needs of the service, continue on active duty if they are chosen by a selection board with the approval of the secretary of the Air Force. Captains may not continue on active duty under this program for a period that extends beyond the last day of the month in which they complete twenty years of active commissioned service unless they are promoted to the regular grade of major. Majors may not continue on active duty under this program for a period that extends beyond the last day of the month in which they complete twenty-four years of active commissioned service unless they are promoted to the regular grade of lieutenant colonel.

Officers selected for continuation on active duty who are not subsequently promoted or continued on active duty and who are not on a list of officers recommended for continuation or for promotion to the next high grade shall, unless sooner retired or discharged under another provision of law, be discharged upon the expiration of the period of continued service or, if eligible, be retired. Officers who would otherwise be discharged and who are within two years of qualifying for retirement under some provision of law shall continue on active duty until qualified for retirement under that law, and then be retired.

Lieutenant Colonels, Colonels, Brigadier Generals, and Major Generals. Officers with the regular grade of lieutenant colonel, colonel, brigadier general, or major general who are subject to retirement for years of service may, subject to the needs of the service, defer retirement and continue on active duty if chosen by a selection board with the approval of the secretary of the Air Force.

Above Major General. Officers subject to retirement for years of service who are serving in a grade above major general may, subject to the needs of the service, defer retirement and continue on active duty by order of the president.

Length of Deferral. Any deferrals of retirement and continuation on active duty under the Selection Continuation Program shall be for a period not to exceed five years, and not to extend beyond the date of the officer's sixty-second birthday.

Declining Deferral. Officers selected for continuation on active duty who decline to continue on active duty shall be discharged, retired, or retained on active duty, as appropriate. Officers who decline continuation are not eligible to receive involuntary separation pay.

VOLUNTARY SEPARATION

The right of officers to resign their commissions or to request release from active duty is subject to certain restrictions dependent on their military status. The president or the secretary of the Air Force may accept a resignation or request for release, as appropriate, through any properly designated office.

Normally, a tendered resignation or request for release from extended active duty will be approved. However, an application for separation may be disapproved when an officer is under investigation; is under charges or awaiting result of trial; is absent without leave; is absent in hands of civil authorities; is insane; is in default with respect to public property or funds; is serving under a suspended sentence to dismissal; has an unfulfilled active-duty service obligation or agreement; is serving in time of war or when war is imminent, or in a period of emergency declared by the president or Congress; or in any other instance where the best interest of the Air Force requires retention. See AFI 36-3206, *Administrative Discharge Procedures for Commissioned Officers* or the *Manual for Courts-Martial* for information on the above separation reasons, other than those for war or emergency.

AFI 36-3207, *Separating Commissioned Officers*, outlines the rationales and procedures pertaining to voluntary separation. The following are key provisions in this AFI:

- Hardship. Traditionally, an officer may request hardship separation when active duty causes personal or family hardship; however, normal inconvenience caused by military service, such as living away from family members, is not considered undue hardship.
- Assuming civil office. To comply with 10 U.S.C. 973, eligible officers request separation on a date prior to their assuming civil office, providing satisfactory evidence of election or appointment to any office as a partisan candidate, a civil office requiring full-time service as a nonpartisan candidate, or a civil office requiring full-time service.
- Completing required active service. Officers may apply to separate when they complete all active-duty service commitments.
- Enlisting and retiring. Officers apply by completing a retirement application and a letter requesting a grade determination. If approved, the officer receives a date of separation (DOS) scheduled three days before the end of the month; retirement is effective on the first day of the following month.
- A secretary of the Air Force–approved early separation program. Officers applying to separate under a SECAF-approved voluntary early separation program must meet the program's eligibility criteria. The DOS normally falls on the date requested by the officer, or as directed by the separation program.
- Withdrawal of ecclesiastical endorsement. Officers may resign ASAP when they lose the approval they need to serve as chaplains.
- Physician redeferment program. If selected for the redeferment program, medical officers may request a DOS effective at least thirty days before, but not earlier than, the start-date of the training program.
- Attending school. Officers applying for separations in order to enter a recognized institution of higher education in a full-time resident course of instruction must show school acceptance and the ability and willingness to pay entrance fees or proof of payment; demonstrate that delaying enrollment until the established DOS date would cause hardship or academic disadvantage; and the DOS is within thirty days of the established DOS or ADSCD.
- Conscientious objector (CO). Officers may resign immediately upon approval of CO status as outlined in AFI 36-3204, *Disposition of Conscientious Objectors*.

- Transfer to another service. Eligible active-duty officers may apply for transfer to another uniformed service by submitting a statement of how the transfer benefits both national defense and the officer's career. Transfer is contingent on appointment in the gaining uniformed service and the officer receiving a DOS before his or her appointment. Officers may not apply for transfer if they have a DOS scheduled within three months of the date of application, receive notice of mandatory retirement, are under investigation, have had charges preferred against them or have been convicted by court-martial, are awaiting separation for cause, have an assignment selection date or are serving overseas, are enrolled in technical or flying training or await disposition after removal from such training, or were considered but not selected for promotion in the primary promotion zone as defined in Part I of AFI 36-2501, *Officer Promotions and Selective Continuation.*
- Separating instead of acquiring an ADSC for an assignment, training, or education course. Officers requesting the seven-day option in lieu of assignment must meet the criteria in AFI 36-2110, *Assignments.*
- Transfer to reserve components under Palace Chase. The DOS of officers approved under AFI 36-3205, *Applying for the Palace Chase and Palace Front Programs*, is normally set on the requested date.
- Medal of Honor. Medal of Honor recipients traditionally receive the requested DOS date.
- Pregnancy. If an officer wants to separate no later than the expected date of confinement, she must provide a physician's statement confirming pregnancy and the EDC. Officers whose pregnancies end by other than live birth receive their applications back from their commander if HQ AFPC has not already processed the application.
- Selective service system. Guard or reserve officers assigned to the selective service system may request release from extended active duty on their requested DOS date.
- Insufficient PCS qualifications on return from overseas. Reserve officers with six or more years of active service may request earlier DOS when they have less than thirty-two calendar days remaining to their current DOS on arrival at CONUS base. Make these requests by memorandum (see AFI 36-3207, *Separating Commissioned Officers*, Attachment 5).
- Miscellaneous reasons. Officers may apply based on unique or unusual reasons not covered in the AFI. They may request a DOS that falls no earlier than six months from the date of application and if HQ AFPC determines the separation is in the best interests of the Air Force, then it normally approves the requested DOS.

24

Retirement

Retirement from the Air Force, in most cases, ends a successful military career and opens the way to a new career or to years of modest leisure. There are, however, other mandatory or voluntary versions of retirement. Some such retirements are the result of dire physical disability. The dangers inherent in many Air Force jobs make disability retirements not uncommon.

The Air Force Personnel Center at Randolph Air Force Base maintains a web page at www.retirees.af.mil that provides information on retiree issues. The website allows access to a variety of resources. *News for USAF Retired Personnel (Afterburner)*, the official Air Force retiree newsletter, is published periodically and mailed to every retiree who receives retired pay. It is also available online at the Randolph website listed above. *Afterburner* is an excellent way to keep current on legislative and other changes that affect retired members and their dependents and survivors. In addition, you can access free publications like the *2013 U.S. Military Retired Handbook* at www.military handbooks.com. This handbook is a very good complement to AFI 36-3203, *Service Retirements.*

TRANSITION TO RETIRED STATUS

Retirement should be a time of pleasure and opportunity—a time to relax or a point of departure for a second career. Success in either depends on how well you prepare yourself for this major transition in your life and your family's life. The following actions can help you enjoy your retirement more.

Have a positive attitude. A positive attitude is a good starting point for a successful retirement. People often think about retirement as the end of a career, the beginning of a lifestyle of leisure, or a transition from the past to the future. Those who think of retirement as an end to a career may find their retirement rather difficult, especially if they try to hang on to the past. Those who think of retirement only as a time for relaxation may fail to prepare to face future challenges. A more realistic outlook toward retirement is to think of it as a time of transition and a time of moving out of past responsibilities and relationships into new ones. In other words, it is a time of change during which you let go of some of the past, take part of the past with you, and develop new strategies for the future. The way you go about making this transition will influence how successful your retirement will be. Remember that it is natural to experience anxiety due to the uncertainties of retirement. That said, service-members often change directions during their military careers, and they can view retirement as just one more change of direction.

Prepare early. You began preparing for retirement as a young officer when you started your career and realized that at some time in the future you would retire. Over your years of active service, you should take a number of steps to prepare for retirement. The more preparation you make, the easier your retire-ment transition will be. Every career officer needs to have a retirement plan, one that factors in financial, health, and family considerations.

Develop a variety of interests. People who put 100 percent into their work may experience a highly successful career but a devastating retirement. On the other hand, those who develop a variety of skills and interests while remaining dedicated to their work will experience an easier transition into retirement. Think about your interests and start developing friendships and activities you want to have and to participate in during your retirement.

Make a realistic appraisal of your accomplishments. Retirement is often a time when people think about what they wanted to accomplish during their career and compare their desired accomplishments with what they have actu-ally achieved. Be realistic about what you have accomplished and focus on your achievements. You cannot go back and change the past. Now is the time to think about the future and set realistic goals for your retirement.

Structure your activities. People who retire with the idea that they will do what they want when they feel like it often become dissatisfied. On the other hand, those who have made some decisions about what activities they want to do, and have scheduled specific times for them, usually experience more satis-faction in retirement. Many people follow through with their past work skills by working part-time, consulting, or doing volunteer work. Others use different skills they have developed, and many people go back to school. Create a new routine for yourself.

Live within your means. Many people look forward to a comfortable retirement only to find that their retirement pay does not go as far as they thought it would. Those who saved, invested, and insured themselves for their retirement will be more comfortable financially than those who did not. Regardless of your financial resources, it is important that you adapt to a lifestyle that is within your means.

Be prepared for different levels of responsibilities. The levels of responsi-bility people experience after retirement are often much different than during their military career. A new career may bring new and rewarding responsibili-ties; however, being the world's best grandparent has rewards all unto itself.

Understand the impact of your retirement on your family. Your family and friends will also need to adjust to your retirement. The changes associated with retirement will have an impact on each of them. Discussing these changes with them can ease potential problems in your relationship with them.

Develop new support systems. Next to your family, your work group may be the strongest emotional support system you have experienced. The loss of your work group can be emotionally painful and leave a void in your life. Getting involved in new groups, such as clubs, sports, or church, can be very important for a successful retirement transition.

Prepare for a move. If you move to a new geographical location in conjunction with your retirement, there will be many more factors to adjust to than if you remain in the same community. There are often a number of community resources that can ease your move and help you and your family get established in the new location. Find out about these resources, and get involved in your new community. Plan your retirement move using many of the same tools used in your military changes in duty station.

Your choices and actions will directly influence the success of your transition into retirement. By preparing early and developing a sound retirement plan, you can significantly reduce the problems many retirees face.

VOLUNTARY RETIREMENT

After Twenty Years' Service (or More). Twenty years' service is still the basis for a full military career and retirement. After twenty years on active duty, officers are eligible for retirement pay. Retirement plans tie retired pay to basic pay, not including bonuses and allowances. Whereas active-duty officers begin drawing retired pay immediately after separation, eligible reservists must wait until their sixtieth birthdays to begin drawing retired pay.

In efforts to reduce the burden of military retired pay on the federal treasury, Congress changed the retired pay compensation formulas twice in the 1980s. The government can again change the formula in the future. Currently, there are three formulas for computing twenty-year retired pay. Which formula is used depends on the date an officer entered military service, usually the day an officer reported for active duty. Reservists, military academy cadets, and ROTC cadets, however, are eligible for the retirement system in effect when they entered the reserves, a federal military academy, or a delayed-entry program, such as ROTC.

Excluding the requirements for retirements based on physical disabilities, the three formulas now in effect are as follows:

- **Final Pay.** For retirees who entered military service before 8 September 1980, the plan bases monthly checks on retired grade and number of years served on active duty. Beginning at half basic pay after twenty years' service, this plan adds 2.5 percent of basic pay for each additional year served. For example, after thirty years' active service, the retiree draws 75 percent of basic pay. Annual cost-of-living adjustments (COLAs), based on the Consumer Price Index (CPI), attempt to compensate for inflation.

- **High-3 Year Average.** For those who entered military service after 7 September 1980 and before 1 August 1986, the "high three" formula applies. This plan bases retired pay on the average basic pay for the thirty-six months with the highest earnings, rather than on basic pay at retirement. The High-3 plan multiplies the yearly average by 2.5 percent for each year on active duty to determine retired pay. Officers retiring under this formula will receive less retirement compensation than those who entered military service before 8 September 1980. These retirees are also entitled to annual COLAs inflation adjusted based on the CPI.

- **CSB/REDUX.** Instead of retiring under High-3, servicemembers may choose to receive a $30,000 Career Status Bonus at fifteen years of service in exchange for agreeing to serve a minimum of another five years and then retiring under the less generous REDUX plan. This plan calculates each of the first twenty years of service using a 2-percent-per-year multiplier. Each year after twenty is worth 3.5 percent. Thus, the plan at the thirty-year career point results in the same 75 percent multiplier; however, it applies the multiplier to the average of the member's highest thirty-six months of basic pay. The REDUX plan computes COLAs using CPI *minus* 1 percent based upon the High-3 basic pay. The plan recomputes retired pay at age sixty-two so that REDUX and High-3 retirement salaries are equal; however, REDUX COLAs for later years will continue to be CPI minus 1 percent.

RETIREMENT FOR PHYSICAL DISABILITY

The Career Compensation Act established a very important departure in remuneration following separation from active service as a result of physical disability. No member can be retired for physical disability if the disability is less than 30 percent, unless the member has at least twenty years' service.

The first stage in any proceeding for separation for physical reasons is a finding by the service that members, by reason of a disability, are not qualified to perform their duties. If the service keeps members on duty, there are, of course, no separation proceedings. However, if a finding is made that the members *cannot* be retained in service, the proceedings enter a second stage. If the disability resulted from "intentional misconduct" or "willful neglect" or was incurred during unauthorized absence, the government gives the members nothing, but merely separates them.

If the disability was *not* due to misconduct or neglect, the next question is: Is the disability 30 percent or more under the VA standard rating? If the disability is less than 30 percent, and the member has less than twenty years' service, no retirement is given. Instead, the servicemember is given *severance pay*, which is two months' basic active-duty pay for each year of active service, to a maximum of two full years' active pay.

Types of Disability Retirement. There are two types of disability retirement lists: the Temporary or Permanent Disability Retirement Lists (TDRL or PDRL). A Physical Evaluation Board (PEB) will determine if a disability qualifies for retirement (or separation for those with fewer than twenty years of service). The Air Force then determines which list, TDRL or PDRL, is appropriate for the individual. Persons who have completed twenty years' active service are entitled to retirement even if their disability is less than 30 percent. However, through this process, if the Air Force determines the disability is service related; if the disability rated 30 percent or higher, it will authorize retirement versus separation.

If you are facing retirement for disability, you should study all methods of compensation—including VA compensation—weighing the income-tax factor, if any, before making a decision. The Defense Accounting and Finance Service (DFAS) website at www.dfas.mil/retiredmilitary.html details the various disability plans. You can find the Air Force AFIs specific to Air Force requirements and processes for retirement at www.e-publishing.af.mil.

Disability Claims. Regardless of whether or not a member is retired for disability from the Air Force, he or she should file a claim with the VA at the time of retirement through the military personnel facility. As part of the disability determination, the VA will determine if you qualify for Combat-Related Special Compensation (CRSC) or Concurrent Retirement and Disability Pay (CRDP). Congress created these two programs to allow disabled military retirees to receive additional compensation beyond retirement pay related to service-related disability.

The CRSC program compensates veterans with combat-related disabilities and is a tax-free entitlement paid monthly and in addition to retirement pay. To qualify, one must be retired, have a VA disability rating of at least 10 percent, accept this pay in lieu of other VA pay, and have specifically applied for it through the Air Force. This program accounts for disabilities for injuries, including those from armed conflict, hazardous duty, from an instrumentality of war, or from simulated war. You can ask questions regarding your eligibility by calling 800-321-1080, or by visiting your servicing MPF. Keep in mind, *you must apply* for CRSC.

The Congressional provisions for CRDP allow you to receive both disability pay and retirement pay without the former decrementing the latter, as was the case prior to 2004. It is important to note that you do not need to apply for CRDP, as the Air Force will automatically enroll you in this VA program as part of your retirement process. Keep in mind that the VA pays this entitlement separately from your Air Force retirement pay.

VA pays disability compensation based upon the percent of disability. These payment rates are subject to change annually according to the law providing cost-of-living adjustments. The DFAS website has a disability retirement calculator to help you know what your payment should be for your disability. In addition, depending on your disability level, your dependents may be entitled to additional allowances.

STATUTORY/MANDATORY AGE RETIREMENT

Unless you retire or separate earlier, commissioned officers will be retired on the first day of the month following the month in which they become sixty-two years of age. The SECDEF or president may defer the retirement of an officer serving in a position that carries a grade above major general, up to age sixty-eight.

Unless provided otherwise by some provision of law, mandatory retirement for lieutenant colonels is twenty-eight years of active service; colonels and brigadier generals, thirty years; major generals, thirty-five years; after thirty-eight years of active commissioned service for O9s; and after forty years of active commissioned service for O10s.

For health care professional officers and chaplains, the secretary of the Air Force may defer retirement until the age of sixty-eight. For permanent professors at service schools, the mandatory retirement age is sixty-four.

RETIRED GRADE, RANK, AND STATUS

Commissioned officers shall be retired in the highest grade in which they satisfactorily served on active duty for not less than six months, as determined by the secretary of the Air Force. To be eligible for voluntary retirement in a grade above major or below lieutenant general, commissioned officers must have served on active duty in that grade for not less than three years.

Officers whose length of service in the highest grade held while on active duty does not meet the service-in-grade requirements specified will be retired in the next lower grade in which they served on active duty satisfactorily for not less than six months. Upon retirement, officers who are serving in or have served in a position of importance and responsibility designated by the president to carry the grade of general or lieutenant general, at the discretion of the president and with the consent of the Senate, may be retired in the highest grade held by them while serving on active duty. DOD or the Air Force grant exceptions to service-in-grade requirements to facilitate force-shaping necessities, such as after the end of the Cold War and to reduce force strength through Palace Chase and the Limited Active Duty Service Commitment Waiver Program.

Increases of Retired Pay. The government increases retired pay based on the Consumer Price Index. Congress, however, has altered the amount of increase in the past.

MISCELLANEOUS

Medical Care. For retiree medical benefits, see chapter 22.

Government Employment of Officers after Retirement. In 1964, Congress authorized the federal government to employ retired regular officers on a basis of compensation, making it feasible for the retired regular officer to accept such employment. It is now possible for the retired regular officer to receive the full pay of a civilian government job, plus the officer's full retirement pay. By law (5 U.S.C. 3326), DOD cannot hire retired members for at least six months after their retirement. However, since 2001, a presidential national emergency act allows DOD to hire retirees once they are retired or on terminal leave. The president extended this act on 11 September 2012.

Residence and Travel Abroad. Permission to travel and reside in a foreign country is not required of retired Air Force personnel, except for personnel who occupied "sensitive" positions or acquired sensitive information before
retirement. Officers restricted because of access to sensitive counterintelligence
information should correspond with Headquarters, Air Force Office of Special
Investigations. Retirees must observe the travel documents requirements to
leave the U.S. (passport) or for visited countries (visa or entry/exit permits) just
as any citizen traveler would need to do.

Officers' requests for retirement at foreign service stations, if otherwise
appropriate, normally will be approved by the Department of the Air Force.
Such approval will not be given if it becomes necessary to return them to the
United States for hospitalization or other purposes of the government, and they
will not be returned to an overseas station solely for the purpose of retirement
there. The officers may, however, obtain authority for foreign residence or
travel, after retirement, as indicated above.

Travel to Home. Officers of the Regular Air Force are presumed to have
no established home. They may select and proceed to a home at government
expense, so far as authorized, at any place they intend to establish a bona fide
home at any time within one year after retirement. You can apply for exten-
sions to the one year time, if desired.

Travel of Retired Personnel by Military Transport. An important privilege for specified retired personnel is space-available (space-A) transportation.
Space-A means space unassigned after all space requirement travel assignments have been made and space that would otherwise be unused if not authorized and assigned to the use indicated. There is a nominal charge to cover
meals and service.

Applications for space-available travel are to be submitted to the appropriate terminal authority, which acts on them on a first-come, first-served basis.
Retirees have the lowest priority for space-A seats. Return transportation cannot be ensured; return by commercial transportation may be necessary at personal expense.

Retired Officer Status. An Air Force officer placed on the retired list is
still an officer of the United States.

Change in Status after Retirement. In the absence of fraud, the retirement of an officer under a particular statute exhausts the power of the president
and the secretary of the Air Force, and the record of executive action cannot be
revoked or modified so as to make retirement relate to another statute, even
though the case were one to which more than one statute properly applied at
the time retirement was accomplished. Further, the statutes relating to retirement apply only to officers on the active list, and there is no authority for the
restoration of a retired officer to the active list for the purpose of being again
retired.

RETIREMENT OF AIR NATIONAL GUARD AND AIR FORCE RESERVE OFFICERS

Retirement for Physical Disability. The laws governing retirement for physical disability apply equally to all officers on active military duty whether of the Regular Air Force or the Air Reserve Forces.

Retirement for Age and Length of Service. Chapter 67, Title 10, U.S. Code, establishes retirement opportunities for AF Reserve and Air National Guard officers who attain age sixty and who satisfy stated requirements of service or service credits described in the law as "points." Officers of the Air National Guard and AF Reserve should have their own records of service carefully checked and verified establishing their retirement credits.

Retirement pay does not reduce other retirement benefits, such as that which may accrue from Social Security legislation or civil service retirement pay, nor should it serve to reduce retirement pay earned by participating in retirement programs of corporations or other employers.

MILITARY OFFICERS ASSOCIATION OF AMERICA

The purpose of the Military Officers Association of America (MOAA) is to aid all personnel of the various services and components. This nonprofit veterans association is dedicated to maintaining a strong national defense and to preserving the earned entitlements of members of the uniformed services, their families, and survivors. Regardless of years in service, all military officers should belong to this association. Membership is open to active-duty, National Guard, Reserve, retired, and former commissioned officers and warrant officers of the following uniformed services: Army, Marine Corps, Navy, Air Force, Coast Guard, Public Health Service, and National Oceanic and Atmospheric Administration. Auxiliary memberships also are available for surviving spouses of deceased officers. You can contact MOAA at, 201 N. Washington Street, Alexandria, VA 22314-2539; 800-234-6622; or www.moaa.org.

25

Benefits after Separation

During military service, all servicemembers accrue certain rights and privileges under various public laws that will be available to them after discharge, release from active duty, or retirement. The administration and payment of these benefits are the responsibility of the Department of Veterans Affairs (VA). Entitlement to benefits varies with length, time, and type of service, as well as disabilities incurred in service. In all cases in which veterans desire to apply for one or more of these statutory benefits, they should obtain all necessary information from the nearest VA office or consulting the Department of Veterans Affairs website at www.va.gov.

Federal Benefits for Veterans and Dependents, a publication of the VA Office of Public Affairs, is another excellent source of information. It is available through www.va.gov (you can download a free copy at www.va.gov/opa/publications/benefits_book.asp). The physical handbook may be ordered by contacting the Superintendent of Documents, U.S. Government Printing Office, via the Internet at bookstore.gpo.gov; by phone, toll free at 866-512-1800, or in Washington, D.C., at 202-512-1800. You can fax your order to 202-512-2104, or mail your request to: Stop IDCC, Washington, DC 20401. The GPO uses the International Standard Book Number (ISBN) 978-0-16-091835-3 for this publication (the 0-16 indicates a GPO product).The remainder of this chapter is extracted from this handbook.

Eligibility for most VA benefits is based on discharge from active military service under other-than-dishonorable conditions for a minimum period specified by law. Honorable and general discharges qualify a veteran for most VA benefits; dishonorable and some bad-conduct discharges issued by general courts-martial bar VA benefits. Veterans with similar service are entitled to the same VA benefits. Certain VA benefits and medical care require wartime service. All veterans must safeguard their service discharge forms; they document service dates and type of discharge and are necessary for filing claims.

HOME LOAN GUARANTIES
VA guarantees loans made to veterans and unremarried surviving spouses (see the handbook for specific conditions for surviving spouses) for the purchase or

refinancing of homes, condominiums, and manufactured homes. VA guarantees part of the total loan, permitting the veteran to obtain a mortgage with a competitive interest rate, even without a down payment if the lender agrees. VA requires a down payment for the purchase of a manufactured home. VA also requires a down payment for a home or condominium if the purchase price exceeds the reasonable value of the property or the loan has a graduated payment feature. With a VA guaranty, the lender is protected against loss up to the amount of the guaranty if the borrower fails to repay the loan. A VA loan guaranty can be used to do the following:

- Buy or build a home.
- Buy a residential condominium unit.
- Repair, alter, or improve a residence owned by the veteran and occupied as a home.
- Refinance an existing home loan.
- Buy a manufactured home and/or lot.
- Install a solar heating or cooling system or other energy efficient improvements.

Eligibility. Applicants must have a good credit rating, have an income sufficient to support mortgage payments, a valid certificate of eligibility (COE), and agree to live on the property. To obtain a VA COE, complete VA Form 26-1880, *Request for Determination of Eligibility and Available Loan Guaranty Entitlement* (available at www.vba.va.gov/pubs/forms/vba-26-1880-are.pdf), and submit it along with required supporting documents to the nearest VA regional office. For additional information or to obtain VA loan guaranty forms, visit www.benefits.va.gov/homeloans.

DISABILITY COMPENSATION

Monetary benefits, called disability compensation, are paid to veterans who are disabled by injury or disease incurred or aggravated during active military service. Monetary benefits are related to the residual effects of the injury or disease. Congress sets the amounts of the benefits, which are not subject to federal or state income tax. Refer to chapter 24 for the discussion on disability retirements under CRDP and CRSC conditions.

The payment of military retirement pay, disability severance pay, and separation incentive payments known as SSB and VSI (Special Separation Benefits and Voluntary Separation Incentives) may affect the amount of VA compensation payable. Since 2004, concurrent receipt of retired pay and disability pay for disabled retirees with 50 percent or more disability is allowed. Compensation for the severely disabled is payable for those with 60 percent or higher disability. For additional details on types of disability claims and how to apply, go to benefits.va.gov/benefits.

Allowances for Family Members. Veterans whose service-connected disabilities are rated at 30 percent or more are entitled to additional allowances for family members.

EDUCATION AND TRAINING

Eligibility and benefits of the various types of the GI Bill and the Veterans' Educational Assistance Program are complicated. For the most up-to-date information, consult the handbook and the "Education and Training" page at www.benefits.va.gov/gibill. The VA continually updates the webpage, so look here for the latest alerts and information.

Montgomery GI Bill—Active Duty (MGIB-AD).

Eligibility. The MGIB-AD is a program of education benefits for individuals who entered active duty for the first time after 30 June 1985. It is available for both enlisted members and for officers who received their commissions through Officer Training School or AFROTC (but did not receive ROTC scholarships). "Active duty" for benefit purposes also includes full-time National Guard duty performed after 29 November 1989. An honorable discharge is required. To receive the maximum benefit over a period of up to thirty-six months for a full-time student, the participant must have served continuously on active duty for three years.

An individual also may qualify for the full benefit by initially serving two continuous years on active duty, followed by four years of Selected Reserve service, beginning within one year of release from active duty. Individuals who initially serve a continuous period of at least three years of active duty, even though they were initially obligated to serve less, will be paid the maximum benefit.

For the most part, benefits end ten years from the date of the veteran's last discharge or release from active duty. VA can extend this ten-year period under certain circumstances. You can confirm eligibility at the VA website at www.benefits.va.gov/gibill/, or contact the VA's education and training telephone service at 1-888-442-4551.

Participation Requirements. Participation in the Montgomery GI Bill requires that servicemembers have their military pay reduced by $100 a month for the first twelve months of active duty or pay a $1,200 lump-sum contribution. This money is not refundable. If an individual decides not to participate in this program, this decision cannot be changed at a later date, except in special circumstances. An exception is made for servicemembers who are involuntarily separated from active duty with an honorable discharge after 2 February 1991. A second exception is made for those who voluntarily separate from active duty after 4 December 1991. If the servicemember decides to participate before separation, military pay will be reduced before separation, and education or training may take place following separation.

Vietnam Era GI Bill and VEAP Conversions. Also eligible for Montgomery GI Bill benefits are those individuals who had remaining entitlement under the Vietnam Era GI Bill on 31 December 1989, served on active duty without a break sometime between 19 October 1984 and 1 July 1985, and continued to serve on active duty to 1 July 1988, or to 1 July 1987, followed by four years in the Selected Reserve. Individuals who were eligible for the post–Vietnam Era Veterans' Educational Assistance Program (VEAP) must elect to receive benefits under the Montgomery GI Bill and apply for a refund of the contributions to VEAP.

Discharges and Separations. For the Montgomery GI Bill program, the discharge must be honorable. Discharges designated "under honorable conditions" and "general" do not establish eligibility. A discharge for one of the following reasons may result in a reduction of the required length of active duty: convenience of the government, disability, hardship, a medical condition existing before service, force reductions, or physical or mental conditions that prevent satisfactory performance of duty.

Education and Training Available. The following are available under the Montgomery GI Bill:

- Courses at colleges and universities leading to associate, bachelor, or graduate degrees, and accredited independent study. Cooperative training programs are also available to individuals not on active duty. Certain overseas courses may qualify for VA assistance.
- Courses leading to a certificate or diploma from business, technical, or vocational schools, including preparatory courses for tests required for admission to schools of higher learning or graduate school.
- Apprenticeships or on-the-job training programs for individuals not on active duty.
- Correspondence courses, under certain conditions.
- Flight training. Before beginning training, the veteran must have a private pilot license and meet the physical requirements for a commercial license. Benefits also may be received for solo flying hours up to the minimum required by the FAA for the rating or certification being pursued.
- Tutorial assistance benefits if individual is enrolled in school half-time or more. Remedial, deficiency, and refresher training also may be available.

Montgomery GI Bill—Selected Reserve (MGIB-SR).

Eligibility. The Montgomery GI Bill—Selected Reserve is an educational assistance program enacted by Congress to attract high-quality people into the reserve branch of the armed forces. This program is for members of the Selected Reserves of the four services, plus the Coast Guard and the Army and Air Force National Guard. The MGIB-SR provides financial assistance to eligible persons for a wide variety of education and training programs. It does not require service in the active Armed Forces in order to qualify for eligibility. To be eligible for the program, a reservist must meet the following criteria:

- Have a six-year obligation to serve in the Selected Reserve signed after 30 June 1985 or, if an officer, agree to serve six years in addition to the original obligation.
- Complete Initial Active Duty for Training (IADT).
- Meet the requirements for a high school diploma or equivalency certificate before completing IADT.
- Remain in good standing in a Selected Reserve unit.

There are eligibility caveats to U.S. Air Force Academy graduates and those receiving ROTC scholarships. Your best option is to confirm eligibility at the VA website at www.benefits.va.gov/gibill/, or contact the VA's education and training telephone service at 1-888-442-4551.

Education and Training Available. Reservists may seek an undergraduate degree or graduate training or take technical courses at colleges and universities. Those who have a six-year commitment beginning after 30 September 1990, may take courses leading to a certificate or diploma from business, technical, or vocational schools; cooperative training; apprenticeship or on-the-job training; correspondence courses; independent study programs; flight training; tutorial assistance; and remedial, refresher, and deficiency training.

Work-Study. Reservists training at the three-quarter or full-time rate are eligible for the work-study program. Terms of participation are the same as under the MGIB-AD program, except that reservists can also work at a military facility if the work is related to Selected Reserve education.

Period of Eligibility. If a reservist stays in the Selected Reserve, benefits end ten years from the date the reservist became eligible for the program. VA can extend this ten-year period under certain circumstances.

BENEFITS FOR SURVIVORS

Consult AFPAM 36-3028, *Benefits and Entitlements for Family Members of Retired Air Force Deceased*, which is available at http://www.e-publishing. af.mil, for the most up-to-date information.

Dependency and Indemnity Compensation. The VA pays Dependency and Indemnity Compensation (DIC) to surviving spouses, unmarried children under eighteen, children with disabilities, children between eighteen and twenty-three if attending a VA-approved school, and low-income parents of service retirees who died from a disease or injury incurred or aggravated while on active duty or active duty for training; an injury incurred or aggravated in line of duty while on inactive-duty training; or a disability compensable by VA. Death cannot be the result of willful misconduct.

In addition, the VA pays DIC compensation to surviving spouses, unmarried children under eighteen, helpless children, and those between eighteen and twenty-three if attending a VA-approved school, of veterans who were totally service-connected disabled at time of death but whose death was not the result of the service-connected disability, if the veteran was continuously rated totally disabled for a period of ten or more years immediately preceding death or the veteran was so rated for a period of not less than five years from the date of discharge from military service. Payments under this provision are subject to offset by the amount received from judicial proceedings brought on account of the veteran's death. When death occurred after service, the veteran's discharge must have been under conditions other than dishonorable.

Remarriage makes a spouse ineligible for survivor benefits; however, the VA may restore payment if the remarriage ends in death, divorce, or annulment. The VA casualty assistance representative or the nearest VA office will explain survivor benefits to you and help you complete the necessary claim forms.

Nonservice-Connected Death Pension. If the VA regional office determines a surviving spouse is not eligible for DIC, the survivor may be eligible to apply for a nonservice-connected death pension. Surviving spouses of deceased members with wartime service and unmarried children under age eighteen, or age twenty-three if attending a VA-approved school, may be eligible for this pension if they meet income limitations prescribed by law. Qualifying children who become incapable of self-support due to disability prior to age eighteen may be eligible for a pension as long as the condition exists, unless the child marries or the child's income exceeds the prescribed income threshold. The rate of pension depends on the amount of income the surviving spouse or child receives from other sources. A pension is not payable to those whose estates are so large that it is reasonable to assume the estate will maintain them financially. Eligible survivors should make application through the local VA office. The VA will determine the survivor's eligibility.

Educational Benefits. The Dependents' Educational Assistance Program provides educational opportunities for the survivors of a retiree who dies from a service-related injury or illness, including the surviving spouse, children between the ages of eighteen and twenty-six, and children under eighteen, under certain conditions. Eligible survivors may receive up to forty-five months of schooling (or the equivalent if enrolled part-time) in VA-approved schools and colleges. In addition to the Dependents' Educational Assistance Program, various programs are available to help children reach their educational goals. To obtain additional information, contact the nearest VA regional office. In addition, many states, universities, and other groups sponsor scholarship programs for the children of deceased servicemembers, particularly those with wartime service. Survivors should contact their high school guidance counselor and check the local library for additional information.

Educational Loans. Loans are available to spouses who qualify for educational assistance benefits. Spouses who have passed their ten-year period of eligibility may be eligible for an educational loan. During the first two years after the end of their eligibility period, they may borrow up to $2,500 per academic year to continue a full-time course leading to a college degree or to a professional or vocational objective that requires at least six months to complete. VA may waive the six-month requirement. The loan program is based on financial need.

Home Loan Guaranties. A GI loan guaranty to acquire a home may be available to an unremarried spouse of a veteran or servicemember who died as a result of service-connected disabilities, or to a spouse of a servicemember who has been officially listed as missing in action or as a prisoner of war for more than ninety days. Spouses of those listed as a POW or MIA are limited to one loan.

Montgomery GI Bill (Active Duty) Death Benefit. VA will pay a special Montgomery GI Bill death benefit to a designated survivor if the servicemember's death is in service or is service-connected and within one year after discharge or release. The deceased must have been a participant in the Montgomery GI Bill program. The death benefit also will be paid if the servicemember would have been eligible to participate but for the high school diploma requirement and the length-of-service requirement. The amount paid will be equal to the participant's actual military pay reduction less any education benefits paid.

INSURANCE

Service-Disabled Veterans' Insurance (S-DVI). This program was first issued in April 1951 and continues to be issued today. It is restricted to veterans who have service-connected disabilities at the time they retire or separate from active duty. The insurance is issued to these individuals at standard premium rates regardless of the severity of the service-connected disability. The insurance is offered in many plans, including unlimited five-year term with a maximum face value of $10,000.

Servicemembers' Group Life Insurance (SGLI). Servicemembers currently on active duty and most categories of reservists are covered by Servicemembers' Group Life Insurance. SGLI is a group insurance purchased from a commercial company and administered by the Office of Servicemembers' Group Life Insurance. The program is supervised by the VA. The insurance is term insurance and has no cash value, with the maximum amount of coverage fixed at $400,000. The government computes the SGLI monthly premium at 6.5 cents per $1,000 of coverage and automatically deducts the premium from your base pay. The premium includes an additional $1.00 per month for Traumatic Injury Protection coverage (TSGLI). There is also a 120-day period of free coverage following separation from active duty. This can be extended to one year if disabled at retirement.

Veterans' Group Life Insurance (VGLI). Upon leaving active duty, and after the period of free SGLI, members are eligible to obtain a like amount of SGLI coverage in a five-year term plan known as Veterans' Group Life Insurance. The VA makes VGLI coverage available in increments of $10,000 up to a maximum of $400,000; however, your initial VGLI coverage amount cannot exceed your SGLI coverage amount in force at the time of separation/retirement from service. At the end of the five-year term, individuals may renew or convert their coverage to any permanent plan of insurance with any of a number of participating commercial insurance companies at standard premium rates regardless of health or military status.

ADDITIONAL VA PROGRAMS

In addition to the benefits mentioned above, there are numerous other VA benefits and programs for veterans and their dependents. Other disability benefits include specially adapted homes and automobiles. There are a variety of pensions, few of which apply to officers or their dependents. There are also vocational rehabilitation and life insurance programs. Health-care benefits include hospital, nursing home, and domiciliary care; outpatient medical, pharmacy, and dental treatment; alcohol and drug dependence treatment; and services for the blind. And there are burial benefits, including national cemeteries, headstones, and flags.

Complete, current information on VA benefits and programs is available at benefits.va.gov/benefits/ and in the handbook *Federal Benefits for Veterans and Dependents*, as cited at the beginning of this chapter. Also consult *Veteran's Guide to Benefits* (Stackpole Books).

STATE BENEFITS

Some states offer benefits to veterans that are independent of federal VA benefits. These benefits differ from state to state. Often eligibility is dependent on the state being the place of residency or home of record at the time the officer entered military service. For information, consult your state veterans office.

PART VI

Personal Affairs

26

Legal Documents and Assistance

All officers of the U.S. Air Force may expect sudden changes of station or in their personal status. Personnel affected by such movements may anticipate months of separation from their families, during which time they may be unable to properly attend to their personal affairs and welfare.

Efficiency of job performance is directly related to servicemembers' peace of mind and mental stability. Servicemembers do not want to expose their families to distress, want, or insecurity. Consequently, officers should arrange their personal affairs adequately to protect and provide for their families and to prevent legal entanglement or embarrassment that could be caused by their absence.

The time to prepare for the sudden separation caused by military transfer is now, while personal matters are moving along in a routine manner, rather than during that turbulent and busy period immediately preceding departure upon a change of station or temporary duty. It is imperative that military personnel keep their personal affairs properly arranged to provide the maximum protection and security for their families, and ensure that their dependents have ample knowledge of and receive all rights and benefits to which they are entitled. Because individual preparations are determined by the needs of the individuals concerned, it is impossible to prescribe an exact set of preparations applicable to all Air Force officers. The status of some may require only simple adjustments, while others may require complicated and minutely detailed arrangements. To help officers properly arrange their personal affairs, this chapter sets forth in detail the varied subjects that Air Force personnel should consider to provide for the welfare, protection, and security of their families at all times.

The Air Force is acutely conscious of the importance to its members of sound guidance in providing assistance in the solution of personal problems. For this reason, each base has a personal affairs staff. Air Force officers who need advice on personal matters should go first to their personal affairs or legal office, state their problems candidly and completely, and ask for guidance. These offices will extend services willingly, authoritatively, and without cost.

ALLOTMENTS OF PAY AND DEDUCTIONS
All military personnel on active duty may authorize pay allotments to the following people and organizations:

- Individuals or banks for the support of dependents or to savings or checking accounts.
- Life insurance companies for the payment of premiums on life insurance.
- Federal savings and loan associations.
- Lending institutions holding loans insured by the Federal Housing Administration or the Housing and Home Finance Agency.
- Air Force Aid Society and American Red Cross for payment of loans made by these organizations to military personnel.

Officers may allot as much of their basic pay, monthly subsistence allowance, and quarters allowance as will leave sufficient balance equal to or greater than the amount of Social Security and income tax to be withheld according to current Internal Revenue Service regulations.

In exceptional cases, where persons in active service have not made adequate provision for the support of certain dependents, the secretary of the Air Force may act in their behalf to make allotments for the well-being and protection of their dependents. The person whose pay is charged may terminate such allotments.

FAMILY CARE PLAN

Single-parent servicemembers and dual-service parents are required to plan the financial, legal, and medical care for their families in the duty absence of the parents. Unit first sergeants help complete AF Form 357, Family Care Certification.

LEGAL ASSISTANCE PROGRAM

If members of the armed forces have problems of such a nature that the services of an attorney are desirable or necessary, they may go to the nearest base legal assistance office. The legal assistance office will counsel, advise, carry on necessary correspondence, negotiate, and draw up any legal papers necessary. Assistance includes separation and divorce agreements; child support, custody, and alimony payments; adoption; naturalization and citizenships; contracts for home purchase; and claims against the government. Legal assistance officers cannot represent servicemembers or their families in criminal matters under civilian law.

Wills of Air Force Personnel. All servicemembers should consider the making of a will. Whether a will is necessary or desirable and the form it should take depend on the desires and circumstances of the individual, and the laws of the place of execution and of the probable place of probate. State laws govern the execution and probate of wills, and the requirements in these respects vary considerably among states.

When people die without having made a will, the law says they have died "intestate." In such event, the estate is administered and distributed according to the statute of "descent and distribution" of the state of legal domicile or, in the case of real property, the state or states in which such real property is located. This law, in effect, creates a will for the individual, which is administered by an administrator appointed by the court, and the estate is distributed to the family members in the manner prescribed by the applicable state's statutes.

If the manner of distribution so prescribed by law does not meet your desires or needs, you can direct a distribution of your estate according to your wishes by making a will. Officers with children should seriously consider a revocable living trust, rather than a will.

Review of a Will. You should review an executed will from time to time, especially when such events as marriage, birth of children, divorce, or death of a named beneficiary occur. Changes of status such as these often affect the provisions of a will. A will is not effective until death and you can update a will or change it by a codicil at any time you feel it necessary to do so. Unless the will is extremely complicated, you should avoid the use of codicils. If you replace a will with a new one, then you should destroy all copies of the previous will. Whenever circumstances change, officers should review their wills with the aid of legal counsel.

Safekeeping. Military personnel, because of their transient status, should not keep the only original copy of the will in their possession. After completion, you should mail an original copy of the new will to the named executor and/or chief beneficiary for safekeeping or place it in some other secure place where it will be available in the event of death. It is advisable, for reference purposes, to keep a copy of the will, with a notation as to the location of the original will. The servicemember should advise the principal beneficiary of the location of the original will.

Emergency Will. If an emergency necessitates the immediate execution of a will, officers should write out their desires as to the distribution of possessions and have them attested by three competent witnesses. Such a handwritten will should state the full name, grade, Social Security number, and permanent address of the officer, the exact desires as to the distribution of possessions, the name and address of the person desired to be the executor, and the date, place, and circumstances of execution. You should replace such a will as soon as possible by one prepared with the aid of legal counsel.

Power of Attorney. A power of attorney is a legal instrument by which you may designate another person to act on your behalf in legal or personal matters. The one executing the power of attorney is usually referred to as the principal, and the one to whom the authority is given is usually referred to as the attorney-in-fact or simply as the attorney for the principal. You may grant the authority of a power of attorney to a member of your family or to any other person of legal age; however, when appointing your attorney-in-fact, you should select somebody in whom you have complete trust. The authority given in a power of attorney, unlike that of a will, becomes invalid upon the death of the principal.

You can make the power of attorney very general and unlimited in scope, or restricted to certain specific functions, depending on the needs and desires of the principal. A power of attorney may or may not be honored, depending on its acceptance by the individual to whom it may be presented for a transaction in the principal's name. The law holds the principal responsible for the actions of an attorney-in-fact performed within the limits of the power of attorney; it is therefore advisable not to execute power of attorney until a specific need or use for it exists. As a rule, a restricted power of attorney will accomplish the specific needs of the individual.

Preparation and Legal Counsel. The requirements as to preparation of the form and content of a legally effective power of attorney vary considerably under the laws of the various states. For this reason, and to properly fulfill the needs and desires of the principal, each power of attorney should be individually prepared under the guidance of legal counsel with due regard to the laws of the state of execution and of the probable place of exercise of the powers granted. You should consult legal counsel for the preparation of a power of attorney when the need for such an instrument exists.

Estates. A person accumulates various types of possessions during a lifetime, which are referred to collectively as an estate. This estate may consist of real estate, which is land and any buildings on it; personal, which includes all items of personal property, such as clothes, household furnishings, automobiles, money, stocks, bonds, jewelry, and, in general, any property that is not real estate; or a combination of both real estate and personal property.

Importance of Joint Tenancy. Air Force personnel, in their arrangements of personal matters for the protection of their families, should consider the importance and advantages of arranging title to most of their property by joint tenancy. In this way, officers will enable the joint tenants to use and control the property during their lifetime, and in the event of their death, to obtain full title as the survivor without the property being subject to administration through the courts. Property owned in joint tenancy cannot be disposed of by a will if the joint tenants survive. Officers can more effectively meet their obligation to provide for the care, welfare, and comfort of their families in the event of prolonged absence or death through the establishment of title to property by joint tenancy than by a power of attorney and a will. The rights of control of property by the joint tenant are full and absolute when title is kept in joint tenancy, and upon the death of the officer, the property will pass automatically into full possession of the joint tenant without judicial proceedings. Personal property held in joint tenancy may, however, make it subject to tax because the Soldiers' and Sailors' Civil Relief Act does not protect dependents.

Sound appraisement on the part of the owner concerning the capabilities and integrity of the contemplated joint owner should be exercised, and, in general, it is not advisable to establish joint property title with a person of short acquaintance.

Except as limited by state statutes, the law grants titles by joint tenancy with right of survivorship for various types of property. Joint owners can hold deeds establishing ownership of real estate, and bills of sale for personal property, such as automobiles and household goods, in joint tenancy with right of survivorship. Joint owners can open bank accounts and purchase stocks and bonds with the right of survivorship.

The government can issue U.S. savings bonds to joint owners with right of survivorship if the purchaser so requests. In addition, the government can reissue a savings bond, previously issued to a single owner (without a designated beneficiary), to joint owners upon proper application to the Treasury Department. Bonds issued to a single owner with a designated beneficiary can be cashed only by the owner during the owner's lifetime, and on death of the owner do not become part of the estate but go directly to the named beneficiary. The Treasury cannot reissue such bonds without the consent of the beneficiary. A bond held in joint ownership can be cashed by either joint owner with or without the consent of the other joint tenant.

Legal Assistance. You should obtain legal advice before creating a joint tenancy title on property. Gift, inheritance, or other taxes may often affect the enactment of joint tenancy titles. Competent legal assistance can explain the advantages and disadvantages of holding the various kinds of property in joint tenancy and can also facilitate the proper establishment of such an estate with due regard to all applicable laws.

Safe-Deposit Boxes. Many banks maintain safe-deposit boxes and rent them for a yearly fee that varies with the size of the box. When available, a safe-deposit box in a conveniently located and reputable bank is usually the best place to keep valuable papers, such as stocks, bonds, deeds to property, house insurance policies, receipts, and a copy of one's will. The bank will seal the box on the renter's death; so do not keep the original will or life insurance policies in a safe-deposit box.

Automobiles. The certificate of title in the state of registration determines proper ownership of a vehicle, not the simple possession of the vehicle. If the title of the automobile is in the name of one person, the automobile, in the event of the death of the owner, would become part of the estate, subject to that person's will, if executed, or the laws of "descent and distribution" of the appropriate state. The actual determination as to disposition of the automobile, pending the result of probate, would rest with the state authorities. Subject to statutory limitations of the state of registration, a married couple may jointly hold title to an automobile. Under such title, in the event of death of one, the automobile would become the property of the survivor. This method is usually the most effective for providing for the use of and title to the automobile for the spouse in the case of prolonged absence or death of the officer. It has its disadvantages, however, in the statutory limitations mentioned above and in the fact that difficulties are sometimes encountered in effecting transfer of the automobile without the presence and signatures of both joint owners, and in the spouse's being subject to personal property taxes in some states.

Changing of Title. Because state laws govern the transfer of title to an automobile, officers should exercise extreme care to ensure all provisions of law relative to such transfer are met. If you want to transfer title to an automobile from yourself to your spouse and you jointly, you should check with the bureau of motor vehicles in the state in which the automobile is registered, requesting the exact procedure necessary to accomplish the transfer.

Importance of Insurance. In many cases, an automobile is the most valuable single item of property owned by a young officer. It is, therefore, essential to protect this property with adequate insurance. The insurance policy should cover the owner, spouse, and all other persons who may have occasion to drive the vehicle. Lack of adequate insurance protection may result in extreme financial, legal, and personal difficulties.

Most states have enacted compulsory insurance laws, and strict compliance with these laws is obligatory. Although a few states do not have compulsory insurance laws, it is foolish not to carry automobile insurance. Officers should not be deceived into a false state of security by possessing only the amount of insurance required by law. In some states, compulsory insurance provides only minimum protection rather than adequate insurance protection.

Soldiers' and Sailors' Civil Relief Act. The purpose of this act is to relieve members of the armed forces from worry over the inability to meet their civil obligations by providing adequate representation for the servicemember during an absence and postponement of certain civil proceedings and transactions until release from such military service. Nothing in the act relieves one from the actual payment of the debts or other obligations; however, if the servicemember is unable to pay premiums on commercial insurance policies, to pay taxes, or to perform other obligations with reference to right and claims to lands of the United States, certain relief may be afforded by this act. If there is legal action based on a servicemember's breach of obligation, the relief afforded under this act is within the discretion of the court and depends upon whether the ability of the servicemember to discharge the obligations or to prosecute the action or defense is materially affected because of military service.

Insurance. Article IV of this act may protect the payment of premiums on commercial life insurance.

Other Protections. In addition to the protection of commercial life insurance, the Soldiers' and Sailors' Civil Relief Act provides arrangements for adequate legal representation and stays of execution for servicemembers on the following legal matters:

- Eviction for nonpayment of rent.
- Court proceedings arising from mortgages, leases, liens, and other contractual obligations.

- Payment of taxes may be deferred in some cases. Officers are not required to pay local taxes in the state where they are stationed unless, by some act of the officers, they become legal residents, provided the officers maintain legal residence in another state and discharge their liability in that state.

Importance of Legal Assistance. This summary of the Soldiers' and Sailors' Civil Relief Act has mentioned only the major points contained in the act. It is very important that officers suddenly presented with a tax bill, or threatened with legal action of any kind while away from their state of domicile, immediately report the matter to their legal assistance officer. The legal team can then study the case and possibly avert court action through implementation of some of the points of the Soldiers' and Sailors' Civil Relief Act. Too often, people delay in notifying the legal assistance officer of their legal difficulties until the case has already reached the litigation stage, with the result that the legal assistance officer is unable to help. One cannot overemphasize the importance of prompt notification and use of base legal assistance facilities in any legal entanglement.

Joint Bank Accounts. A joint bank account is one in which two persons have full authority to perform the functions of depositing and withdrawing funds from the same account. Such an account may be either a savings account or a checking account and the legal system considers them the joint property of the persons concerned. It is possible in most states to maintain joint accounts, and most banks have a specially prepared contract form setting out the legal status of such accounts in accordance with the state laws that govern the operations of the bank. Such a contract and the accompanying passbook usually contain a phrase somewhat as follows: "John Doe and Mary Doe, jointly or either, with rights of survivorship and not as tenants in common."

The chief advantage of a joint account is that the funds are readily available to either or both of the parties at any time. This situation is especially important to Air Force personnel because by maintaining their accounts in such a status, they enable their spouses to obtain the funds even though the servicemember is absent. If officers carry bank accounts in their names only, the legal system could deprive their spouses of the use of the money at a time when a spouse most urgently needs it. Another great advantage is that in the event of death of one of the parties, the survivor automatically becomes sole owner of the money in the account, usually without having a probate court freezing the account while the will of the deceased goes through the probate process. Thus, the spouse or other family members will have the money available to them when it is needed most.

Allotments to Joint Bank Accounts. You must credit to one person any allotments to a bank for deposit in a savings or checking account. It is permissible, however, to make an allotment to a bank even though the one to whom the allotment is credited is a party in a joint account. In addition, you must make proper arrangements for acceptance and depositing of the allotment with the desired financial institution before initiation of such an allotment.

Credit Unions. The Air Force assists the establishment of credit union facilities on Air Force installations as cooperative organizations to encourage systematic savings and create a source of credit for Air Force personnel and their families. Typically, you will find a credit union on any good-sized base or within the local community.

PERSONAL AFFAIRS RECORD

It is very important that you keep an up-to-date record of your personal affairs and property. Both you and your family will probably have many occasions to refer to such a record during your military service. You will find a property record of great importance when filing for possible damages that can occur during a permanent change of duty station.

Fill in your record carefully and completely and then make as many copies of your record as you will need for your family or for other persons whom you wish to trust with such information. Be sure you consider each item and make the record as complete and accurate as possible.

Remember to keep your records up-to-date, as changes or additions occur, by amending the original record or preparing a completely new record, and send copies to whomever you gave copies of the original record.

Start now to get the necessary information and to prepare your record, and do not stop until it is complete.

FAMILY SUPPORT CENTER PROGRAMS

At each Air Force base, an organization exists to aid Air Force personnel and their families in solving personal problems. Air Force members know this operation as the Family Support Center, which is part of a DOD-focused support network. The Armed Forces Family Support Center home page can be accessed at www.militaryonesource.mil and at www.afcrossroads.com. The Family Support Center's One Source help line can be reached at 800-342-9647 (877-888-0727 for Spanish). This program provides assistance to military families in the following areas:

- Information/referral center, where airmen or officers can get information or specialized assistance.
- Relocation assistance, for help when moving to another base.
- Support during family separations, mobilization, and deployment.
- Personal financial management programs, including Air Force Aid.
- Spouse employment programs, which offer information about job opportunities and programs on how to develop job-hunting skills.
- Heart Link program, an Air Force–wide standardized spouse orientation, is a one-day class held quarterly to acclimatize military spouses with Air Force life. Its target group is military spouses with five years or less of military affiliation.
- Family life education programs, such as on parenting, stress management, building self-esteem.
- Special-needs programs, such as single parents' groups.

- Family skills, which offer programs on communication and enhancing a family's quality of life.
- Private and professional assistance for personal crisis issues, such as marital, child-related, and so forth.
- Transition assistance and relocation assistance for those separating from the Air Force.

AIR FORCE AID SOCIETY

Mission. The Air Force Aid Society (AFAS) is the emergency relief organization for the U.S. Air Force. Its mission is to support the mission of the Air Force by reducing financial distress of Air Force personnel and their dependents. The AFAS augments the relief available to the servicemember through the American Red Cross; however, AFAS does not compete with or replace the work of the Red Cross because congressional charter makes the Red Cross the primary relief organization for the armed forces.

Eligibility. The following classes of individuals are eligible for assistance:

- Active-duty Air Force personnel and their eligible family members.
- Retired Air Force personnel and their eligible family members, but not on a continuing basis, and based on a case-by-case review.
- Air National Guard or Air Force Reserve personnel on extended active duty fifteen days or more under Title 10 USC.
- Spouses and dependent-age children of deceased Air Force personnel who died on active duty or in retired status.

In addition, Army, Navy, and Marine personnel and their dependents may receive assistance through the Air Force Aid Society when an Army Emergency Relief or Navy Relief Services office is not readily accessible and it is not feasible to refer the applicant to the Red Cross.

Eligible dependents are the spouse and minor children of Air Force personnel. The AFAS may consider as eligible dependents parents who are wholly dependent upon the servicemember. The existence of an allotment to a relative other than the spouse or child of an officer is acceptable as reasonable evidence of an officer's acceptance of responsibility to support the relative. The existence of a voluntary allotment in an amount constituting substantial support, regular maintenance as a member of an officer's household, or other reliable indication of true dependency will be accepted as evidence that an officer's dependent is eligible for AFAS assistance.

Assistance. AFAS renders assistance in the form of non-interest-bearing loans or cash grants or combinations of both. Those entitled to assistance can obtain help by contacting the Aid Society officer at any Air Force installation. Persons eligible for assistance that are not connected with or living at or near an Air Force base should make application for assistance from the AFAS through their local chapter of the American Red Cross. If you have questions or comments for the HQ AFAS staff, please e-mail the appropriate department:

- afas@afas-hq.org — For general questions or comments about the organization or website.
- ea@afas-hq.org — For questions concerning emergency assistance policy and procedures.
- ed@afas-hq.org — For questions concerning General Henry H. Arnold Education Grants or other AFAS education programs.
- LoanMgt@afas-hq.org — For questions concerning Loan Management such as repayment of AFAS loans, allotments, and Paymatic issues.
- Donations@afas-hq.org — For donating to the Air Force Aid Society.
- To contact AFAS by mail, correspondence should be addressed to: Headquarters Air Force Aid Society, 241 18th Street S., Suite 202, Arlington, VA 22202. The AFAS headquarters can be reached by phone at 703-972-2650.

The Air Force Aid Society is a charitable organization. It receives no government funds that it can use for relief purposes. The income of the AFAS comes from gifts and contributions, royalties from books and songs given to the Aid Society, legacies, and interest on the invested capital. The limited resources of the Aid Society and the very large number of persons eligible under its charter for assistance make it mandatory for assistance to be limited to cases of emergency only and also make it essential that Aid Society assistance be restricted to those cases that do not rightfully belong to some other welfare organization.

AMERICAN RED CROSS
Consistent with the congressional charter of the American Red Cross, the Red Cross has the primary responsibility for a broad program of volunteer aid to military personnel and their families. The Air Force Aid Society coordinates its functions with the American Red Cross in such a manner as to avoid duplication of effort in providing for the welfare of military personnel and their dependents. The American Red Cross carries out its responsibilities through personnel assigned to military establishments and through the home service program of local Red Cross chapters.

AIR FORCE CHAPLAINS
Religious Services.

Worship Services. Chaplains conduct worship services as are required for the religious practice of the members of each faith. The Air Force affords its personnel every opportunity to attend individual religious services. Chapels at most bases also offer religious instruction, such as Sunday school and catechism classes.

Marriage. The Air Force authorizes chaplains, but does not require them, to perform the marriage rite, if such ceremony meets all local laws and proper individuals obtain required legal permission in each case. The Air Force urges persons contemplating marriage to confer with a chaplain of their faith to ensure they make proper arrangements for the wedding.

Funerals. The commander or his representative will assist in making funeral arrangements, and a chaplain will conduct appropriate burial services at the interment of members of the military service, active and retired, and for their family members, when requested. If the family of a servicemember who dies in the United States requests transportation of the body to a home burial ground instead of permitting burial in a local or national cemetery, the family will normally be expected to provide a clergyman for the burial services because the chaplain's other duties preclude absence for an extended period.

Conferences and Retreats. The service authorizes chaplains, assisted by civilian religious leaders, to conduct religious conferences and retreats for Air Force personnel. For the purpose of attending such conferences and retreats, Air Force personnel may be placed on temporary duty. Chaplains may conduct these programs at either military or civilian locations.

PERSONAL AFFAIRS OFFICER

Air Force Casualty Services. The Air Force Casualty Services branch provides guidance to commanders, casualty assistance representatives, family liaison officers, and many other support agencies to ensure members and their families are taken care of as expeditiously as possible in a family emergency. A personal affairs officer can refer dependents to related agencies in regard to civil service preference, Social Security benefits, state benefits, transportation of dependents and household goods, and issuance of grave markers. Members or dependents can report the death of an active-duty airman by calling 800-433-0048.

Other Assistance. Personal affairs officers advise military personnel and their dependents as to their rights in securing benefits from the government and as to sources of information and procedures, but are strictly forbidden by law from acting as an agent or attorney for such persons other than in the discharge of their official duties. In their capacity as advisor to military personnel and their dependents, personal affairs officers maintain liaison with the American Red Cross director, the Air Force Aid Society officer, and other agencies, so they may bring to the attention of these organizations servicemembers and their families who are in financial need or in need of other assistance.

SCHOLARSHIPS FOR DEPENDENTS OF AIR FORCE PERSONNEL

Air Force Aid Society General Arnold Grant Program. Those eligible for this program qualify in any of the following categories:

- Dependent sons and daughters of Air Force members in one of the following categories:
  - Active Duty, Title 10 AGR/Reserve on extended active duty, and Title 32 AGR performing full-time active duty. All members must be on active duty through December 1, 2014 (all other Guard and reserve are not eligible).

- — Retired due to length of active duty service or disability, or retired AGR/Reserve with 20-plus satisfactory service years creditable for retired pay (all others are not eligible).
- — Deceased while on active duty or in retired status.
- Spouses of active-duty members and Title 10 AGR/Reservists on extended active duty. Member's active-duty status must extend through December 1, 2014. Eligible spouses must be legally married to member (not separated or pending divorce) at time of application and disbursement of award.
- Surviving spouses of Air Force members who died while on active duty or in retired status.
- Will be a high school graduate enrolled or accepted as a full-time undergraduate student in the 2014–15 academic year. *Note:* Students enrolled exclusively in distance education courses should check with their school official to verify their enrollment as meeting that school's full-time status requirements.
- Will be enrolled or accepted in an accredited college, university, or vocational/trade school approved by the U.S. Department of Education for participation in federal aid programs.
- Maintain at least a cumulative 2.0 grade point average (GPA) on a 4.0 grading scale.

Applicants or interested persons who desire additional information should contact their local Family Support Center.

Air Force Clubs' and Spouses Clubs' Scholarships. Air Force Clubs and many servicemembers spouses' clubs grant small annual scholarships on a competitive basis.

APPOINTMENT TO THE FEDERAL SERVICE ACADEMIES

The president is authorized by law to appoint a limited number of cadets from the United States at large to be selected from sons and daughters of members of the armed services who were killed or died in service as the result of wounds, injuries, or disease received or aggravated in active service. All such appointees must be otherwise qualified and the academy selects candidates in order of merit as established by competitive examination.

The president may appoint as cadets from the U.S. at large sons and daughters of persons that have been awarded the Medal of Honor.

IN-SERVICE HOUSING LOANS

If officers have been on extended active duty for at least two years, they may finance the purchase of a home with an FHA loan. The law provides a system of mortgage insurance that enables officers to more easily build or purchase homes. You qualify for FHA eligibility through the same criteria as used for a VA loan. This includes a VA certificate of eligibility, which verifies your military status for the FHA.

PAY, ALLOWANCES, AND ALLOTMENTS OF PERSONNEL
REPORTED MISSING

Pay and Allowances. When a service officially classifies a member as missing, the affected member remains entitled pay and allowance credited to his or her accounts for the period the service carries the member in such status. Such entitlement shall terminate upon the date of receipt by the Department of the Air Force of evidence or determination of death for the servicemember. Such entitlement, however, shall not terminate upon expiration of term of service during absence, and in case of death during absence shall not terminate earlier than the dates stated herein. No pay and allowances accrue to such missing persons for any period during which they may be officially determined absent from their posts of duty without authority, and they shall be indebted to the government for any payments from amounts credited to their accounts during such period of absence.

Allotments. The service continues to pay allotments instituted before the absence of a missing person who is entitled to accrued pay and allowances for a period of twelve months from the date of absence. In the absence of an allotment for support for dependents or payment of insurance premiums, or if an existing allotment is insufficient for its purposes, the secretary of the Air Force can direct that adequate allotments be instituted. The Air Force makes such determinations based upon information listed on DD Form 93 (*Record of Emergency Data*). The total of all allotments, however, may not exceed the total pay and allowances to which the missing person is entitled.

When the twelve-month period from date of commencement of absence is about to expire in the case of a missing person, the secretary of the Air Force shall cause a full review of the case to be made by appropriate authorities.

27

Financial Security
for Your Family

Few newly commissioned Air Force officers think about their retirement, and fewer still about the aftermath of their own death. Consequently, some do not give serious attention to the need for estate planning. Yet, all officers should study the financial needs of their families and make provisions to meet them.

Unmarried officers should also begin financial planning, systematic savings, and probably insurance programs. One of the most important aspects of building an estate is time; the earlier begun, the more that can accumulate. Officers should approach estate planning systematically. They should assess their responsibilities (or potential future responsibilities), determine the long-term needs of their families, understand benefits due them as active-duty and retired officers, take out insurance to make up the difference between the needs of their families and their current assets, and begin systematic financial investment programs. For more information, consult Stackpole Books' *Armed Forces Guide to Personal Financial Planning*; AFPAM 36-3028, *Benefits and Entitlements for Family Members of Retired Air Force Deceased*; and the Department of Veterans Affairs' *Federal Benefits for Veterans and Dependents*.

LONG-TERM RESPONSIBILITIES
Every Air Force family's needs vary, and every family's needs change over time. It is important to consider the long-term needs of the officer's spouse and children should the officer die. Is the spouse prepared to earn an adequate income? Do the children have special needs? What do the officer and spouse believe are their responsibilities for their children's education, and what level of comfort is desired for the survivors? Will the officer's or the spouse's parents or other relatives require support? The servicemember should also consider the family's needs should the spouse die: What is required to carry on as a single parent? Other factors to consider are inflation, when the family's financial needs will peak, and how assets will change over time and after retirement. Each Air Force family should reassess its long-term needs every few years or when a significant event, such as the birth of a child, makes a significant change.

GOVERNMENT BENEFITS

Government benefits vary depending on the officer's status: active-duty less than twenty years, active-duty over twenty years, retired, retired with disability, or eligible for Social Security. Benefits also vary depending on the ages of the surviving spouse and children. Every officer has the moral obligation to know what survivor benefits are available for family members—and to provide for shortfalls between anticipated needs and government benefits. For additional details, consult AFPAM 36-3028, *Benefits and Entitlements for Family Members of Retired Air Force Deceased.*

Death Gratuity. Death gratuity is a tax-free, lump-sum payment of $100,000 made by the Air Force to the eligible beneficiary of a member who dies on active duty, or a $12,400 payment if a servicemember dies within 120 days after retirement or separation. Usually paid within forty-eight hours of death, its purpose is to help the survivors in their readjustment and to aid in their meeting immediate expenses incurred. Death gratuity is paid to survivors in the following order: spouse, children, parents, siblings. The government does not pay the death gratuity to any other person when there are no survivors as listed. A will is not a legal designation for death gratuity, since the death gratuity is not money or a debt due the member and cannot be part of the estate.

Unpaid Pay and Allowances. Upon death of an active-duty or retired member, the government pays any pay and allowances due, but not paid to the member, to the designated beneficiary. Unpaid pay and allowances may include unpaid basic or retired pay, payment for accrued leave (not to exceed sixty days), amounts due for travel, per diem, and transportation of dependents and shipment of household goods. DFAS audits the decedent's pay record, and issues a check for any amount due to the designated beneficiary.

Burial Benefits. For members who die on active duty, the mortuary affairs officer will assist the survivors in making funeral arrangements. The Air Force will provide services and benefits that will cover, within reason, most funeral expenses. In addition, the Social Security Administration pays a small lump sum payment and the VA will pay up to $2,000 toward burial expenses for service-related deaths occurring on or after September 11, 2001.

Normally, the Air Force does not provide burial benefits when a retiree dies. The only exception is if the retired member was a patient in a U.S. military hospital while on active duty and continued to be a patient, physically in the hospital, until the date of death. The mortuary affairs officer at the nearest Air Force base will assist survivors of retirees in this category.

Other government agencies provide the following burial benefits in the case of a retired member's death:

- A lump sum is paid by the Social Security Administration.
- The VA pays a modest burial allowance under certain conditions of service-related disability or disability compensation. The Veterans' Benefit Act of 2010 allows payments of up to $700 toward burial and funeral expenses and a $700 plot-interment allowance for deaths that occur after

1 October 2011. Refer to the VA website for conditions and application forms.

Dependency and Indemnity Compensation. The Survivors Dependency and Indemnity Compensation Act of 1974 provides for compensation to survivors for the loss of a servicemember whose death is attributable to military service. All service-connected deaths that occur in peace or wartime in the line of duty qualify the eligible survivors for the Dependency and Indemnity Compensation (DIC). Retired officers' survivors may qualify also, provided the VA rules the death to have been from service-connected causes. The government pays DIC based upon the deceased member's pay grade. Once established, however, the DIC rate is fixed. Rate increases are only by separate congressional action. The law does not allow DIC payments to the survivors of a retired officer whose death was not service-connected. However, the law provides for payment of a small pension to the widow or widower, as discussed later, provided her or his income is below a stated minimum. This gap must receive consideration in developing a total family security plan.

Compensations may be increased for widows and widowers with children under eighteen or with a child over eighteen who is incapable of self-support. The DIC program may award an additional sum for each child between eighteen and twenty-three who attends a VA-approved school. All such compensations are exempt from federal income tax. The officer's surviving children will receive compensations if the spouse dies. Dependent parents likewise qualify for compensations. Your finance officer or any VA regional office can assist you in computing the various possible compensations and pensions for your particular family situation.

Survivor Benefit Plan (SBP). The Survivor Benefit Plan allows members of the uniformed services to elect to receive a reduced retirement pay in order to provide annuities for their survivors, for another person with an insurable interest in the servicemember, or under certain conditions, for an ex-spouse. Under SBP, the federal government pays a substantial portion of the overall cost. Participation in the SBP is open to all future retirees, including members of the reserve forces when they attain age sixty and become entitled to retired or retainer pay.

Under SBP, future retirees may elect to leave up to 55 percent of their retired pay to their selected annuitants. Participation in SBP is automatic at the 55 percent rate for those still on active duty who have a spouse or children and who have a minimum of twenty years' service at the time of their death. Before retirement, the member may elect a reduced coverage or the minimum base amount, or may decline to participate. However, the spouse must concur in the election of reduced or no coverage.

The plan bases costs for spouse-only coverage under SBP on a percentage of the minimum base amount, plus a percentage. The program may revise threshold amounts from time to time. You can find current SBP coverage costs at www.retirees.af.mil/factsheets/factsheet.asp?id=11654. Note that the plan bases its cost upon the total retired pay used to compute the SBP annuity and not upon the amount of the annuity. Extension of the coverage to a child or children costs about .05 percent of the annuity amount a month. The program bases children-only SBP on the age of the youngest child and on the age of the retiree, as well as the base amount.

There are a number of points about the SBP that deserve careful consideration. Most decisions are irrevocable, but deductions under the plan cease during any month in which there is no eligible beneficiary. Further, you can switch the coverage to a new spouse if you remarry. An important advantage of SBP is that the plan ties the amount of coverage to the Consumer Price Index (CPI). Whenever retired pay is adjusted based on the CPI, the amount selected by the retiree as an annuity base, the deduction from retired pay covering the adjusted base, and the annuity payable to selected beneficiaries will be adjusted accordingly. The survivor receives 55 percent of the base amount of retired pay until the survivor begins to draw Social Security, at which time the amount drops to 35 percent of the base amount of retired pay, which continues for the life of the survivor. After intensive lobbying by retirees, Congress approved a resolution that removes this inequity over the next few years. Subsequently, survivors will receive both their Social Security and their full retirement annuities. Furthermore, Congress approved a measure that ends the SBP premium deduction when the retiree has paid the SBP premium for 360 months and has reached seventy years of age.

The plan also provides that if a retiree dies of a service-connected cause, as a result of which survivors are entitled to DIC payments (see "Dependency and Indemnity Compensation" above), the SBP payment will be reduced so that the total of the two payments—DIC and SBP—will be equal to the full amount otherwise payable under SBP. Thus, the total income to the survivors from SBP, DIC, and Social Security can equal or be slightly higher than the SBP income alone, depending upon the extent of the offset for Social Security. On the other hand, since the plan ties SBP (as well as Social Security) to the Consumer Price Index, the retired member also is assured, unless Congress again alters the program, that the spending power provided through SBP will remain relatively constant regardless of the effects of inflation.

It is apparent that participation in SBP has definite advantages and, perhaps, disadvantages that call for study, obtaining advice, and care in deciding if coverage is desired and in selecting the amount. SBP is not necessarily a panacea for all military retirees, but it deserves careful consideration as a benefit accruing to you because of military service, which is available for use in planning your estate.

SOCIAL SECURITY

Military personnel accrue Social Security benefits for active service as an important element of their overall financial security program. Participation is mandatory. Under the Social Security program, the Internal Revenue Service taxes your base pay at a prescribed rate. The IRS increases the maximum taxable earnings as average wage levels rise. At the same time, the benefits payable also increase. The amount of the benefit received from Social Security will depend upon the average monthly earnings and the number of years of credit that have been accrued. The benefit of most general interest is the monthly income that an officer and eligible members of the officer's family attain when the officer reaches the eligibility age for Social Security. Congress has recently increased the retirement age for certain year groups; you should anticipate further changes, perhaps even radical ones, in this program.

The government also provides payments for disabled officers and for their spouses and children. It authorizes a monthly income for an officer's widow or widower with children under eighteen years of age, for children alone, for the widow or widower at age sixty, or for dependent parents. These important benefits supplement other insurance-type security programs. Survivors can make application for benefits at any Social Security office.

Note: It is important that you ensure that the Social Security Administration has credited you with the correct contributions. You can request information on the status of your account at approximately three-year intervals. Postcard-type forms are available at any Social Security office to use for this request.

Pension for Dependents of Retired Personnel and Veterans Whose Death Was Not Service-Connected. A modest survivor pension may be payable to dependents of veterans or retired personnel when retirement was for a reason other than physical disability or death occurred for a reason other than a service-connected cause. However, the spouse and children of the veteran or retired individual are the only ones eligible.

The government does not consider the following payments as part of death pension payments:

- Government life insurance proceeds and, in some cases, commercial life insurance proceeds.
- The death gratuity.
- Donations from public or private relief or welfare organizations.
- Payments of VA pension, compensation, and dependency compensation.
- Survivor Benefit Plan.
- Lump-sum Social Security death payments.
- Payments to a person under public or private retirement annuity, endowment, or similar plans or programs equal to that person's contributions.
- Proceeds of a fire insurance policy.
- Amounts equal to amounts paid by a spouse or a child of a deceased veteran for just debts, the expenses of the last illness, and the expenses of burial that are not reimbursed by the VA.

For pension and other benefit rates, consult your personal affairs office.

INSURANCE

There are many variations of insurance, some inexpensive, some very expensive. Never lose sight of the basic fact that the primary object of life insurance is to provide for the well-being of your survivors after your death; this includes having tax-free cash assets to meet pressing financial obligations without having to liquidate savings. Everything else is incidental; in other words, insurance is not an investment program. See to it that your insurance program gives your family a reasonable chance for an acceptable standard of living after your death.

Timing. In general, the time to take out insurance policies is at the earliest age you can afford them. All types of policies involve increased premiums with increased age. Remember that insurance is paid off in dollars that are subject to inflation; in other words, the purchasing power of insurance dollars may become less with passing years. Therefore, along with your insurance program and throughout your active service, you should follow a sound investment program in mutual funds, common stocks, and so on.

Educational Policies. Insurance firms design educational policies to produce a given amount of money for the education of your children. Such a policy matures and is payable to you at a stipulated age of your child or is payable to your child at the time of your death. These are worthwhile policies, but they can be relatively expensive. Many states offer "tomorrow funds" for public and/or private colleges and universities within the state originating the policy. Such policies might be suitable for your family situation.

Ordinary Life Insurance. Companies term this form of life insurance whole, or straight, life insurance. Although it does have a cash surrender value that you can use in circumstances of acute financial stress, its main characteristic is that it provides a high level of financial security for your family at a low cost, especially if purchased while you are young. You may use the proceeds of such a policy to serve the purposes of educational and endowment policies when protection is no longer needed. After years of advocating term insurance, many financial advisors are again stressing the importance of whole-life insurance.

Term Life Insurance. You will hear that term insurance is far less expensive than whole-life insurance—and it is, for a limited period. However, you must renew term policies based on your age, often resulting in either increased cost or reduced coverage. Moreover, upon retirement or later, you may become uninsurable because of physical disability or age. If, however, your need for insurance (or for additional insurance) is temporary, term insurance may best meet this special need. Term insurance provides the most coverage for the money when an officer is young. If you save systematically, the need for life insurance will decrease as term premiums increase with your age. However, you will always need some life insurance even if you accumulate a large estate, because life insurance will provide cash for your survivors.

Servicemembers' Group Life Insurance (SGLI). In 1965, Congress approved a group life insurance program for all members of the armed forces. This program now authorizes $400,000 life insurance policies to any active-duty or reserve component servicemember. The government pays the benefits of this insurance to the beneficiary named by the servicemember (spouse, children, parents, next of kin, or executor), with minimum limitation as to place or manner of death.

The SGLI program costs the servicemember a small monthly premium, which DFAS automatically deducts from monthly pay with the government providing for any additional premium costs. You must decline in writing if you choose to opt out of this coverage. The insurance is valid until 120 days after termination of active duty; within that 120 days, you may convert the insurance into a commercial life insurance policy without physical examination if desired. Although coverage under this program is optional, its advantages to Air Force members are so obvious and considerable that it should not be necessary to urge it upon you. In no other way can you obtain so much life insurance so inexpensively.

Long Term Care Insurance. Long term care (LTC) insurance is a way to protect your income and assets should you need long-term care services at home, in a nursing home, or at another long-term care facility. Most government health insurance programs, including the Federal Employee Health Benefit Program, TRICARE, and TRICARE For Life, provide little or no coverage for long-term care, which can be very expensive. The U.S. Office of Personnel Management (OPM) sponsors a LTC insurance program known as the Federal Long Term Care Insurance Program (FLTCIP). Eligible members include federal and U.S. Postal Service employees and annuitants, active and retired members of the uniformed services, and their qualified relatives. Information is available at www.ltcfeds.com. Many private insurance companies also provide LTC programs. You should review your options carefully, as plans vary; in addition, financial planners have varying opinions on the need for LTC coverage, so do your homework before investing in a program.

Mutual Insurance Associations for Servicemembers. There are mutual associations of officers of the military services. Eligible officers may assume with confidence that these organizations are carefully administered and that the services provided are tailored to fit military requirements.

Air Force Association Life Insurance. AFA provides a selection of insurance plans at low rates. Write to AFA Insurance Division, 1501 Lee Highway, Arlington, VA 22209-1198; call 800–727–3337; or visit www.afa.org/AFA/memberbenefits/memberbenefitsinsurance.

The Armed Forces Benefit Association. This nonprofit service organization offers group life and health insurance at low cost to supplement an officer's permanent program. Rates are low because it is group insurance. At death, AFBA can pay the life insurance in a lump sum or part in lump sum, part in installments, all in installments, or as an annuity.

In addition to life and health insurance plans, AFBA offers banking services and long-term care insurance. Membership is open to regular officers and to reserve officers on extended active duty. Although this insurance is limited to active officers, there are provisions for conversion to other forms of insurance with the John Hancock Mutual Life Insurance Company, one of the underwriters of the program. For more information, write to The Armed Forces Benefit Association, 909 N. Washington St., Alexandria, VA 22314-1556; call 800-776-2322 (extension 2265 for banking services); or visit www.afba.com.

Armed Forces Insurance. This group offers insurance against losses to personal and household effects, regardless of station or duty and at actual cost to members. The company offers an array of home and vehicle polices. Coverage is worldwide and premium rates are low. AFI works to ensure settlements are prompt and fair to all concerned. Eligibility is open to any serving or honorably retired or discharged servicemember—active, Guard, reserve, or civilian. Other agencies may be eligible. Spouses and children of eligible servicemembers may also join AFI. For information, visit www.afi.org or call 800-495-8234.

The Army and Air Force Mutual Aid Association. This association provides a wide array of insurance and financial planning services. It serves current and former members of the four services and the Coast Guard. Write to 102 Sheridan Ave., Fort Myer, VA 22211; call 800-522-5221; or visit www.aafmaa.com.

United Services Automobile Association. This association provides a full range of home, life, and vehicle insurance and banking and investment services. USAA arranges its programs to meet the specific conditions of officer and enlisted; active, Guard, and reserve; and retired persons with worldwide coverage. It also offers its services to spouses and children of current or retired servicemembers. For information: call 800-531-8722, or visit www.usaa.com.

INVESTMENTS

You can use life insurance to make up the difference between a family's needs and the financial benefits available from the government. However, investments are the real basis of financial security and independence. Furthermore, you do not have to die to enjoy their fruits.

To devise an investment strategy, you should evaluate the financial obligations and needs of your family. The objective should be to arrange your spending habits so that you not only live within your income, but also save systematically. From your income, you must first meet your financial obligations, and then you should save a fixed amount monthly. The priority order is first obligations, then savings, and only then nonessentials. Financial discipline, like any other discipline, pays dividends. Systematic savings in well-chosen investment instruments, compounded with interest over time, result in financial security and independence. Because time is so important, you should begin a systematic investment plan now. You can never regain time forfeited today.

There are a variety of investment instruments available, such as: the military's tax-deferred Thrift Savings Plan (www.tsp.gov), bank savings accounts, government savings bonds, treasury notes and bills, certificates of deposit, annuities, municipal bonds, individual stocks, and mutual funds. Some of these instruments offer fixed rates of return, and others variable rates of return—or loss. Some are conservative and secure; others are risky. The greatest potential for high return comes from risky instruments. For the average investor, this means individual stocks or mutual funds whose objective is growth, not income.

Unless you have the skills, interest, and time to be your own financial expert, you need to select an investment instrument and/or an investment advisor. Conventional wisdom identifies mutual funds as the instrument of choice for those who cannot personally manage their investments, but want their investments professionally managed. There are hundreds of funds to choose from, focusing on differing needs and inclinations of investors: growth, income, or both; high or low risk; and so on. Selecting a fund can be a daunting task. Conventional wisdom recommends no-load or low-load funds—those without brokerage fees. However, for the novice investor, especially one unwilling to do a good deal of research before selecting a fund, professional advice may be of more value than saving the load fees. But do not let the task of selecting long-term investment instruments stop you from beginning saving now; use the military's Thrift Savings Plan or a bank or a credit union savings account until you have made your long-term financial investment plan.

Thrift Savings Plan. The Thrift Savings Plan for Uniformed Services works to help provide sufficient retirement income to members of the uniformed services. It has the same types of savings and tax benefits as 401(k) plans. Each TSP participant chooses a plan from a selection of TSP investment funds. You contribute to TSP by allotment. Information on the Thrift Savings Plan is available online at www.tsp.gov, or from your military personnel flight, family support center financial counselors, or the Air Force Personnel Center.

Professional Help. A professional financial planner can assist officers in providing for the financial security of their families. Some financial investment and planning institutions cater to officers and senior NCOs. That they are in business to make money does not negate their usefulness as advisors. If you feel unprepared to do your own estate planning, a perfectly realistic feeling for the majority of officers, consult the professionals. Ask several senior officers to recommend estate-planning professionals, or consult *Armed Forces Guide to Personal Financial Planning*, published by Stackpole Books.

Precious metals and stones, fine arts, antiques, and other collectibles are best left to the experts or gamblers. If you acquire these, you should like to live with them, because they may very well turn out to be poor investments.

Credit or Debit Cards. Credit or debit cards are convenient. Use them as a convenience only. Misuse of credit cards can cause financial disaster, especially if interest on accrued debt grows so large it exceeds the original charged amount. Pay off your monthly credit card balance in full each billing cycle; carry over debt only in an emergency.

Except in unusual circumstances, an Air Force officer's income is sufficient to meet financial obligations, maintain a reasonable lifestyle, systematically invest, and indulge in an occasional luxury. Each officer must recognize the moral obligation and responsibility to provide his or her family financial security. Government benefits paid to survivors of deceased officers are inadequate to meet the needs of most Air Force families. Insurance can cover the gap between government benefits and family needs, but only systematic investment can build real financial security and independence.

28

Overseas Assignment

One of the benefits of service in the Air Force is travel. Most Air Force families look back on overseas assignments as the highlight of their careers. For those who take advantage of living abroad, there are numerous life-enriching opportunities. Living abroad broadens perspective—on culture, values, history, and the perspectives of others of the United States and its people. There are opportunities for friendships, entertainment, recreation, and sightseeing that are not available in the United States or that are restricted to those with the financial wherewithal to travel abroad. For all the advantages, however, there is also some trepidation. You can mitigate this natural response to the unknown by asking questions and by thoroughly planning for your travel. The Air Force, and especially other Air Force families, can provide many of the answers as you prepare for overseas travel and/or assignment.

Air Force officers expect to spend some of their careers at overseas stations. Depending on where the Air Force posts its officers, they may go unaccompanied to an overseas assignment, leaving their families behind in the United States for some months, the period varying with different overseas stations. This separation of officers and their families may be the result of military hostilities, unstable politico-military situations, or limited housing available at overseas bases. On arrival in the overseas area, officers who are allowed to bring dependents sign up on a priority list for family housing. Housing Offices govern this list by the length of the period of separation that has occurred. In some overseas areas, the Air Force permits officers to obtain private rental housing for themselves and families; however, the overseas command must approve such housing before one can use it as a basis for dependent travel. Other overseas assignments are designated unaccompanied; families cannot join their sponsors.

ACTION BEFORE DEPARTURE

The military personnel flight (MPF) team counsels officers on travel procedures and tour elections when alerted for an overseas move. When the service authorizes dependent travel, officers should file, with MPF assistance, an advance application for concurrent travel in order to move their families overseas.

Official orders of the Department of the Air Force assigning officers to an overseas command prescribe the timing, the method of transportation, and other essential information about the journey. Officers must set their official and personal houses in order so that no unfinished official or personal business will arise before or after departure.

At every step, officers must bear in mind that their spouses (and children), if not authorized to travel concurrently, will have need for certain documents in connection with later movement to the overseas area. Officers must therefore ensure that their family members have all necessary documents, such as titles to automobiles, copies of officers' orders, passports, insurance policies, inventories of household goods, children's school records, birth certificates, and the like. Officers must also ensure that their spouses have sufficient money (an allotment may be needed) to cover family needs during the period of separation, including the period of movement overseas.

Receipt of Passport Authorization. After the overseas commander approves the officer's application for dependent travel, MPF personnel furnish a letter authorizing the family members to apply for a no-fee passport. Upon receipt of passport authorization, family members should make application for a no-fee passport through the military personnel flight at the nearest military base, preferably an Air Force base. When making application, family members must present these documents:

- A birth certificate for each member of the family going overseas.
- Two identical photographs not smaller than 2 inches by 2 inches and taken full face and without a hat.
- Proof of American citizenship, if not native born.

Immunizations Required. All family members going overseas at government expense are required to receive certain immunizations before leaving the United States. Immunization requirements may change without notice; the base medical facility has current information to help the family prepare to travel overseas.

Shipment of Household Goods. The officer's overseas sponsor has the best information as to specific recommendations about the household goods the officer will ship to a particular foreign country. The family must make decisions as to what, if any, items of their household goods should be left in storage in the United States. The departure base's transportation officer will arrange for storage of all or any portion of the family's household goods in commercial facilities located in the general vicinity of the base. The transportation officer will also oversee shipment of other household goods to the overseas base. Some commands limit the weight and nature of household goods that officers can ship overseas.

ACTIONS ON RECEIPT OF PORT CALL

When the family has received its port call—that is, information as to the exact time for reporting to the aerial port of embarkation—they must make final decisions on the following points:

- The exact time for household goods to be picked up by the commercial carriers for delivery to the overseas base of assignment or the commercial storage facility.
- What will be shipped as unaccompanied baggage. Transportation rules limit unaccompanied baggage by weight. This baggage may include clothes, kitchen utensils, light housekeeping items, and collapsible items, such as cribs and playpens, when necessary for the care of an infant. The family should expect that the unaccompanied baggage would arrive in the overseas area several weeks after the arrival of the family members.
- What to do about the automobile. If the servicemember's orders authorized the shipment of a privately owned vehicle (POV), the officer oversees delivery of the vehicle to the port of shipment.

Movement of POV. The privately owned vehicle turned in for shipment will move to a seaport in the area to which the family is traveling. The automobile will be about one month in transit. It will arrive at a port, where the officer, or his/her agent, must pick up the vehicle. Port authorities will notify the officer upon arrival of the automobile at the port.

Shipment of Pets to Overseas Areas. The owner, at own risk, can ship certain pets at no expense to the government. The United Kingdom, which does not have rabies, restricts the importation of pets. Officers should check pet importation regulations at overseas destinations and intermediate stops that might result in the impoundment of a pet.

Exchange Facilities Overseas. Air Force personnel preparing for overseas assignments should *not* assume that they must take with them all things needed for a three-year tour. The exchanges overseas are excellent. They are prepared to meet every conceivable need, from clothing to washing machines, electronics, and automobiles. The Air Force family can obtain virtually everything needed to thrive in the new location from their base exchange. The exchanges are complete in themselves, because regulations allow overseas exchanges to stock and sell items denied to exchanges in the United States. Moreover, many local economies offer Air Force families numerous supplementary sources of goods and services.

Commissaries Overseas. Military commissaries overseas meet all normal food needs. Food prices in the overseas commissaries are comparable to those in military facilities in the United States. Military families who buy food at the local markets do so merely because they prefer that option.

Medical Care Overseas. The Air Force ensures the family has adequate medical care overseas for adults or children, including prenatal treatment. Excellent clinics are available in most areas. Optical and dental services are available for family members in the military facilities.

Schools Overseas. The DOD school system provides elementary, middle, and high school facilities in all established commands. Standards are closely supervised. Most parents believe their children benefit by the overseas experience, especially considering the intangible values of new locations and new cultures. In the unusual case where the military does not control or provide schools, parents should learn about facilities used by American citizens in the area or explore the possibilities of home schooling. Unless there are very unusual circumstances, the overseas school situation should not cause separations in Air Force families.

Movement of Dependent Students to and from Overseas Areas. Student dependents of military personnel stationed outside the continental United States are authorized transportation on a space-available basis to the port of embarkation in the United States to attend school in the United States, and between the United States and an overseas port to spend their summer vacations with their families. The service authorizes one round-trip a year, normally taken during the summer vacation period. The Air Force authorizes dependents over the age of twenty-one years, while engaged in full-time undergraduate study, the same transportation privilege.

Postal Service. The Army—Air Force Postal Service provides mail service overseas for Air Force and Army personnel. Postal rates are identical to those in the continental United States.

Merchandise Subject to U.S. Customs. Service overseas provides an opportunity for the purchase of merchandise made in foreign countries. Often families can purchase items at lesser cost than they would pay for similar items in the United States. The officer and spouse who make a real study of these possibilities and purchase wisely may acquire unusual possessions they will cherish throughout their lives.

All such purchases should be made with due regard to U.S. and host country customs regulations. The laws and regulations governing the entry of merchandise purchased abroad into the United States are quite liberal. The entry or attempt at entry of merchandise purchased abroad without the required customs declaration is an evasion of the law. It is smuggling, and it is subject to severe penalties. Find out what you can bring into the United States openly and legally. For articles of personal use and enjoyment in a household, the quantity authorized for free entry should be sufficient. Taking certain items, especially antiquities, out of some countries is a crime. Learn the laws.

Housing in Overseas Areas. Each foreign country presents the Air Force officer and family with new and challenging living conditions. Conditions vary widely among countries. Therefore, you should study individually each new foreign station; generalizations are worthless and misleading. Officers and their families who are on orders to a foreign country should learn about the local conditions, such as housing, cost of living, currency, operation of appliances, furniture, clothes, and pets.

Will your electrical equipment work on the current (voltage and cycle) in the overseas area? A transformer can reduce a 220-volt system to 110 volts and you will find these devices available at the overseas exchange or a thrift shop.

Housing available to officers overseas varies considerably among areas. Government quarters are, however, generally adequate, and some are excellent.

Although the standard of government quarters in any overseas area approximates that of quarters on bases in the United States, there are exceptions.

Private housing is an entirely different proposition. The price of private housing is often very high. The cost of utilities is also higher than in the United States. On the other hand, finance may authorize officers required to find housing within the local economy a station allowance that partly compensates for the increased costs encountered off base. The amount of the COLA (cost-of-living allowance) varies with overseas stations.

Travel and Recreation Opportunities in Overseas Areas. One of the great attractions of life overseas is the opportunity provided to travel in foreign countries and to take advantage of the recreational facilities available. By using the facilities of the various U.S. military installations sprinkled over Europe, it is possible to visit a vast number of interesting places at a reasonable cost. In the Far East, distances become a problem; nonetheless, it is possible for officers to arrange to visit countries other than their duty location. In Europe and in Japan, facilities for sports of all kinds are not only available, but also close at hand. Where the overseas station is somewhat isolated, such as in Korea, DoD arranges facilities and/or opportunities to serve sports enthusiasts of all types.

TOURS OF DUTY
The Air Force seeks to ensure equitable distribution of overseas assignments to its personnel. Although the policy is on a "first to return, first to go" basis, specific requirements must influence actual selections, and lengths of tours may change with the military situation.

LEARNING THE LANGUAGE
If possible, you should learn the language of your host country, resulting in skills that are both personally rewarding and of value upon return to the United States. Off-duty classes, mixing with the nationals, and studying the local culture and government are methods you can use to learn the local language. Even if the language is a difficult one, you and your family should learn at least the phrases of courtesy and of the social amenities. These will carry you a long way.

CULTURAL DIFFERENCES
Some of the most exciting, and at times most confusing and even exasperating, experiences of living overseas are based on cultural differences. Living overseas requires constant observation—similar to prudent behavior anywhere or anytime you do not know what to expect and what others expect of you.

As an observation applicable to life in almost all overseas areas, it is possible to say this: You will find the situation not at all difficult, nor nearly as different as you might have thought. So, relax. You are not going to the moon, but rather, in most cases, to highly civilized and industrialized countries whose cultures were ancient when the United States was a wilderness.

Before venturing afield, acquaint yourself with cultural differences that have the potential to offend the sensitivities of your host nation. Be particular about religion, appropriate clothing and public behavior for men and women, use of tobacco and alcohol, and social customs regarding eating and being introduced to host nationals. Be aware that the freedoms you are accustomed to as an American may be restricted or may not even exist—freedoms regarding religious observation, public speech (including written materials), and gender equality. You must always remember that all Americans abroad are unofficial ambassadors of the United States; this fact is all the more important for employees of the U.S. government: you and your family members.

Appendix A

Initial Active-Duty and Follow-On Assignments

You may find reporting to your initial active-duty assignment after commissioning somewhat traumatic. Officers always experience some uneasiness as they move from assignment to assignment: Will I like the location, the work, my fellow workers, and my boss? Moreover, will they like me? Will I be up to what is required of me? Chances are that the answers to all these questions will be "yes." Except under the most unusual circumstances, professional success, fulfillment, and happiness are under your control.

Your preparation can dispel much of the uneasiness you might feel about your first active-duty assignment or subsequent follow-on assignments. The more you know about your assignment, the more comfortable you will be. Try to find out as much as possible from your commissioning source and take advantage of a "sponsor" should your new unit provide one for you and your family. In any case, each new assignment will involve recurring tasks. You'll learn to do them in your sleep—and sponsors, checklists, and all the personnel at the in-processing section of your military personnel flight (MPF) will help you make it a smooth transition.

INITIAL ASSIGNMENT

Notification of Assignment. The Air Force Personnel Center (AFPC) will send you a notification of assignment letter, or extended active-duty order. It will give you your duty unit, generally a specialty course in one of Air Education and Training Command's schools. As most officers begin their service as officer students, transition to active duty is eased somewhat. The letter will tell you when and where to report. Read and understand this letter. For follow-on assignments, officers receive permanent-change-of-station (PCS) orders.

Sponsorship. Training schools do not typically assign sponsors to incoming personnel. If you are one of the few officers with a direct-duty assignment,—your gaining unit will provide you a sponsor who will ease your PCS in many ways. This also applies to all follow-on assignments.

Shipping Household Goods. If you have more household goods than you can carry in your automobile, contact the traffic management office (TMO) at

301

the nearest Air Force base (see appendix C). If you're going to school, you will probably live in the bachelor officer quarters (BOQ), so you will want to store your household goods at government expense. Question the TMO on this. Don't exceed the weight limit of 10,000 pounds for single, and 12,000 pounds for married second lieutenants.

Travel. Most officers will drive their own automobiles to their first assignments. The government reimburses a set amount per mile for the official distance from your home of record to your initial base and a daily rate, called per diem, for lodging and food up to the number of travel days authorized in your orders. If you will not be driving, talk with the TMO about commercial travel, such as by air.

Paperwork and Documents. You will need to have ready access to certain documents during your Air Force career. Bring them with you when you report for your first duty assignment. You will not need all of them, but it is better to have them if required than to have to hunt them down later. Carry those documents that you will not need immediate access to in a small fireproof metal box. Of course, it is always a good practice to have photocopies of your most important personal documents. The threat of identity theft dictates that you always safeguard your personal documents, especially your credit card, bank account, and Social Security card numbers. After reaching your PCS assignment, you should consider renting a safe-deposit box in a local bank. In an age of identity theft, it is crucial that you safeguard documents such as these. You should include the following documents:

- Any remaining copies of travel orders and amendments
- Transportation request (TR)
- Household goods shipping documents
- Driver's license
- Car registration and title
- Car insurance policies
- Personal property insurance policies
- Checkbook
- Financial and investment records
- Credit cards
- Immunization records
- Official copies of birth certificates for all family members
- Naturalization papers, if applicable
- Passports
- Copy of will
- Social Security card
- Official college transcripts
- Marriage certificate
- Divorce or death certificates terminating any previous marriages
- Certified true copies of adoption papers for any adopted children
- Children's school records

Uniforms. When going to your first assignment, at the minimum take one dress uniform (coat and trousers or skirt) and at least two service uniforms (shirt and trousers or skirt) for the season of the year (coat if necessary); have all accessories, including hat and shoes. You can buy additional uniforms and uniform items at the Clothing Sales store at your first base.

Expenses. Take enough money (cash, checks, credit card) to handle your travel expenses and at least the first two weeks at your new base; base finance should start your pay within two weeks.

Actions on Arrival. Report during the time window indicated on your orders. If no times are indicated, you have until midnight of your report-not-later-than date (RNLTD), although you should arrive during unit duty hours. The security police at the gate will give you a temporary pass if necessary, and direct you to your unit during duty hours or to the twenty-four-hour arrival point during nonduty hours (generally the base billeting office). In any case, you'll want to take care of your billeting, especially if you have a family with you. If you are single or unaccompanied, the lodging office will probably billet you in the visiting officer quarters (VOQ) or bachelor officer quarters (BOQ). If your family accompanies you, the lodging office should provide quarters in the temporary lodging facility (TLF). In any case, the billeting office will help you. (If you have a sponsor, he or she may have made billeting arrangements for you.) If you arrive after duty hours, call your sponsor if you have one, or call your unit first thing in the morning. Your unit may expect you to in-process immediately, or to report to the unit first and then into the base. If this is your first assignment, you'll probably be at an Air Education and Training Command base, where there will be more than ample instructions. In either case, unit or in-processing personnel will expect you to be in uniform; remember the importance of a good first impression.

In-Processing. All bases have well-organized, easy-to-follow in-processing. If you're at a school, you'll be led through the process. Otherwise, you'll have to in-process with your unit's orderly room and/or your military personnel flight (MPF), accounting and finance office, various briefings, and unit processing. It all begins at the MPF. For your first assignment take all the documents listed above (just leave them locked in your car); you may not need them all, but it's better to come prepared.

Permanent Housing. If your first assignment is an Air Force Education and Training Command school and if you're single or unaccompanied, the lodging office will almost certainly billet you on base. However, if you have a direct-duty assignment or a follow-on assignment, and you bring your family, you will need to find housing. The housing office can help you find a place to live, either in on-base housing or in the local community. It can also help you with location advice and any restrictions to location in the area. Your unit or school will recognize that you will not really be settled and ready to devote all your efforts to the job until you have housing, especially if you arrive with family. Be assured that they will help you get settled. The base Family Services

Center can provide loaned household items such as bedding, small appliances, cooking and eating utensils, and baby needs.

Starting Work. As a newly commissioned officer arriving on active duty for a first tour, you will find that no one expects you to be expert in performing your duties or in knowing about the Air Force. You will also find, however, that seniors and contemporaries will expect you to work hard to improve your technical capabilities and expand your knowledge. Practically everyone on the base, from the airman to the commander, military and civilian, will be ready to assist you in any way they can. As a new officer, you should neither bluff nor be too proud to seek information and assistance. Simply proceed to learn your job and your way around. Always remember: the only stupid question is the one not asked.

CHANGE OF STATION

When you, as an officer already assigned on active duty, receive orders reassigning you to a different base, you must perform certain tasks before you leave. Although the most important of these duties relates to securing release from responsibility for unit property and funds, you must also take care of certain personal responsibilities when departing a station. For example, you must turn in equipment drawn from the base supply officer. Generally, you can clear the base from one central location. If you have outstanding debts or bills in the local civilian community, you should either pay these obligations or make satisfactory arrangements with your creditors.

ASSUMPTION OF NEW DUTIES

Many of the rapidly occurring changes in the lives and careers of Air Force officers involve physical movement from one base to another; quite often, the change confronting an Air Force officer is in the nature of the assumption of a new duty. Command is a very infrequent duty assignment. By far the majority of the officers of the Air Force are engaged in duties, most frequently staff assignments that do not involve exercising command over units of the Air Force.

Assuming a Staff Position. Staff work is extremely important; commanders could not function without their staffs. Every officer must be determined to perform every assignment in an outstanding manner.

Upon reporting for duty on staff assignments, officers should report to the executive officer of the staff agency to which they are assigned and thereafter to the chiefs of sub-branches or sections as directed by the exec. (Your sponsor should direct you in this and accompany you on your orientation.) Usually, a well-administered headquarters will have published a manual for staff officers setting forth the organization and the particular staff procedures desired by the commander of the headquarters. On joining a staff, you should find one of these manuals and study it with care. Another step is to become acquainted with the other members of the staff, especially with those members of staff sections closely allied with your own.

Having mastered the organization and the procedures, and having become acquainted with the members of the staff to which you are assigned, you should get acquainted with officers in staffs senior and junior to you. For example, as an officer assigned to the operations section of a group headquarters, you should become acquainted with the operations personnel in the wing headquarters and in each of the squadron headquarters within your own group. These personal relationships often go far in mitigating misunderstanding among staffs of various levels.

As a staff officer, you must constantly bear in mind that you are not a commander and do not have the power of command. Occasionally, however, you may act for the commander in matters of considerable importance. In doing so, you must strictly adhere to the policies of the commander. Never use your commander's name, rank, title, or position to affect actions that are, in fact, your own preferences. Do not pretend to represent your commander when, in fact, you are actually representing yourself. On the other hand, you certainly should not evade your own responsibilities by seeking to discover the views of the commander in every specific instance. You must act within the scope of the commander's authority and policies, and you must act as if you bear the sole responsibility for your actions. Consider these questions whenever you have to make decisions for or in other ways act for your commander: (1) Would I be willing to undertake the execution of the decision I recommend were I a subordinate element commander receiving orders of this staff? (2) Would I, if I were chief of staff, be willing to accept the full responsibility for the effects of this decision?

Assuming a Command Position. See chapter 4.

Appendix B

Professional Reading Guide

Professional competence demands that all Air Force officers study air and space power, service doctrine, employment concepts, and the Air Force contribution to joint and combined operations. For these reasons, former Chief of Staff of the Air Force General Ronald Fogleman created the first CSAF Professional Reading List in 1996. The list is updated annually and can be found at static.dma.mil/usaf/csafreadinglist/index.html. As a supplement to that list, this appendix contains the 2000 Air University Professional Reading Guide. Although it is no longer published (it was superseded by the CSAF list), it still provides Air Force officers the foundation for developing professional expertise.

All officers should read *Air and Space Power Journal* in addition to books selected from the following list.

SERVICE READING LISTS
Below you will find the reading list of each of the Service Chiefs and the Chairman of the Joint Chiefs of Staff. While the lists vary, you will find many titles repeating across them. In addition, the differences between the lists give insight into issues and ideas that are important to the different services.

The source URLs take you to the websites where you will find additional information and, in some cases, more detailed synopses of the books.

Chief of Staff of the Air Force Reading List
(http://static.dma.mil/usaf/csafreadinglist/01_books.html)
Glines, Carroll V. *The Doolittle Raid.*
> On 18 April 1942, sixteen B-25s launched from the carrier *Hornet*, under the command of Lt. Col. Jimmy Doolittle, flew 650 miles to Japan, dropped their bombs on Tokyo and other targets, and escaped to China and neutral Soviet territory. Although a very small affair in comparison with the B-29 strikes three years later, the Doolittle raid was a severe psychological blow to Japanese military leaders and had far-reaching strategic effects, providing an electrifying boost to American morale.

Makos, Adam with Larry Alexander. *A Higher Call.*
> Four days before Christmas 1943, a badly damaged American bomber struggled to fly over wartime Germany. At its controls was a 21-year-old

pilot. Half his crew lay wounded or dead. It was their first mission. Suddenly, a sleek, dark shape pulled up on the bomber's tail—a German Messerschmitt fighter. Worse, the German pilot was an ace, a man able to destroy the American bomber in the squeeze of a trigger.

Lambeth, Benjamin S. *The Unseen War*.

The Unseen War offers a comprehensive assessment of the air contribution to the three weeks of major combat that ended the rule of Iraq's Saddam Hussein in 2003. In contrast to Operation Desert Storm in 1991, the role of allied air power in the nation's second war against Iraq was not apparent to most observers, due to the concurrent land and air offensives coupled with the overwhelming majority of reporters embedded with ground troops.

Grossman, Dave and Loren W. Christensen. *On Combat*.

On Combat looks at how the stresses of deadly battle affect the human body: the impact on the nervous system, heart, breathing, visual and auditory perception, and memory. The reader will learn what measures warriors take to prevent such debilitations to stay in the fight, survive, and win. *On Combat* presents emerging research for inoculating the mind to stress, fear, and even pain.

Biank, Tanya. *Undaunted*.

Since 9/11, more than 240,000 women soldiers have fought in Iraq and Afghanistan—more than 140 have died there, and they currently make up 14 percent of the total active-duty forces. Despite advances, today's servicewomen are constantly pressed to prove themselves, to overcome challenges men never face, and to put the military mission ahead of all other aspects of their lives, particularly marriage and motherhood.

Blehm, Eric. *Fearless*.

When Navy SEAL Adam Brown woke up on 17 March 2010, he did not know he would die that night in the Hindu Kush Mountains of Afghanistan, but he was ready. In a letter to his children, he wrote, "I'm not afraid of anything that might happen to me on this earth, because I know no matter what, nothing can take my spirit from me."

Bellavia, David and John R. Bruning. *House to House*.

One of the great heroes of the Iraq War, Staff Sergeant David Bellavia captures the brutal action and raw intensity of leading his Third Platoon, Alpha Company, into the lethally choreographed kill zone of booby-trapped, explosive-laden houses of Fallujah's militant insurgents.

Heath, Chip and Dan Heath. *Switch: How to Change Things When Change Is Hard*.

Why is it so hard to make lasting changes in our companies, in our communities, and in our own lives? The primary obstacle is a conflict that is built into our brains, say Chip and Dan Heath, authors of the critically acclaimed bestseller *Made to Stick*. Psychologists have discovered that our minds are ruled by two different systems—the rational mind and the emotional mind—that compete for control.

Bowden, Mark. *Worm: The First Digital World War.*

Despite the growing importance and virtual ubiquity of the Internet, the open nature of this twentieth-century innovation makes the Internet vulnerable to attack. *Worm: The First Digital World War*, by veteran journalist and bestselling author Mark Bowden, looks at the evolving cyber arena and the serious threats that will continue to challenge the security of all Internet users, including individuals, the private sector, and governments.

Clark, Dan. *The Art of Significance.*

We're socialized from birth to pursue success at all costs. Day after day, we build our careers and our personal lives around getting what we want. But Dan Clark thinks we're missing something important: the difference between success and significance. For example, successful people think wealth flows to them. Significant people know wealth flows through them. The successful say "knowledge is power."

Greeny, Joseph, Ron McMillan, Kerry Patterson, and Al Switzler. *Crucial Conversations.*

A crucial conversation, as opposed to a casual exchange, is a discussion between two or more people about tough issues where opinions vary, stakes are high, and emotions run strong. When a topic needs to be breached that could easily lead to disaster, such as approaching a boss who is breaking his or her own safety or quality policies, or critiquing a colleague's work, or talking to a team member who isn't keeping commitments, talking openly is a must, but can be very difficult. Through the art of dialogue, a free flow of meaning between two or more people, we are able to put all the relevant information out in the open. We safely share our ideas and as a group are able to use the most accurate and relevant information to make better decisions.

Shaw, Haydn. *Sticking Points.*

This is the first time in American history that we have had four different generations working side by side in the workplace: the Traditionalists (born before 1945), the Baby Boomers (born 1945–1964), Generation X (born 1965–1980), and the Millennials (born 1981–2001). Haydn Shaw, popular business speaker and generational expert, has identified twelve places where the four generations typically come apart in the workplace (and in life as well).

USMC: Commandant's Reading List

(http://guides.grc.usmcu.edu/content.php?pid=408059&sid=3340387)

Commandant's Choice Books

Hubbard, Elbert. *A Message to Garcia.*

The story of an American soldier charged with delivering a critical message to a leader of Cuban rebel forces during the Spanish American War. He delivers the urgent missive with no questions asked, no complaining, and no hedging. The enduring and almost unbelievably simple message of the essay is this: When asked to perform a task, don't ask "How?" or "Why?" or "Wouldn't it be better if?" Just do it. This book is also on the Sergeant Major of the Marine Corps Reading List and Chairman, Joint Chiefs of Staff, Reading List.

Pressfield, Steven. *The Warrior Ethos*.
Do we fight by a code? If so, what is it? What is the Warrior Ethos? Where did it come from? What form does it take today? How do we (and how can we) use it and be true to it in our internal and external lives? The Warrior Ethos is intended not only for men and women in uniform, but artists, entrepreneurs and other warriors in other walks of life. The book examines the evolution of the warrior code of honor and "mental toughness." It goes back to the ancient Spartans and Athenians, to Caesar's Romans, Alexander's Macedonians, and the Persians of Cyrus the Great (not excluding the Garden of Eden and the primitive hunting band). Sources include Herodotus, Thucydides, Plutarch, Xenophon, Vegetius, Arrian, and Curtius—and on down to General George Patton, Field Marshal Erwin Rommel, and Israeli Minister of Defense Moshe Dayan.

United States Marine Corps. *Leading Marines (MCWP 6-11)*.
This publication describes a leadership philosophy that reflects the traditional strengths of the Marine Corps as an institution and attempts to define the very ethos of being a Marine. It is about the inseparable relationship between the leader and the led, and is as much about the individual Marine—the bedrock upon which the Corps is built—as it is about any leader.

United States Marine Corps. *Warfighting (MCDP-1)*.
This Marine Corps doctrinal publication explains the code of conduct and moral quality of a Marine. The message delivered, if taken as a how-to-book, empowers the reader to plan, fearlessly expect the unexpected, and, finally, get things done.

United States Marine Corps. *Sustaining the Transformation (MCRP 6-11D)*.
Our warfighting capability depends upon a lasting transformation: every Marine must possess the intellect, skill, and solid moral foundation to fight in the increasingly chaotic battlespace of the twenty-first century. *MCRP 6-11D* is designed to aid Marine leaders at all levels in their efforts to sustain the transformation process.

Enlisted
Entry Level: Recruit–Poolee
Uris, Leon. *Battle Cry*.
Battle Cry follows the fortunes of a Marine outfit from boot camp to Guadalcanal, Tarawa, and elsewhere in the Pacific during World War II. Many of the events are based on the author's WWII experience with the

6th Marine Regiment. The interactions of the characters and their ability to develop *esprit de corps* is a central theme.

Miller, Zell. *Corps Values*.

The author recounts the simple but powerful lessons he learned as a United States Marine: the core values we must embrace if we are to be successful as individuals and as a nation. Only by incorporating such time-honored Marine qualities as pride, discipline, courage, brotherhood, and respect into our personal and professional lives can we meet the challenges that lie ahead.

Ricks, Thomas E. *Making the Corps*.

This book follows recruit of Platoon 3086 through Marine Corps boot camp in Parris Island, South Carolina, and the drill instructors who instill in them the principles of discipline, teamwork, and commitment. Ricks also examines changes in recruit training and how the Corps deals with critical social and political issues like race relations, gender equality, and sexual orientation, as well as the growing divide between the military and the rest of America. As the author follows these men from their home-towns, through boot camp, and into their first year as Marines, he paints a picture not only of individual Marines but the Corps as a whole.

Crane, Stephen. *The Red Badge of Courage*.

This book is about a young soldier's experience during the American Civil War and is well known for its realistic depiction of battle. Henry Fleming, a private in the Union Army, runs away from the field of war. Afterward, the shame he feels at this act of cowardice ignites his desire to receive an injury in combat—a red badge of courage that will redeem him.

Primary Level: Private–Private First Class–Lance Corporal–Corporal

Card, Orson Scott. *Ender's Game*.

In this science fiction novel, child genius Ender Wiggin is chosen by inter-national military forces to save the world from destruction by a deadly alien race. His skills make him a leader yet Ender suffers from isolation and rivalry from his peers, pressure from adults, and fear of the enemy. His psychological battles include loneliness and fear that he is becoming like his cruel brother. The novel's major theme is the concept of a "game," and all of the other important ideas in the novel are interpreted through this concept. Some of the important ideas in the book include the relationship between children and adults, compassion, ruthlessness, friends and ene-mies, and the question of humanity.

Pressfield, Steven. *Gates of Fire: An Epic Novel of the Battle of Thermopylae*.

In the battle of Thermopylae (480 BCE), seven thousand Greeks led by three hundred Spartans held an enormous Persian army of two hundred thousand at bay for several days—an army that would have changed our civilization had the Greeks not died fighting it. Never before or since has such a badly outnumbered army fought so valiantly nor effectively. This book is also on the Sergeant Major of the Marine Corps Reading List.

Davis, Burke. *Marine! The Life of Lt. Gen. Lewis B. (Chesty) Puller, USMC (Ret.).*

Biography of real-life hero Chesty Puller, the most decorated Marine in history. From commanding the Horse Marines in Peking to leading the Inchon landing, Puller was a legend in his own time. But his popularity added to his blunt honesty earned him many enemies in Washington, and when the war was done they no longer needed a fighter like Chesty. Winner of five Navy Crosses, no officer ever inspired greater courage, loyalty, and devotion from his men, pushed them harder, or served them better.

Kasal, Brad. *My Men Are My Heroes.*

Account of Marine First Sergeant Brad Kasal's courageous mission to rescue fallen comrades while under intense enemy fire during the Battle of Fallujah. During the fight, Kasal was shot seven times, almost losing his leg, and sustained forty-seven shrapnel wounds using his body to shield a wounded Marine from an enemy grenade. He was awarded the Navy Cross, the nation's second highest award for heroism, for his actions.

Forester, C. S. *Rifleman Dodd.*

Study of one man's commitment to duty taking precedence over his own personal survival. It shows how one man with ability, courage, and initiative can make a difference to the outcome of a war. This book is also on the Sergeant Major of the Marine Corps Reading List.

Drury, Bob. *The Last Stand of Fox Company: A True Story of U.S. Marines in Combat.*

During the Korean War, 234 heroic Marines from Fox Company, First Division, held off a force of 10,000 Chinese soldiers in subzero weather to secure the Toktong Pass. This is their story. This book is also on the Sergeant Major of the Marine Corps Reading List.

McLaurin, Melton Alzona. *The Marines of Montford Point: America's First Black Marines.*

Collection of interviews with members of the Montford Point Marines Association, organized by chronology and theme. This recognizes and honors the men who desegregated the Marine Corps and loyally served their country in three major wars. It is about the first black recruits who received Marine Corps basic training at the segregated Camp Montford Point (adjacent to Camp Lejeune). Between 1942 and 1949, more than twenty thousand men trained at Montford Point, most of them going on to serve in the Pacific Theater in World War II as members of support units. This book is also on the Sergeant Major of the Marine Corps Reading List.

Career Level: Sergeant–Staff Sergeant

Krulak, Victor H. *First to Fight: An Inside View of the U.S. Marine Corps.*

This book examines the foundation on which the Marine Corps is built.

The author, Lt. Gen. Victor "Brute" Krulak (USMC, Ret.), offers an insider's chronicle of Marines, on the battlefield and off. He takes a close look at the Marine experience during WWII, Korea, and Vietnam—wars in which he was a participant—and, in doing so, helps answer the question of what it means to be a Marine and how the Corps has maintained such an outstanding reputation. This book is also on the Sergeant Major of the Marine Corps Reading List.

Burgin, R. V. *Islands of the Damned: A Marine at War in the Pacific.*

Personal narrative of the author's experiences as a Marine during WWII in the Pacific Theater where he confronted snipers, ambushes along narrow jungle trails, abandoned corpses of hara-kiri victims, and howling banzai attacks. During his two years of service, the author rose from green private to seasoned sergeant, and earned a Bronze Star for his valor at Okinawa.

Gladwell, Malcolm. *Outliers: The Story of Success.*

An intellectual journey through the world of "outliers"—the best and the brightest, the most famous and the most successful. The author challenges the reader to answer the question: What makes high-achievers different? His answer is that we pay too much attention to what successful people are like and too little attention to where they are from: that is, their culture, their family, their generation, and the idiosyncratic experiences of their upbringing.

Fraser, George MacDonald. *Quartered Safe Out Here.*

Action-packed memoir of the author's experiences in Burma during WWII. Although only 19 years old when he arrived during the war's final year, he offers a firsthand glimpse at the camaraderie, danger and satisfaction of service.

Kaplan, Robert D. *Soldiers of God: With Islamic Warriors in Afghanistan and Pakistan.*

This book is about the mujahidin—"soldiers of god"—whose unwavering devotion to Islam fueled their mission to oust the formidable Soviet invaders from Afghanistan. The thwarted Soviet invasion then gave rise to the ruthless Taliban and the defining international conflict of the twenty-first century. Traveling alongside Islamic guerrilla fighters, sharing their food, observing their piety in the face of deprivation, and witnessing their determination, the author offers a unique opportunity to increase our understanding of a people and a country that are at the center of current world events. This book is also on the Sergeant Major of the Marine Corps Reading List.

Junger, Ernst. *Storm of Steel.*

This book illuminates not only the horrors but also the fascination of total war, seen through the eyes of an ordinary German soldier. Leading raiding parties, defending trenches against murderous British incursions, and enduring as shells tore his comrades apart, the author was constantly tested by the Great War, which he saw not just as a war but as a personal struggle.

Swinton, E. D. *The Defence of Duffer's Drift*.
> Insightful analysis of small unit tactics in defending a strategic objective given limited communications, resources, and manpower. Although some advice is outdated, three of the twenty-two lessons learned presented are of extreme relevance to a new platoon leader: the urgency and importance of first setting security and preparing defenses, the use of cover and concealment, and the creation of clear fields of fire.

Sajer, Guy. *The Forgotten Soldier*.
> Recounts the horror of WWII on the Eastern Front as seen through the eyes of a teenage German soldier. It depicts a desperate struggle for survival against cold, hunger, and terrifying Soviet artillery. Photos show the hardships and destructiveness of war, such as troops battling through snow, mud, burned villages, and rubble-strewn cities.

Shaara, Michael. *The Killer Angels: The Classic Novel of the Civil War*.
> This book centers around the key battle of the American Civil War: the battle of Gettysburg. In a day-by-day chronicle, the events immediately before and during the battle of Gettysburg unfold through the eyes of Confederate and Union generals and officers. The author's ability to convey the thoughts of men in war as well as their confusion—the so-called "fog of battle"—is outstanding.

United States of America. *U.S. Constitution*.
> The U.S. Constitution is the supreme law of the United States of America. Amendments 1–10 constitute what is known as the Bill of Rights. Several changes and additions have been made over the past two-hundred-plus years (Amendments 11–27).

Sledge, E. B. *With the Old Breed at Peleliu and Okinawa*.
> First-person account of fighting at Peleliu and Okinawa. Eugene Sledge was part of WWII's famous 1st Marine Division, 3rd Battalion, 5th Marines. It is based on notes Sledge secretly kept in a copy of the New Testament, and documents what saved, threatened, and changed his life. It is also a story of how Sledge learned to hate and kill—and came to love—his fellow man. This book is also on the Sergeant Major of the Marine Corps Reading List.

Intermediate Level: Gunnery Sergeant–Master Sergeant–First Sergeant

Remarque, Erich Maria. *All Quiet on the Western Front*.
> This book is about Paul Baumer, who enlists with his classmates in the German army of WWI. They become soldiers with youthful enthusiasm. Through years of vivid horror, Paul holds fast to a single vow: to fight against the principle of hate that meaninglessly pits young men of the same generation but different uniforms against each other, if only he can come out of the war alive.

Warren, James. *American Spartans: A Combat History from Iwo Jima to Iraq*.
> Authoritative battle history of the Marines from the islands of the Pacific to Korea to the Middle East. It reveals how "the few and the proud" have

drawn on their timeless precepts across six decades while reinventing themselves in the face of political change to forever remain America's finest warriors.

Webb, James. *Fields of Fire.*

A novel about three young men from different worlds plunged into jungle warfare in the An Hoa Basin of Vietnam in 1969. The author captures the journey of one Marine platoon through a man-made hell as in the heat and horror of battle they took on new identities and took on each other until each man found his fate.

Bradley, James. *Flags of Our Fathers.*

The true story behind the immortal photograph that has come to symbolize the courage and indomitable will of America. In February 1945, U.S. Marines plunged into the surf at Iwo Jima—and into history. Through a hail of machine gun and mortar fire that left the beaches strewn with comrades, they battled to the island's highest peak and raised the American flag.

Leckie, Robert. *Helmet for My Pillow: From Parris Island to the Pacific: A Young Marine's Stirring Account of Combat in World War II.*

This book follows the author's journey from basic training on Parris Island, South Carolina, to the raging battles in the Pacific, where some of the war's fiercest fighting took place. Recounting his service with the 1st Marine Division and the brutal action on Guadalcanal, New Britain, and Peleliu, the author spares no detail of the horrors and sacrifices of war, painting an unvarnished portrait of how real warriors are made, fight, and often die in the defense of their country.

Grossman, Dave. *On Killing: The Psychological Cost of Learning to Kill in War and Society.*

Study of the techniques the military uses to overcome the powerful reluctance to kill, of how killing affects soldiers, and of the societal implications of escalating violence. It includes information on twenty-first-century military conflicts, recent trends in crime, suicide bombings, school shootings, and more.

Ramo, Joshua Cooper. *The Age of the Unthinkable: Why the New World Disorder Constantly Surprises Us and What We Can Do About It.*

Presents a new model for understanding our dangerously unpredictable world. Drawing upon history, economics, complexity theory, psychology, immunology, and the science of networks, the author describes a new landscape of inherent unpredictability—and remarkable, wonderful possibility.

Van Creveld, Martin. *The Changing Face of War: Combat from the Marne to Iraq.*

Examines the path that led to the impasse in Iraq, why powerful standing armies are now helpless against ill-equipped insurgents, and how the security of sovereign nations may be maintained in the future. Paying close attention to the unpredictability of the human element, the author takes the reader on a journey from the last century's clashes of massive armies to today's short, high-tech, lopsided skirmishes and frustrating quagmires.

Fehrenbach, T. R. *This Kind of War: The Classic Korean War History.*
History of the Korean War written from the perspective of those who fought it. Partly drawn from official records, operations journals, and histories, it is based largely on the compelling personal narratives of small-unit commanders and their troops. As Americans and North Koreans continue to face each other across the 38th Parallel, this book offers vital lessons for the future.

United States of America. *U.S. Constitution.*
The U.S. Constitution is the supreme law of the United States of America. Amendments 1–10 constitute what is known as the Bill of Rights. Several changes and additions have been made over the past two hundred-plus years (Amendments 11–27).

Moore, Harold G. *We Were Soldiers Once and Young: Ia Drang: The Battle That Changed the War in Vietnam.*
This book is about a group of men persevered, sacrificed themselves for their comrades, and never gave up. In November 1965, some four hundred fifty men of the 1st Battalion, 7th Cavalry, fought against two thousand North Vietnamese soldiers in the Ia Drang Valley—one of the most savage and significant battles of the Vietnam War. This book is also on the Sergeant Major of the Marine Corps Reading List.

Senior Level: Master Gunnery Sergeant–Sergeant Major

Shay, Jonathan. *Achilles in Vietnam: Combat Trauma and the Undoing of Character.*
Examines the psychological devastation of war by comparing the soldiers of Homer's *Iliad* with Vietnam veterans suffering from post-traumatic stress disorder. Although the *Iliad* was written twenty-seven centuries ago, it has much to teach about combat trauma, as do the more recent, compelling voices and experiences of Vietnam vets. This book is also on the Sergeant Major of the Marine Corps Reading List.

Smith, Perry M. and Daniel M. Gerstein. *Assignment: Pentagon: How to Excel in a Bureaucracy.*
Essential guide for newly assigned military personnel, fresh civilians, and interested outsiders to the Pentagon's informal set of arrangements, networks, and functions that operate in the service and joint-service world. It delivers practical advice and helpful hints about surviving the pressures and problems of working in "The Building." If you've been assigned to the Pentagon or are starting work for any large company, you need to read this book.

Muth, Jörg. *Command Culture: Officer Education in the U.S. Army and the German Armed Forces, 1901–1940, & the Consequences for World War II.*
The U.S. Army and the German Armed Forces traveled different paths to select, educate, and promote their officers in the crucial time before

WWII. The author explores the paradox that in Germany officers came from a closed authoritarian society but received an extremely open-minded military education, whereas their counterparts in the United States came from one of the most democratic societies but received an outdated military education that harnessed their minds and limited their initiative. While German officer candidates learned that in war everything is possible and a war of extermination acceptable, American officers, raised in a democracy, learned that certain boundaries could never be crossed.

Hammes, Thomas. *Forgotten Warriors: The 1st Provisional Marine Brigade, the Corps Ethos, and the Korean War.*
At the outbreak of the Korean War, the Marine Corps was ordered to deploy an air-ground brigade in less than ten days, even though no such brigade existed at the time. Assembled from the woefully understrength 1st Marine Division and 1st Marine Air Wing units, the Brigade shipped out only six days after activation, sailed directly to Korea, and was in combat within ninety-six hours of landing. Despite these enormous handicaps and numerically superior enemy forces, the 1st Provisional Marine Brigade won every one of its engagements and helped secure the Pusan Perimeter.

Friedman, Thomas L. *Hot, Flat, and Crowded: Why We Need a Green Revolution and How It Can Renew America.*
A provocative look at the biggest challenge facing us today—our hot, flat, and crowded world. Climate change and rapid population growth mean that it's no longer possible for businesses (or the rest of us) to keep doing things the same old way. Things are going to have to change—and fast. The author provides a bold strategy for clean fuel, energy efficiency, and conservation that he calls "Code Green." It will change everything, including what we put into our equipment to bring to battle.

Walzer, Michael. *Just and Unjust Wars: A Moral Argument with Historical Illustrations.*
Examines the moral issues surrounding military theory, war crimes, and the spoils of war. The author studies a variety of conflicts over the course of history, as well as the testimony of those who have been most directly involved—participants, decision makers, and victims. He specifically addresses the moral issues surrounding the war in and occupation of Iraq, reminding us once again that "the argument about war and justice is still a political and moral necessity."

Twining, Merril B. *No Bended Knee: The Battle for Guadalcanal: The Memoir of Gen. Merril B. Twining, USMC (Ret.).*
In this military memoir by the 1st Marine Division's operations officer during the 1942 battle for Guadalcanal, Twining gives us an appreciation for Marines at war from the strategic, operational, and tactical levels. His firsthand report details the fierce fighting and horrid conditions endured by Marines on the ground and the decision of U.S. Navy to pull away from Guadalcanal, as well as addressing the role of the MAGTFs, conducting

amphibious operations, hostility between the armed forces, and understanding joint and combined theater logistics.

Keegan, John. *The Face of Battle.*

This book looks at military history from the battlefield and at the direct
experience of individuals at the "point of maximum danger." In the
author's scrupulous reassessment of three battles representative of three
different time periods, he manages to convey what the experience of combat meant for the participants, whether they were facing the arrow cloud at
the battle of Agincourt, the musket balls at Waterloo, or the steel rain of
the Somme. This book is also on the Sergeant Major of the Marine Corps
Reading List.

Keegan, John. *The Mask of Command.*

This book asks the reader to consider questions that are seldom asked:
What makes a great military leader? Why is it that men, indeed sometimes
entire nations, follow a single leader, often to victory, but with equal dedication also to defeat? Keegan applies these questions to four commanders
who profoundly influenced the course of history: Alexander the Great, the
Duke of Wellington, Ulysses S. Grant, and Adolf Hitler. All powerful
leaders, each cast in a different mold, each with diverse results. This book
is also on the Sergeant Major of the Marine Corps Reading List.

Officers
Entry Level: Candidate–Midshipmen

Uris, Leon. *Battle Cry.*

Battle Cry follows the fortunes of a Marine outfit from boot camp to
Guadalcanal, Tarawa, and elsewhere in the Pacific during World War II.
Many of the events are based on the author's WWII experience with the
6th Marine Regiment. The interactions of the characters and their ability to
develop *esprit de corps* is a central theme.

Miller, Zell. *Corps Values.*

The author recounts the simple but powerful lessons he learned as a United
States Marine: the core values we must embrace if we are to be successful
as individuals and as a nation. Only by incorporating such time-honored
Marine qualities as pride, discipline, courage, brotherhood, and respect
into our personal and professional lives can we meet the challenges that lie
ahead.

Proser, Jim and Jerry Cutler. *I'm Staying with My Boys: The Heroic Life of Sgt.
John Basilone, USMC.*

The only family-authorized biography of Sgt. John Basilone, the only
World War II Marine to win the Medal of Honor, the Navy Cross, and a
Purple Heart. The book is written in the first-person, allowing the reader to
experience his significant achievements at Guadalcanal and Iwo Jima as
perhaps he did himself.

Ricks, Thomas E. *Making the Corps*.

This book follows recruit of Platoon 3086 through Marine Corps boot camp in Parris Island, South Carolina, and the drill instructors who instill in them the principles of discipline, teamwork, and commitment. Ricks also examines changes in recruit training and how the Corps deals with critical social and political issues like race relations, gender equality, and sexual orientation, as well as the growing divide between the military and the rest of America. As the author follows these men from their hometowns, through boot camp and into their first year as Marines, he paints a picture not only of individual Marines but the Corps as a whole.

Kasal, Brad. *My Men are My Heroes*.

Account of Marine First Sergeant Brad Kasal's courageous mission to rescue fallen comrades while under intense enemy fire during the Battle of Fallujah. During the fight, Kasal was shot seven times, almost losing his leg, and sustained forty-seven shrapnel wounds using his body to shield a wounded Marine from an enemy grenade. He was awarded the Navy Cross, the nation's second highest award for heroism, for his actions.

Shaara, Michael. *The Killer Angels: The Classic Novel of the Civil War*.

This book centers around the key battle of the American Civil War: the battle of Gettysburg. In a day-by day chronicle, the events immediately before and during the battle of Gettysburg unfold through the eyes of Confederate and Union generals and officers. The author's ability to convey the thoughts of men in war as well as their confusion—the so-called "fog of battle"—is outstanding.

Primary Level: Warrant Officer–Second Lieutenant–First Lieutenant

Remarque, Erich Maria. *All Quiet on the Western Front*.

This book is about Paul Baumer, who enlists with his classmates in the German army of WWI. They become soldiers with youthful enthusiasm. Through years of vivid horror, Paul holds fast to a single vow: to fight against the principle of hate that meaninglessly pits young men of the same generation but different uniforms against each other, if only he can come out of the war alive.

Von Schell, Adolf. *Battle Leadership*.

Collection of lessons learned by the author, who served as a small unit infantry commander (German army) during WWI. It includes observations on tactics and psychological reactions of troops in battle.

Pressfield, Steven. *Gates of Fire: An Epic Novel of the Battle of Thermopylae*.

In the battle of Thermopylae (480 BCE), seven thousand Greeks led by three hundred Spartans held an enormous Persian army of two hundred thousand at bay for several days—an army that would have changed our civilization had the Greeks not died fighting it. Never before or since has such a badly outnumbered army fought so valiantly nor effectively. This book is also on the Sergeant Major of the Marine Corps Reading List.

Davis, Burke. *Marine! The Life of Lt. Gen. Lewis B. (Chesty) Puller, USMC (Ret.)*.

Biography of real-life hero Chesty Puller, the most decorated Marine in history. From commanding the Horse Marines in Peking to leading the Inchon landing, Puller was a legend in his own time. But his popularity added to his blunt honesty earned him many enemies in Washington, and when the war was done they no longer needed a fighter like Chesty. Winner of five Navy Crosses, no officer ever inspired greater courage, loyalty, and devotion from his men, pushed them harder, or served them better.

Marlantes, Karl. *Matterhorn: A Novel of the Vietnam War*.

Story of a young Marine lieutenant and his comrades who are dropped into the mountain jungle of Vietnam as boys and forced to fight their way into manhood. Standing in their way are the North Vietnamese, monsoon rain and mud, leeches and tigers, and disease and malnutrition. Almost as daunting are the obstacles they discover between each other: racial tension, competing ambitions, and duplicitous superior officers. This book is also on the Sergeant Major of the Marine Corps Reading List.

Tzu, Sun. *The Art of War*.

Written more than two thousand years ago, *The Art of War* is the first known study of the planning and conduct of military operations. In addition to military theory and strategy, the author examines relevant economic, political, and psychological factors. The timeless principles of *The Art of War* are often applied outside the military realm in the areas of business and management. This book is also on the Sergeant Major of the Marine Corps Reading List.

Swinton, E. D. *The Defence of Duffer's Drift*.

Insightful analysis of small unit tactics in defending a strategic objective given limited communications, resources, and manpower. Although some advice is outdated, three of the twenty-two lessons learned presented are of extreme relevance to a new platoon leader: the urgency and importance of first setting security and preparing defenses, the use of cover and concealment, and the creation of clear fields of fire.

Sajer, Guy. *The Forgotten Soldier*.

Recounts the horror of WWII on the Eastern Front as seen through the eyes of a teenage German soldier. It depicts a desperate struggle for survival against cold, hunger, and terrifying Soviet artillery. Photos show the hardships and destructiveness of war, such as troops battling through snow, mud, burned villages, and rubble-strewn cities.

Drury, Bob. *The Last Stand of Fox Company: A True Story of U.S. Marines in Combat*

During the Korean War, 234 heroic Marines from Fox Company, First Division, held off a force of 10,000 Chinese soldiers in subzero weather to secure the Toktong Pass. This is their story. This book is also on the Sergeant Major of the Marine Corps Reading List.

McLaurin, Melton Alonza. *The Marines of Montford Point: America's First Black Marines.*

Collection of interviews with members of the Montford Point Marines Association, organized by chronology and theme. This recognizes and honors the men who desegregated the Marine Corps and loyally served their country in three major wars. It is about the first black recruits who received Marine Corps basic training at the segregated Camp Montford Point (adjacent to Camp Lejeune). Between 1942 and 1949, more than twenty thousand men trained at Montford Point, most of them going on to serve in the Pacific Theater in World War II as members of support units. This book is also on the Sergeant Major of the Marine Corps Reading List.

United States of America. *U.S. Constitution.*

The U.S. Constitution is the supreme law of the United States of America. Amendments 1–10 constitute what is known as the Bill of Rights. Several changes and additions have been made over the past two-hundred-plus years (Amendments 11–27).

Sledge, E. B. *With the Old Breed at Peleliu and Okinawa.*

First-person account of fighting at Peleliu and Okinawa. Eugene Sledge was part of WWII's famous 1st Marine Division, 3rd Battalion, 5th Marines. It is based on notes Sledge secretly kept in a copy of the New Testament and documents what saved, threatened, and changed his life. It is also a story of how Sledge learned to hate and kill—and came to love—his fellow man. This book is also on the Sergeant Major of the Marine Corps Reading List.

Career Level: Chief Warrant Officer 2 and 3–Captain

Rommel, Erwin. *Attacks.*

Reprint of Field Marshal Erwin Rommel's World War I military classic, *Infanterie Greift An.* In his autobiography, Rommel traces his development from a "green" lieutenant to a confident, seasoned, and singularly success-ful commander. Providing keen insight into his mind and character, it is an important treatise on combat leadership and psychology, containing many valuable lessons for those who would raise and train armies. Prime among these lessons is the reminder that men are the key element in combat; that it is the will, spirit and skill of men, led by competent and courageous offi-cers that win battles; and that high morale is developed by the accomplish-ment of difficult tasks.

Frederick, Jim. *Black Hearts.*

Story of a small group of soldiers from the 101st Airborne Division's fabled 502nd Infantry Regiment—"the Black Heart Brigade." Deployed in late 2005 to Iraq's "Triangle of Death," the Black Hearts found themselves in the country's most dangerous location at its most dangerous time. It is a story about men in combat, the fragility of character in the savage crucible of warfare, and a warning of new dangers emerging in the way American soldiers are led on the battlefields of the twenty-first century.

Krulak, Victor H. *First to Fight: An Inside View of the U.S. Marine Corps*.
This book examines the foundation on which the Marine Corps is built.
The author, Lt. Gen. Victor "Brute" Krulak (USMC, Ret.), offers an
insider's chronicle of Marines, on the battlefield and off. He takes a close
look at the Marine experience during WWII, Korea, and Vietnam—wars
in which he was a participant—and in doing so helps answer the question
of what it means to be a Marine and how the Corps has maintained such an
outstanding reputation. This book is also on the Sergeant Major of the
Marine Corps Reading List.

Infantry School, Fort Benning, Ga. *Infantry in Battle (FMFRP 12-2)*.
This publication covers small unit tactic as illustrated by examples drawn
from WWI. It checks the ideas acquired from peacetime instruction
against the experience of battle.

Petersen, Frank E. *Into the Tiger's Jaw: America's First Black Marine Aviator*.
Autobiography of the first black aviator in the United States Marine Corps.
After earning his wings in 1952, Petersen saw combat in Korea and Vietnam where he flew more than three hundred and fifty missions. He commanded at the squadron, group, brigade, and Marine Aircraft levels during
his career as a Marine aviator.

Burgin, R. V. *Islands of the Damned—A Marine at War in the Pacific*.
Personal narrative of the author's experiences as a Marine during WWII in
the Pacific Theater where he confronted snipers, ambushes along narrow
jungle trails, abandoned corpses of hara-kiri victims, and howling banzai
attacks. During his two years of service, the author rose from green private
to seasoned sergeant, and earned a Bronze Star for his valor at Okinawa.

Grossman, Dave. *On Killing: The Psychological Cost of Learning to Kill in
War and Society*.
Study of the techniques the military uses to overcome the powerful reluctance to kill, of how killing affects soldiers, and of the societal implications
of escalating violence. It includes information on twenty-first-century
military conflicts, recent trends in crime, suicide bombings, school shootings, and more.

Gladwell, Malcolm. *Outliers: The Story of Success*.
An intellectual journey through the world of "outliers"—the best and the
brightest, the most famous, and the most successful. The author challenges
the reader to answer the question: What makes high-achievers different?
His answer is that we pay too much attention to what successful people are
like and too little attention to where they are from: that is, their culture,
their family, their generation, and the idiosyncratic experiences of their
upbringing.

Fraser, George MacDonald. *Quartered Safe Out Here*.
Action-packed memoir of the author's experiences in Burma during
WWII. Although only 19 years old when he arrived during the war's final
year, Fraser offers a firsthand glimpse at the camaraderie, danger and satisfaction of service.

Klein, Gary. *Sources of Power: How People Make Decisions.*
> This book discusses the naturalistic decision-making approach, which views people as inherently skilled and experienced. It is based on observations of humans acting under such real-life constraints as time pressure, high stakes, personal responsibility, and shifting conditions. The professionals studied include firefighters, critical care nurses, pilots, nuclear power plant operators, battle planners, and chess masters.

Pressfield, Steven. *The Virtues of War.*
> A novel in which Alexander the Great recounts with a warrior's unflinching eye for detail the blood, terror, and tactics of his greatest battlefield victories. He never denies the hard realities of the code by which he lives: The Virtues of War. As much as he is feared by his enemies, he is loved and revered by his friends, generals, and the men who follow him into battle. Alexander conquered every enemy the world stood against him— except the one he never saw coming.

United States of America. *The U.S. Constitution.*
> The U.S. Constitution is the supreme law of the United States of America. Amendments 1–10 constitute what is known as the Bill of Rights. Several changes and additions have been made over the past two-hundred-plus years (Amendments 11–27).

Boot, Max. *War Made New: Technology, Warfare, and the Course of History.*
> Focuses on four revolutions in military affairs and describes how inventions ranging from gunpowder to GPS-guided air strikes have remade the field of battle and shaped the rise and fall of empires. The author argues that even as cutting-edge technologies have made America the greatest military power in world history, advanced communications systems have allowed decentralized irregular forces to become an increasingly significant threat.

Intermediate Level: Chief Warrant Officer 4 and 5–Major–Lieutenant Colonel

McPherson, James M. *Battle Cry of Freedom: The Civil War Era.*
> Recounts the momentous episodes that preceded the American Civil War, is a chronicle of the war itself, and includes the author's view on such matters as the slavery expansion issue in the 1850s, the origins of the Republican Party, the causes of secession, internal dissent and anti-war opposition in the North and the South, and the reasons for the Union's victory. This book is also on the Sergeant Major of the Marine Corps Reading List.

Gladwell, Malcolm. *Blink: The Power of Thinking without Thinking.*
> This is a book about how we think without thinking, about choices that seem to be made in an instant—in the blink of an eye—that actually aren't as simple as they seem. Why are some people brilliant decision makers while others are consistently inept? Why do some people follow their instincts and win while others end up stumbling into error? It reveals that great decision makers are not those who process the most information or

spend the most time deliberating, but those who have perfected the art of "thin-slicing"—filtering the very few factors that matter from an overwhelming number of variables.

Coram, Robert. *Boyd: The Fighter Pilot Who Changed the Art of War.*
John Boyd, considered by many to be the greatest U.S. fighter pilot ever, is the man who, in simulated air-to-air combat, defeated every challenger in less than forty seconds. His manual of fighter tactics changed the way every air force in the world flies and fights. Boyd was a rebel who cared not for his reputation or fortune but for his country.

Coram, Robert. *Brute: The Life of Victor Krulak, U.S. Marine.*
Biography of Lt. Gen. Victor "Brute" Krulak (USMC, Ret.). He went on daring spy missions, was badly wounded, pioneered the use of amphibious vehicles and use of helicopters in warfare, and masterminded the invasion of Okinawa. In Vietnam, he developed a holistic military strategy in stark contrast to the Army's "Search and Destroy" methods. Yet it can be argued that all of these accomplishments pale in comparison to what he did after WWII and again after Korea: He almost single-handedly stopped the U.S. government from abolishing the Marine Corps.

Hanson, Victor. *Carnage and Culture: Landmark Battles in the Rise of Western Power.*
Examines nine landmark battles from ancient to modern times, from Salamis where outnumbered Greeks devastated the slave army of Xerxes, to Cortes's conquest of Mexico, to the Tet offensive. Looking beyond popular explanations such as geography or superior technology, the author argues that it is in fact Western culture and values—the tradition of dissent, the value placed on inventiveness and adaptation, and the concept of citizenship—that have consistently produced superior arms and soldiers. This book is also on the Sergeant Major of the Marine Corps Reading List.

Muth, Jörg. *Command Culture: Officer Education in the U.S. Army and the German Armed Forces, 1901–1940, & the Consequences for World War II.*
The U.S. Army and the German Armed Forces traveled different paths to select, educate, and promote their officers in the crucial time before WWII. The author explores the paradox that in Germany officers came from a closed authoritarian society but received an extremely open minded military education, whereas their counterparts in the United States came from one of the most democratic societies but received an outdated military education that harnessed their minds and limited their initiative. While German officer candidates learned that in war everything is possible and a war of extermination acceptable, American officers, raised in a democracy, learned that certain boundaries could never be crossed.

Field Marshal Viscount Slim. *Defeat into Victory: Battling Japan in Burma and India 1942–1945.*
This detailed autobiography by British Field Marshal Viscount Slim (1891–1970) is a first-person account of the retaking of Burma during

World War II. In this book, Slim honestly examines his decisions as a leader and consequences of those decisions, both good and bad. Defeat into Victory is widely regarded as a classic memoir of high command. This book is also on the Sergeant Major of the Marine Corps Reading List.

Hammes, Thomas. *Forgotten Warrior: The 1st Provisional Marine Brigade, the Corps Ethos, and the Korean War.*

At the outbreak of the Korean War, the Marine Corps was ordered to deploy an air-ground brigade in less than ten days, even though no such brigade existed at the time. Assembled from the woefully understrength 1st Marine Division and 1st Marine Air Wing units, the Brigade shipped out only six days after activation, sailed directly to Korea and was in combat within ninety-six hours of landing. Despite these enormous handicaps and numerically superior enemy forces, the 1st Provisional Marine Brigade won every one of its engagements and helped secure the Pusan Perimeter.

Friedman, Thomas L. *Hot, Flat, and Crowded: Why We Need a Green Revolution and How It Can Renew America.*

A provocative look at the biggest challenge facing us today—our hot, flat, and crowded world. Climate change and rapid population growth mean that it's no longer possible for businesses (or the rest of us) to keep doing things the same old way. Things are going to have to change—and fast. The author provides a bold strategy for clean fuel, energy efficiency, and conservation that he calls "Code Green." It will change everything, including what we put into our equipment and bring to battle.

Walzer, Michael. *Just and Unjust Wars: A Moral Argument with Historical Illustrations.*

Examines the moral issues surrounding military theory, war crimes, and the spoils of war. The author studies a variety of conflicts over the course of history, as well as the testimony of those who have been most directly involved—participants, decision makers, and victims. He specifically addresses the moral issues surrounding the war in and occupation of Iraq, reminding us once again that "the argument about war and justice is still a political and moral necessity."

Murray, Williamson R. and Allan R. Millett (editors). *Military Innovation in the Interwar Period.*

This volume of comparative essays studies major military innovations in the 1920s and 1930s and explores differences in innovating exploitation by the seven major military powers. It investigates how and why innovation occurred or did not occur, and explains much of the strategic and operative performance of the Axis and Allies in WWII.

Hanson, Victor Davis. *Ripples of Battle: How Wars of the Past Still Determine How We Fight, How We Live, and How We Think.*

The effects of war refuse to remain local: They persist through the centuries, sometimes in unlikely ways far removed from the military arena.

The author explains how the Athenian defeat at Delium in 424 BCE brought tactical innovations to infantry fighting; it also assured the influence of the philosophy of Socrates, who fought well in the battle. Perhaps most resonant for our time, the book discusses how the agony of Okinawa spurred the Japanese toward state-sanctioned suicide missions.

Ramo, Joshua Cooper. *The Age of the Unthinkable: Why the New World Disorder Constantly Surprises Us and What We Can Do About It.*
Presents a new model for understanding our dangerously unpredictable world. Drawing upon history, economics, complexity theory, psychology, immunology, and the science of networks, the author describes a new landscape of inherent unpredictability—and remarkable, wonderful possibility.

Gray, J. Glenn. *The Warriors: Reflections on Men in Battle.*
A philosophical meditation on what warfare does to us and an examination of the reasons soldiers act as they do. The author explains the attractions of battle—the adrenaline rush, the *esprit de corps*—and analyzes the many rationalizations made by combat troops to justify their actions. The author notes that "War reveals dimensions of human nature both above and below the acceptable standards for humanity."

Fehrenbach, T. R. *This Kind of War: The Classic Korean War History.*
History of the Korean War written from the perspective of those who fought it. Partly drawn from official records, operations journals, and histories, it is based largely on the compelling personal narratives of small-unit commanders and their troops. As Americans and North Koreans continue to face each other across the 38th Parallel, this book offers vital lessons for the future.

Senior Level: Colonel–General

Gray, Colin. *Another Bloody Century: Future Warfare.*
This book looks into the future to provide some intriguing answers about the ways Western armed forces—which have traditionally been trained to fight conventional, not guerrilla, warfare—may need to evolve.

Smith, Perry M. and Daniel M. Gerstein. *Assignment: Pentagon: How to Excel in a Bureaucracy.*
Essential guide for newly assigned military personnel, fresh civilians, and interested outsiders to the Pentagon's informal set of arrangements, networks, and functions that operate in the service and joint-service world. It delivers practical advice and helpful hints about surviving the pressures and problems of working in "The Building." If you've been assigned to the Pentagon or are starting work for any large company, you need to read this book.

McMaster, H. R. *Dereliction of Duty: Lyndon Johnson, Robert McNamara, the Joint Chiefs of Staff, and the Lies That Led to Vietnam.*
Analysis of how and why the United States became involved in an all-out war in Southeast Asia. Based on transcripts and personal accounts of crucial meetings, confrontations, and decisions, it re-creates what happened

and why. The book focuses on President Lyndon Johnson, Robert McNamara, General Maxwell Taylor, McGeorge Bundy, and other top officials.

Kissinger, Henry. *Diplomacy.*

Overview of the history and an account of Henry Kissinger's negotiations with world leaders. The author describes how the art of diplomacy has created the world in which we live, and how America's approach to foreign affairs has always differed vastly from that of other nations.

Rose, Gideon. *How Wars End: Why We Always Fight the Last Battle: A History of American Intervention from World War I to Afghanistan.*

This book recreates the choices that presidents and their advisers have confronted during the final stages of each major conflict from WWI through Iraq. The author "puts readers in the room" with U.S. officials as they make decisions that affect millions of lives and shape the modern world—seeing what they saw, hearing what they heard, and feeling what they felt. He argues that American leaders have repeatedly ignored the need for careful postwar planning, but can (and must) do a better job in order to create a stable and sustainable political outcome once the "real" military work is over.

Biddle, Stephen. *Military Power: Explaining Victory and Defeat in Modern Battle.*

Systematic account of force employment's role and how this account holds up under rigorous, multi-method testing. The results challenge a wide variety of standard views, from current expectations for a revolution in military affairs, to mainstream scholarship in international relations, and orthodox interpretations of modern military history. The author argues that force employment is central to modern war, and has become increasingly important since 1900 as the key to surviving ever more lethal weaponry. Technological change produces opposite effects depending on how forces are employed; to focus only on materiel is thus to risk major error—with serious consequences for both policy and scholarship.

Gray, Colin S. *Modern Strategy.*

The book is a major contribution to the general theory of strategy; it makes sense of the strategic history of the twentieth century and provides understanding of what that strategic history implies for the century to come.

Cohen, Eliot A. *Supreme Command: Soldiers, Statesmen, and Leadership in Wartime.*

This book offers compelling proof that, as Clemenceau put it, "War is too important to leave to the generals." By examining the shared leadership traits of four politicians (Abraham Lincoln, Georges Clemenceau, Winston Churchill, and David Ben-Gurion) who triumphed in extraordinarily varied military campaigns, the author argues that active statesmen make the best wartime leaders, pushing their military subordinates to succeed where they might have failed if left to their own devices.

Goodwin, Doris Kearns. *Team of Rivals: The Political Genius of Abraham Lincoln.*
Biography of Abraham Lincoln, centered on his mastery of men and how it shaped the most significant presidency in the nation's history. Throughout the turbulent 1850s, each of his "rivals" energetically sought the presidency as the conflict over slavery was leading inexorably to secession and civil war. Lincoln's understanding of human behavior and motivation enabled him to bring his disgruntled opponents together, create the most unusual cabinet in history, and marshal their talents to the task of preserving the Union and winning the war.

Hamilton, Alexander, James Madison, and John Jay. *The Federalist Papers.*
This book explains the complexities of a constitutional government—its political structure and principles based on the inherent rights of man. Scholars have long regarded this work as a milestone in political science and a classic of American political theory. It is commonly referred to the third "sacred writing" of American political history, behind the Declaration of Independence and the U.S. Constitution.

Tuchman, Barbara W. *The Guns of August.*
This book brings to life the people and events that led up to WWI. The author clearly articulates just how the war started, why, and why it could have been stopped but wasn't.

Strassler, Robert B. (editor). *The Landmark Thucydides: A Comprehensive Guide to the Peloponnesian War.*
Comprehensive guide to the Peloponnesian War. It includes several maps, brief informative appendices by classical scholars, explanatory marginal notes on each page, an index of unprecedented subtlety, and numerous other useful features.

Gaddis, John Lewis. *The Landscape of History: How Historians Map the Past.*
A look at the historian's craft as well as a strong argument for why a historical consciousness should matter to us today. For example: What is history and why should we study it? Is there such a thing as historical truth? Is history a science? This book is a "historical method" for beginners, a reaffirmation of it for practitioners, a challenge to social scientists, and essential for anyone who reads, writes, teaches, or cares about history.

Ip, Greg. *The Little Book of Economics: How the Economy Works in the Real Word.*
From inflation to the Federal Reserve, taxes to the budget deficit, the author walks us through how the economy really works and its role in our everyday life. Contains plain-English explanations of important economic terms, concepts, events, historical figures, and major players.

Kaplan, Robert D. *The Revenge of Geography: What Maps Tell Us about Coming Conflicts and the Battle against Fate.*
This book offers a new prism through which to view global upheavals and to understand what may lie ahead for continents and countries around the

world. The author builds on the insights, discoveries, and theories of great geographers and geopolitical thinkers of the past to look back at critical points in history, and then to look forward at the evolving global scene.

Chief of Naval Operations Reading List
(http://navyreading.dodlive.mil)

Warfighting First
Daughan, George C. *1812: The Navy's War.*

This Essential category Warfighting First book provides an engaging account of the War of 1812. At the outbreak of the War of 1812, America's prospects looked dismal. It was clear that the primary battlefield would be the open ocean but America's war fleet, only twenty ships strong, faced a practiced British navy of more than a thousand men of war. Still, through a combination of nautical deftness and sheer bravado, the American navy managed to take the fight to the British on the Great Lakes, in the Atlantic, and even in the eastern Pacific, and turn the tide of the war.

Clarke, Richard A. *Cyber War.*

This Essential category Warfighting First book details the nature and scope of the cyber threat to U.S. national security through very readable technical descriptions and gripping real-world examples of cyber attacks. *Cyber War* is a powerful book about technology, government, and military strategy; and about criminals, spies, soldiers, and hackers. It explains clearly and convincingly what cyber war is, how cyber weapons work, and how vulnerable we are as a nation and as individuals to the vast and looming web of cyber criminals. The author, Richard A. Clarke, is an internationally recognized expert on security and served in various capacities under four presidents. This important book provides a comprehensive overview of one of the greatest national security threats that America confronts today. This selection supports Department of Defense and U.S. Navy priorities for countering cyber warfare.

Williams, Gary. *SEAL of Honor.*

This Essential category Warfighting First book tells the compelling tale of the late Navy SEAL, Lt. Michael Murphy. A young man of great character, he is the subject of Naval Special Warfare courses on leadership. An Arleigh Burke–class guided missile destroyer, naval base, school, post office, ball park, and hospital emergency room have all been named in his honor. In his bestselling book *Lone Survivor* (formerly listed on the CNO Professional Reading Program), Marcus Luttrell, the only survivor of Operation Red Wing, called Michael "the best officer I ever knew, an iron-souled warrior of colossal, almost unbelievable courage in the face of the enemy." *SEAL of Honor* tells the story of Lt. Michael Murphy's life and how he came to be a man of selfless courage and honor. This book offers a sterling example of Navy core values lived out in his life, his service, and his sacrifice. It's a gripping and often emotionally moving book, and honors all who have made the ultimate sacrifice in the war against terrorism.

Marolda, Edward J. and Robert J. Schneller Jr. (editors). *Shield and Sword*. More than a decade after the United States forged a diverse international coalition to drive Saddam Hussein's invading forces out of Kuwait, the vital role seapower played in that mission has received far less recognition than the land and air campaigns. Yet U.S. Navy surface ships and submarines launched hundreds of cruise missile attacks against Iraqi targets throughout the war, and carriers in surrounding waters sent air strikes deep into the enemy's territory. The battleships *Missouri* and *Wisconsin* bombarded hostile targets while U.S. sailors fought naval actions beside U.S. Army and Royal Navy helicopter crews. SEAL missions, global sealift actions, mine countermeasures, and operations in support of the economic embargo all contributed to this complex joint war effort that became one of the most successful campaigns in American military history. This book details those naval operations and includes candid observations of leadership effectiveness, interservice relations, and methods of command and control.

Ricks, Thomas E. *The Gamble*. This Essential category Warfighting First book uses hundreds of hours of exclusive interviews with top officers in Iraq and extraordinary on-the-ground reportage to document the inside story of the Iraq War since late 2005. *The Gamble* offers news-breaking information, revealing behind-the-scenes disagreements between top commanders. We learn that almost every single officer in the chain of command fought against implementing the surge. Many of General Petraeus's closest advisers went to Iraq extremely pessimistic, doubting that the surge would have any effect. *The Gamble* examines the congressional hearings through the eyes of Petraeus and Ambassador Ryan Crocker, and their views of the questions posed by the 2008 presidential candidates. Thomas E. Ricks's stunning conclusion, stated in the last line of the book, is that "the events for which the Iraq war will be remembered by us and by the world have not yet happened." This title provides a comprehensive and highly readable presentation of how a complex problem in Iraq was addressed by U.S. military and political leaders.

Sterling, Forest J. *Wake of the Wahoo*. This Essential category Warfighting First book was an almost forgotten WWII classic that has been brought back into the spotlight by the CNO Professional Reading Program. From Pearl Harbor to her last and fatal voyage, this is the heroic true story of America's most daring World War II submarine, as told by one of the only surviving members of her crew, retired Chief Petty Officer Forest J. Sterling. The USS *Wahoo* (SS-238) was the most successful American submarine in the World War II Pacific Fleet. This riveting account of five combat sea patrols of the *Wahoo* captures life aboard a WWII submarine with a witty and inspiring deck-plates perspective of the boat's yeoman (YN1 Sterling). The superb leadership and tactical acumen of the *Wahoo*'s famed commanding officer, Commander Dudley "Mush" Morton and Executive Officer Commander Dick O'Kane are vividly illustrated in Sterling's book. *Wake of the Wahoo* is an unforgettable and invaluable read.

Operating Forward

Lewis, Bernard. *The Crisis of Islam.*

This timely book examines the historical roots of the resentments that dominate the Islamic world and that all too often have manifested themselves in acts of terrorism. Expanded from an award-winning *New Yorker* article, *The Crisis of Islam* looks at the theological origins of political Islam and takes the reader through the rise of militant Islam in Egypt, Saudi Arabia, and Iran, examining the impact of radical Wahhabi proselytizing and Saudi oil money, on the rest of the Islamic world. *The Crisis of Islam* ranges widely across thirteen centuries of history, but in particular it charts the key events of the twentieth century leading up to the violent confrontations of today: the creation of the state of Israel, the Cold War, the Iranian revolution, the defeat of the Soviet Union in Afghanistan, the Gulf War, and 9/11. While hostility toward the West has a long and varied history in the lands of Islam, its current concentration on America is new. So too is the cult of the suicide bomber. Brilliantly disentangling the cross-currents of Middle Eastern history from the rhetoric of its manipulators, author Bernard Lewis helps the reader understand the increasingly dogmatic rejection of modernity by many in the Muslim world in favor of a return to a sacred past. *The Crisis of Islam* is essential reading for anyone who wants to know what Osama bin Laden represents and why his murderous message resonates so widely in the Islamic world.

Holwitt, Lt. Joel, USN. *Execute Against Japan.*

This Essential category Operate Forward book was written by active-duty Submarine Warfare Officer Lt. Joel Holwitt. Less than five hours after the Japanese attack on Pearl Harbor, a telegram from the U.S. Chief of Naval Operations ordered, "Execute against Japan unrestricted air and submarine warfare." Mere hours after the attack, the United States abandoned its longstanding adherence to freedom of the seas, under which commercial vessels were immune from attack. From that moment, the American war effort in the Pacific would target not only military assets but all Japanese shipping. This surprising shift in U.S. policy expanded the limits of warfare in the Pacific. *Execute Against Japan* offers a new understanding of U.S. military policy during World War II. This book offers valuable lessons on the interplay of law, diplomacy, politics, and military doctrine and strategy in the conduct of war.

Kaplan, Robert. *Monsoon*.

This Essential category Operate Forward book offers a pivotal examination of the countries known as "Monsoon Asia," which include India, Pakistan, China, Indonesia, Burma, Oman, Sri Lanka, Bangladesh, and Tanzania. Bestselling author Robert D. Kaplan shows how crucial this dynamic area has become to American power. It is here that the fight for democracy, energy independence, and religious freedom will be lost or won, and it is here that American foreign policy must be concentrated if the United States is to remain relevant in an ever-changing world. From the Horn of Africa to the Indonesian archipelago and beyond, Kaplan exposes the effects of population growth, climate change, and extremist politics on this unstable region, demonstrating why Americans can no longer afford to ignore this important area of the world. This informative and engaging book truly is essential professional reading for those serving in the twenty-first-century U.S. Navy.

Hornfischer, James D. *Neptune's Inferno*.

This Essential category Operate Forward book is the most epic and intimate account ever written of the contest for control of the seaways of the Solomon Islands. Those who enjoyed *The Last Stand of the Tin Can Sailors*, on the previous edition of the CNO Professional Reading Program, will find *Neptune's Inferno* equally impressive. *Neptune's Inferno* details the grim, protracted campaign for Guadalcanal that has long been heralded as a Marine victory. Now, with his powerful portrait of the Navy's sacrifice—three sailors died at sea for every man lost ashore—Hornfischer tells for the first time the full story of the Navy men who fought in the deadly waters of "Ironbottom Sound." In addition to the rich Navy history and heritage that is contained in this book, there are many insightful lessons on leadership and the high cost of tactical failures in combat. This gripping book offers valuable lessons for sailors and officers of all pay grades.

Yoshihara, Toshi and James Holmes. *Red Star over the Pacific*.

This Essential category Operate Forward book assesses how the rise of Chinese sea power will affect U.S. maritime strategy in Asia. Combining a close knowledge of Asia and an ability to tap Chinese-language sources with naval combat experience and expertise in sea-power theory, the authors argue that China is laying the groundwork for a sustained challenge to American primacy in maritime Asia. To defend this hypothesis, they look back to Alfred Thayer Mahan's seapower theories, now popular with the Chinese. The book considers how strategic thought about the sea shapes Beijing's deliberations and compares China's geostrategic predicament to that of the Kaiser's Germany a century ago. It examines the Chinese navy's operational concepts, tactics, and capabilities, and appraises China's ballistic-missile submarine fleet. The authors conclude that unless Washington adapts, China will present a challenge to America's strategic position in Asia. This selection supports Department of Defense and U.S.

Navy priorities for increased focus on the Pacific Rim. Rich with historical examples and superb scholarship, *Red Star over the Pacific* is a thoughtful and informative analysis on the rise of Chinese naval power.

Collins, Catherine and Douglas Frantz. *The Man from Pakistan.*

In this Essential category Operate Forward book, investigative journalists Douglas Frantz and Catherine Collins tell an alarming tale of international intrigue through the eyes of the European and American officials who had suspicions about Pakistani nuclear scientist A. Q. Khan, tracked him, and ultimately shut him down, but only after the nuclear "genie" was out of the bottle. This well-researched book tells the story of how Khan managed to steal enough nuclear secrets to give Pakistan atomic weapons and then to go into business selling atomic secrets to Libya, Iraq, Iran, North Korea, and others. *The Man from Pakistan* provides an excellent foundation of knowledge for one of the greatest threats confronting the United States in the twenty-first century. It explains the origin of the emerging nuclear proliferation threats in North Korea and Iran, as well as technical descriptions of the process of manufacturing nuclear materials into weapons-grade materials. It offers valuable lessons for Navy personnel who must confront this threat as they operate forward in an increasingly dangerous environment.

Be Ready

Cutler, Thomas. *A Sailor's History of the U.S. Navy.*

The winner of the 2006 U.S. Maritime Literature Award, this highly readable book offers a fresh approach to naval history. Adopted by the U.S. Navy for issue to all new sailors, *A Sailor's History* vividly and excitingly brings to life the events that have shaped and inspired the Navy of today. Its perspective is thoroughly and decidedly democratic, highlighting the role of all sailors—from seaman to admiral. Rather than focus entirely on such naval icons as Jones, Decatur, and Nimitz, as most histories tend to do, author Thomas J. Cutler (a former gunner's mate and retired lieutenant commander) brings to the forefront the contributions of enlisted people, such as Quartermaster Peter Williams, who steered the ironclad *Monitor* into history, and Hospital Corpsman Tayinikia Campbell, who saved lives on the USS *Cole* after the terrorist attack in Yemen. The book's structure is unique; rather than a straightforward chronological arrangement, the work is grouped thematically in sections named after the Navy's core principles of honor, courage, and commitment; its traditions of "Don't Tread on Me" and "Don't Give Up the Ship"; and other significant aspects. The result is a unique account that captures Navy heritage as well as history, that provides inspiration as well as information, and that celebrates that most essential element of the Navy's history: the sailor.

Welle, Joshua, John Ennis, Katherine Kranz, and Graham Plaster. *In the Shadow of Greatness.*

This Essential category Be Ready book provides a glimpse into the lives of some of the post-9/11 generation of warriors. The stories of the Naval

Academy Class of 2002 are representative of an entire generation of sailors and officers who volunteered for service with the knowledge that they would serve in combat. Each story depicted in this book provides a glimpse into the lives of modern-day military officers who were faced with unique challenges. Their stories bring to light the trials of war and reveal a world most outside of the military do not understand. Refreshingly candid, their narratives take readers on a journey from Annapolis to the far corners of the world to experience operations at sea, on the land, and in the skies.

Williams Sr., Melvin G. and Melvin G. Williams, Jr. *Navigating the Seven Seas.*

This Essential category Be Ready book showcases important leadership lessons. The authors are the first African-American father and son to have served at the top in the U.S. Navy. In addition to the engaging biographical content of the book are the Seven C's of Leadership—Character, Courage, Competence, Commitment, Caring, Community, and Communicating— explained through vivid examples that will serve to guide sailors and officers to a successful life and Navy career. The father and son authors share inspirational lessons that cover all areas of the leadership spectrum, from the makings of a command master chief to the makings and distinct achievement of a flag officer. Navy heritage embraces both men's contributions since both father and son had to open doors that were closed to them due to their race. Melvin G. Williams Senior's ability to make Fleet improvements and positive recommendations for others was passed on to his own son, who served as Commander, U.S. 2nd Fleet and obtained the rank of Vice Admiral.

Orend, Brian. *The Morality of War.*

This Essential category Be Ready book provides the modern Navy warrior with an accessible and important reference to draw upon in the planning and execution of combat operations. *The Morality of War* thoughtfully analyzes every military conflict of recent decades as a means of illustrating the evolution of just war theory. The vivid historical examples from past wars and more recent conflicts in Bosnia, Iraq, and Afghanistan make this an intellectually engaging and important book for our age. *The Morality of War* is considered by many warriors and scholars to be the most accessible and comprehensive work on the important questions pertaining to morality and war. *The Morality of War* is an excellent introduction into just war theory and supports Department of Defense priorities for Counter Terrorism and Information Warfare.

Morgenstern, Julie. *Time Management from the Inside Out.*

This is an updated, expanded version of the definitive guide to managing and freeing up that most precious of commodities—time. Applying her trademark from-the-inside-out approach, author Julie Morgenstern sets a new standard for the time-management ideal. Her system has helped countless readers uncover their mental/emotional stumbling blocks and strengths, and cultivate a time-management methodology that suits individual needs. By applying the prescribed three-step program—Analyze, Strategize, Attack—readers of *Time Management from the Inside Out* will find more room in life for work, family, self-improvement, or whatever is deemed most important. Time management is a learnable skill, and in this completely revised edition of her work, Morgenstern provides the ultimate tools to combine, delegate, and eliminate unnecessary tasks; put technology to work; and, above all, stop procrastinating, for once and for all. This revised edition includes a new chapter on getting started in the method, new "time maps" for people with irregular schedules, new four-, eight-, and twelve-week program guides for improving time-management skills, and a fully updated resource guide.

Singer, P. W. *Wired for War.*

This Essential category Be Ready book explores the greatest revolution in military affairs since the atom bomb: the dawn of robotic warfare. Noted author P. W. Singer argues that we are on the cusp of a massive shift in military technology that threatens to make real the stuff of *I, Robot* and *The Terminator*. Blending historical evidence with interviews of an amazing cast of characters, Singer shows how technology is changing not just how wars are fought, but also the politics, economics, laws, and the ethics that surround war itself. Traveling from the battlefields of Iraq and Afghanistan to modern-day "skunk works" in the midst of suburbia, Singer illustrates that the robotics revolution has arrived. *Wired for War* is a must-read for all modern-day warriors who need to understand the impact of this revolution and how it is changing the way we operate and fight.

Army Chief of Staff Reading List
(history.army.mil/html/books/105/105-1-1)

The Army Profession

Puryear Jr., Edgar F. *19 Stars: A Study in Military Character and Leadership.*
This valuable work studies the lives and careers of Generals Dwight D. Eisenhower, Douglas MacArthur, George C. Marshall, and George S. Patton through their own eyes as well as the recollections of hundreds of others who worked with and knew them personally. Elements common to their success are examined, including obvious attributes such as their thorough preparation and capacity for work, as well as the more subtle qualities of character and, of course, luck. This is a great work for up-and-coming officers to better understand the fundamentals of leadership, preparation, and the need for luck.

Ambrose, Stephen E. *Band of Brothers: E Company, 506th Regiment, 101st Airborne from Normandy to Hitler's Eagle's Nest.*
Historian Stephen Ambrose tells the story of the men of Company E, 506th Parachute Infantry, 101st Airborne Division, from recruitment

through the end of World War II in Europe. The author compiled hours of interviews with many of the veterans themselves and poured through journals and letters as well. The book is a story of sacrifice and heroism by a unit that suffered a 150-percent casualty rate and considered the Purple Heart a badge of honor.

Moten, Matthew (editor). *Between War and Peace: How America Ends Its Wars*.

This is a collection of essays by prominent military historians who discuss how America rarely terminates its conflicts in a neat or absolute fashion. The covered wars span our history from the Revolutionary War to Operations Desert Shield and Desert Storm. Each essay has a unique perspective, and many contain assertions that contradict traditional views. Several common themes tie the essays together. Most prominently, wars, once launched, irrevocably change facts and acquire momentum of their own, distorting and altering initial military and political goals.

Coram, Robert. *Boyd: The Fighter Pilot Who Changed the Art of War*.

The author recounts the life of U.S. Air Force Col. (Ret.) John Boyd (1927–1997), who was a brilliant fighter pilot, tactician, and strategist. Colonel Boyd wrote the first manual on jet aerial combat, which proved to be instrumental in redesigning the Air Force after the Vietnam War and led to success in Desert Storm. His writings and theories on military strategy remain influential today, particularly his concept of the Observation, Orientation, Decision, Action (OODA) Loop, which all the military services and many business strategists use to this day.

Muth, Jörg. *Command Culture: Officer Education in the U.S. Army and the German Armed Forces, 1901–1940, and the Consequences of World War II*.

Jörg Muth examines the educational system of the German and American officer corps from 1901 to 1940 that shaped the outcome of World War II. His unique observation is that the German officers who came from a closed society were allowed greater intellectual freedom than their American counterparts, who came from an open society but received an outdated education that limited initiative. German officer candidates learned that in war everything is possible and that a war of extermination is acceptable. By contrast, American officers, raised in a democracy, were taught certain boundaries could never be crossed, and they succeeded not because of their military education but despite it.

United States of America. *Constitution of the United States*.

As soldiers and civilians, we swear an oath to defend this document as the basis of our government and way of life. It is time to revisit our nation's foundational document to refresh our understanding of the principles that organize and balance our society and remind us what we are swearing to "support and defend."

McMaster, H. R. *Dereliction of Duty: Lyndon Johnson, Robert McNamara, the Joint Chiefs of Staff, and the Lies That Led to Vietnam.*

In a masterful study of military strategy gone awry, the author (a professional soldier) argues persuasively that President Lyndon B. Johnson wanted to fight the war on poverty, not the war in Vietnam, and that the president made decisions he believed would allow him to do both. The result was a recipe for disaster that the Joint Chiefs of Staff exacerbated by failing to provide the president with their best advice. *Dereliction of Duty* is a cautionary tale about how military and civilian leadership failed at the highest levels and stumbled into a war that appeared to have no logical culmination.

D'Este, Carlo. *Eisenhower: A Soldier's Life.*

Perhaps the most renowned American general of the twentieth century, Dwight D. Eisenhower remains a subject of intense interest. A lieutenant colonel at the age of fifty with little combat experience and no military future ahead of him in the stifling between-the-wars promotion system, Eisenhower became, in little more than three years, a five-star general who would later lead the nation as president for two terms of office. D'Este's work focuses only on World War II, discussing the emerging general's skill at building the Allied coalition and keeping its disparate elements pointed at a common objective. The author also covers Eisenhower's weaknesses, indicting the supreme commander for keeping incompetent favorites in key positions, failing to make decisive decisions at key junctures in the war, and generally ignoring the dimension of logistics. The balanced account provides an accurate picture of the dilemmas faced by military commanders beset by conflicting objectives and courses of action.

Keegan, John. *The Face of Battle: A Study of Agincourt, Waterloo, and the Somme.*

One of the classics of modern military history, *The Face of Battle* brings to life three major battles: Agincourt (1415), Waterloo (1815), and the first battle of the Somme (1916). The author describes the sights, sounds, and smells of battle, providing a compelling look at what it means to be a soldier and how hard it is to describe realistically the dynamics of combat.

Angers, Trent. *The Forgotten Hero of My Lai: The Hugh Thompson Story.*

On 16 March 1968, soldiers belonging to Task Force Barker, 23rd Infantry Division (commonly known as the Americal Division), killed approximately five hundred Vietnamese civilians in the village of Son My. Because 347 of those victims died in the hamlet of My Lai-4, the event is generally referred to as the My Lai massacre, one of the darkest episodes in the history of the U.S. Army. This book describes the events that took place at My Lai and uncovers the courageous acts of CWO Hugh Thompson and his helicopter crew. They risked their lives to intervene, ultimately saving the lives of hundreds of innocent civilians. Army professionals should not ignore any aspect of My Lai. The episode provides a case study for soldiers and leaders to examine the role of integrity, selfless service, and personal courage in the Army profession.

Cox, Edward. *Grey Eminence: Fox Conner and the Art of Mentorship.*

Because Fox Conner's name was synonymous with mentorship, he was nicknamed the "Grey Eminence" within the Army. His influence and mentorship helped shape the careers of George S. Patton, George C. Marshall, and, most notably, President Dwight D. Eisenhower. While little is known about Conner himself, the author uses stories about Conner's relationship with Eisenhower. Fox Conner's four-step model for developing strategic leaders still holds true today. First, be a master of your craft. Second, recognize and recruit talented subordinates. Third, encourage and challenge protégés to develop their strengths and overcome their weaknesses. Fourth, do not be afraid to break the rules of the organization to do it. Everyone can learn something to apply to his or her life from Fox Conner.

McManus, John C. *Grunts: Inside the American Infantry Combat Experience, World War II through Iraq.*

Historian John C. McManus covers six decades of warfare, from the fight on the island of Guam in 1944 to today's counterinsurgency in Iraq. He demonstrates that the foot soldier has been the most indispensable and much overlooked factor in wartime victory despite the advancement of weaponry. McManus stresses that the importance of the human element in protecting the United States is too often forgotten and advances a passionate plea for fundamental change in our understanding of war.

William, T. Harry. *Lincoln and His Generals.*

First published in 1952, *Lincoln and His Generals* remains one of the definitive accounts of Abraham Lincoln's wartime leadership. In it, Williams dramatizes Lincoln's long and frustrating search for an effective leader of the Union Army and traces Lincoln's transformation from a politician with little military knowledge into a master strategist of the Civil War. Explored in-depth are Lincoln's often fraught relationships with generals such as George B. McClellan, John Pope, Ambrose E. Burnside, Joseph Hooker, John C. Fremont, and of course, Ulysses S. Grant. In this superbly written narrative, Williams demonstrates how Lincoln's persistent "meddling" into military affairs was crucial to the Northern war effort and utterly transformed the president's role as commander in chief.

Hubbard, Elbert. *A Message to Garcia.*

This classic essay from 1899, based on the true story of Lt. Andrew Rowan, is a notable testament of initiative and responsibility. This work provides common-sense advice on the importance of personal responsibility, loyalty, hard work, and enterprise.

Myrer, Anton. *Once an Eagle.*

An exciting historical novel, *Once an Eagle* traces the career of a fictitious soldier from World War I to Vietnam. The book realistically portrays the confusion of combat, the bonds that form between fighting men, the tensions between line and staff officers, and the heavy responsibility of command. This is a great work for young leaders contemplating a career in the profession of arms and looking for a deeper understanding of Army culture.

Perry, Mark. *Partners in Command: George Marshall and Dwight Eisenhower in War and Peace.*

The book is a balanced biographical view of the relationship between Generals George C. Marshall and Dwight D. Eisenhower. It provides an illustrative glimpse at the connection between the two men as they developed a grand alliance and forged the strategies that led to victory in Europe in World War II. It accurately and evenly portrays their relationship with each other and their contemporary American and British military and civilian counterparts. The volume is a good read for strategic leaders who wish to better understand the complexities of coalition, joint, and civil-military relations.

Grant, Ulysses S. *Personal Memoirs: Ulysses S. Grant.*

A classic and honest study by one of America's greatest generals, this is one of the finest autobiographies of a military commander ever written. It has valuable insights into leadership and command that apply to all levels and in all times. Grant's resiliency under almost unimaginable stress during critical junctures of America's most bloody war makes him a fascinating and human case study of the "epitomized" soldier.

Hackett, John Winthrop. *The Profession of Arms.*

This book traces the lineage of armies, from the ancient world to today, in a concise and insightful manner. Hackett focuses on the relationship between military forces and the countries they represent on the battlefield. Based on his vast military experience and career, the author offers some interesting opinions about training future leaders in the armed services.

Cohen, Eliot A. *Supreme Command: Soldiers, Statesmen, and Leadership in Wartime.*

This work examines four case studies in leadership and civil-military relations. Cohen focuses on Abraham Lincoln, Georges Clemenceau, Winston Churchill, and David Ben-Gurion and their relationships with subordinate military commanders. The author argues that rather than adhere to traditional civilian and military roles in directing war, some of the most successful civilian leaders have inserted themselves into what many have asserted were "purely military" spheres of strategic and operational art. Cohen's study provides an accessible treatment of long-standing issues in the field of civil-military relations.

Mullaney, Craig M. *The Unforgiving Minute: A Soldier's Education.*

A West Point graduate, Rhodes scholar, Airborne Ranger, and U.S. Army captain, Craig Mullaney recounts the hard lessons that only war can teach while fighting al-Qaeda in Afghanistan. This is an unforgettable portrait of a young soldier grappling with the weight of war and coming to terms with what it means to be a man.

The Force of Decisive Action

McCullough, David. *1776*.

This is a fast-paced narrative of the Revolutionary War from the summer of 1775 to Washington's stunning twin victories at Trenton and Princeton in late 1776. McCullough shows that persistence, dedication to the American cause, and Washington's remarkable leadership drove a small, ill-equipped American army to overcome severe hardships and numerous defeats to save the American Revolution from collapse during the war's most tumultuous year.

Grotelueschen, Mark E. *The AEF Way of War: The American Army and Combat in World War I*.

This exemplary case study of doctrinal and tactical innovation under fire shows how four divisions of the American Expeditionary Forces adapted, or failed to adapt, to conditions on the Western Front during World War I. The 1st and 2nd Divisions perfected artillery-infantry liaison so that by November 1918 they had achieved "state of the art" tactical skills as practiced by the Allied armies. Both the 26th and 77th Divisions failed to achieve this level of skill—the 26th because its commander failed to maintain control of his subordinate units and the 77th because its commander remained wedded to prewar doctrine.

Stewart, Richard W. (editor). *American Military History, Vol. 2, The United States Army in a Global Era, 1917–2008*.

Created initially as a Reserve Officers' Training Corps textbook, this second volume in a two-volume overview of the Army's story covers the period from World War I to the early days of the wars in Afghanistan and Iraq. Written in an engaging style and enhanced by sophisticated graphics and recommended readings, the work is an excellent source of general service history in the modern world.

Atkinson, Rick. *An Army at Dawn: The War in North Africa, 1942–1943*

In the first volume of his highly anticipated *Liberation Trilogy* series, Atkinson shows why no modern reader can understand the ultimate victory of the Allied Powers in May 1945 without a solid understanding of the events that took place in North Africa in 1942 and early 1943. He convincingly demonstrates that the first years of the Allied war effort were a pivotal point in American history—the moment when the United States began to act like a great military power. He also chronicles without apology the many false steps taken before the new and untested U.S. Army could emerge as a coherent and capable force.

McPherson, James M. *Battle Cry of Freedom: The Civil War Era*.

McPherson has written a brilliant account of the American Civil War—the war that made the country what it is today. He discusses in clear, incisive detail the causes of the war, the military operations, the soldiers, the leaders, and the political, economic, and social aspects of life in the Union and the Confederacy before and during the war. With many experts judging it to be the best one-volume history of the Civil War, it provides an excellent introduction to the most significant war fought by the American Army.

Whiting, Charles. *The Battle of Hürtgen Forest (Spellmount Siegfried Line Series, Vol. 4)*.

This is the story of the longest battle fought in the Army's history, in which thirty thousand soldiers were killed or wounded. The battle has been ignored for so long and, as the author claims, is one that should never have been fought. From September 1944 to February 1945, ten American divisions fought the Germans and sustained a casualty rate of over 50 percent. The author alleges that commanders failed to realize the limited value of the military objectives to the overall strategy and therefore poured more men into the meat grinder. This is a classic account of the price fighting men pay for the prideful blunders of their commanders.

Sheehan, Neil. *A Bright Shining Lie: John Paul Vann and America in Vietnam*.

The book centers on the career of Lt. Col. John Paul Vann, whose story illuminates America's failures and disillusionment in Southeast Asia. Vann, a field adviser to the South Vietnamese Army, became appalled at the corruption of the South Vietnamese regime, South Vietnam's incompetence in fighting the Communists, and the regime's brutal alienation of the South Vietnamese people. He found his superiors too blinded by political lies to understand that the war was being thrown away, and he secretly briefed reporters on what was really happening. This is a valuable read for those who want to understand the inherent conflict between trust and loyalty to one's superiors and organization and trust and loyalty to the American people.

Parker, Geoffrey (editor). *Cambridge Illustrated History of Warfare: The Triumph of the West*.

Written in a digestible, compelling manner, Parker's authors cover the gamut of Western warfare from antiquity to the present, including the development of warfare on land, sea, and air; weapons and technology; strategy, operations, and tactics; and logistics and intelligence. Throughout, there is an emphasis on the socioeconomic aspects of war, the rise of the West to global dominance, and the nature of the aggressive military culture that has been its hallmark.

Appleman, Roy E. *East of Chosin: Entrapment and Breakout in Korea, 1950*.

This book tells the riveting story of three thousand soldiers of the U.S. 7th Infantry Division who fought in a four-day, five-night battle on the east side of the Changjin (Chosin) Reservoir in November and December 1950 during the initial Communist Chinese intervention in the Korean War. During this brief battle, Task Force MacLean/Faith endured frigid cold, privation, and exhaustion before meeting with disaster. Although not as well known as other tactical disasters in Korea, such as the earlier Task Force Smith, this book says a great deal about the overall condition of the U.S. Army during the early days of the war.

Keegan, John. *Intelligence in War: Knowledge of the Enemy from Napoleon to Al-Qaeda.*

Keegan brings to life the split-second decisions that went into waging war before the benefit of aerial surveillance and electronic communications. He explains how espionage and decryption have changed the face of battle, such as thwarting the Japanese attack on Midway by an early warning. Keegan illustrates that timely information is only the beginning of decision making during war, where brute force is often more critical.

Shaara, Michael. *The Killer Angels.*

The late Shaara's Pulitzer Prize–winning novel (1974) recounts the battle of Gettysburg from a fictional point of view and was the basis for the 1993 film *Gettysburg.* The author tells the events immediately before and during the battle as seen through the eyes of Confederate generals Robert E. Lee, James Longstreet, and Lewis A. Armistead; Federal general John Buford and Colonel Joshua L. Chamberlain; and a host of others. The author's ability to convey the thoughts of men in war as well as their confusion in the "fog of battle" is outstanding.

Grossman, Dave. *On Killing: The Psychological Cost of Learning to Kill in War and Society.*

The book investigates the psychology of killing in combat and stresses that human beings have a powerful, innate resistance to the taking of life. The author examines the techniques developed by the military to overcome that aversion during the Vietnam War, revealing how an American soldier was more lethal during this conflict than at any other time in history. Grossman argues that the combination of the breakdown of American society, the pervasive violence in the media, and interactive video games is conditioning our children to kill in a manner similar to the Army's conditioning of soldiers.

Strassler, Robert B. (editor). *The Landmark Thucydides: A Comprehensive Guide to the Peloponnesian War.*

This is an annotated, new translation of the classic Greek historian's account of the war between Athens and Sparta fought between 431 and 404 BCE. It has explanatory footnotes and appendixes on war and society in fifth-century BCE Greece that do much to place the war in context. The Peloponnesian War is not only an excellent chronicle of ancient warfare, but also a thoughtful dissertation on the relationship between politics and war, government and empire, and the strong and the weak. This volume should be on every soldier's and diplomat's bookshelf.

Catton, Bruce. *A Stillness at Appomattox.*

The book narrates the final year of the Civil War from Wilderness through Petersburg, Virginia, and finally to the climax at Appomattox. Catton provides an emotionally charged account of the surrender scene, when Generals Ulysses S. Grant and Robert E. Lee finally meet. This is the third book in Catton's *Army of the Potomac* trilogy.

Palmer, Dave R. *Summons of the Trumpet: U.S.-Vietnam in Perspective.*
This work is a clear, concise history of the Vietnam War from 1954 to 1973 written by someone who witnessed it firsthand as a combat adviser to the South Vietnamese Army. It is especially useful for those seeking a broad overview of an extremely lengthy and confusing conflict and a summary of the war's main military and political trends.

Van Creveld, Martin. *Supplying War: Logistics from Wallenstein to Patton.*
Surveying four centuries of military history, the noted historian Martin Van Creveld clearly points out the reasons "amateurs study tactics; professionals study logistics." Most battlefield results would not have been possible without the careful organization and allocation of logistical resources. Leaders who fail to consider logistics in all of their plans and operations will do so at their peril.

Fehrenbach, T. R. *This Kind of War: The Classic Korean War History.*
This volume is a dramatic account of the Korean War written from the perspective of those who fought in it. Taken from records, journals, and histories, it is based largely on the compelling personal narratives of the small-unit commanders and their troops. It provides both a broad overview and a direct account of American troops in fierce combat. Fifty years later, *This Kind of War* commemorates the past and offers vital lessons for the future.

Hoffman, Jon T. (editor). *Tip of the Spear: U.S. Army Small-Unit Action in Iraq, 2004–2007.*
This is a collection of short combat action studies from the war in Iraq that took place during the growing insurgency that followed the highly successful invasion and initial occupation of the country in 2003. Each account illustrates the everyday challenges that U.S. soldiers faced in the struggle against an inventive and elusive enemy. The stories also highlight the personal bravery, resourcefulness, and courage of our modern Army as it adapts to the constantly changing circumstances that existed in Iraq at the time.

Macgregor, Douglas A. *Transformation Under Fire: Revolutionizing How America Fights.*
Through this book, Colonel (Ret.) Macgregor captured the attention of key leaders and inspired a genuine public debate on military reform. The author's controversial ideas would reduce timelines for deployment, enhance responsiveness to crises, and permit rapid decision making and planning. Macgregor pointedly argues that today's Army faces potential failure in a modern war. Without a conceptual redefinition of warfare as a joint operation, a new military culture that can execute joint expeditionary warfare will not emerge. The author's visionary plan to integrate ground

maneuver forces with powerful strike assets is the foundation for a true revolution in military affairs and has sparked heated debates in policy and military circles.

Yates, Lawrence A. *The U.S. Military Intervention in Panama: Origins, Planning, and Crisis Management, June 1987–December 1989.*

In this first of a planned two-volume history of Operation Just Cause, Yates, a noted historian of the U.S. intervention in the Dominican Republic in 1965, discusses the critical events, planning, and undercurrents that lay behind the U.S. military intervention in Panama in late 1989. He skillfully weaves military planning, high-level strategic debates, and interagency priorities and confusion into a masterful story of crisis management in a post–Goldwater-Nichols world. This is essential reading for any student of regional combatant commands, their powers, and their limitations as they attempt to influence strategy and national policy.

Moore, Harold G. and Joseph L. Galloway. *We Were Soldiers Once . . . and Young: Ia Drang—the Battle That Changed the War in Vietnam.*

This is a gripping firsthand account of the November 1965 battle of the Ia Drang by the commander of the 1st Battalion, 7th Cavalry, 1st Cavalry Division. The Ia Drang was the first major combat test of the airmobile concept and the first major battle between U.S. forces and the North Vietnamese Army.

Broadening Leaders

Ramo, Joshua Cooper. *The Age of the Unthinkable: Why the New World Disorder Constantly Surprises Us and What We Can Do about It.*

This book challenges conventional assumptions, world views, and thinking in an increasingly complex world. The author proposes controversial ways of considering global challenges, such as studying why Hezbollah is the most efficiently run Islamic militant group. Ramo uses economics, history, complexity theory, and network science to describe an ambiguous reality that has many innovative possibilities.

Johnson, Chalmers. *Blowback: The Costs and Consequences of American Empire.*

Author Chalmers Johnson writes about how poorly formed policy can lead to disastrous and unintended consequences. Using America's experience in Okinawa, Korea, and other Asian countries, he discusses the danger of overextending American power, both militarily and economically. He cites the need for the United States to reevaluate its strategic requirements and to formulate a new foreign policy that relies less on military presence and economic coercion.

America's misguided foreign policy, according to Johnson, drains enormous resources from taxpayers, fails to provide the nation with beneficial results, and harms our image abroad.

Cowper-Coles, Sherard. *Cables from Kabul: The Inside Story of the West's Afghanistan Campaign.*

The British ambassador to Afghanistan from 2007 to 2010 provides a pessimistic view of the war in Afghanistan and a unique frankness of the inner workings of diplomacy. In his view, the military continues to give overoptimistic assessments. The author looks at the transatlantic alliance and the ambitious U.S. military strategy and offers conclusions on the war. Broader than just Afghanistan, this book furnishes insights on current Western diplomacy and the way the North Atlantic Treaty Organization operates, particularly in hostile territories.

Freedman, Lawrence. *A Choice of Enemies: America Confronts the Middle East.*

A leading professor from the United Kingdom provides an objective study of U.S. engagements in the Middle East. This volume looks at U.S. strategies from President Jimmy Carter to President George W. Bush, evaluating the evolution of U.S. policy toward the region and offering thoughtful analysis of how and why the United States has confronted regional issues with global impact during five presidencies.

Kouzes, James M. and Barry Z. Posner. *Credibility: How Leaders Gain and Lose It, Why People Demand It.*

After thirty years of research, Kouzes and Posner conclude that credibility is the cornerstone of leadership. Leaders must "say what you mean and mean what you say." The three sources of credibility are honesty, competence, and inspiration. Army leaders cannot achieve their potential without considering and addressing the expectations of those whom they lead.

al-Jezairy, Zuhair. *The Devil You Don't Know: Going Back to Iraq.*

Twenty-five years after fleeing Iraq for defying Saddam Hussein, Iraqi journalist al-Jezairy returns and travels throughout the country. He captures the essence of a country emerging from thirty-five years of totalitarianism, subsequent decent into hopeless violence, and the bravery of the Iraqi people. He provides an inspirational account of post-Saddam Iraq while offering great insights into the culture and society.

Machiavelli, Niccolò. *Discourses on Livy.*

These discourses have captivated scholars of political thought for five centuries. Machiavelli eloquently explains how to maintain vibrancy in a republic through "new modes and orders." The discourses, written in the early sixteenth century, offer a unique perspective on world history through frequent references to the virtuous aspects of ancient Greek or Roman history, the conformity of the Middle Ages, and the Renaissance. Army professionals should study this book to gain insights into the origins of modern political thought, which is the sphere in which our joint force operates.

Knox, MacGregor and Williamson Murray (editors). *The Dynamics of Military Revolution, 1300–2050.*

The editors provide a conceptual framework and historical context for understanding the patterns of change, innovation, and adaptation that have marked war in the Western world since the fourteenth century. Case studies and a conceptual overview offer all Army leaders an indispensable introduction to military change.

Zegart, Amy B. *Flawed by Design: The Evolution of the CIA, JCS, and NSC.*

The book looks at the current interagency process and challenges the traditional opinion that the key national security institutions (composed of the Central Intelligence Agency, Joint Chiefs of Staff, and National Security Council) operate as the National Security Act of 1947 intended. The reality has been that politics and bureaucratic and budgetary turf wars effectively impair the original purpose of these organizations and have caused systematic failures. Reforms over the years were made, including the 1986 Goldwater-Nichols Act and the recent legislation after 11 September 2001 that created the director of national intelligence. However, according to the author, proposals for reform of the entire interagency process must be carefully considered based on the historical record of its performance. This is an important read for those who wish to learn how key institutions were intended to work and how they actually work today in an era of increasing uncertainty.

Hemingway, Ernest. *For Whom the Bell Tolls.*

This is a classic novel of a man fighting on the side of the Loyalists in the Spanish Civil War and coming to terms with violence, death, and the ultimate futility of war.

Seidman, Dov. *How: Why How We Do Anything Means Everything . . . in Business (and in Life).*

In today's fast-changing, hyper-connected, and hyper-transparent world, what we do no longer sets us apart from others because every task is a commodity, easily duplicated or reverse-engineered. How we do what we do determines whether we achieve a sustainable advantage. Seidman examines how we interact, how we think, how we behave, and how we govern. He argues that sustainable values that were once afterthoughts— trust, integrity, values, and reputation—are now the ultimate drivers of success. *How* is an important book to help Army professionals critically examine their personal performance and organizational cultures in this fast-changing era.

Wolman, David. *The Instigators: How a Small Band of Digital Activists Risked Their Lives and Helped Bring Down the Government of Egypt.*

Wolman argues that social media does not stand on its own as a change agent. People have to act in the real world to leverage the potential of the cyber world. The author, a journalist with *Wired* magazine, gives a very personal tour of the Egyptian revolution, tracing the use of social media by the leaders of one Arab Spring group. This book is useful in illuminating the key role that social media, social networking, bloggers, and the virtual world played in conceiving a revolution. It also provides a useful primer on forms of social media and current digital tools such as Facebook, blogs, e-mail, Twitter, Google Earth, and others.

Kotter, John P. *Leading Change*.

In this now-classic book on leadership, Kotter describes a proven eight-step change process: establishing a sense of urgency, creating the guiding coalition, developing a vision and strategy, communicating the change vision, empowering others to act, creating short-term wins, consolidating gains and producing even more change, and institutionalizing new approaches in the future. Leaders across the Army and at all levels should study and use Kotter's change process to assist in leading complex Army organizations through uncertainty and difficult circumstances.

Paret, Peter (editor). *Makers of Modern Strategy: From Machiavelli to the Nuclear Age*.

This is a wonderful anthology on the evolution of strategic thought. Moving from Machiavelli to the present in twenty-eight insightful essays, the authors examine such topics as the role of doctrine, the genius of Napoleon, the limits of airpower, and nuclear strategy. A primer for all military leaders who must think strategically on a variety of issues, *Makers of Modern Strategy* summarizes the classic military thinkers in a highly digestible manner, underlining the enduring lessons that remain relevant today.

Builder, Carl H. *The Masks of War: American Military Styles in Strategy and Analysis*.

This volume presents a look at the different styles and personalities of the Army, Navy, and Air Force. The Army considers itself a servant of the nation. The Navy sees itself mainly as an heir to a glorious tradition. The Air Force is the embodiment of a single idea. Within this context, this book evaluates the problems, interests, and aspirations of American military institutions in terms of their approaches to military strategy, planning, and analysis. The author argues that the roots of modern American military strategies lie buried in the nation's three most powerful institutions and provides insights on why these roots are obstacles to military reform.

Morozov, Evgeny. *The Net Delusion: The Dark Side of Internet Freedom*.

Morozov argues against the conventional wisdom that the Internet and social media will automatically promote and expand freedom around the world. While social networking may enable popular mobilization, authoritarian regimes can use the same tools to suppress free speech, monitor their opposition, and disseminate propaganda. The author asserts that while digital diplomacy and Internet freedom sound good rhetorically, foreign policy based on these terms may actually hinder the promotion of democracy, cause dictators to become more repressive, and harm the reform efforts of dissidents.

McIvor, Anthony D. *Rethinking the Principles of War.*
> This series of articles seeks to review, validate, or discard various tenets of the principles of today's globalized and information interconnected world. The book examines five key themes: the American way of war, conventional warfare, irregular warfare, post-conflict and stability operations, and intelligence—winning the silent wars. The volume provides all Army professionals with the context to evaluate the last ten years of war and assess and improve our Army profession and general understanding of war itself.

Brafman, Ori and Rod Beckstrom. *The Starfish and the Spider: The Unstoppable Power of Leaderless Organizations.*
> A traditional top-down organization is like a spider: If you cut off its head, it dies. By contrast, if you cut off a starfish's leg, it grows a new one, and that leg can grow into an entirely new starfish. *The Starfish and the Spider* explores what happens when starfish companies, such as Wikipedia and eBay, take on spiders. It reveals how established companies and institutions, from IBM to U.S. government agencies, are also learning how to incorporate starfish principles to achieve success. The Army's success over the past decade hinged on distributed, networked operations and operational adaptability at every level. Every indication is these trends will continue into the future. This book is an excellent primer to generate thought on how the Army should adapt as an institution to meet future challenges.

Heath, Chip and Dan. *Switch: How to Change Things When Change Is Hard.*
> After decades of research, the Heaths are clearly two of the worldwide experts on change efforts. In *Switch*, they describe trends from their research that illuminate what causes success—or failure—in efforts to achieve transformative change. The outcome is a pattern—or game plan—that leaders can use to change their organizations or even their individual lives. There are few subjects more worthy of study for Army professionals.

Neustadt, Richard E. and Ernest R. May. *Thinking in Time: The Uses of History for Decision Makers.*
> History is a valuable tool for decision makers, but, if used without careful consideration, it can blind the unwary by false analogies. A true classic, this book offers senior leaders meaningful suggestions on how to use and avoid misusing the experience that history can provide.

Singer, P. W. *Wired for War: The Robotics Revolution and Conflict in the 21st Century.*
> P. W. Singer explores robotic warfare as a revolution in military affairs on a par with the atom bomb or gunpowder. The author discusses the impact of new military technology on the ways war is fought and the influence robots will have on the future battlefield, as well as the ramifications robotic warfare will have on ethics, law, politics, and economics.

The Strategic Environment

Ferguson, Niall. *The Ascent of Money: A Financial History of the World*.
   Economic historian and Harvard professor Niall Ferguson provides a historical narrative on the ascent of money and how it has both contributed to the expansion of the global marketplace and caused conflict. This is a cautionary tale that relates to the current fiscal crisis in Europe and the United States; interdependence between the United States and Chinese economies; the financial crash of 2008; and the subsequent Occupy Wall Street Movement and slow economic growth around the world. It is an important read for those who want to understand how the global fiscal and economic crisis could impact our defense strategy and defense force structure.

Lewis, Michael. *Boomerang: Travels in the New Third World*.
   Lewis describes in clear language the complex financial engineering that has led to the current global financial crisis. He traces the domestic and global origins of the bubbles that led to the collapse of the Icelandic, Irish, and Greek economies; describes how the Germans unwittingly enabled the debt crises in Europe; and explores similar challenges that do not bode well for the United States. Though *Boomerang* does not explicitly discuss national security implications, the volume does explain sources of economic weakness that have the potential to pose challenges for the United States and its allies for investing in defense and other security-related areas.

Kissinger, Henry A. *On China*.
   This is a sweeping and insightful history of China by a distinguished international scholar, diplomat, and statesman. It provides a fascinating historical view of China and its relations with its neighbors and the United States over the last forty years. It is useful for readers to understand the world's second largest economy and the rising global player, which will impact U.S. national and economic security for decades to come.

Huntington, Samuel P. *The Clash of Civilizations and the Remaking of World Order*.
   The late Harvard social scientist Samuel Huntington warns of the increasing threat of renewed conflicts originating in countries and cultures that base their traditions on religious faith and dogma. Moving past the issues of race and nationality as sources of future conflict, he cites the growing influence of a handful of major cultures—Western, Eastern Orthodox, Latin American, Islamic, Japanese, Chinese, Hindu, and African—in current struggles across the globe. His study underlines the importance of cultural awareness in dealing with crises throughout the globe and the significant role that awareness plays in implementing effective policies and programs on the ground.

Rashid, Ahmed. *Descent into Chaos: The United States and the Failure of Nation Building in Pakistan, Afghanistan, and Central Asia*
   Rashid, a Pakistani writer, describes how the war against Islamic extremism is being lost in Pakistan, Afghanistan, and central Asia. He examines

the region and the corridors of power in Washington and Europe to see how the promised nation-building in these countries has progressed. His conclusions are devastating: an unstable and nuclear-armed Pakistan, a renewed al-Qaeda profiting from a booming opium trade, and a Taliban resurgence and reconquest. He argues that failing states pose a graver threat to global security than the Middle East.

Reid, Michael. *Forgotten Continent: The Battle for Latin America's Soul.* In examining a vast continent that is often overlooked by the West, Reid argues that Latin America's efforts to build more equitable and more prosperous societies make that region one of the most dynamic places in the world. In that area, a series of democratic leaders is attempting to lay the foundations for faster economic growth and more inclusive politics while addressing the region's seemingly intractable problems of poverty, inequality, and social injustice. Failure will not only increase the flow of drugs and illegal immigrants, but also will jeopardize the stability of a region rich in oil and other strategic commodities and threaten some of the world's most majestic natural environments. The study provides a vivid, current, and informed account of a dynamic continent and its struggle to compete in a globalized world.

Luttwak, Edward N. *The Grand Strategy of the Byzantine Empire.* In this book, the author follows the pattern of his earlier classic on the grand strategy of the Roman Empire and presents the grand strategy of the eastern Roman Empire, or the Byzantine Empire, as we know it today. The Byzantine Empire lasted more than twice as long as the more familiar western empire. Luttwak tries to explain that the eastern empire outlasted its western counterpart because its rulers were able to adapt strategically to diminished circumstances. They devised new ways of coping with successive enemies, including a life or death struggle—a "long war"—with the new and highly militant religion of Islam. Without extensive resources, the Byzantines relied less on military strength and more on persuasion to recruit allies and divide enemies.

Abrahamian, Ervand. *A History of Modern Iran.* In a reappraisal of Iran's modern history, the author traces Iran's traumatic journey across the twentieth century, through the discovery of oil, imperial interventions, the rule of the Pahlavis, and, in 1979, revolution and the birth of the Islamic republic. In the intervening years, the country has experienced a bitter war with Iraq, the transformation of society under the clergy, and, more recently, the expansion of the state and the struggle for power between the old elites, the intelligentsia, and the commercial middle class. As Iran emerges at the beginning of the twenty-first century as one of the most powerful states in the Middle East, it is important to understand its culture and history.

Brown, John Sloan. *Kevlar Legions: The Transformation of the U.S. Army, 1989–2005.*

Former Chief of Military History and retired Brig. Gen. John S. Brown brings his formidable analytical skills to bear in a detailed study of how the senior Army leadership formulated, managed, and executed a multiyear transformational effort after the end of the Cold War. A consistent vision from the Army senior leadership allowed the Army to cope with the changed international environment after the collapse of the Soviet Union, with high operational tempo contingency operations, and with the opening salvos of the Global War on Terrorism, and still craft a flexible, adaptable Army that is the premier ground force in the world today. This is a mustread for all those who served in the Army during this transitional period and for future Army leaders who will face an uncertain future in times of dwindling resources but who still need to prepare the force for victory.

Habeck, Mary. *Knowing the Enemy: Jihadist Ideology and the War on Terror.*

In this primer on a small splinter group of Islam, Habeck traces current jihadism from an early fourteenth-century scholar and the eighteenth-century founder of the harshly restrictive Islam (predominantly in Saudi Arabia) to four twentieth-century figures that inspired a host of radical reactionary organizations, including Hamas and al-Qaeda. The author's purpose is to reveal the origins of jihadism. In so doing, she contributes in considerable detail and with admirable clarity one of the most valuable books on the ongoing Middle East—and global—conflicts. This is an important volume for all leaders to understand what drives people to attack democracies.

Hiro, Dilip. *The Longest War: The Iran-Iraq Military Conflict.*

Lasting eight years and costing over a trillion dollars and a million casualties, this conflict (which featured chemical weapons and genocide against the Kurds), is largely unknown to most Westerners. The author, an expert on Middle Eastern affairs, traces the ancient animosities and territorial aspirations that animated the slaughter, describes in detail the actual fighting, and connects the war to the "great powers" that covertly aided the belligerents. Despite current fears of excessive Iranian influence in newly democratic Iraq, the war, revolving around oil, access to the sea, and religious tensions, is not yet over.

Kaplan, Robert D. *Monsoon: The Indian Ocean and the Future of American Power.*

Kaplan provides a sweeping examination of the countries that compose "Monsoon Asia"—China, India, Pakistan, Indonesia, Burma, Oman, Sri Lanka, Bangladesh, and Tanzania. This book is a must-read for Army professionals, especially those whose focus has been weighted toward the challenges in Iraq and Afghanistan over the past decade. As the United States pivots strategically to the Pacific, Kaplan's unique perspective on the implications of rising powers, the shifting global balance, and the potential contingencies that might arise is timely and important.

Behrman, Greg. *The Most Noble Adventure: The Marshall Plan and How America Helped Rebuild Europe.*
This is a comprehensive review of the Marshall Plan and how successful civilian-military teams applied unity of effort to rebuild Europe after World War II. The book can be used as a comparative analysis between how the Marshall Plan was prepared and executed in Europe and its application to the current conflicts in Iraq and Afghanistan.

Zaeef, Abdul Salam. *My Life with the Taliban.*
This is an autobiography of a former senior member of Afghanistan's Taliban. Zaeef served as ambassador to Pakistan at the time of the terrorist attack on the United States on 11 September 2001. In 2002, Zaeef was delivered to U.S. forces operating in Pakistan and spent four and a half years in prison. His reflections give insights into rural Pashtun communities and help explain what drives men like him to take up arms against foreigners.

Kitfield, James. *Prodigal Soldiers: How the Generation of Officers Born of Vietnam Revolutionized the American Style of War.*
The book examines how a generation of officers, such as Colin Powell, H. Norman Schwarzkopf, and Barry R. McCaffrey, experienced Vietnam and the subsequent hollowing of the force and helped put in place the systems and policies that aided the Army in achieving victory in Desert Storm. This volume is a good read for today's officer corps as it prepares to transition from a decade of conflict to a reduction in force structure and resources, and attempts to balance the need for a rapid drawdown with the requirement that the Army remain the force of decisive action for the nation.

Yergin, Daniel. *The Quest: Energy, Security, and the Remaking of the Modern World.*
For the past twenty years, Yergin has been widely recognized as the most authoritative voice on the geopolitics of energy and resource competition. His new book is the most comprehensive, even-handed, and current work now available on the topic and will likely stand as the definitive work for the indefinite future. While he has long been part of the "optimist school" of energy experts (dismissing the idea, for example, of "peak oil" and its near-term depletion), he remains worried about security, financial, technological, and ecological problems stemming from the role of fossil fuels in global energy production. This volume not only explains the deeper history of energy production and the dramatic changes of the past decade, but also provides valuable policy advice for minimizing the potential for catastrophic disruptions in energy security and the conflicts this could produce.

Friedman, Thomas L. and Michael Mandelbaum. *That Used to Be Us: How America Fell Behind in the World It Invented and How We Can Come Back.*

This book looks at current U.S. challenges stemming from increasing globalization, changing information technology, rising national debt, and growing energy consumption, and argues that the country must take assertive steps to maintain its position in the international system. Though deficit spending must be reduced, U.S. greatness is based on five historical pillars that also require revitalization to foster future economic growth. These pillars are public education, infrastructure, immigration, research and development, and public regulation of private economic activity. With regard to the last of these, there is a particularly urgent need for a comprehensive energy policy that also addresses climate change. The authors argue that the world will be a poorer and more dangerous place if the United States cannot successfully renew itself.

Smith, Rupert. *The Utility of Force: The Art of War in the Modern World*. Drawing on his experience as a commander during Operations Desert Shield and Desert Storm and in Bosnia, Kosovo, and Northern Ireland, British general Smith gives us a probing analysis of modern war and questions why we try to use military force to solve our political problems and why, when our forces win military battles, we still fail to solve the problems. He demonstrates why today's conflicts must be understood as intertwined political and military events and makes clear why the current model of total war has failed in Iraq, Afghanistan, and other recent campaigns.

Friedman, Thomas L. *The World Is Flat: A Brief History of the Twenty-first Century*.

Friedman, a *New York Times* foreign-affairs columnist and pundit, sees the globalization process entering an entirely new phase. Advances in information technologies, an intensified world division of labor, stepped-up competition, and economic practices such as outsourcing have joined with the political opening of the world following the collapse of communism to produce a progressive "flattening" of the world. The author believes that states and individuals have no option but to accept this dynamic and develop the skills to survive the flattened world. A best seller, Friedman's book presents much food for thought for today's strategist.

Kissinger, Henry A. *A World Restored: Metternich, Castlereagh and the Problems of Peace, 1812–1822*

A World Restored examines a misunderstood and overlooked historical era that offers strategic insights that remain very relevant today. Austrian Foreign Minister Prince Klemens Wenzel von Metternich and British Foreign Secretary Viscount Castlereagh served in the tumultuous period following the fall of Napoleon I. They sought national greatness for their respective nations while walking a fragile line between peace and war. Kissinger's book reveals timeless strategic issues that endure throughout all eras and reminds us that our counterparts from previous times experienced challenges and uncertainty at least as significant as those we are experiencing today.

Chairman Joint Chiefs of Staff Reading List
(http://whs.mil.campusguides.com/content.php?pid=324900&sid=2697482)

Krepinevich, Andrew F. *7 Deadly Scenarios*.
  What if the worst that could happen actually happens? How would we
  respond? Are we ready?
    These are the questions that Andrew Krepinevich asks—and
  answers—in this timely and often chilling new book, which describes the
  changing face of war in the twenty-first century and identifies seven
  deadly scenarios that threaten our security in the crucial years ahead. As
  president of the Center for Strategic and Budgetary Assessments and
  consultant to secretaries of defense, the CIA, the Homeland Security
  Council, and the Joint Forces Command, Krepinevich's job is to think the
  unthinkable—and prepare a response in the event our worst nightmares
  become reality.
Ramo, Joshua Cooper. *The Age of the Unthinkable*.
  Today the very ideas that made America great imperil its future. Our plans
  go awry and policies fail. History's grandest war against terrorism creates
  more terrorists. Global capitalism, intended to improve lives, increases the
  gap between rich and poor. Decisions made to stem a financial crisis guarantee its worsening. Environmental strategies to protect species lead to
  their extinction.
Tzu, Sun (Denma Translation Group with commentaries by Translator). *The
  Art of War*.
  The Art of War is more than just an ancient Chinese war manual: It is a
  store of wisdom that answers the perennial question, How are we to act
  effectively within a never-ending flow of change? The living quality of
  Sun Tzu's strategic masterpiece has never been clearer than in this simple,
  bold new translation. The result is text that provides us with an understanding of how to achieve victory over war—how we can win without
  fighting—in practical terms that anyone can apply to conflicts in our
  everyday lives. This new edition includes engaging essays and commentary to deepen the reader's understanding of how to apply Sun Tzu's
  insights in modern day life. In *The Art of War*, Sun Tzu teaches us how to
  overcome our adversaries without destroying them. The essence of this
  approach lies in the concept of "taking whole"—bringing the opponent
  into one's own sphere. How can readers apply this wisdom? If they
  assume the perspective of the Sage Commander, noting the conditions
  of every conflict, then skillful action becomes apparent in any given
  situation. Original essays and commentary clearly articulate this perspective. Awareness of the present moment, the translators show, holds the key
  to implementing Sun Tzu's principles in our daily lives. "Develop an
  intimate understanding of the text as a living practice," they advise.
  "Then, like its earlier lineage holders, we can move outward into our
  world and act."

de Jomini, Antone Henri (G. H. Mendell and W. P. Craighill, translators; James H. Ford, editor). *The Art of War by Baron de Jomini—Special Edition.*

The Art of War by Baron de Jomini was considered by most military experts of the day, at the time of the American Civil War, to be the definitive work on strategy and warfare. Even today, it is highly regarded as a seminal work in the development of strategy. Antoine Henri de Jomini was one of Napoleon's most capable generals and contributed to almost all of Napoleon's major battles. Napoleon regarded him so highly he made him Baron de Jomini. At the close of the Napoleonic Wars, de Jomini became general and aide de camp for the Tsar of Russia. His firsthand accounts and rigorous analysis of important battles are still a major resource on tactics, strategy, and warfare.

Taleb, Nassim Nicholas. *The Black Swan.*

A black swan is a highly improbable event with three principal characteristics: It is unpredictable, it carries a massive impact, and, after the fact, we concoct an explanation that makes it appear less random—and more predictable—than it was. The astonishing success of Google was a black swan; so was 9/11. For Nassim Nicholas Taleb, black swans underlie almost everything about our world, from the rise of religions to events in our own personal lives.

Coram, Robert. *Boyd: The Fighter Pilot Who Changed the Art of War.*

A great American hero—a twentieth-century warrior and military strategist who lived outside the spotlight but whose work has been enormously influential—is brought brilliantly to life in this acclaimed biography. John Boyd was the finest fighter pilot in American history. From the proving ground of the Korean War, he went on to win notoriety as the instructor who defeated, in less than forty seconds, every pilot who challenged him. But what made Boyd a man for the ages was what happened after he left the cockpit. He transformed the way military aircraft—in particular the F-15 and F-16—were designed with his revolutionary Energy-Maneuverability Theory. Boyd dedicated his later years to a radical theory of conflict that was largely ignored during Boyd's lifetime but is now widely considered to be the most influential thinking about conflict since Sun Tzu's *The Art of War.*

Douhet, Giulio (Joseph P. Harahan and Richard H. Kohn, editors and introduction; Dino Ferrari, translator). *The Command of the Air.*

The Italian General Giulio Douhet reigns as one of the twentieth century's foremost strategic air power theorists. As such scholars as Raymond Flugel have pointed out, Douhet's theories were crucial at a pivotal pre-World War II Army Air Force institution, the Air Corps Tactical School.

Higginbotham, Donald. *George Washington and the American Military Tradition.*

In *George Washington and the American Military Tradition*, Don Higginbotham investigates the interplay of militiaman and professional soldier, of soldier and legislator, that shaped George Washington's military career and ultimately fostered the victory that brought independence to our nation. Higginbotham then explores the legacy of Washington's success, revealing that the crucial blending of civil and military concerns characteristic of the Revolution has been variously regarded and only seldom repeated by later generations of American soldiers.

Mahan, Alfred Thayer. *The Influence of Sea Power on History, 1660–1783.* Though technological advances over the last century have revolutionized warfare, *The Influence of Sea Power upon History, 1660–1783* remains a classic text on the history, strategy, and comprehension of commercial and military command of the high seas. The first president of the U.S. Naval War College, Alfred Thayer Mahan demonstrates through historical examples that the rise and fall of sea power and the wealth of nations have always been linked with commercial and military command of the sea. Mahan describes successful naval strategies employed in the past—from Greek and Roman times through the Napoleonic Wars—with an intense focus on England's rise as a sea power in the eighteenth century. This book provides not only an overview of naval tactics but also a lucid exposition of geographic, economic, and social factors governing the maintenance of sea power.

Corbett, Julian Stafford. *Principles of Maritime Strategy.* The respected naval historian emphasizes precise definitions of terminology and ideas as the antidote to purposeless discussion and the direct path to the fundamental data on which all are agreed. He places naval warfare within the larger framework of human conflict, proposing that the key to maritime dominance lies in the effective use of sea lines.

Kaplan, Robert D. *Monsoon.* On the world maps common in America, the Western Hemisphere lies front and center, while the Indian Ocean region all but disappears. This convention reveals the geopolitical focus of the now-departed twentieth century, but in the twenty-first century that focus will fundamentally change. In this pivotal examination of the countries known as "Monsoon Asia"—which include India, Pakistan, China, Indonesia, Burma, Oman, Sri Lanka, Bangladesh, and Tanzania—bestselling author Robert D. Kaplan shows how crucial this dynamic area has become to American power. It is here that the fight for democracy, energy independence, and religious freedom will be lost or won, and it is here that American foreign policy must concentrate if the United States is to remain relevant in an ever-changing world. From the Horn of Africa to the Indonesian archipelago and beyond, Kaplan exposes the effects of population growth, climate change, and extremist politics on this unstable region, demonstrating why Americans can no longer afford to ignore this important area of the world.

Von Clausewitz, Carl (Anatol Rapoport, editor and introduction). *On War.* "War . . . is an act of violence intended to compel our opponent to fulfil our will." Writing at the time of Napoleon's greatest campaigns, Prussian soldier and writer Carl von Clausewitz created this landmark treatise on the art of warfare, which presented war as part of a coherent system of political thought. In line with Napoleon's military actions, Clausewitz illustrated the need to annihilate the enemy and to make a strong display of one's power in an "absolute war" without compromise. But he was also careful to distinguish between war and politics, arguing that war could only be justified when debate was no longer adequate, and that, if undertaken, its aim should ultimately be to improve the well-being of the nation. Combining military theory and practice, *On War* has had a profound influence on subsequent thinking on warfare. This edition contains a detailed introduction examining Von Clausewitz's skill and reputation as a writer, philosopher, and political thinker, as well as a bibliography, notes, and a glossary.

Myrer, Anton. *Once an Eagle*.

Once an Eagle is the story of one special man, a soldier named Sam Damon, and his adversary over a lifetime, fellow officer Courtney Massengale. Damon is a professional who puts duty, honor, and the men he commands above self interest. Massengale, however, brilliantly advances by making the right connections behind the lines and in Washington's corridors of power.

Huntington, Samuel P. *The Soldier and the State*.

In a classic work, Samuel P. Huntington challenges most of the old assumptions and ideas on the role of the military in society. Stressing the value of the military outlook for American national policy, Huntington has performed the distinctive task of developing a general theory of civil-military relations and subjecting it to rigorous historical analysis.

Brafman, Ori and Rod Beckstrom. *The Starfish and the Spider*.

If you cut off a spider's head, it dies; if you cut off a starfish's leg it grows a new one, and that leg can grow into an entirely new starfish. Traditional top-down organizations are like spiders, but now starfish organizations are changing the face of business and the world.

Sinek, Simon. *Start with Why*.

Why are some people and organizations more innovative, more influential, and more profitable than others? Why do some command greater loyalty? In studying the leaders who've had the greatest influence in the world, Simon Sinek discovered that they all think, act, and communicate in the exact same way—and it's the complete opposite of what everyone else does. People like Martin Luther King Jr., Steve Jobs, and the Wright Brothers might have little in common, but they all started with why. Drawing on a wide range of real-life stories, Sinek weaves together a clear vision of what it truly takes to lead and inspire.

Stoler, Mark A. *Twentieth Century American Biography Series: George C. Marshall*.

General George C. Marshall played a pivotal role in American history between 1939 and 1951. In this fascinating work, Mark Stoler integrates an extensive variety of primary and secondary sources, including Marshall's private papers, in the story of the frustrations and successes of Marshall's attempts to forge a workable military policy in World War II consistent with the basic principles of American democracy. Marshall, best remembered for the Marshall Plan, is made comprehensible as a strategist at the center of the most destructive conflict in world history.

2000 AIR UNIVERSITY PROFESSIONAL READING GUIDE

The books listed in the Air University Professional Reading Guide are divided into three categories. *Warfare Studies* builds a foundation of knowledge about war and deals with particular types and periods of warfare. It includes historical and analytical readings, as well as firsthand accounts. *Command and Leadership* examines the challenges of military leadership and management and includes the biographies and autobiographies of some whose measure of success is now a matter of public record. *National Security Affairs and Strategy* deals with the theory and practice of creating and implementing military strategies and policies. Included in this category are studies of air warfare, from its infancy through its maturation in Desert Storm.

Warfare Studies
General Military History, Strategy, and Doctrine

Brodie, Bernard, and Fawn M. Brodie. *From Crossbow to H-bomb*. Bloomington: Indiana University Press, 1973. 320 pp. A historical survey of science and technology in warfare.

Builder, Carl H. *The Icarus Syndrome*. New Brunswick, NJ: Transaction Publishers, 1993. 299 pp. A provocative and critical look at the role of air power theory in the development of the U.S. Air Force.

Clausewitz, Carl von. *On War*. Edited and translated by Peter Paret and Michael Howard. Princeton, NJ: Princeton University Press, 1984 (1976). 732 pp. The military classic on the nature and art of waging war.

Douhet, Guilio. *The Command of the Air*. Translated by Dino Ferrari. Washington, DC: Office of Air Force History, 1983. First published 1942 by Coward-McCann. 394 pp. The first and most passionate exposition of a comprehensive air warfare theory.

Freedman, Lawrence. *War*. New York: Oxford University Press, 1994. 385 pp. Excellent anthology of articles on all aspects of war.

Hallion, Richard P. *Strike from the Sky: The History of Battlefield Air Attack, 1911–1945*. Washington, DC: Smithsonian Institution Press, 1989. 323 pp. Comprehensive look at the development of tactical airpower.

Howard, Michael E. *War in European History*. New York: Oxford University Press, 1976. 165 pp. Short but brilliant study that links society, politics, economics, and technology to explain the changes in war on that continent.

Liddell Hart, Sir Basil H. *Strategy: The Indirect Approach*. London: Praeger, 1954. 420 pp. The author explains through historical examples his concept of the indirect approach.

McNeill, William H. *The Pursuit of Power: Technology, Armed Force, and Society Since A.D. 1000.* Chicago: University of Chicago Press, 1982. 405 pp. Postulates that the West's rise to military dominance has roots in the military and economic diversity that characterized Europe's situation after the fall of Rome.

Meilinger, Phillip S. *10 Propositions Regarding Air Power.* Washington, DC: Air Force History and Museums Program, 1995. 86 pp. Provocative propositions to instill an appreciation for airpower.

Millett, Allan R., and Peter Mazlowski. *For the Common Defense: A Military History of the United States of America.* New York: Free Press, 1984. 621 pp. A balanced, thorough one-volume examination of American military policy from the colonial period to the Reagan era.

Millis, Walter. *Arms and Men: A Study in American Military History.* Revised edition. New Brunswick, NJ: Rutgers University Press, 1981. First published 1956 by G. P. Putnam's Sons. 382 pp. Though concerned with American military policy, Millis's real contribution is his discussion of revolutions in warfare and how they contributed to the appearance of total war.

Preston, Richard A., Sidney F. Wise, and Alex Roland. *Men in Arms: A History of Warfare and Its Interrelationships with Western Society.* Fort Worth: Holt, Rhinehart and Winston, 1991. 458 pp. Sets military history in the broad spectrum of social, economic, political, and technological change in world history.

Strachan, Hew. *European Armies and the Conduct of War.* Boston: Allen and Unwin, 1983. 224 pp. Modern European military history analyzed by examining the principal military theorists and practitioners.

Sun Tzu. *The Art of War.* Translated by T. R. Phillips. New York: Delta, 1988. 82 pp. This short treatise lays down the basic and timeless principles dealing with strategy, tactics, communications, supply, intelligence, etc.

United States Air Force. *AFM 1–1, Volumes I and II: Basic Aerospace Doctrine of the United States Air Force.* Washington, DC: Government Printing Office, March 1992. Vol. I: 20 pp. Vol. II: 308 pp. Volume I contains the definitive statement of U.S. Air Force basic doctrine. Volume II contains a set of background essays explaining and supporting Air Force basic doctrine. You can find these publications at your base library or obtain them through interlibrary loan from Air University.

Warden, John A., III. *The Air Campaign: Planning for Combat.* Washington, DC: Pergamon-Brassey's, 1989. 160 pp. A new look at the theory of air warfare that links the theory to practical application at the operational level of war.

Weigley, Russell F. *The American Way of War.* Bloomington: Indiana University Press, 1977 (1973). 584 pp. Analyzes the historical roots of American military strategy.

Period-Specific Studies

Atkinson, Rick. *Crusade: The Untold Story of the Persian Gulf War.* New York: Houghton Mifflin Company, 1993. 575 pp. Balanced journalistic account of Operation Desert Storm.

Baucom, Donald K. *The Origins of SDI, 1944–1983.* Lawrence: University Press of Kansas, 1992. 276 pp. An insider's account of the development of the Strategic Defense Initiative Program through the post–Cold War era.

Clodfelter, Mark. *The Limits of Airpower: The American Bombing of Vietnam.* New York: The Free Press, 1989. 297 pp. An excellent study of the use and misuse of airpower.

Futrell, Robert F. *The United States Air Force in Korea, 1950–1953.* Washington, DC: Office of Air Force History, 1983 (1961). 823 pp. Official history and analysis of air power in Korea.

Greer, Thomas H. *The Development of Air Doctrine in the Army Air Arm, 1917–1941.* Washington, DC: Office of Air Force History, 1985. 154 pp. The evolution of air doctrine between the world wars.

Herring, George C. *America's Longest War: The United States and Vietnam, 1950–1975.* New York: Knopf, 1986. 316 pp. Review of the politico-military issues of the Vietnam War.

Mann, Edward C., III. *Thunder and Lightning: Desert Storm and the Air Power Debates.* Montgomery, AL. Air University Press, 1995. 220 pp. Volume II on the Operation Desert Storm air campaign.

Morrow, Robert. *The Great War in the Air.* Washington, DC: Smithsonian Institution Press, 1993. 300 pp. The best overall book available on airpower in World War I.

Murray, Williamson. *Strategy for Defeat: The Luftwaffe, 1933–1945.* Montgomery, AL: Air University Press, 1983. 365 pp. Well-balanced analysis of the Luftwaffe in World War II.

Overy, R. J. *The Air War, 1939–1945.* Chelsea, MI: Scarborough House, 1981. 263 pp. Excellent one-volume work on the role of air forces in World War II.

Perret, Geoffrey. *Winged Victory: The Army Air Forces in World War II.* New York: Random House, 1993. 549 pp. The best treatment of the Air Force's World War II experience.

Reynolds, Richard T. *Heart of the Storm.* Montgomery, AL. Air University Press, 1995. 147 pp. Volume I on the genesis of the air campaign against Iraq.

Spector, Ronald H. *Eagle Against the Sun: The American War with Japan.* New York: Free Press, 1985. 589 pp. The best single-volume history of the Pacific War.

Stokesbury, James L. *A Short History of World War.* New York: William Morrow & Company, 1981. 348 pp. Stokesbury's survey is the best brief account of the war.

Weinberg, Gerhardt L. *A World at Arms: A Global History of World War II*. New York: Cambridge University Press, 1994. 1,178 pp. A comprehensive look at World War II.

Topic-Specific Studies

Freedman, Lawrence. *The Evolution of Nuclear Strategy*. New York: St. Martin's Press, 1989. 522 pp. Examination of the theories and theorists of the nuclear age.

Hough, Harold. *Satellite Surveillance*. Port Townsend, WA: Loompanics Unlimited, 1991. 196 pp. Explores spaceborne imagery and details uses and abuses of satellite technology.

Joint Chiefs of Staff. *Joint Publication 30: Doctrine for Joint Operations*. Washington, DC: Government Printing Office, September 9, 1993. 203 pp. The fundamental principles and concepts for joint and multinational operations.

Laquer, Walter. *Guerrilla: A Historical and Critical Study*. Boston: Little, Brown, 1976. 462 pp. A comparative study of guerrilla and terrorist theory.

Levine, Alan J. *The Missile and Space Race*. Westport, CT: Praeger, 1994. 247 pp. Comprehensive look at the U.S. and Soviet space and missile program development.

Mason, Tony. *Air Power: A Centennial Appraisal*. Washington, DC: Brassey's, 1994. 320 pp. Comprehensive look at airpower in theory and practice.

Pagonis, William G. *Moving Mountains: Lessons in Leadership and Logistics from the Gulf War*. Boston: Harvard Business School Press, 1992. 248 pp. Reviews leadership, management, and logistics in the Gulf War.

Van Creveld, Martin L. *Supplying War: Logistics from Wallenstein to Patton*. Cambridge, UK: Cambridge University Press, 1977. 284 pp. Examines the practical art of moving and supplying armies.

Command and Leadership

Frisbee, John L. *Makers of the United States Air Force*. Washington, DC: Pergamon-Brassey's International Defense Publishers, 1989. 347 pp. A must-read on those who helped develop the USAF.

Gardner, John. *On Leadership*. New York: Free Press, 1990. 220 pp. A searching examination of leadership as it is practiced, or malpracticed, in America today.

Hackett, John Winthrop. *The Profession of Arms*. London: Times Publishing Co., 1963. 68 pp. Traces the development, meaning, and implications of our military traditions.

Keegan, John. *The Face of Battle*. New York: Penguin, 1978 (1976). 364 pp. Classic work that examines the battles at Agincourt (1415), Waterloo (1815), and the Somme (1916).

Puryear, Edgar F. *Nineteen Stars: A Study in Military Character and Leadership*. Novato, CA: Presidio Press, 1981. 437 pp. This purely leadership-oriented work highlights the careers of four outstanding Army officers.

Toner, James H. *True Faith and Allegiance: The Burden of Military Ethics*. Lexington: The University Press of Kentucky, 1995. 202 pp. An officer's ethical foundation is based on true faith and allegiance and the knowledge to do the right thing.

National Security Affairs and Strategy

Brodie, Bernard. *Strategy in the Missile Age*. Princeton, NJ: Princeton University Press, 1965. 423 pp. One of this era's wisest thinkers reviews the relationship between military policy, strategy, and nuclear weapons.

Builder, Carl H. *The Mask of War*. Baltimore: The Johns Hopkins University Press, 1989. 242 pp. A provocative study arguing that institutional personalities determine how the services approach strategy and planning.

Huntington, Samuel P. *The Soldier and the State: The Theory and Politics of Civil-Military Relations*. Cambridge, MA: Belknap Press of Harvard University, 1957. 534 pp. Classic realist exposition on American civil-military relations.

Paret, Peter, ed. *Makers of Modern Strategy: From Machiavelli to the Nuclear Age*. Princeton, NJ: Princeton University Press, 1986. 941 pp. Twenty-eight essays tracing the evolution of military thought. An essential book on the subject of strategy.

Schelling, T. C. *The Strategy of Conflict*. Cambridge, MA: Harvard University Press, 1960. 272 pp. One of the earliest and best books on modern strategy. Ideas are extremely relevant for a post–Cold War environment.

Wright, Q. *A Study of War*. Chicago: University of Chicago Press, 1965. 365 pp. The classic account of why wars occur, with a masterful blend of history and international relations.

Appendix C

Major USAF Installations

Altus AFB, Okla. 73523-5000; 120 mi. SW of Oklahoma City. Phone: 580-482-8100; DSN 312-866-1110. Majcom: AETC. Host: 97th Air Mobility Wing. Mission: trains aircrew members for C-17 and KC-135 aircraft. History: activated January 1943; inactivated May 1945; reactivated January 1953. Area: 6,593 acres. Runways: 13,440 ft., 9,000-ft. parallel runway, and 3,515-ft. assault strip. Altitude: 1,381 ft. Personnel: permanent party military, 1,333; DOD civilians, 1,285 Housing: single family, 797; visiting, VOQ/VAQ, 315; TLF, 30. Clinic. Website: www.altus.af.mil.

JB Anacostia-Bolling, includes Bolling AFB, D.C. 20032-5000; 3 mi. S of US Capitol. Phone: 703-545-6700; DSN 312-297-0450. Host: 11th Wing, which includes the USAF Band and USAF Honor Guard. Mission: Provides support responsibilities for Hq. USAF and 40,000 USAF members worldwide. Major tenants: Air Force Chief of Chaplains; Air Force District of Washington; Air Force Surgeon General; Air Force Medical Operations Agency; Defense Intelligence Agency; Air Force Legal Services Agency; 497th Intelligence Gp. (ACC). History: activated October 1917. Named for Col. Raynal C. Bolling, first high-ranking Army Air Service officer killed in WWI. Consolidated with Naval Support Facility Anacostia as a joint base October 1, 2010. Area: 607 acres. Runway: Helipad only. Altitude: 20 ft. Personnel: permanent party military, 1,408; DOD civilians, 822. Housing: single family, officer, 285, enlisted, 950; unaccompanied, UAQ/UEQ, 262; visiting, VOQ, 62, VAQ/VEQ, 87, TLF, 100. Clinic. Website: www.cnic.navy.mil/regions/ndw/installations/jbab.html.

Andersen AFB, Guam, APO AP 96543-5000; 2 mi. N of Yigo. Phone: (cmcl, from CONUS) 671-366-1110; DSN 315-366-1110. Majcom: PACAF. Host: 36th Wing. Mission: Pacific center for power projection, regional cooperation, and multinational training; serves as a logistic support and staging base for aircraft operating in the Pacific and Indian Oceans. Major tenants: Det. 5, 22nd Space Operations Sq. (AFSPC); 613th Contingency Response Gp. (AMC); 734th Air Mobility Sq. (AMC); Helicopter Combat Support Sq. 5 (US Navy). History: activated 1945. Named for Gen. James Roy Andersen, who was chief of staff, Hq. AAF, Pacific Ocean Areas, and lost at sea in February 1945. Area: 20,270 acres. Runways: 11,182 ft. and 10,555 ft. Altitude: 612 ft. Personnel: permanent party military, 1,762; DOD civilians, 1,561. Housing:

single family, officer, 236, enlisted, 1,153; unaccompanied, UOQ, 74, UAQ/UEQ, 1,018; visiting, VOQ, 23, VAQ/VEQ, 519, TLF, 232. Clinic. Website: www.andersen.af.mil.

JB Andrews, includes Andrews AFB, Md. 20762-5000; 10 mi. SE of Washington, D.C. Phone: 301-981-1110; DSN 312-858-1110. Majcom: AMC. Host: 89th Airlift Wing. Mission: gateway to nation's capital and home of Air Force One. Provides worldwide airlift for the President, vice president, top US officials, and foreign heads of state. Also responsible for Presidential support and base operations; supports all branches of the armed services, several major commands, and federal agencies. Major tenants: Air Force Flight Standards Agency; Hq. AFOSI; AFOSI Academy; Air National Guard Readiness Center; 113th Wing (ANG), F-16; 459th ARW (AFRC), KC-135; Naval Air Facility; Marine Aircraft Gp. 49, Det. A; Air Force Review Boards Agency. History: activated May 1943. Named for Lt. Gen. Frank M. Andrews, military air pioneer and WWII commander of the European Theater, killed in aircraft accident May 3, 1943 in Iceland. Consolidated with Naval Air Facility Washington as a joint base 2009. Area: 6,853 acres. Runways: 9,755 ft. and 9,300 ft. Altitude: 281 ft. Personnel: permanent party military, 5,502; DOD civilians, 3,247. Housing: single family, officer, 383 (including 96 govt. leased), enlisted, 1,667 (including 318 govt.-leased); unaccompanied, UAQ/UEQ, 923; visiting, VOQ, 136, VAQ/VEQ, 66, TLF, 68. Hospital. Website: www.andrews.af.mil.

Arnold AFB, Tenn. 37389; approx. 7 mi. SE of Manchester. Phone: 931-454-3000; DSN 312-340-4574. Majcom: AFMC. Host: Arnold Engineering Development Center. Mission: supports acquisition and sustainment of aerospace systems by conducting flight simulation research, development, and evaluation testing for DOD, other government agencies, and commercial aerospace firms with the world's largest complex of wind tunnels, jet and rocket engine test cells, space simulation chambers, and hyperballistic ranges. History: base dedicated June 25, 1951. Named for Gen. of the Army H.H. "Hap" Arnold, wartime Chief of the Army Air Forces. Area: 39,081 acres. Runway: 6,000 ft. Altitude: 1,100 ft. Personnel: permanent party military, 58; DOD civilians, 240. Housing: single family, officer, 12, enlisted, 28; visiting, 40. Medical aid station and small VA clinic. Website: www.arnold.af.mil.

Aviano AB, Italy, APO AE 09604; adjacent to Aviano, 50 mi. N of Venice. Phone: (cmcl, from CONUS) 011–39–0434–307111; DSN 314–632–7111. Majcom: USAFE. Host: 31st Fighter Wing. Mission: maintains two LANTIRN-equipped F-16 fighter squadrons, the 510th and the 555th, and 603rd Air Control Sq. Major tenants: Hq. 401st Air Expeditionary Wing (USAFE). Geographically Separated Units (GSUs): Det. 2, 401st AEW Pristina (Kosovo) Serbia; Det. 1, 401st AEW, Sarajevo, Bosnia; 774th Expeditionary Air Base Gp., Istres AB, France; 31st RED HORSE Flt. and 31st Munitions Sq., Camp Darby, Italy; 31st Munitions Support Sq., Ghedi AB, Italy; 99th Ex. Recon. Sq., RAF Akrotiri, Cyprus; 496th Air Base Sq., Morón AB, Spain. History: one of the oldest Italian air bases, dating to 1911. USAF began

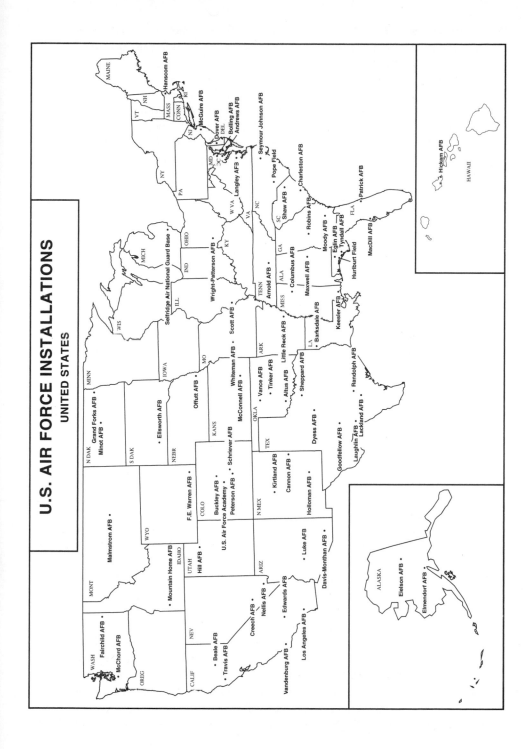

U.S. AIR FORCE INSTALLATIONS
UNITED STATES

Hanscom AFB
McGuire AFB
Dover AFB
Bolling AFB
Andrews AFB
Seymour Johnson AFB
Langley AFB
Pope Field
Charleston AFB
Patrick AFB
Shaw AFB
Robins AFB
Moody AFB
Eglin AFB
Tyndall AFB
Hurlburt Field
MacDill AFB
Maxwell AFB
Columbus AFB
Arnold AFB
Keesler AFB
Barksdale AFB
Little Rock AFB
Sheppard AFB
Randolph AFB
Wright-Patterson AFB
Selfridge Air National Guard Base
Scott AFB
Whiteman AFB
Vance AFB
Tinker AFB
Altus AFB
Dyess AFB
Goodfellow AFB
Laughlin AFB
Lackland AFB
Kirtland AFB
Cannon AFB
Holloman AFB
Offutt AFB
Ellsworth AFB
Grand Forks AFB
Minot AFB
McConnell AFB
Schriever AFB
Buckley AFB
Peterson AFB
U.S. Air Force Academy
F.E. Warren AFB
Malmstrom AFB
Mountain Home AFB
Hill AFB
Luke AFB
Davis-Monthan AFB
Creech AFB
Nellis AFB
Edwards AFB
Los Angeles AFB
Fairchild AFB
McChord AFB
Beale AFB
Travis AFB
Vandenburg AFB

Hickam AFB
HAWAII

Eielson AFB
Elmendorf AFB
ALASKA

MAINE
NH
VT
MASS
CONN
RI
NJ
DEL
MD
SC
NY
PA
W VA
VA
NC
FLA
GA
ALA
MISS
LA
TENN
KY
OHIO
IND
ILL
WIS
MICH
IOWA
MO
ARK
MINN
N DAK
S DAK
NEBR
KANS
OKLA
TEX
COLO
WYO
IDAHO
UTAH
N MEX
ARIZ
MONT
NEV
CALIF
OREG
WASH

operations 1954. Area: 1,467 acres. Runway: 8,596 ft. Altitude: 413 ft. Personnel: permanent party military, 3,700; DOD civilians, 164. Housing: 681 govt.-leased (189 officer, 592 enlisted); unaccompanied, UAQ/UEQ, 812; visiting, 74, DV, 6. Clinic (contracted with local hospital). Website: www.aviano.af.mil.

Barksdale AFB, La. 71110-5000; in Bossier City. Phone: 318-456-1110; DSN 312-781-1110. Majcom: ACC. Host: 2nd Bomb Wing. Mission: B-52H operations and training, nuclear deterrence, and global strike operations. Major tenants: 8th Air Force (ACC); 917th Wing (AFRC), A-10, B-52H; 8th Air Force Museum. History: activated Feb. 2, 1933. Named for Lt. Eugene H. Barksdale, WWI airman killed in an August 1926 crash. Area: 22,000 acres (18,000 acres reserved for recreation). Runway: 11,756 ft. Altitude: 166 ft. Personnel: permanent party military, 5,300; DOD civilians, 1,800. Housing: single family, officer, 135, enlisted, 594; unaccompanied, 876; visiting, VOQ, 118, VAQ, 102, TLF, 24. Superclinic. Website: www.barksdale.af.mil.

Beale AFB, Calif. 95903-5000; 13 mi. E of Marysville. Phone: 530-634-3000; DSN 312-368–3000. Majcom: ACC. Host: 9th Reconnaissance Wing. Mission: U-2, and Global Hawk missions. Major tenants: 940th ARW (AFRC), KC-135; 7th Space Warning Sq. (AFSPC), PAVE PAWS; 548th Intelligence Gp. (ACC). History: originally US Army's Camp Beale; transferred to Air Force in 1948; became Air Force base in April 1951. Named for Brig. Gen. E. F. Beale, Indian agent in California prior to Civil War. Area: 22,944 acres. Runway: 12,000 ft. Altitude: 113 ft. Personnel: permanent party military, 3,742; DOD civilians, 718. Housing: single family, officer, 159, enlisted, 1,294; unaccompanied, 545; visiting, VOQ, 53, VAQ/VEQ, 125, TLF, 46. Clinic. Website: www.beale.af.mil.

Buckley AFB, Colo. 80011-9524; 8 mi. E of Denver. Phone: 720-847-9011 DSN 312-847-9011. Majcom: AFSPC. Host: 460th Space Wing. Mission: space-based missile warning data. Major tenants: 2nd SWS, 140th Wing (ANG); Aerospace Data Facility; Navy/Marine Reserve Center; Air Reserve Personnel Center; Army Aviation Support Facility; Defense Finance and Accounting Center-Denver. History: activated April 1, 1942 as a gunnery training facility. Named for 1st Lt. John H. Buckley, a WWI flier, killed Sept. 17, 1918. ANG assumed control from US Navy in 1959. Became active-duty Air Force base Oct. 2, 2000. Area: 3,832 acres. Runway: 11,000 ft. Altitude: 5,663 ft. Personnel: permanent party military, 3,114; DOD civilians, 3,365. Housing: unaccompanied, UAQ/UEQ, 380 Clinic. Website: www.buckley.af.mil.

Cannon AFB, N.M. 88103-5000; 7 mi. W of Clovis. Phone: 575-784-4228; DSN 312-681-4228. Majcom: ACC. Host: 27th FW. Mission: F-16 operations; infiltration, exfiltration, and resupply to support special operations missions. History: activated August 1942. Named for Gen. John K. Cannon, WWII commander of all Allied air forces in the Mediterranean Theater and former commander, Tactical Air Command. Area: 3,789 acres, excluding range. Runways: 10,000 ft. and 8,200 ft. Altitude: 4,295 ft. Personnel: permanent party military, 3,126; DOD civilians, 610. Housing: single family, officer,

143, enlisted, 1,501; unaccompanied, 835; visiting, 57, TLF, 36. Ambulatory care clinic. Website: www.cannon.af.mil.

JB Charleston, includes Charleston AFB, S.C. 29404-5000; 10 mi. from downtown Charleston. Phone: 843-963-1110; DSN 312-673-1100. Majcom: AMC. Host: 437th AW. Mission: C-17 operations. Major tenant: 315th AW (AFRC assoc.), C-17. History: activated October 1942; inactivated March 1946; reactivated August 1953. Consolidated with Naval Support Activity Charleston as a joint base October 1, 2010. Area: 6,033 acres (including auxiliary airfield). Runway: 9,000 ft.; joint-use airfield. Altitude: 46 ft. Personnel: permanent party military, 3,553; DOD civilians, 962. Housing: single family, officer, 148, enlisted, 1,178; unaccompanied, UAQ/UEQ, 587; visiting, VOQ, 156, VAQ/VEQ, 40, TLF, 40. Clinic. Website: www.charleston.af.mil/units/index.asp.

Columbus AFB, Miss. 39710-1000; 7.5 mi. NW of Columbus. Phone: 662-434-1110; DSN 312-742-110. Majcom: AETC. Host: 14th Flying Training Wing. Mission: Specialized Undergraduate Pilot Training (T-1, T-37, T-38). History: activated 1942 for pilot training. Area: 5,325 acres. Runways: 12,000 ft., 8,000 ft., and 6,300 ft. Altitude: 219 ft. Personnel: permanent party military, 1,409; DOD civilians, 585. Housing: single family, 538; unaccompanied, UOQ, 234, UAQ/UEQ, 166; visiting, 73, DV, 4, TLF, 20. Clinic. Website: www.columbus.af.mil.

Davis-Monthan AFB, Ariz. 85707-5000; within Tucson. Phone: 520-228-1110; DSN 312-228-1110. Majcom: ACC. Host: 355th Wing. Mission: Deploy, employ, and sustain expeditionary combat and combat support forces while enabling critical JFACC and HLS operations. Major tenants: 12th Air Force (ACC); Aerospace Maintenance and Regeneration Center (AFMC), DOD's single location for regeneration, maintenance, parts reclamation, preservation, storage, and disposal of excess DOD and government aerospace vehicles; 943rd Rescue Gp. (AFRC), HH-60; 55th ECG (ACC); 563rd RQG (AFSOC); US Customs and Border Protection. History: activated 1927. Named for two local aviators: 2nd Lt. Samuel H. Davis, killed Dec. 28, 1921, and 2nd Lt. Oscar Monthan, killed March 27, 1924. Area: 10,633 acres. Runway: 13,643 ft. Altitude: 2,404 ft. Personnel: permanent party military, 6,671; DOD civilians, 3,197. Housing: single family, officer, 125, enlisted, 1,129; unaccompanied, 756; visiting, VOQ, 20, VAQ/VEQ, 61, DV, 165, TLF, 50. Clinic. Website: www.dm.af.mil.

Dover AFB, Del. 19902-7209; 6 mi. SE of Dover. Phone: 302-677-3000; DSN 312-445-3000. Majcom: AMC. Host: 436th AW. Mission: C-5 operations; operates largest DOD aerial port facility; houses military's East Coast mortuary. Major tenant: 512th AW (AFRC assoc.). History: activated December 1941; inactivated 1946; reactivated February 1951. Area: 3,908 acres. Runways: 12,900 ft. and 9,600 ft. Altitude: 28 ft. Personnel: permanent party military, 3,350; DOD civilians, 1,040. Housing: single family, officer, 139, enlisted, 866; unaccompanied, UAQ/UEQ, 533; visiting, VOQ, 238, VAQ/VEQ, 34, TLF, 19. Clinic. Website: www.dover.af.mil.

U.S. AIR FORCE INSTALLATIONS
ATLANTIC—PACIFIC

Dyess AFB, Tex. 79607-1980; WSW border of Abilene. Phone: 325-696-1110; DSN 312-461-1110. Majcom: ACC. Host: 7th BW. Mission: B-1 operations. Major tenant: 317th Airlift Gp. (AMC), C-130. History: activated April 1942; deactivated December 1945; reactivated as Abilene AFB September 1955. In December 1956, renamed for Lt. Col. William E. Dyess, WWII fighter pilot who escaped from a Japanese prison camp, killed in P-38 crash in December 1943. Area: 6,342 acres (including off-base sites). Runway: 13,500 ft. Altitude: 1,789 ft. Personnel: permanent party military, 4,884; DOD civilians, 412. Housing: single family, officer, 153, enlisted, 824; unaccompanied, 808; visiting, 160, TLF, 39. Clinic. Website: www.dyess.af.mil.

Edwards AFB, Calif. 93524; adjacent to Rosamond. Phone: 661-277-1110; DSN 312-527-3510. Majcom: AFMC. Host: 95th Air Base Wing. Mission: The Air Force Flight Test Center is AFMC's center of excellence for conducting and supporting research, development, test, and evaluation of aerospace systems from concept to combat. It operates the US Air Force Test Pilot School and is home to NASA's Dryden Research Center and considerable test activity conducted by America's commercial aerospace industry. Major tenants: AFRL's Propulsion Directorate (AFMC); Dryden Flight Research Center (NASA); USMC Air Reserve helicopter squadrons and detachments HMM 764 and HMH 769. History: activities began in September 1933 when the Muroc Bombing and Gunnery Range was established. In 1942, it was designated Muroc Army Air Base. Renamed in 1949 for Capt. Glen W. Edwards, killed June 5, 1948 in crash of a YB-49 "Flying Wing." Area: 301,000 acres. Runways: 21, from 4,000 to 39,000 ft. Altitude: 2,302 ft. Personnel: permanent party military, 1,701; DOD civilians, 3,471. Housing: single family, officer, 194; enlisted, 603. Medical and dental clinics. Website: www.edwards.af.mil.

Eglin AFB, Fla. 32542; 2 mi. SW of the twin cities of Niceville and Valparaiso; 7 mi. NE of Fort Walton Beach. Phone: 850-882-1110; DSN 312-872-1110. Majcom: AFMC. Host: 96th ABW. Mission: supporting the Eglin Air Armament Center and associate units. Major tenants: AFRL's Munitions Directorate (AFMC); 33rd FW (ACC), F-15; 53rd Wing (ACC); 919th Special Operations Wing (AFRC) at Duke Field, MC-130; Air Force Armament Museum; Army 6th Ranger Training Battalion; Naval School Explosive Ordnance Disposal. History: activated 1935. Named for Lt. Col. Frederick I. Eglin, WWI flier killed in aircraft accident Jan. 1, 1937. Area: 463,452 acres. Eglin is the nation's largest Air Force base in terms of acreage, covering an area roughly two-thirds the size of Rhode Island. Runways: 12,000 ft. and 10,000 ft. Altitude: 85 ft. Personnel: permanent party military, 7,854; DOD civilians, 3,884 (excluding Hurlburt Field). Housing: single family, officer, 218, enlisted, 2,116; unaccompanied, UAQ/UEQ, 1,212; visiting, VOQ, 169, VAQ/VEQ, 156, TLF, 87. Hospital. Website: www.eglin.af.mil.

Eielson AFB, Alaska 99702-5000; 26 mi. SE of Fairbanks. Phone: 907-377-1110; DSN 317-377-1110. Majcom: PACAF. Host: 354th FW. Mission: operates and maintains PACAF's largest air-to-ground bombing range complex and conducts the premier large force exercise, Red Flag – Alaska; supports operations, maintenance, mission support, and medical group functions. Major tenants: Arctic Survival School (AETC); 168th Air Refueling Wing (ANG), KC-135; 353rd Combat Training Sq. History: activated October 1944. Named for Carl Ben Eielson, Arctic aviation pioneer who died in an Arctic rescue mission in November 1929. Area: 19,790 acres (including 16 remote sites, 63,195 acres). Runway: 14,500 ft. Altitude: 534 ft. Personnel: permanent party military, 2,930; DOD civilians, 633. Housing: single family, officer, 181, enlisted, 1,243; unaccompanied, UOQ, 8, UAQ, 522, UEQ, 16; visiting, VOQ, 206, VAQ/VEQ, 328, TLF, 40. Outpatient clinic. Website: www.eielson.af.mil.

Ellsworth AFB, S.D. 57706-5000; 12 mi. ENE of Rapid City. Phone: 605-385-1110; DSN 312-675-0111. Majcom: ACC. Host: 28th BW. Mission: B-1 operations. Major tenants: Det. 21, Belle Fourche Electronic Scoring Site; Det. 8, 372nd Training Sq. (AETC); Det. 226, AFOSI. History: activated January 1942 as Rapid City AAB; renamed June 13, 1953 for Brig. Gen. Richard E. Ellsworth, killed March 18, 1953 in RB-36 crash. Area: 5,411 acres. Runway: 13,500 ft. Altitude: 3,276 ft. Personnel: permanent party military, 3,144; DOD civilians, 451. Housing: single family, officer, 311, enlisted, 1,535, unaccompanied, 728; visiting, 80, TLF, 29. Clinic. Website: www.ellsworth.af.mil.

JB Elmendorf-Richardson, includes Elmendorf AFB, Alaska 99506-5000; bordering Anchorage. Phone: 907-552-1110; DSN 317-552-1110. Majcom: PACAF. Host: 3rd Wing. Mission: C-12, C-130, E-3 Airborne Warning and Control System, F-15C/D, and F-15E operations. Hub for air traffic to and from Far East. Major tenants: Alaskan Command; 11th Air Force (PACAF); Alaskan NORAD Region. History: activated July 1940. Named for Capt. Hugh Elmendorf, killed Jan. 13, 1933. Consolidated with U.S. Army's Ft. Richardson as a joint base 2010. Area: 13,100 acres. Runways: 10,000 ft. and 7,500 ft. Altitude: 213 ft. Personnel: permanent party military, 6,642; DOD civilians, 898. Housing: single family, officer, 172, enlisted, 1,640; unaccompanied, UAQ/UEQ, 1,044; visiting, VOQ, 196, VAQ/VEQ, 203, TLF, 86. Hospital. Website: www.jber.af.mil.

Fairchild AFB, Wash. 99011-9588; 10 mi. WSW of Spokane. Phone: 509-247-1212; DSN 312-657-1212. Majcom: AMC. Host: 92nd Air Refueling Wing. Mission: KC-135R operations. Major tenants: 2nd SS (ACC) Munition Maintenance; 336th Training Gp. (USAF Survival School, AETC); 141st ARW (ANG), KC-135E. History: activated January 1942. Named for Gen. Muir S. Fairchild, USAF vice chief of staff at his death in 1950. Area: 5,823 acres; 530,205 acres used for survival school. Runway: 13,901 ft. Altitude: 2,426 ft. Personnel: permanent party military, 2,759; DOD civilians, 787. Housing: single family, officer, 144, enlisted, 1,092; unaccompanied, UAQ/UEQ, 642; visiting, VOQ, 85, VAQ/VEQ, 222, TLF, 18. Clinic. Website: www.fairchild.af.mil.

F. E. Warren AFB, Wyo. 82005-5000; adjacent to Cheyenne. Phone: 307-773-1110; DSN 312-481-1110. Majcom: AFSPC. Host: 90th SW. Mission: Minuteman III ICBMs; UH-1N. Major tenants: 20th Air Force (AFSPC); Air

Force ICBM Museum. History: activated as Ft. D.A. Russell July 4, 1867; under Army jurisdiction until 1949, when reassigned to USAF; renamed in 1930 for Francis Emory Warren, Wyoming senator and first state governor. Area: 5,866 acres. Missile site area covering more than 12,600 sq. mi. in Wyoming, Colorado, and Nebraska. Runway: none. Altitude: 6,142 ft. Personnel: permanent party military, 3,078; DOD civilians, 1,017. Housing: single family, officer, 114, enlisted, 717; unaccompanied, officer, 12, enlisted, 767; visiting, 30, TLF, 39. Clinic. Website: www.warren.af.mil.

Goodfellow AFB, Tex. 76908-4410; SE of San Angelo. Phone: 325-654-1110; DSN 312-477-1110. Majcom: AETC. Host: 17th Training Wing. Mission: trains intelligence, fire protection, and special instruments personnel for US military and DOD and international agencies. Major tenants: 344th Military Intelligence Battalion (Army); Center for Information Dominance det. (Navy); USMC det.; NCO Academy. History: activated January 1941. Named for Lt. John J. Goodfellow Jr., WWI observation airplane pilot killed in combat Sept. 14, 1918. Area: 1,136 acres. Runway: none. Altitude: 1,900 ft. Personnel: permanent party military, 1,387; DOD civilians, 689. Housing: single family, officer, 2, enlisted, 296; unaccompanied, UOQ, 51, UAQ/UEQ, 206; visiting, VOQ, 206, VAQ/VEQ, 351, TLF, 31. Clinic. Website: www.goodfellow.af.mil.

Grand Forks AFB, N.D. 58205-5000; 16 mi. W of Grand Forks. Phone: 701-747-3000; DSN 312-362-3000. Majcom: AMC. Host: 319th ARW. Mission: KC-135R operations. History: activated 1956. Named after town of Grand Forks, whose citizens bought the property for the Air Force. Area: 5,418 acres. Runway: 12,351 ft. Altitude: 911 ft. Personnel: permanent party military, 1,986; DOD civilians, 366. Housing: single family, officer, 168, enlisted, 1,036; unaccompanied, UAQ/UEQ, 587; visiting, VOQ, 31, VAQ/VEQ, 17, TLF, 27. Hospital. Website: www.grandforks.af.mil.

Hanscom AFB, Mass. 01731-5000; 17 mi. NW of Boston. Phone: 781-225-1110; DSN 312-845-1110. Majcom: AFMC. Host: 66th ABW. Mission: Electronic Systems Center manages development and acquisition of command and control systems. Major tenants: AFRL's Space Vehicles Directorate-Hanscom; AFRL's Sensors Directorate-Hanscom. History: activated 1941. Named for Laurence G. Hanscom, a pre-WWII advocate of private aviation, killed in a lightplane accident in 1941. Area: 846 acres. Runway: no flying mission; transient USAF aircraft use runways of Laurence G. Hanscom Field, state-operated airfield adjoining the base. Altitude: 133 ft. Personnel: permanent party military, 1,229; DOD civilians, 2,051. Housing: single family, officer, 314, enlisted, 383; unaccompanied, UAQ/UEQ, 122; visiting, 148, TLF, 47. Clinic. Website: www.hanscom.af.mil.

Hill AFB, Utah 84056-5990; 25 mi. N. of Salt Lake City. Phone: 801-777-1110; DSN 312-777-1110. Majcom: AFMC. Host: 75th ABW. Mission: provide quality products and services that equip, maintain, and sustain operational forces as they execute national defense policy around the world; dominant combat airpower and world-class test and training opportunities. Major tenants:

388th FW (ACC); 419th FW (AFRC), F-16; Hill Aerospace Museum; Defense Enterprise Computing Center (DISA); Defense Distribution Depot Hill Utah; Defense Logistics Agency; 372nd Recruiting Gp. (USAF). History: activated 1940. Named for Maj. Ployer P. Hill, killed Oct. 30, 1935 while test flying the first B-17. Area: 6,797 acres; manages 962,076 acres (Utah Test and Training Range). Runway: 13,500 ft. Altitude: 4,789 ft. Personnel: permanent party military, 6,200; DOD civilians, 17,000. Housing: single family, officer, 178, enlisted, 960; unaccompanied, UAQ/UEQ, 786; visiting, VOQ, 13, VAQ/VEQ, 147, TLF, 61. Clinic. Website: www.hill.af.mil.

Holloman AFB, N.M. 88310; 8 mi. SW of Alamogordo. Phone: 575-572-1110; DSN 312-572-1110. Majcom: ACC. Host: 49th FW. Mission: F-117A operations; Basic Expeditionary Airfield Resources (BEAR Base Assets) and two air transportable clinics. Major tenants: 46th Test Gp. (AFMC); 4th Space Control Sq. (AFSPC); German Air Force Flying Training Center. History: activated 1941. Named for Col. George Holloman, guided-missile pioneer. Area: 58,000 acres. Runways: 12,000 ft., 10,500 ft., and 8,000 ft. Altitude: 4,350 ft. Personnel: permanent party military, 3,751; DOD civilians, 1,049. Housing: single family, officer, 190, enlisted, 1,223; unaccompanied, 945; visiting, 192, TLF, 49. Clinic. Website: www.holloman.af.mil.

Hurlburt Field, Fla. 32544-5000; 5 mi. W of Fort Walton Beach. Phone: 850-884-1110; DSN 312-579-1110. Majcom: AFSOC. Host: 16th Special Operations Wing. Mission: specialized airpower, equipped with AC-130H/U, MC-130E/H, MC-130P (located at Eglin), MH-53J/M, U-28A. Major tenants: AFSOC; 823rd RED HORSE Sq.; USAF Combat Weather Center; USAF Special Operations School; Joint Special Operations University; 505th Command and Control Wing; 605th Test and Evaluation Sq.; 25th Information Operations Sq.; 18th Flight Test Sq.; 720th Special Tactics Gp.; Det. 3, 342nd Training Sq. History: activated 1943. Named for Lt. Donald W. Hurlburt, WWII pilot killed Oct. 1, 1943. Area: 6,600 acres. Runway: 6,900 ft. Altitude: 38 ft. Personnel: permanent party military, 7,340; DOD civilians, 800. Housing: single family, officer, 52, enlisted, 628; unaccompanied, UAQ/UEQ, 1,231; visiting, VOQ, 163, VAQ/VEQ, 51, TLF, 24. Clinic. Website: www2.hurlburt.af.mil.

Incirlik AB, Turkey, APO AE 09824; 6 mi. E of Adana. Phone: (cmcl, from CONUS) 011-90-322-316-1110; DSN (from CONUS) 314-676-1110. Majcom: USAFE. Host: 39th ABW. Mission: provides full spectrum, forward operating base support to expeditionary forces. History: activated May 1954. Present unit began operations March 1966. Incirlik, in Turkish, means fig orchard. Area: 3,400 acres. Runway: 10,000 ft. Altitude: 240 ft. Personnel: permanent party military, 1,358; DOD civilians, 696. Housing: single family, 750; unaccompanied, UOQ, 105, UEQ, 756; visiting, VOQ, 91, VAQ/VEQ, 192, DV, 18, TLF, 80. Clinic. Website: www.incirlik.af.mil.

Kadena AB, Japan, APO AP 96368-5000; 15 mi. N of Naha. Phone: (cmcl, from CONUS) 011-81-6117-34-1110; DSN 315- 634-1110. Majcom: PACAF. Host: 18th Wing. Mission: E-3, F-15C/D, KC-135R, and HH-60 operations. Major tenants: 353rd Special Operations Gp. (AFSOC); 390th Intelligence Sq.; 82nd Reconnaissance Sq. (ACC); 733rd Air Mobility Support Sq. (AMC); Commander, Fleet Activities Okinawa (Navy). History: occupied by US forces in April 1945. Named for city of Kadena, Okinawa. Area: 11,210 acres. Runway: 12,100 ft. Altitude: 146 ft. Personnel: permanent party military, 8,000; DOD civilians, 1,800. Housing: single family, officer, 1,677, enlisted, 5,800; unaccompanied, UOQ, 47, UAQ/UEQ, 2,080; visiting, VOQ, 226, VAQ/VEQ, 222, TLF, 122. Clinic. Website: www.kadena.af.mil.

Keesler AFB, Miss. 39534-5000; located in Biloxi. Phone: 228-377-1110; DSN 312-591-8728. Majcom: AETC. Host: 81st TRW. Mission: Train airmen across the spectrum of technical, medical, and airmanship to build overwhelming combat power for the Air Force. Major tenants: 2nd Air Force (AETC); 45th Airlift Sq. (AETC), C-21; 403rd Wing (AFRC), C-130, WC-130. History: activated June 12, 1941. Named for 2nd Lt. Samuel R. Keesler Jr., a native of Mississippi and WWI aerial observer killed in action Oct. 9, 1918. Area: 3,554 acres, excluding off-base housing. Runway: 6,600 ft. Altitude: 33 ft. Personnel: permanent party military, 3,956; DOD civilians, 3,483. Housing: single family, officer, 280, enlisted, 1,551; unaccompanied, UAQ/UEQ, 809; visiting, 1,306, TLF, 79. Keesler Medical Center. Website: www.keesler.af.mil.

Kirtland AFB, N.M. 87117 5606; SE quadrant of Albuquerque. Phone: 505-846-0011; DSN 312-246-0011. Majcom: AFMC. Host: 377th ABW. Mission: provide world-class nuclear surety, expeditionary forces, and support to base operations. Major tenants: 498th Armament Systems Wing (AFMC); 58th SOW (AETC), HC-130, MC-130, HH-60, MH-53, UH-1, receiving CV-22 in 2006; Airborne Laser Program Office; Air Force Nuclear Weapons and Counterproliferation Agency; Air Force Pararescue and Combat Officer School; Air Force Office of Aerospace Studies; Air Force Operational Test and Evaluation Center; Air Force Research Laboratories (AFMC); 150th FW (ANG), F-16; Defense Threat Reduction Agency; Nuclear Weapons Center (AFMC); Nuclear Weapons Directorate (AFMC); Sandia National Laboratories; National Nuclear Security Administration (DOE); Space and Missile Systems Center Det. 12 (AFSPC); Defense Nuclear Weapons School; Air Force Inspection Agency; Air Force Safety Center. History: activated January 1941. Named for Col. Roy C. Kirtland, aviation pioneer who died May 2, 1941. Area: 52,678 acres. Runways: two, each 13,000 ft.; 10,000 ft.; and 6,000 ft. Altitude: 5,352 ft. Personnel: permanent party military, 3,057; DOD civilians, 3,459. Housing: single family, officer, 136, enlisted, 892; unaccompanied, UAQ/UEQ, 828; visiting, VOQ, 181, VAQ/VEQ, 216, DV, 38, TLF, 39. Air Force-VA joint medical center. Website: www.kirtland.af.mil.

Kunsan AB, South Korea, APO AP 96264-5000; 8 mi. SW of Kunsan City. Phone: (cmcl, from CONUS) 011-82-63-470-1110; DSN 315-782-1110. Majcom: PACAF. Host: 8th FW. Mission: F-16C/D operations; home of the "Wolf Pack" and the first active overseas F-16 wing (September 1981). Major tenants: US Army's Charlie and Delta Batteries, 2nd Battalion, 1st Air Defense

Artillery; US Army Contracting Command Korea. History: built by the Japanese in 1938. Area: 2,157 acres. Runway: 9,000 ft. Altitude: 29 ft. Personnel: permanent party military, 2,550; DOD civilians, 31. Housing: unaccompanied, UOQ, 245, UAQ/UEQ, 2,475; visiting, VOQ, 26, VAQ/VEQ, 60. Clinic. Website: www.kunsan.af.mil.

Lajes Field, Azores, Portugal, APO AE 09720-5000; Terceira Island, 900 mi. W of Portugal. Phone: (cmcl, from CONUS) 011-351-295-57-5178; DSN from US 312-535-5178. Majcom: USAFE. Host: 65th ABW. Mission: provides support to US and allied aircraft and personnel transiting the Atlantic, through US military and host-nation coordination. Major tenants: 65th ABW; 729th AMS (AMC). History: US operations began at Lajes Field 1943. Area: 1,192 acres. Runway: 10,865 ft. Altitude: 180 ft. Personnel: permanent party military, 655; DOD civilians, 151. Housing: single family, officer, 80, enlisted, 336; unaccompanied, UOQ, 20, UAQ/UEQ, 269; visiting, 252, TLF, 30. Clinic. Website: www.lajes.af.mil.

JB Langley-Eustis, includes Langley AFB, Va. 23665-5000; 3 mi. N of Hampton. Phone: 757-764-4169; DSN 312-574-4169. Majcom: ACC. Host: 1st FW. Mission: F-15 and F-22A air dominance operations. Major tenants: Air Combat Command; Air Force Rescue Coordination Center; Aerospace C2ISR Center; USAF Heritage of America Band; 480th Intelligence Wg. (ACC); Air and Space Expeditionary Force Center (ACC). History: activated Dec. 30, 1916. Langley is the first military base in the US purchased and built specifically for military aviation. Named for aviation pioneer and scientist Samuel Pierpont Langley, who died in 1906. Consolidated with U.S. Army's Ft. Eustis as a joint base October 1, 2010. Area: 2,900 acres. Runway: 10,000 ft. Altitude: 11 ft. Personnel: permanent party military, 8,057; DOD civilians, 2,264. Housing: single family, officer, 328, enlisted, 1,053; unaccompanied, 1,053; visiting, VOQ, 78, VAQ/VEQ, 153, TLF, 60. Hospital. Website: www.jble. af.mil.

Laughlin AFB, Tex. 78843-5000; 6 mi. E of Del Rio. Phone: 830-298-5620; DSN 312-732-5620. Majcom: AETC. Host: 47th FTW. Mission: SUPT (T-1, T-6, T-38). History: activated July 1942. Named for 1st Lt. Jack Thomas Laughlin, Del Rio native, B-17 pilot, killed Jan. 29, 1942. Area: 5,343 acres. Runways: 8,858 ft., 8,316 ft., and 6,236 ft. Altitude: 1,081 ft. Personnel: permanent party military, 929; DOD civilians, 982. Housing: single family, officer, 298, enlisted, 218; unaccompanied, UOQ, 320, UAQ/UEQ, 184; visiting, 96, TLF, 20. Clinic. Website: www.laughlin.af.mil.

JB Lewis-McChord, includes McChord AFB, Wash. 98438-1109; 8 mi. S of Tacoma. Phone: 253-982-1110; DSN 382-1110. Majcom: AMC. Host: 62nd AW. Mission: C-17 operations. Base is adjacent to Ft. Lewis, its primary customer for strategic airlift worldwide. Major tenant: 446th AW (AFRC assoc.). History: activated May 5, 1938. Named for Col. William C. McChord, killed Aug. 18, 1937. Consolidated with U.S. Army's Ft. Lewis as a joint base October 1, 2010. Area: 4,639 acres. Runway: 10,100 ft. Altitude: 4,639 ft.

Personnel: permanent party military, 3,750; DOD civilians, 1,128. Housing: single family, officer, 113, enlisted, 867; unaccompanied, UOQ, 2, UAQ/UEQ, 752; visiting, VOQ, 68, VAQ/VEQ, 232, TLF, 20. Dispensary. Madigan Army Medical Center is located 4 mi. SE. Website: www.lewis-mcchord.army.mil.

Little Rock AFB, Ark. 72099-4940; 17 mi. NE of Little Rock (Jacksonville). Phone: 501-987-1110; DSN 312-731-1110. Majcom: AETC. Host: 314th AW. Mission: largest C-130 training base in the world; trains crew members from all services and 28 allied nations. Major tenants: 463rd Airlift Gp. (AMC), C-130; 189th AW (ANG), C-130; US Air Force Mobility Weapons School (AMC); Hq. Ark. ANG. History: activated Oct. 9, 1955. Area: 6,130 acres. Runway: 12,000 ft. Altitude: 310 ft. Personnel: permanent party military, 5,340; DOD civilians, 570. Housing: single family, officer, 185, enlisted, 1,286; unaccompanied, 840; visiting, VOQ, 102, VAQ/VEQ, 52. Clinic. Website: www.littlerock.af.mil.

Los Angeles AFB, Calif. 90245-4657; in El Segundo, 3 mi. SE of Los Angeles Arpt.; base housing and support facilities 18 mi. S of the main base, in San Pedro. Phone: 310-363-1110; DSN 312-833-1110. Majcom: AFSPC. Host: Space and Missile Systems Center. Mission: responsible for research, development, acquisition, on-orbit testing, and sustainment of military space and missile systems. History: activated as Air Research and Development Command's Western Development Division July 1, 1954. Area: 112 acres at Los Angeles AFB and 127 acres at Ft. MacArthur Military Family Housing Annex. Runway: none. Altitude: 95 ft. Personnel: permanent party military, 1,076; DOD civilians, 1,257. Housing: 645 units, TLF, 25. Clinic. Website: www.losangeles.af.mil.

Luke AFB, Ariz. 85309-5000; 20 mi. WNW of downtown Phoenix. Phone: 623-856-6550; DSN 312-896-6550. Majcom: AETC. Host: 56th FW. Mission: F-16 operations; conducts USAF and allied F-16 pilot and crew chief training. Major tenant: 944th FW (AFRC), F-16. History: activated 1941. Named for 2nd Lt. Frank Luke Jr., observation balloon-busting ace of WWI and first American aviator to receive the Medal of Honor, killed in action Sept. 29, 1918. Luke is the largest fighter training base in the world. Area: 4,200 acres, plus 1.9-million-acre Barry M. Goldwater Range. Runways: 10,000 ft. and 9,910 ft. Altitude: 1,090 ft. Personnel: permanent party military, 5,008; DOD civilians, 935. Housing: single family, 724; unaccompanied, UAQ/UEQ, 730; visiting, 186, TLF, 84. Clinic. Website: www.luke.af.mil.

MacDill AFB, Fla. 33621-5000; on the Interbay Peninsula in southern Tampa. Phone: 813-828-1110; DSN 312-968-1110. Majcom: AMC. Host: 6th AMW. Mission: KC-135 operations; provides worldwide air refueling and combatant commander support. Major tenants: SOCOM; CENTCOM; Joint Communications Support Element; NOAA Aircraft Operations Center. History: activated April 15, 1941. Named for Col. Leslie MacDill, killed in aircraft accident Nov. 8, 1938. Area: 5,767 acres. Runways: 11,420 ft. and 7,167 ft. Altitude: 6 ft. Personnel: permanent party military, 3,650; DOD civilians,

1,417. Housing: single family, officer, 45, enlisted, 629; unaccompanied, UAQ/UEQ, 610; visiting, VOQ, 112, VAQ/VEQ, 130, TLF, 5. Hospital. Website: www.macdill.af.mil.

Malmstrom AFB, Mont. 59402-5000; 1.5 mi. E of Great Falls. Phone: 406-731-1110; DSN 312-632-1110. Majcom: AFSPC. Host: 341st SW. Mission: Minuteman III ICBM operations, UH-1N. Major tenant: 819th RED HORSE Sq. (ACC). History: activated Dec. 15, 1942. Named for Col. Einar A. Malmstrom, WWII fighter commander killed in air accident Aug. 21, 1954. Site of SAC's first Minuteman wing. Area: 3,716 acres, plus about 23,500 sq. mi. for missile sites. Runway: closed. Altitude: 3,460 ft. Personnel: permanent party military, 3,382; DOD civilians, 607. Housing: single family, officer, 210, enlisted, 974; unaccompanied, UAQ/UEQ, 834; visiting, 53, TLF, 30. Clinic. Website: www.malmstrom.af.mil.

Maxwell AFB, Ala. 36112-5000; 1 mi. WNW of Montgomery. Phone: 334-953-1110; DSN 312-493-1110. Majcom: AETC. Host: 42nd ABW. Mission: Air University conducts professional military, graduate, and professional continuing education for precommissioned and commissioned officers, enlisted personnel, and civilians. Major tenants: Air University; Air War College; Air Command and Staff College; Air University Library; College of Aerospace Doctrine, Research, and Education; School of Advanced Air and Space Studies; Air Force Officer Accession and Training Schools; Ira C. Eaker College for Professional Development; College for Enlisted Professional Military Education; Community College of the Air Force; Air Force Institute for Advanced Distributed Learning; Squadron Officer College; Civil Air Patrol; 908th AW (AFRC), C-130; Air Force Historical Research Agency; Air Force Doctrine Center; Headquarters Operations and Sustainment Systems Gp.; USAF Counterproliferation Center. History: activated 1918. Named for 2nd Lt. William C. Maxwell, killed in air accident Aug. 12, 1920. Area: 4,221 acres (includes Gunter Annex). Runway: 8,000 ft. Altitude: 172 ft. Personnel: permanent party military, 3,466; DOD civilians, 5,395. Housing: single family, officer, 372, enlisted, 588; unaccompanied, UAQ/UEQ, 280; visiting, 2,304, TLF, 30. Clinic. Website: www.maxwell.af.mil.

McConnell AFB, Kan. 67221-5000; SE corner of Wichita. Phone: 316-759-6100; DSN 312-743-6100. Majcom: AMC. Host: 22nd ARW. Mission: KC-135 operations. Major tenants: 184th ARW (ANG); 931st Air Refueling Gp. (AFRC assoc.). History: activated June 5, 1951. Named for the three McConnell brothers, WWII B-24 pilots from Wichita—Lt. Col. Edwin M. McConnell (died Sept. 1, 1997), Capt. Fred J. McConnell (died in a private airplane crash Oct. 25, 1945), and 2nd Lt. Thomas L. McConnell (killed July 10, 1943). Area: 3,533 acres. Runways: two, 12,000 ft. each. Altitude: 1,371 ft. Personnel: permanent party military, 2,722; DOD civilians, 403. Housing: single family, officer, 83, enlisted, 506; unaccompanied, UAQ/UEQ, 615; visiting, VOQ, 42, VAQ/VEQ, 44, TLF, 45. Clinic. Website: www.mcconnell.af.mil.

JB McGuire-Dix-Lakehurst, includes McGuire AFB, N.J. 08641-5000; 18 mi. SE of Trenton. Phone: 609-754-1100; DSN 312-650-3628. Majcom: AMC. Host: 305th AMW. Mission: C-17 and KC-10 operations. Major tenants: 21st Expeditionary Mobility Task Force (AMC); Air Mobility Warfare Center, Ft. Dix, N.J.; N.J. Civil Air Patrol; 108th ARW (ANG), KC-135; 514th AMW (AFRC assoc.). History: adjoins Army's Ft. Dix. Formerly Ft. Dix AAB; activated as Air Force base 1949. Named for Maj. Thomas B. McGuire Jr., P-38 pilot, second leading US ace of WWII, Medal of Honor recipient, killed in action Jan. 7, 1945. Consolidated with U.S. Army's Ft. Dix and Naval Air Engineering Station Lakehurst as a joint base October 1, 2009. Area: 3,598 acres. Runways: 10,001 ft. and 7,129 ft. Altitude: 133 ft. Personnel: permanent party military, 5,189, DOD civilians, 3,812. Housing: single family, officer, 223, enlisted, 1,658; unaccompanied, UAQ/UEQ, 1,162; visiting, VOQ, 33, VAQ/VEQ, 385, TLF, 55. Clinic. Website: www.jointbasemdl.af.mil.

Minot AFB, N.D. 58705-5000; 13 mi. N of Minot. Phone: 701-723-1110; DSN 312-453-1110. Majcom: ACC. Host: 5th BW. Mission: B-52 operations. Major tenant: 91st SW (AFSPC), Minuteman III, UH-1N. History: activated January 1957. Named after the city of Minot, whose citizens donated $50,000 toward purchase of the land for USAF. Area: 4,732 acres, plus additional 330 acres for missile sites spread over 8,500 sq. miles. Runway: 13,200 ft. Altitude: 1,668 ft. Personnel: permanent party military, 5,370; DOD civilians, 569. Housing: single family, officer, 324, enlisted, 1,521; unaccompanied, 813; visiting, 51, TLF, 15. Clinic. Website: www.minot.af.mil.

Misawa AB, Japan, APO AP 96319-5000; within Misawa city limits. Phone: (cmcl, from CONUS) 011-81-3117-66-1100; DSN 315-226-1110. Majcom: PACAF. Host: 35th FW. Mission: F-16C/D operations. Major tenants: 301st Intelligence Sq. (ACC); Naval Air Facility; Naval Security Gp. Activity; 750th Military Intelligence Det. (Army); Co. E, US Marine Support Battalion; Northern Air Defense Force (JASDF). History: occupied by US forces September 1945. Area: 3,865 acres. Runway: 10,000 ft. Altitude: 119 ft. Personnel: permanent party military, 3,769; DOD civilians, 398. Housing: single family, officer, 298, enlisted, 1,810; unaccompanied, UOQ, 40, UAQ/UEQ, 951; visiting, VOQ, 82, VAQ/VEQ, 44, TLF, 40. Hospital. Website: www. misawa.af.mil.

Moody AFB, Ga. 31699-5000; 10 mi. NNE of Valdosta. Phone: 229-257-4211; DSN 312-460-4211. Majcom: AFSOC. Host: 347th Rescue Wing. Mission: HC-130 and HH-60 operations. Major tenants: 479th Flying Training Gp. (AETC); 820th Security Forces Gp. (ACC). History: activated June 1941. Named for Maj. George P. Moody, killed May 5, 1941. Area: 6,050 acres. Runways: 9,300 ft. and 8,000 ft. Altitude: 235 ft. Personnel: permanent party military, 5,349; DOD civilians, 439. Housing: single family, officer, 32, enlisted, 271; unaccompanied, 714; visiting, VOQ, 37, VAQ/VEQ, 19, TLF, 32. Clinic. Website: www.moody.af.mil.

Mountain Home AFB, Idaho 83648-5000; 50 mi. SE of Boise. Phone: 208-828-1110; DSN 312-728-2110. Majcom: ACC. Host: 366th FW. Mission: F-15C and F-15E operations. Major tenants: Air Warfare Battlelab; 266th Range Sq. History: activated August 1943. Area: 9,112 acres. Runway: 13,500 ft. Altitude: 3,000 ft. Personnel: permanent party military, 3,985; DOD civilians, 535. Housing: single family, officer, 175, enlisted, 1,170; unaccompanied, 883; visiting, VOQ, 43, VAQ/VEQ, 54, TLF, 15. Hospital. Website: www. mountainhome.af.mil.

Nellis AFB, Nev. 89191-5000; 8 mi. NE of Las Vegas. Phone: 702-652-1110; DSN 312-682-1110. Majcom: ACC. Host: 99th ABW. Mission: USAF Warfare Center manages advanced pilot training and tactics development and integrates test and evaluation programs. Its 98th Range Wing oversees a 15,000-sq.-mile Nellis Range Complex and two emergency airfields. 57th Wing, A-10A, F-15C/D/E, F-16C/D, HH-60G, and Predator MQ-1/9 UAV. 57th Wing missions include Red Flag exercises (414th Combat Training Sq.); graduate-level pilot training (USAF Weapons School); support for Army exercises (549th Combat Training Sq.); training for international personnel in joint firepower procedures and techniques (Hq. USAF Air Ground Operations School); and USAF Air Demonstration Sq. (Thunderbirds). 53rd Wing, at 17 locations nationwide, serves as focal point for combat air forces in electronic warfare, armament and avionics, chemical defense, reconnaissance, and aircrew training devices, and operational testing and evaluation of proposed new equipment and systems. 505th Command and Control Wing builds the predominant air and space command and control ability for combined joint warfighters through training, testing, exercising, and experimentation. Major tenants: Aerospace Integration Center; Triservice Reserve Center; 58th and 67th Intelligence Gp. (ACC); 58th and 66th RQS (AFSOC); 820th RED HORSE Sq. (ACC); and 896th Munitions Sq. (AFMC). History: activated July 1941 as Las Vegas AAF with Army Air Corps Flexible Gunnery School; closed 1947; reopened 1948. Named for 1st Lt. William H. Nellis, WWII P-47 fighter pilot, killed Dec. 27, 1944. Area: Main base is 14,000 acres. NRC occupies 3 million acres of restricted air-land use and an additional 7,000-sq.-mile military operating area shared with civilian aircraft. Runways: 10,119 ft. and 10,051 ft. Altitude: 1,868 ft. Personnel: permanent party military, 8,636; DOD civilians, 3,748. Housing: single family, officer, 88, enlisted, 1,190; unaccompanied, 1,190; visiting, VOQ, 340, VAQ/VEQ, 354, TLF, 60. Air Force–VA joint hospital. Website: www.nellis.af.mil.

Offutt AFB, Neb. 68113-5000; 8 mi. S of Omaha. Phone: 402-294-1110; DSN 312-271-1110. Majcom: ACC. Host: 55th Wing. Mission: provides worldwide reconnaissance, command and control, and combat support to warfighting commanders and national leadership. Major tenants: STRATCOM; Joint Intelligence Center (STRATCOM); Air Force Weather Agency; National Airborne Operations Center (JCS); USAF Heartland of America Band. History: activated 1896 as Army's Ft. Crook. Landing field named for 1st Lt. Jarvis J. Offutt,

WWI pilot who died Aug. 13, 1918. Area: 4,039 acres. Runway: 11,700 ft. Altitude: 1,048 ft. Personnel: permanent party military, 5,741; DOD civilians, 1,984. Housing: single family, officer, 344, enlisted, 2,256; unaccompanied, 793; visiting, 171, TLF, 60. Clinic. Website: www.offutt.af.mil.

Osan AB, South Korea, APO AP 96278-5000; 38 mi. S of Seoul. Phone: (cmcl, from CONUS) 011-82-31-661-1110; DSN 315-784-1110. Majcom: PACAF. Host: 51st FW. Mission: A/OA-10, C-12, and F-16C/D operations. Major tenants: 7th Air Force (PACAF); 5th RS (ACC); 31st SOS (AFSOC); 33rd Rescue Sq. (PACAF); 303rd Intelligence Sq. (AIA); 731st Air Mobility Sq. (AMC); Charlie and Delta Batteries, 1st Battalion, 43rd Air Defense Artillery (Army). History: originally designated K-55; runway opened December 1952. Renamed Osan AB in 1956 for nearby town that was the scene of first fighting between US and North Korean forces in July 1950. Area: 1,674 acres. Runway: 9,000 ft. Altitude: 38 ft. Personnel: permanent party military, 5,700; DOD civilians, 280. Housing: single family, 211; unaccompanied, UOQ, 457, UAQ/UEQ, 3,615; visiting, VOQ, 57, VAQ/VEQ, 20, DV, 350, TLF, 15. Hospital. Website: www.osan.af.mil.

Patrick AFB, Fla. 32925-3237; 2 mi. S of Cocoa Beach. Phone: 321-494-1110; DSN 312-854-1110. Majcom: AFSPC. Host: 45th SW. Mission: supports DOD, NASA, Navy (Trident), and other government agency and commercial missile and space programs. Host responsibilities include Cape Canaveral AFS and tracking stations on Antigua and Ascension islands. Major tenants: Defense Equal Opportunity Management Institute; Air Force Technical Applications Center; 920th Rescue Wing (AFRC), HC-130, HH-60; 2nd Brigade, 87th Division (Army); Naval Ordnance Test Unit (Navy); Joint Task Force for Joint STARS at Melbourne, Fla. History: activated 1940. Named for Maj. Gen. Mason M. Patrick, Chief of AEF's Air Service in WWI and Chief of the Air Service/Air Corps, 1921-27. Area: 2,341 acres. Runway: 9,000 ft. Altitude: 9 ft. Personnel: permanent party military, 3,109; DOD civilians, 1,766. Housing: single family, enlisted, 550; unaccompanied, UAQ/UEQ, 204; visiting, VOQ, 52, VAQ/VEQ, 163, TLF, 51. Clinic. Website: www.patrick.af.mil.

JB Pearl Harbor-Hickam, includes Hickam AFB, Hawaii 96853-5000; 9 mi. W of Honolulu. Phone: 808-449-7110 (Oahu military operator); DSN 315-449-7110. Majcom: PACAF. Host: 15th AW. Mission: provides base and logistical support for 140 associate and tenant units in Hawaii and other Pacific-region locations; airlift for commander, PACOM, and commander, PACAF; and maintenance and refueling support for aircraft transiting between the US mainland and the western Pacific. Major tenants: PACAF; 13th AF/Kenney Warfighting Hq. (Provisional); 154th Wing (ANG), C-17, C-130, F-15, KC-135R; Joint POW/MIA Accounting Command. History: activated September 1938. Named for Lt. Col. Horace M. Hickam, aviation pioneer killed in crash Nov. 5, 1934. Consolidated with Naval Base Pearl Harbor as a joint base 2010. Area: 2,761 acres. Runways: Four joint-use runways shared with Honolulu Arpt.: 12,357 ft., 12,000 ft., 9,000 ft., and 6,952 ft. Altitude: 13

ft. Personnel: permanent party military, 5,016; DOD civilians, 1,405. Housing: single family, officer, 553, enlisted, 1,628; unaccompanied, UAQ/UEQ, 588; visiting, VOQ, 149, VAQ/VEQ, 83, TLF, 40. Clinic. Website: www.cnic.navy. mil/regions/cnrh/installations/jb_pearl_harbor_hickam.html.

Peterson AFB, Colo. 80914-5000; at eastern edge of Colorado Springs. Phone: 719-554-7321; DSN 312-834-7321. Majcom: AFSPC. Host: 21st SW. Mission: provides missile warning and space control; detects, tracks, and catalogs objects in space. Major tenants: NORAD; AFSPC; NORTHCOM; US Army Space and Missile Defense Command; 302nd AW (AFRC), C-130. History: activated 1942. Named for 1st Lt. Edward J. Peterson, killed Aug. 8, 1942. Area: 1,277 acres. Runway: shared with city. Altitude: 6,200 ft. Personnel: permanent party military, 6,152; DOD civilians, 2,302. Housing: single family, officer, 103, enlisted, 384; unaccompanied, UAQ/UEQ, 704; visiting, VOQ, 100, VAQ/VEQ, 54, TLF, 68. Clinic. Website: www.peterson.af.mil.

Pope AFB, N.C. 28308-2391; 12 mi. NNW of Fayetteville. Phone: 910-394-1110; DSN 312-486-1110. Majcom: AMC. Host: 43rd AW. Mission: C-130 operations. Adjoins Army's Ft. Bragg and provides intratheater combat airlift and close air support for airborne forces and other personnel, equipment, and supplies. Major tenants: 23rd Fighter Gp. (ACC), A/OA-10; 18th Air Support Operations Gp. (ACC); 21st and 24th STSs (AFSOC); USAF Combat Control School. History: activated 1919. Named after 1st Lt. Harley H. Pope, WWI pilot, killed Jan. 7, 1919. Area: 2,198 acres. Runway: 7,500 ft. Altitude: 218 ft. Personnel: permanent party military, 3,166; DOD civilians, 559. Housing: single family, officer, 84, enlisted, 543; unaccompanied, UAQ/UEQ, 668; visiting, VOQ, 8, VAQ/VEQ, 159, TLF, 22. Clinic. Website: www.pope.af.mil.

RAF Lakenheath, UK, APO AE 09461-5000; 70 mi. NE of London; 25 mi. NE of Cambridge. Phone: (cmcl, from CONUS) 011-44-1638-52-3000; DSN 314-226-1110. Majcom: USAFE. Host: 48th FW (USAFE). Mission: F-15C and F-15E operations. GSU: 85th Group, NAS Keflavik, Iceland. History: activated 1941. US forces arrived August 1948; the 48th FW arrived January 1960. Named after nearby village. Area: 2,290 acres. Runway: 9,000 ft. Altitude: 32 ft. Personnel: permanent party military, 4,500; DOD civilians, 250; Housing: single family, officer, 196, enlisted, 1,869; unaccompanied, UAQ/UEQ, 984; visiting, VOQ, 88, VAQ/VEQ, 48, TLF, 33. Regional medical center. Website: www.lakenheath.af.mil.

RAF Mildenhall, UK, APO AE 09459-5000; 20 mi. NE of Cambridge. Phone: (cmcl, from CONUS) 011-44-1638-54-1110; DSN 314-238-3000. Majcom: USAFE. Host: 100th ARW. Mission: KC-135R operations. Major tenants: 16th Air Force (USAFE); 352nd SOG (AFSOC), MC-130, MH-53; 95th RS (ACC); 488th Intelligence Sq. (ACC); Naval Air Facility. History: activated 1934; US presence began July 1950. Named after nearby town. Area: 1,144 acres. Runway: 9,227 ft. Altitude: 33 ft. Personnel: permanent party military, 3,053; DOD civilians, 331. Housing: single family, officer, 64, enlisted, 137; unaccompanied, UAQ/UEQ, 783; visiting, 328, TLF, 36. Website: www. mildenhall.af.mil.

Ramstein AB, Germany, APO AE 09094-0385; adjacent to the city of Ramstein, 10 mi. W of Kaiserslautern. Phone: (cmcl, from CONUS) 011-49-6371-47-113; DSN 314-480-1110. Majcom: USAFE. Host: 86th AW. Mission: C-20, C-21, C-40, and C-130E operations; provides expeditionary airlift for first-in base opening capabilities; 86th AW commander also serves as commander of the Kaiserslautern Military Community; also at Ramstein is the 435th Air Base Wing and the 38th Combat Support Wing. The 435th ABW provides expeditionary combat support and quality of life services for the Kaiserslautern community; the 38th CSW provides mission support to geographically separated units delivering American and European alliance combat support. Major tenant: USAFE. History: activated and US presence began 1953. Area: 3,212 acres. Runways: 10,498 ft. and 8,015 ft. Altitude: 782 ft. Personnel: permanent party military, 13,876; DOD civilians, 7,544. Housing: single family, officer, 473, enlisted, 4,588; unaccompanied, UOQ, 32, UAQ/UEQ, 1,795; visiting, 547, TLF, 70. Clinic. Website: www.ramstein.af.mil.

Robins AFB, Ga. 31098; 15 mi. SSE of Macon at Warner Robins. Phone: 478-926-1113; DSN 312-468-1113. Majcom: AFMC. Host: 78th ABW. Mission: Warner Robins Air Logistics Center provides worldwide logistics management for the C-5, C-17, C-130, E-8, F-15, U-2, and various special operations forces aircraft and helicopters. Support for general-purpose computers, avionics, missiles, aircraft propellers, vehicles, airborne electronic warfare and communications equipment, airborne bomb- and gun-directing systems, fire-fighting equipment, Joint Tactical Information Distribution System, and emergency software programming of Air Force, other DOD, and allied electronic warfare systems. Major tenants: Air Force Reserve Command; 116th Air Control Wing (ACC), E-8; 19th ARG (AMC), KC-135; 5th Combat Communications Gp. (ACC). History: activated March 1942. Named for Brig. Gen. Augustine Warner Robins, an early chief of the Materiel Division of the Army Air Corps, who died June 16, 1940. Area: 8,700 acres. Runway: 12,000 ft. Altitude: 294 ft. Personnel: permanent party military, 6,210; DOD civilians, 13,815. Housing: single family, officer, 108, enlisted, 1,043; visiting, VOQ, 134, VAQ/VEQ, 157, TLF, 50. Clinic. Website: www.robins.af.mil.

JB San Antonio, includes Lackland AFB, Tex. 78236-5000; 8 mi. SW of downtown San Antonio. Phone: 210-671-1110; DSN 312-473-1110. Majcom: AETC. Host: 37th TRW. Mission: One of the largest USAF training wings. Provides basic military training for civilian recruits entering Air Force, ANG, and AFRC; conducts courses in ground combat (base support) functions, English language training for international and US military students, and specialized maintenance and security training in Spanish to military forces and government agencies from 26 Latin American nations. Major tenants: Air Intelligence Agency; 433rd AW (AFRC); 149th FTW (ANG); 67th Information Operations Wing (ACC); National Security Agency/Central Security Service Texas; 59th Medical Wing; Air Force Security Forces Center; Force Protection Battlelab; Cryptologic Systems Gp. History: activated 1941. Named for Brig. Gen. Frank D. Lackland, early commandant of Kelly Field advanced flying school, who died in 1943. Consolidated with U.S. Army's Ft. Sam Houston and Randolph AFB as a joint base October 1, 2010. Area: 9,572 acres. Runway: 11,550 ft. Altitude: 691 ft. Personnel: permanent party military, 20,303; DOD civilians, 7,797. Housing: single family, officer, 151, enlisted, 1,060; unaccompanied, enlisted, 1,477; visiting, 2,838, TLF, 96. Wilford Hall Medical Center. Website: www.jbsa.af.mil.

JB San Antonio, includes Randolph AFB, Tex. 78150-5000; 17 mi. NE of San Antonio. Phone: 210-652-1110; DSN 312-487-1110. Majcom: AETC. Host: 12th FTW. Mission: conducts T-1, T-6, T-37, and T-38 instructor pilot training and combat systems officer training in the T-43. Major tenants: AETC; 19th Air Force; Air Force Personnel Center; Air Force Manpower Agency; Air Force Services Agency; Air Force Recruiting Service. History: dedicated June 1930. Named for Capt. William M. Randolph, killed Feb. 17, 1928. Consolidated with U.S. Army's Ft. Sam Houston and Lackland AFB as a joint base October 1, 2010. Area: 5,044 acres. Runways: two, 8,350 ft. each. Altitude: 761 ft. Personnel: permanent party military, 4,626; DOD civilians, 4,318. Housing: single family, officer, 218, enlisted, 427; unaccompanied, UOQ, 200, UEQ, 276; visiting, VOQ, 376, VAQ/VEQ, 164, TLF, 30. Clinic. Website: www.jbsa.af.mil.

Schriever AFB, Colo. 80912-5000; 10 mi. E of Colorado Springs. Phone: 719-567-1110; DSN 312-560-1110. Majcom: AFSPC. Host: 50th SW. Mission: command and control of DOD satellites. Major tenants: Joint National Integration Center; Space Battlelab; 310th Space Gp. (AFRC). History: designated as Falcon AFB June 1988. Renamed in June 1998 for Gen. Bernard A. Schriever. Area: 3,840 acres. Runway: none. Altitude: 6,267 ft. Personnel: permanent party military, 2,000; DOD civilians, 627. Housing: none. Medical and dental clinics. Website: www.schriever.af.mil.

Scott AFB, Ill. 62225-5000; 6 mi. ENE of Belleville. Phone: 618-256-1110; DSN 312-576-1110. Majcom: AMC. Host: 375th AW. Mission: C-9 and C-21 operations. Major tenants: TRANSCOM; AMC; 18th Air Force; Air Force Communications Agency; Defense Information Technology Contracting Office; 126th ARW (ANG), KC-135; 932nd AW (AFRC), C-9. History: activated June 14, 1917. Named for Cpl. Frank S. Scott, the first enlisted man to die in an aircraft accident, killed Sept. 28, 1912. Area: 3,230 acres. Runways: 10,000 ft. and 8,000 ft. (joint-use airfield). Altitude: 453 ft. Personnel: permanent party military, 5,364; DOD civilians, 5,032. Housing: single family, officer, 298, enlisted, 1,122; unaccompanied, UAQ/UEQ, 569; visiting, VOQ, 222, VAQ/VEQ, 173, TLF, 60. Hospital. Website: www.scott.af.mil.

Seymour Johnson AFB, N.C. 27531; within city limits of Goldsboro. Phone: 919-722-1110; DSN 312-722-1110. Majcom: ACC. Host: 4th FW. Mission: F-15E operations and training. Major tenant: 916th ARW (AFRC), KC-135R. History: activated June 12, 1942. Named for Navy Lt. Seymour A. Johnson, Goldsboro native, killed March 5, 1941. Area: 3,558 acres. Runway:

11,758 ft. Altitude: 110 ft. Personnel: permanent party military, 6,409; DOD civilians, 1,091. Housing: single family, officer, 150, enlisted, 1,210; unaccompanied, 652; visiting, VOQ, 63, VAQ/VEQ, 40, DV, 10, TLF, 49. Clinic. Website: www.seymourjohnson.af.mil.

Shaw AFB, S.C. 29152-5000; 8 mi. WNW of Sumter. Phone: 803-895-1110; DSN 312-965-1110. Majcom: ACC. Host: 20th FW. Mission: F-16CJ operations. Major tenants: 9th Air Force (ACC); CENTCOM Air Forces. History: activated Aug. 30, 1941. Named for 1st Lt. Ervin D. Shaw, one of the first Americans to see air action in WWI, killed in France July 9, 1918. Area: 121,930 acres. Runways: 10,000 ft. and 8,000 ft. Altitude: 242 ft. Personnel: permanent party military, 5,200; DOD civilians, 938. Housing: single family, officer, 164, enlisted, 1,042; unaccompanied, 1,112; visiting, 97, TLF, 39. Hospital (no emergency room). Website: www.shaw.af.mil.

Sheppard AFB, Tex. 76311-5000; 5 mi. N of Wichita Falls. Phone: 940-676-2511; DSN 312-736-2511. Majcom: AETC. Host: 82nd TRW. Mission: second largest of AETC's four technical training centers. Conducts resident training in aircraft maintenance, aircraft avionics, aerospace propulsion, fuels, ammo and munitions, armament, aerospace ground equipment, life support, civil engineering, communications, and various medical and dental specialties; provides instruction in a wide range of specialties at more than 40 USAF installations worldwide. Major tenant: 80th FTW (AETC), conducts T-37 and T-38 UPT, instructor pilot training in the Euro-NATO Joint Jet Pilot Training program, and Introduction to Fighter Fundamentals course with AT-38 aircraft. History: activated June 14, 1941. Named for US Sen. Morris E. Sheppard, who died April 9, 1941. Area: 6,158 acres. Runways: 13,100 ft., 10,000 ft., 7,000 ft., and 6,000 ft. Altitude: 1,019 ft. Personnel: permanent party military, 3,248; DOD civilians, 1,208. Housing: single family, officer, 200, enlisted, 1,010; unaccompanied, UOQ, 196, UAQ/UEQ, 396; visiting, 1,584, TLF, 95. Clinic. Website: www.sheppard.af.mil.

Spangdahlem AB, Germany, APO AE 09126-5000; 20 mi. NE of Trier; 9 mi. E of Bitburg. Phone: (cmcl, from CONUS) 011-49-6565-61-1110; DSN 314-452-1110. Majcom: USAFE. Host: 52nd FW. Mission: HARM-equipped A-10 A/C and F-16C/D operations; air control squadron operations with logistics responsibilities at dozens of GSUs. History: built by the French in 1951 and turned over to US in 1952. Named after nearby town. Area: 1,616 acres. Runway: 10,000 ft. Altitude: 1,196 ft. Personnel: permanent party military, 5,252; DOD civilians, 171. Housing: single family, officer, 126, enlisted, 1,299; unaccompanied, UAQ/UEQ, 856, UOQ, 8; visiting, 114, TLF, 52. Hospital. Website: www.spangdahlem.af.mil.

Tinker AFB, Okla. 73145-3010; 8 mi. SE of Oklahoma City. Phone: N/A. Majcom: AFMC. Host: 72nd ABW. Mission: Oklahoma City Air Logistics Center manages and repairs the engines that power cruise missiles and a variety of Air Force and Navy aircraft. The center also accomplishes aircraft modifications and repairs and maintains bombers, refuelers, and reconnaissance aircraft, including the B-1, B-2, B-52, C/KC-135, E-3 AWACS, and E-6 Mercury. Major tenants: 552nd Air Control Wing (ACC), E-3; Navy Strategic Communications Wing One, E-6; 507th ARW (AFRC), KC-135; 513th Air Control Gp. (AFRC assoc.), E-3; Defense Information Systems Agency; Defense Logistics Agency; Defense Distribution Center Oklahoma; 3rd Combat Communications Gp. (ACC); 38th Engineering Installation Gp. (AFMC). History: activated March 1942. Named for Maj. Gen. Clarence L. Tinker, who went down at sea June 7, 1942 while leading group of LB-30 bombers against Japan. Area: 5,033 acres. Runways: 11,100 ft. and 10,000 ft. Altitude: 1,291 ft. Personnel: permanent party military, 9,174; DOD civilians, 15,911. Housing: single family, officer, 107, enlisted, 587; unaccompanied, UAQ/UEQ, 1,220; visiting, VOQ, 109, VAQ/VEQ, 50, TLF, 40. Clinic. Website: www.tinker.af.mil.

Travis AFB, Calif. 94535-5000; 50 mi. NE of San Francisco at Fairfield. Phone: 707-424-1110; DSN 312-837-1110. Majcom: AMC. Host: 60th AMW. Mission: C-5 and KC-10 operations. Major tenants: 615th Contingency Response Wing; 15th Expeditionary Mobility Task Force (AMC); 349th AMW (AFRC assoc.); USAF Band of the Golden West; Air Museum. History: activated May 17, 1943. Named for Brig. Gen. Robert F. Travis, killed Aug. 5, 1950. Area: 6,383 acres. Runways: two, approx. 11,000 ft. each. Altitude: 62 ft. Personnel: permanent party military, 5,800; DOD civilians, 3,811. Housing: single family, officer, 177, enlisted, 1,143; unaccompanied, UAQ/UEQ, 1,627; visiting, VOQ, 139, VAQ/VEQ, 212, TLF, 84. David Grant Medical Center. Website: www.travis.af.mil.

Tyndall AFB, Fla. 32403-5000; 12 mi. E of Panama City. Phone: 850-283-1110; DSN 312-523-1110. Majcom: AETC. Host: 325th FW. Mission: F-15 and F-22 operations; trains USAF F-15 and F-22 pilots. Major tenants: 1st Air Force (ANG); Southeast Air Defense Sector (ANG); 53rd Weapons Evaluation Gp. (ACC); Air Force Civil Engineer Support Agency. History: activated Dec. 7, 1941. Named for 1st Lt. Frank B. Tyndall, WWI fighter pilot killed July 15, 1930. Area: 29,102 acres. Runways: 10,000 ft., 9,000 ft., and 7,000 ft. Altitude: 18 ft. Personnel: permanent party military, 5,280; DOD civilians, 687. Housing: single family, officer, 111, enlisted, 737; unaccompanied, UAQ/UEQ, 448; visiting, 648, TLF, 52. Clinic. Website: www.tyndall.af.mil.

US Air Force Academy, Colo. 80840-5025; N of Colorado Springs. Phone: 719-333-1110; DSN 312-333-1110. Host: USAFA. Mission: inspires and develops outstanding young men and women to become Air Force officers with knowledge, character, and discipline. History: established April 1, 1954. Moved to permanent location August 1958. Area: 18,500 acres. Runways: 4,500 ft., 3,500 ft., and 2,300 ft. Altitude: 7,200 ft. Personnel: permanent party military, 1,890; DOD civilians, 1,995. Housing: single family, officer, 231, enlisted, 978; unaccompanied, 130; visiting, 90, TLF, 30. Hospital. Website: www.usafa.af.mil.

Vance AFB, Okla. 73705-5000; 3 mi. SSW of Enid. Phone: 580-213-5000; DSN 312-448-5000. Majcom: AETC. Host: 71st FTW. Mission: provides Joint SUPT in T-1, T-6, T-37, and T-38 aircraft. History: activated

November 1941. Named for Lt. Col. Leon R. Vance Jr., Enid native, 1939 West Point graduate, and Medal of Honor recipient, killed July 26, 1944. Area: 3,066 acres. Runways: 9,200 ft., 9,200 ft., and 5,001 ft. Altitude: 1,307 ft. Personnel: permanent party military, 700; DOD civilians, 225. Housing: single family, officer, 115, enlisted, 115; unaccompanied, UOQ, 202, UAQ/UEQ, 108; visiting, 64, TLF, 10. Clinic. Website: www.vance.af.mil.

Vandenberg AFB, Calif. 93437-5000; 8 mi. NNW of Lompoc. Phone: 805-606-1110; DSN 312-276-1110. Majcom: AFSPC. Host: 30th SW. Mission: conducts polar-orbiting space launches and supports R&D tests and launch range operations for DOD, USAF, and NASA space, ballistic missile, and aeronautical systems and commercial space launches; provides test support for DOD space and ICBM systems; furnishes facilities and essential services to more than 36 aerospace contractors. Major tenants: 14th Air Force (AFSPC); 381st Training Gp. (AETC); 576th Flight Test Sq. (Space Warfare Center). History: originally Army's Camp Cooke. Activated October 1941; taken over by USAF June 7, 1957. Renamed for Gen. Hoyt S. Vandenberg, USAF's second Chief of Staff. Area: 98,400 acres. Runway: 15,000 ft. Altitude: 367 ft. Personnel: permanent party military, 2,680; DOD civilians, 1,100. Housing: single family, officer, 403, enlisted,1,566; unaccompanied, dorm rooms, 670, UOQ, 43, UAQ/UEQ, 59; visiting, VOQ, 111, VAQ/VEQ, 124, DV, 18, TLF, 26. Clinic. Website: www.vandenberg.af.mil.

Whiteman AFB, Mo. 65305-5000; 2 mi. S of Knob Noster. Phone: 660-687-1110; DSN 312-975-1110. Majcom: ACC. Host: 509th BW. Mission: B-2 operations. Major tenants: 442nd FW (AFRC), A/OA-10; 1st Battalion, 135th Aviation Regiment (ARNG); Mobile Inshore Undersea Warfare Unit 114 (Navy Reserve). History: activated 1942. Named for 2nd Lt. George A. Whiteman, first pilot to die in aerial combat during the attack on Pearl Harbor. Area: 4,993 acres. Runway: 12,400 ft. Altitude: 871 ft. Personnel: permanent party military, 5,246; DOD civilians, 2,492. Housing: single family, officer, 116, enlisted, 968; unaccompanied, 674; visiting, VOQ, 52, VAQ/VEQ, 35, TLF, 31. Clinic. Website: www.whiteman.af.mil.

Wright-Patterson AFB, Ohio 45433; 10 mi. ENE of Dayton. Phone: 937-257-7411; DSN 312-787-7411. Majcom: AFMC. Host: 88th ABW. Mission: Aeronautical Systems Center develops, acquires, modernizes, and sustains aerospace systems. Major tenants: Air Force Materiel Command; Development and Fielding Systems Gp.; Air Force Research Laboratory (AFMC); Air Force Security Assistance Center (AFMC); 445th AW (AFRC), C-141 (converting to C-5); Air Force Institute of Technology (AETC); National Museum of the US Air Force. History: originally separate, Wright Field and Patterson Field were merged and redesignated Wright-Patterson AFB Jan. 13, 1948. Named for aviation pioneers Orville and Wilbur Wright and for 1st Lt. Frank S. Patterson, killed June 19, 1918. The Wright brothers did much of their early flying on Huffman Prairie, now in Area C of the present base. The prairie is part of the Dayton Aviation Heritage National Historical Park. Site of US Air Force Marathon, held annually on Saturday nearest Sept. 18. Area:

8,357 acres. Runway: 12,600 ft. Altitude: 824 ft. Personnel: permanent party military, 6,698; DOD civilians, 10,199. Housing: single family, officer, 914, enlisted, 1,098; unaccompanied, UAQ/UEQ, 300; visiting, 414, TLF, 41. Wright-Patterson Medical Center. Website: www.wpafb.af.mil.

    Yokota AB, Japan, APO AP 96328-5000; approx. 28 mi. W of downtown Tokyo. Phone: (cmcl, from CONUS) 011-81-311-75-5-1110; DSN 315-225-1110. Majcom: PACAF. Host: 374th AW. Mission: C-12J, C-130H, and UH-1N operations; primary airlift hub for the Western Pacific. Major tenants: US Forces, Japan; 5th Air Force (PACAF); 730th AMS (AMC); Det. 1, Air Force Band of the Pacific-Asia; American Forces Network Tokyo; DFAS-Japan. History: opened as Tama AAF by the Japanese in 1939. Area: 1,750 acres. Runway: 11,000 ft. Altitude: 457 ft. Personnel: permanent party military, 3,414; DOD civilians, 199. Housing: single family, officer, 683, enlisted, 1,956; unaccompanied, UOQ, 184, UAQ/UEQ, 896; visiting, VOQ, 202, VAQ/VEQ, 23, TLF, 189. Hospital. Website: www.yokota.af.mil.

Appendix D

Selected Air Force Publications

The Air Force instructions, manuals, pamphlets, handbooks, and catalogs listed below should be of interest to Air Force officers in general. All officers should identify those additional publications related to their specialties and become familiar with their contents. These documents are found on the Air Force's e-publishing website at www.e-publishing.af.mil. The website contains both publications and forms for the Air Force and the Air National Guard. The Air Force further breaks down the information to the major commands, direct reporting units, field operating agencies, numbered air forces, and bases and units levels.

AIR FORCE INSTRUCTIONS (AFI)

AFI 31-401	*Information Security Program Management*
AFI 31-501	*Personnel Security Program Management*
AFI 34-202	*Protecting Nonappropriated Funds Assets*
AFI 34-1201	*Protocol*
AFI 36-2101	*Classifying Military Personnel*
AFI 36-2107	*Active Duty Service Commitments*
AFI 36-2110	*Assignments*
AFI 36-2116	*Extended Active Duty for Reserve Component Officers*
AFI 36-2301	*Developmental Education*
AFI 36-2302	*Professional Development (Advanced Academic Degrees and Professional Continuing Education)*
AFI 36-2406	*Officer and Enlisted Evaluation Systems*
AFI 36-2501	*Officer Promotions and Selective Continuation*
AFI 36-2504	*Officer Promotions, Continuation and Selective Early Removal in the Reserve of the Air Force*
AFI 36-2608	*Military Personnel Records Systems*
AFI 36-2610	*Appointing Regular Air Force Officers and Obtaining Conditional Reserve Status*
AFI 36-2611	*Officer Professional Development*
AFI 36-2640	*Executing Total Force Development*

AFI 36-2706	*Equal Opportunity Program Military and Civilian*
AFI 36-2803	*The Air Force Awards and Decorations Program*
AFI 36-2903	*Dress and Personal Appearance of Air Force Personnel*
AFI 36-2905	*Fitness Program*
AFI 36-2906	*Personal Financial Responsibility*
AFI 36-2907	*Unfavorable Information File (UIF) Program*
AFI 36-2908	*Family Care Plans*
AFI 36-2909	*Professional and Unprofessional Relationships*
AFI 36-2910	*Line of Duty (Misconduct) Determination*
AFI 36-3003	*Military Leave Program*
AFI 36-3006	*Survivor Benefit Plan (SBP)* (Active, Guard, Reserve, and Retired)
AFI 36-3203	*Service Retirements*
AFI 36-3206	*Administrative Discharge Procedures for Commissioned Officers*
AFI 36-3207	*Separating Commissioned Officers*
AFI 38-101	*Air Force Organization*
AFI 40-101	*Health Promotion*
AFI 40-102	*Tobacco Use in the Air Force*
AFI 40-104	*Health Promotion Nutrition*
AFI 44-120	*Military Drug Demand Reduction Program*
AFI 44-121	*Alcohol and Drug Abuse Prevention and Treatment (ADAPT) Program*
AFI 51-201	*Administration of Military Justice*
AFI 51-202	*Nonjudicial Punishment*
AFI 51-401	*Training and Reporting to Ensure Compliance with the Law of Armed Conflict*
AFI 51-902	*Political Activities by Members of the U.S. Air Force*
AFI 51-903	*Dissident and Protest Activities*
AFI 51-904	*Complaints of Wrongs under Article 138, Uniform Code of Military Justice*
AFI 90-301	*Inspector General Complaints Resolution*
AFI 91-202	*U.S. Air Force Mishap Prevention Program*
AFI 91-204	*Safety Investigations and Reports*
AFI 91-302	*Air Force Occupational and Environmental Safety, Fire Protection, and Health (AFOSH) Program*

AIR FORCE MANUALS (AFMAN)

AFMAN 33-326	*Preparing Official Communications*
AFMAN 36-2203	*Drill and Ceremonies*
AFMAN 36-2643	*Air Force Mentoring Program*

AIR FORCE PAMPHLETS (AFPAM)

AFPAM 10-100   *Airman's Manual*
AFPAM 34-1202   *Guide to Protocol*
AFPAM 36-2506   *You and Your Promotions: The Air Force Officer Promotion Program*
AFPAM 36-2607   *Applicant's Guide to the Air Force Board for Correction of Military Records*
AFPAM 36-3027   *Benefits and Entitlements for Family Members of Air Force Deceased*
AFPAM 36-3028   *Benefits and Entitlements for Family Members of Retired Air Force Deceased*
AFPAM 38-102   *Headquarters United States Air Force Organization and Functions (Chartbook)*

AIR FORCE POLICY DIRECTIVES (AFPD)

AFPD 36-27   *Equal Opportunity (EO)*
AFPD 36-29   *Military Standards*
AFPD 36-30   *Military Entitlements*
AFPD 51-4   *Compliance with the Law of Armed Conflict*

AIR FORCE HANDBOOKS (AFH)

AFH 33-337   *The Tongue and Quill* (Guide to Air Force Communications)

Appendix E

USAF Acronyms and Abbreviations

A1C	airman first class
AA&E	arms, ammunition, and explosives
AAF	Army Air Force
AAFES	Army and Air Force Exchange Service
AB	airman basic; air base
ABC	Aerospace Basic Course
ABU	Airman Battle Uniform
ACC	Air Combat Command
ACE	Allied Command Europe
ACSC	Air Command and Staff College
AD	active duty
ADAPT	alcohol and drug abuse prevention and treatment
ADAPTPM	ADAPT program manager
ADC	Area Defense Counsel; Air Defense Command
ADSC	Active Duty Service Commitment
AECP	Airman Education and Commissioning Program
AEF	air and space expeditionary force; American Expeditionary Force (WWI)
AETC	Air Education and Training Command
AEW	aerospace expeditionary wing
AFAS	Air Force Aid Society
AFBCMR	Air Force Board for Correction of Military Records
AFCFM	Air Force career field manager
AFEM	Armed Forces Expeditionary Medal
AFGCM	Air Force Good Conduct Medal
AFHRA	Air Force Historical Research Agency
AFIA	Air Force Inspection Agency
AFIT	Air Force Institute of Technology
AFLSA	Air Force Longevity Service Award
AFMC	Air Force Materiel Command
AFMIA	Air Force Manpower and Innovation Agency
AFOEA	Air Force Organizational Excellence Award

AFOMS	Air Force Occupational Measurement Squadron
AFOR	Air Force Overseas Ribbon
AFOSI	Air Force Office of Special Investigations
AFOUA	Air Force Outstanding Unit Award
AFPC	Air Force Personnel Center
AFR	Air Force Reserve
AFRC	Air Force Reserve Command
AFRH	Armed Forces Retirement Home
AFROTC	Air Force Reserve Officer Training Corps
AFS	Air Force specialty
AFSC	Air Force specialty code
AFSM	Armed Forces Service Medal
AFSNCOA	Air Force Senior NCO Academy
AFSOC	Air Force Special Operations Command
AFSPC	Air Force Space Command
AFTR	Air Force Training Ribbon
AGR	active guard or reserve
ALS	airman leadership school
AMC	Air Mobility Command
Amn	airman
ANG	Air National Guard
AOR	area of responsibility
APOD	aerial port of debarkation
APOE	aerial port of embarkation
APZ	above the promotion zone
ARC	American Red Cross; Air Reserve Component
ASCP	Airman Scholarship and Commissioning Program
AT	antiterrorism
ATC	Air Traffic Controller
ATM	automated teller machine
AWACS	Airborne Warning and Control System
AWC	Air War College
AWOL	absent without official leave
BAH	basic allowance for housing
BAS	basic allowance for subsistence
BDU	battle dress uniform
BMT	basic military training
BOP	base of preference
BOQ	bachelor officers' quarters
BPZ	below the promotion zone
BX	base exchange
C3	command, control, and communications
C3I	command, control, communications, and intelligence
C4	command, control, communications, and computer systems
CAA	career assistance advisor

CAF	Combat Air Forces
CAFSC	control Air Force specialty code
CAP	Civil Air Patrol
CAREERS	Career Airman Reenlistment Reservation System
CASF	composite air strike force
CB	chemical-biological
CCAF	Community College of the Air Force
CCMS	command chief master sergeant
CCRC	common core readiness criteria
CCT	combat controller
CDC	career development course
CENTAF	U.S. Air Force Central Command
CEPME	College for Enlisted Professional Military Education
CFC	Combined Federal Campaign
CFETP	career field education and training plan
CHAMPUS	Civilian Health and Medical Program of the Uniformed Services (former name for TRICARE)
CI	compliance inspection; counterintelligence
CIA	Central Intelligence Agency
CINC	commander in chief
CJCS	Chairman, Joint Chiefs of Staff
CMC	Commandant of the Marine Corps
CMSAF	Chief Master Sergeant of the Air Force
CMSgt	chief master sergeant
COLA	cost-of-living adjustment
COMPUSEC	computer security
COMSEC	communications security
CONUS	continental United States
CPR	cardiopulmonary resuscitation
CRO	change of rating official
CRSC	combat-related special compensation
CRDP	concurrent retirement disability pay
CSA	Chief of Staff, U.S. Army
CSAF	Chief of Staff, U.S. Air Force
CSS	commander support staff; combat service support
CTO	commercial travel office
DANTES	Defense Activity for Nontraditional Education Support
DCS	deputy chief of staff
DFAS	Defense Finance and Accounting Service
DIEMS	date initially entered military service
DLA	Defense Logistics Agency
DOB	date of birth
DOD	Department of Defense
DOPMA	Defense Officer Personnel Management Act
DOR	date of rank

DOS	date of separation
DOT	Department of Transportation
DRU	direct reporting unit
DTRA	Defense Threat Reduction Agency
DUI	driving under the influence
DV	distinguished visitors
EAD	extended active duty; entrance on active duty
EES	Enlisted Evaluation System
EFMP	Exceptional Family Member Program
EFT	electronic funds transfer
E-mail	electronic mail
ELA	educational leave of absence
EML	environmental and morale leave
EMSEC	emissions security
EOT	equal opportunity and treatment
EPA	Environmental Protection Agency
EPR	enlisted performance report
ETS	expiration of term of service
EXORD	execution order
FAC	functional account code
FAP	Family Advocacy Program
FBI	Federal Bureau of Investigation
FICA	Federal Insurance Contributions Act
FITW	Federal income tax withholding
FOA	field operating agency
FOIA	Freedom of Information Act
FOUO	for official use only
FPCON	force protection condition
FSA	family separation allowance
FSA-R	FSA reassignment
FSA-T	FSA temporary
FSC	family support center
FSH	family separation, basic allowance for housing
FSO	financial services office
FSSA	family subsistence supplemental allowance
FTA	first-term airman
FVAP	Federal Voting Assistance Program
FWA	fraud, waste, and abuse
FY	fiscal year
GCE	ground crew ensemble
GCM	general court-martial
GHQ	general headquarters
HAZMAT	hazardous material
HUMINT	human intelligence
ICBM	intercontinental ballistic missile

IG	Inspector General
IMA	individual mobilization augmentee
IO	information operations
IPZ	in the promotion zone
IRA	individual retirement account
IRR	individual ready reserve
ISP	Internet service provider
ISR	intelligence, surveillance, reconnaissance
IW	information warfare
JCS	Joint Chiefs of Staff
JFACC	joint forces air component commander
JFTR	Joint Federal Travel Regulation
JOPS	Joint Operational Planning System
JTF	joint task force
JTR	Joint Travel Regulations
JUMPS	Joint Uniform Military Pay System
JV	Joint Vision
LD/HD	low density/high density
LES	leave and earnings statement
LOA	letter of admonishment
LOAC	law of armed conflict
LOC	letter of counseling; line of communication
LOD	line of duty
LOE	letter of evaluation
LOR	letter of reprimand
LOW	law of war
MAAG	Military Assistance Advisory Group
MAC	Military Airlift Command
MAJCOM	major command
MAF	mobility air forces
MALT	monetary allowance in lieu of transportation
MCM	Manual for Courts-Martial
MDS	Manpower Data System
MEO	military equal opportunity; most effective organization
MFR	memorandum for record
MGIB	Montgomery GI Bill
MilPDS	Military Personnel Data System
MOPP	mission-oriented protective posture
MPF	military personnel flight
MR	memorandum for record
MRE	meal, ready-to-eat
MSgt	master sergeant
MSO	military service obligation
MTF	military treatment facility; medical treatment facility
MTP	master training plan

MTW	major theater war
MWR	morale, welfare, and recreation
NAF	numbered Air Force; non-appropriated fund
NATO	North Atlantic Treaty Organization
NBC	nuclear, biological, and chemical
NBCC	nuclear, biological, chemical, and conventional
NCO	noncommissioned officer
NCOA	noncommissioned officer academy
NDSM	National Defense Service Medal
NOTAM	Notice to Airmen
NSI	nuclear surety inspection
OBAD	operating budget authority document
OJT	on-the-job training
OPLAN	operations plan
OPORD	operations order
OPR	office of primary responsibility; officer performance report
OPSEC	operations security
ORI	operational readiness inspection
ORM	operational risk management
OSD	Office of the Secretary of Defense
OSHA	occupational safety and health administration
OSI	Office of Special Investigations
OTS	Officer Training School
PACAF	Pacific Air Forces
PACOM	Pacific Command
PC	personal computer
PCA	permanent change of assignment
PCM	primary care manager
PCS	permanent change of station
PDA	personal digital assistant
PDS	permanent duty station; personnel data system
PECD	promotion eligibility cutoff date
PERSTEMPO	personnel tempo
PES	promotion eligibility status
PFE	promotion fitness examination
PFW	performance feedback worksheet
PIN	personal identification number
PJ	pararescue
P.L.	public law
PME	professional military education
POV	privately owned vehicle
POW	prisoner of war
PRP	Personnel Reliability Program
PSN	promotion sequence number
PT	physical training

PTDY	permissive temporary duty
QRP	Qualified Recycling Program; Quality Retraining Program
QT	qualification training
RAC	risk assessment code
RHIP	rank has its privileges
RIC	record of individual counseling
RMS	resource management system
RNLTD	report not later than date
ROE	rules of engagement
ROPMA	Reserve Officer Personnel Management Act
ROTC	Reserve Officer Training Corps
SAC	Strategic Air Command
SAF	Secretary of the Air Force
SAM	surface-to-air missile
SAV	staff assistance visit
SBP	survivor benefit plan
SCG	security classification guide
SCM	summary court-martial
SDI	special duty identifier
SEA	senior enlisted advisor
SECAF	Secretary of the Air Force
SECDEF	Secretary of Defense
SEI	special experience identifier
SelRes	selected reserve
SG	surgeon general
SGLI	servicemembers' group life insurance
SII	special interest item
SJA	staff judge advocate
SLA	special leave accrual
SMSgt	senior master sergeant
SNCO	senior noncommissioned officer
SOAR	Scholarships for Outstanding Airmen to ROTC
SOF	special operations force
SOP	standing operating procedure
SPCM	special court-martial
SrA	senior airman
SRB	selective reenlistment bonus
SRID	senior rater identification
SROE	standing rules of engagement
SRP	Selective Reenlistment Program
SSgt	staff sergeant
STEP	Stripes for Exceptional Performers
TAC	Tactical Air Command
TAFMS	total active federal military service
TDP	TRICARE Dental Program

TDY	temporary duty
TFW	tactical fighter wing
TIG	time in grade
TIS	time in service
TJAG	The Judge Advocate General
TMO	traffic/transportation management office
TO	technical order
TOS	time on station
TRW	tactical reconnaissance wing
TSCO	Top Secret control officer
TSgt	technical sergeant
TSP	Thrift Savings Plan
UCMJ	Uniform Code of Military Justice
UETM	unit education and training manager
UFPM	unit fitness program manager
UIF	unfavorable information file
UMD	unit manning document
UN	United Nations
UOCAVA	Uniformed and Overseas Citizens Absentee Voting Act
UPMR	unit personnel management roster
USAAF	U.S. Army Air Forces
USAF	United States Air Force
USAFA	United States Air Force Academy
USAFE	U.S. Air Forces in Europe
USAFR	U.S. Air Force Reserves
U.S.C.	United States Code
USEUCOM	U.S. European Command
UTC	unit type code
UTM	unit training manager
VA	Veterans Affairs
VAO	voting assistance officer
VCJCS	Vice Chairman, Joint Chief of Staff
VEAP	Veterans Education Assistance Program
VIP	very important person
vMPF	virtual Military Personnel Flight
WAPS	Weighted Airman Promotion System
WASP	Women Airforce Service Pilots
WMD	weapons of mass destruction
WOC	wing operations center
WR	war reserve
WWI	World War I
WWII	World War II

Appendix F

USAF Fitness Charts

DETERMINING FITNESS SCORE

Fitness level is determined by adding aerobic fitness, body composition, push-up, and crunch component points.

FITNESS LEVEL	TOTAL SCORE
Excellent	≥ 90
Good	75–89.9
Marginal	70–74.9
Poor	< 70

Members must complete *all* components unless medically exempted. If a member is medically exempted from any component, the total score is calculated as follows:

$$\frac{\text{Total component points achieved}}{\text{Total possible points}} \times 100$$

COMPONENT	POSSIBLE POINTS
Aerobic	50
Body Comp	30
Push-ups	10
Crunches	10

DETERMINING BODY COMPOSITION

To measure abdominal circumference, locate the upper hip bone and the top of the right iliac crest. Place a measuring tape in a horizontal plane around the abdomen at the level of the iliac crest. Before reading the tape measure, ensure that the tape is snug, but does not compress the skin, and is parallel to the floor. The measurement is made at the end of a normal expiration.

Health Risk Category = low, moderate or high risk for current and future cardiovascular disease, diabetes, certain cancers, and other health problems.

Passing Requirements = member *must:* 1.) meet minimum value in each of the four components, *and* 2.) achieve a composite point total ≥ 75 points.

MALES <30 YEARS OF AGE

CARDIORESPIRATORY ENDURANCE

Run Time (mins:secs)	Health Risk Category	Points
≤ 9:12	Low-Risk	60.0
9:13 - 9:34	Low-Risk	59.7
9:35 - 9:45	Low-Risk	59.3
9:46 - 9:58	Low-Risk	58.9
9:59 - 10:10	Low-Risk	58.5
10:11 - 10:23	Low-Risk	57.9
10:24 - 10:37	Low-Risk	57.3
10:38 - 10:51	Low-Risk	56.6
10:52 - 11:06	Low-Risk	55.7
11:07 - 11:22	Low-Risk	54.8
11:23 - 11:38	Low-Risk	53.7
11:39 - 11:56	Low-Risk	52.4
11:57 - 12:14	Low-Risk	50.9
12:15 - 12:33	Low-Risk	49.2
12:34 - 12:53	Moderate Risk	47.2
12:54 - 13:14	Moderate Risk	44.9
13:15 - 13:36*	Moderate Risk	42.3
> 13:36	High Risk	0.0

BODY COMPOSITION

AC (inches)	Health Risk Category	Points
≤ 32.5	Low-Risk	20.0
33.0	Low-Risk	20.0
33.5	Low-Risk	20.0
34.0	Low-Risk	20.0
34.5	Low-Risk	20.0
35.0	Low-Risk	20.0
35.5	Moderate Risk	17.6
36.0	Moderate Risk	17.0
36.5	Moderate Risk	16.4
37.0	Moderate Risk	15.8
37.5	Moderate Risk	15.1
38.0	Moderate Risk	14.4
38.5	Moderate Risk	13.5
39.0*	Moderate Risk	12.6
≥ 39.5	High Risk	0.0

MUSCLE FITNESS

Push-ups (reps/min)	Points	Sit-ups (reps/min)	Points	Push-ups (reps/min)	Points	Sit-ups (reps/min)	Points
≥ 67	10.0	≥ 58	10.0	47	8.0		
62	9.5	55	9.5	46	7.8		
61	9.4	54	9.4	45	7.7		
60	9.3	53	9.2	44	7.5		
59	9.2	52	9.0	43	7.3		
58	9.1	51	8.8	42	7.2		
57	9.0	50	8.7	41	7.0		
56	8.9	49	8.5	40	6.8		
55	8.8	48	8.3	39	6.5		
54	8.8	47	8.0	38	6.3		
53	8.7	46	7.5	37	6.0		
52	8.6	45	7.0	36	5.8		
51	8.5	44	6.5	35	5.5		
50	8.4	43	6.3	34	5.3		
49	8.3	42*	6.0	33*	5.0		
48	8.1	≤ 41	0.0	≤ 32	0.0		

Minimum Component Values
   Run time ≤ 13:36 mins:secs / Abd Circ ≤ 39.0 inches
   Push-ups ≥ 33 repetitions/one minute / Sit-ups ≥ 42 repetitions/one minute

Composite Score Categories: Excellent ≥ 90.0 pts / Satisfactory = 75.0 - 89.9 / Unsatisfactory < 75.0

MALES 30 – 39 YEARS OF AGE

CARDIORESPIRATORY ENDURANCE

Run Time (mins:secs)	Health Risk Category	Points
≤ 9:34	Low-Risk	60.0
9:35 - 9:58	Low-Risk	59.3
9:59 - 10:10	Low-Risk	58.6
10:11 - 10:23	Low-Risk	57.9
10:24 - 10:37	Low-Risk	57.3
10:38 - 10:51	Low-Risk	56.6
10:52 - 11:06	Low-Risk	55.7
11:07 - 11:22	Low-Risk	54.8
11:23 - 11:38	Low-Risk	53.7
11:39 - 11:56	Low-Risk	52.4
11:57 - 12:14	Low-Risk	50.9
12:15 - 12:33	Low-Risk	49.2
12:34 - 12:53	Low-Risk	47.2
12:54 - 13:14	Moderate Risk	44.9
13:15 - 13:36	Moderate Risk	42.3
13:37 - 14:00*	Moderate Risk	39.3
≥ 14:01	High Risk	0.0

BODY COMPOSITION

AC (inches)	Health Risk Category	Points
≤ 32.5	Low-Risk	20.0
33.0	Low-Risk	20.0
33.5	Low-Risk	20.0
34.0	Low-Risk	20.0
34.5	Low-Risk	20.0
35.0	Low-Risk	20.0
35.5	Moderate Risk	17.6
36.0	Moderate Risk	17.0
36.5	Moderate Risk	16.4
37.0	Moderate Risk	15.8
37.5	Moderate Risk	15.1
38.0	Moderate Risk	14.4
38.5	Moderate Risk	13.5
39.0*	Moderate Risk	12.6
≥ 39.5	High Risk	0.0

MUSCLE FITNESS

Push-ups (reps/min)	Points	Sit-ups (reps/min)	Points	Push-ups (reps/min)	Points	Sit-ups (reps/min)	Points
≥ 57	10.0	≥ 54	10.0	39	8.0	≤ 38	0.0
52	9.5	51	9.5	38	7.8		
51	9.4	50	9.4	37	7.7		
50	9.3	49	9.2	36	7.5		
49	9.2	48	9.0	35	7.3		
48	9.2	47	8.8	34	7.0		
47	9.1	46	8.7	33	6.8		
46	9.0	45	8.5	32	6.7		
45	8.9	44	8.3	31	6.5		
44	8.8	43	8.0	30	6.0		
43	8.7	42	7.5	29	5.5		
42	8.6	41	7.0	28	5.3		
41	8.5	40	6.5	27*	5.0		
40	8.3	39*	6.0	≤ 26	0.0		

Minimum Component Values
Run time ≤ 14:00 mins:secs / Abd Circ ≤ 39.0 inches
Push-ups ≥ 27 repetitions/one minute / Sit-ups ≥ 39 repetitions/one minute

Composite Score Categories: Excellent ≥ 90.0 pts / Satisfactory = 75.0 - 89.9 / Unsatisfactory < 75.0

MALES 40 – 49 YEARS OF AGE

CARDIORESPIRATORY ENDURANCE

Run Time (mins:secs)	Health Risk Category	Points
≤ 9:45	Low-Risk	60.0
9:46 - 10:10	Low-Risk	59.8
10:11 - 10:23	Low-Risk	59.5
10:24 - 10:37	Low-Risk	59.1
10:38 - 10:51	Low-Risk	58.7
10:52 - 11:06	Low-Risk	58.3
11:07 - 11:22	Low-Risk	57.7
11:23 - 11:38	Low-Risk	57.1
11:39 - 11:56	Low-Risk	56.3
11:57 - 12:14	Low-Risk	55.4
12:15 - 12:33	Low-Risk	54.3
12:34 - 12:53	Low-Risk	53.1
12:54 - 13:14	Low-Risk	51.5
13:15 - 13:36	Low-Risk	49.8
13:37 - 14:00	Moderate Risk	47.7
14:01 - 14:25	Moderate Risk	45.2
14:26 - 14:52*	Moderate Risk	42.3
≥ 14:53	High Risk	0.0

BODY COMPOSITION

AC (inches)	Health Risk Category	Points
≤ 32.5	Low-Risk	20.0
33.0	Low-Risk	20.0
33.5	Low-Risk	20.0
34.0	Low-Risk	20.0
34.5	Low-Risk	20.0
35.0	Low-Risk	20.0
35.5	Moderate Risk	17.6
36.0	Moderate Risk	17.0
36.5	Moderate Risk	16.4
37.0	Moderate Risk	15.8
37.5	Moderate Risk	15.1
38.0	Moderate Risk	14.4
38.5	Moderate Risk	13.5
39.0*	Moderate Risk	12.6
≥ 39.5	High Risk	0.0

MUSCLE FITNESS

Push-ups (reps/min)	Points	Sit-ups (reps/min)	Points	Push-ups (reps/min)	Points	Sit-ups (reps/min)	Points
≥ 44	10.0	≥ 50	10.0	30	8.0	37	7.5
40	9.5	47	9.5	29	7.5	36	7.0
39	9.4	46	9.4	28	7.3	35	6.5
38	9.2	45	9.2	27	7.2	34*	6.0
37	9.1	44	9.1	26	7.0	≤ 33	0.0
36	9.0	43	9.0	25	6.5		
35	8.8	42	8.8	24	6.0		
34	8.5	41	8.7	23	5.8		
33	8.4	40	8.5	22	5.5		
32	8.3	39	8.0	21*	5.0		
31	8.1	38	7.8	≤ 20	0.0		

Minimum Component Values
  Run time ≤ 14:52 mins:secs / Abd Circ ≤ 39.0 inches
  Push-ups ≥ 21 repetitions/one minute / Sit-ups ≥ 34 repetitions/one minute

Composite Score Categories: Excellent ≥ 90.0 pts / Satisfactory = 75.0 - 89.9 / Unsatisfactory < 75.0

MALES 50 – 59 YEARS OF AGE

CARDIORESPIRATORY ENDURANCE

Run Time (mins:secs)	Health Risk Category	Points
≤ 10:37	Low-Risk	60.0
10:38 - 11:06	Low-Risk	59.7
11:07 - 11:22	Low-Risk	59.4
11:23 - 11:38	Low-Risk	59.0
11:39 - 11:56	Low-Risk	58.5
11:57 - 12:14	Low-Risk	58.0
12:15 - 12:33	Low-Risk	57.3
12:34 - 12:53	Low-Risk	56.5
12:54 - 13:14	Low-Risk	55.6
13:15 - 13:36	Low-Risk	54.5
13:37 - 14:00	Low-Risk	53.3
14:01 - 14:25	Low-Risk	51.8
14:26 - 14:52	Low-Risk	50.0
14:53 - 15:20	Moderate Risk	47.9
15:21 - 15:50	Moderate Risk	45.4
15:51 - 16:22*	Moderate Risk	42.4
≥ 16:23	High Risk	0.0

BODY COMPOSITION

AC (inches)	Health Risk Category	Points
≤ 32.5	Low-Risk	20.0
33.0	Low-Risk	20.0
33.5	Low-Risk	20.0
34.0	Low-Risk	20.0
34.5	Low-Risk	20.0
35.0	Low-Risk	20.0
35.5	Moderate Risk	17.6
36.0	Moderate Risk	17.0
36.5	Moderate Risk	16.4
37.0	Moderate Risk	15.8
37.5	Moderate Risk	15.1
38.0	Moderate Risk	14.4
38.5	Moderate Risk	13.5
39.0*	Moderate Risk	12.6
≥ 39.5	High Risk	0.0

MUSCLE FITNESS

Push-ups (reps/min)	Points	Sit-ups (reps/min)	Points	Push-ups (reps/min)	Points	Sit-ups (reps/min)	Points
≥ 44	10.0	≥ 46	10.0	26	8.2	30	6.5
39	9.5	43	9.5	25	8.0	29	6.3
38	9.4	42	9.4	24	7.5	28*	6.0
37	9.4	41	9.2	23	7.3	≤ 27	0.0
36	9.3	40	9.1	22	7.2		
35	9.3	39	9.0	21	7.0		
34	9.2	38	8.8	20	6.5		
33	9.2	37	8.7	19	6.0		
32	9.1	36	8.5	18	5.8		
31	9.1	35	8.0	17	5.5		
30	9.0	34	7.8	16	5.3		
29	8.8	33	7.5	15*	5.0		
28	8.5	32	7.3	≤ 14	0.0		
27	8.3	31	7.0				

Minimum Component Values
  Run time ≤ 16:22 mins:secs / Abd Circ ≤ 39.0 inches
  Push-ups ≥ 15 repetitions/one minute / Sit-ups ≥ 28 repetitions/one minute

Composite Score Categories: Excellent ≥ 90.0 pts / Satisfactory = 75.0 - 89.9 / Unsatisfactory < 75.0

MALES 60+ YEARS OF AGE

CARDIORESPIRATORY ENDURANCE

Run Time (mins:secs)	Health Risk Category	Points
≤ 11:22	Low-Risk	60.0
11:23 - 11:56	Low-Risk	59.7
11:57 - 12:14	Low-Risk	59.4
12:15 - 12:33	Low-Risk	59.0
12:34 - 12:53	Low-Risk	58.5
12:54 - 13:14	Low-Risk	58.0
13:15 - 13:36	Low-Risk	57.3
13:37 - 14:00	Low-Risk	56.5
14:01 - 14:25	Low-Risk	55.6
14:26 - 14:52	Low-Risk	54.5
14:53 - 15:20	Low-Risk	53.3
15:21 - 15:50	Low-Risk	51.8
15:51 - 16:22	Low-Risk	50.0
16:23 - 16:57	Moderate Risk	47.9
16:58 - 17:34	Moderate Risk	45.4
17:35 - 18:14*	Moderate Risk	42.4
≥ 18:15	High Risk	0.0

BODY COMPOSITION

AC (inches)	Health Risk Category	Points
≤ 32.5	Low-Risk	20.0
33.0	Low-Risk	20.0
33.5	Low-Risk	20.0
34.0	Low-Risk	20.0
34.5	Low-Risk	20.0
35.0	Low-Risk	20.0
35.5	Moderate Risk	17.6
36.0	Moderate Risk	17.0
36.5	Moderate Risk	16.4
37.0	Moderate Risk	15.8
37.5	Moderate Risk	15.1
38.0	Moderate Risk	14.4
38.5	Moderate Risk	13.5
39.0*	Moderate Risk	12.6
≥ 39.5	High Risk	0.0

MUSCLE FITNESS

Push-ups (reps/min)	Points	Sit-ups (reps/min)	Points	Push-ups (reps/min)	Points	Sit-ups (reps/min)	Points
≥ 30	10.0	≥ 42	10.0	19	6.3	30	8.0
28	9.5	39	9.5	18	6.0	29	7.8
27	9.3	38	9.4	17	5.8	28	7.5
26	9.0	37	9.2	16	5.5	27	7.3
25	8.8	36	9.1	15	5.3	26	7.0
24	8.5	35	9.0	14 *	5.0	25	6.8
23	8.0	34	8.9	≤ 13	0.0	24	6.5
22	7.5	33	8.8			23	6.3
21	7.0	32	8.6			22*	6.0
20	6.5	31	8.5			≤ 21	0.0

Minimum Component Values
Run time ≤ 18:14 mins:secs / Abd Circ ≤ 39.0 inches
Push-ups ≥ 14 repetitions/one minute / Sit-ups ≥ 22 repetitions/one minute

Composite Score Categories: Excellent ≥ 90.0 pts / Satisfactory = 75.0 - 89.9 / Unsatisfactory < 75.0

FEMALES <30 YEARS OF AGE

CARDIORESPIRATORY ENDURANCE

Run Time (mins:secs)	Health Risk Category	Points
≤ 10:23	Low-Risk	60.0
10:24 - 10:51	Low-Risk	59.9
10:52 - 11:06	Low-Risk	59.5
11:07 - 11:22	Low-Risk	59.2
11:23 - 11:38	Low-Risk	58.9
11:39 - 11:56	Low-Risk	58.6
11:57 - 12:14	Low-Risk	58.1
12:15 - 12:33	Low-Risk	57.6
12:34 - 12:53	Low-Risk	57.0
12:54 - 13:14	Low-Risk	56.2
13:15 - 13:36	Low-Risk	55.3
13:37 - 14:00	Low-Risk	54.2
14:01 - 14:25	Low-Risk	52.8
14:26 - 14:52	Low-Risk	51.2
14:53 - 15:20	Moderate Risk	49.3
15:21 - 15:50	Moderate Risk	46.9
15:51 - 16:22*	Moderate Risk	44.1
≥ 16:23	High Risk	0.0

BODY COMPOSITION

AC (inches)	Health Risk Category	Points
≤ 29.0	Low Risk	20.0
29.5	Low Risk	20.0
30.0	Low Risk	20.0
30.5	Low Risk	20.0
31.0	Low Risk	20.0
31.5	Low Risk	20.0
32.0	Moderate Risk	17.6
32.5	Moderate Risk	17.1
33.0	Moderate Risk	16.5
33.5	Moderate Risk	15.9
34.0	Moderate Risk	15.2
34.5	Moderate Risk	14.5
35.0	Moderate Risk	13.7
35.5*	Moderate Risk	12.8
≥ 36.0	High Risk	0.0

MUSCLE FITNESS

Push-ups (reps/min)	Points	Sit-ups (reps/min)	Points	Push-ups (reps/min)	Points	Sit-ups (reps/min)	Points
≥ 47	10.0	≥ 54	10.0	31	8.3	40	6.8
42	9.5	51	9.5	30	8.2	39	6.5
41	9.4	50	9.4	29	8.1	38*	6.0
40	9.3	49	9.0	28	8.0	≤ 37	0.0
39	9.2	48	8.9	24	7.0		
38	9.1	47	8.8	23	6.5		
37	9.0	46	8.6	22	6.3		
36	8.9	45	8.5	21	6.0		
35	8.8	44	8.0	20	5.8		
34	8.6	43	7.8	19	5.5		
33	8.5	42	7.5	18*	5.0		
32	8.4	41	7.0	≤ 17	0.0		

Minimum Component Values
Run time ≤ 16:22 mins:secs / Abd Circ ≤ 35.5 inches
Push-ups ≥ 18 repetitions/one minute / Sit-ups ≥ 38 repetitions/one minute

Composite Score Categories: Excellent ≥ 90.0 pts / Satisfactory = 75.0 - 89.9 / Unsatisfactory < 75.0

FEMALES 30 – 39 YEARS OF AGE

CARDIORESPIRATORY ENDURANCE

Run Time (mins:secs)	Health Risk Category	Points
≤ 10:51	Low-Risk	60.0
10:52 - 11:22	Low-Risk	59.5
11:23 - 11:38	Low-Risk	59.0
11:39 - 11:56	Low-Risk	58.6
11:57 - 12:14	Low-Risk	58.1
12:15 - 12:33	Low-Risk	57.6
12:34 - 12:53	Low-Risk	57.0
12:54 - 13:14	Low-Risk	56.2
13:15 - 13:36	Low-Risk	55.3
13:37 - 14:00	Low-Risk	54.2
14:01 - 14:25	Low-Risk	52.8
14:26 - 14:52	Low-Risk	51.2
14:53 - 15:20	Low-Risk	49.3
15:21 - 15:50	Moderate Risk	46.9
15:51 - 16:22	Moderate Risk	44.1
16:23 - 16:57*	Moderate Risk	40.8
≥ 16:58	High Risk	0.0

BODY COMPOSITION

AC (inches)	Health Risk Category	Points
≤ 29.0	Low Risk	20.0
29.5	Low Risk	20.0
30.0	Low Risk	20.0
30.5	Low Risk	20.0
31.0	Low Risk	20.0
31.5	Low Risk	20.0
32.0	Moderate Risk	17.6
32.5	Moderate Risk	17.1
33.0	Moderate Risk	16.5
33.5	Moderate Risk	15.9
34.0	Moderate Risk	15.2
34.5	Moderate Risk	14.5
35.0	Moderate Risk	13.7
35.5*	Moderate Risk	12.8
≥ 36.0	High Risk	0.0

MUSCLE FITNESS

Push-ups (reps/min)	Points	Sit-ups (reps/min)	Points	Push-ups (reps/min)	Points	Sit-ups (reps/min)	Points
≥ 46	10.0	≥ 45	10.0	26	8.5	≤ 28	0.0
40	9.5	42	9.5	25	8.3		
39	9.4	41	9.4	24	8.2		
38	9.3	40	9.0	23	8.0		
37	9.3	39	8.8	22	7.9		
36	9.2	38	8.5	21	7.8		
35	9.1	37	8.3	20	7.6		
34	9.1	36	8.2	19	7.5		
33	9.0	35	8.0	18	7.0		
32	8.9	34	7.8	17	6.8		
31	8.9	33	7.5	16	6.5		
30	8.8	32	7.0	15	6.0		
29	8.7	31	6.8	14*	5.0		
28	8.6	30	6.5	≤ 13	0.0		
27	8.6	29*	6.0				

Minimum Component Values
Run time ≤ 16:57 mins:secs / Abd Circ ≤ 35.5 inches
Push-ups ≥ 14 repetitions/one minute / Sit-ups ≥ 29 repetitions/one minute

Composite Score Categories: Excellent ≥ 90.0 pts / Satisfactory = 75.0 - 89.9 / Unsatisfactory < 75.0

FEMALES 40 – 49 YEARS OF AGE

CARDIORESPIRATORY ENDURANCE

Run Time (mins:secs)	Health Risk Category	Points
≤ 11:22	Low-Risk	60.0
11:23 - 11:56	Low-Risk	59.9
11:57 - 12:14	Low-Risk	59.8
12:15 - 12:33	Low-Risk	59.6
12:34 - 12:53	Low-Risk	59.4
12:54 - 13:14	Low-Risk	59.1
13:15 - 13:36	Low-Risk	58.7
13:37 - 14:00	Low-Risk	58.2
14:01 - 14:25	Low-Risk	57.7
14:26 - 14:52	Low-Risk	56.9
14:53 - 15:20	Low-Risk	56.0
15:21 - 15:50	Low-Risk	54.8
15:51 - 16:22	Low-Risk	53.3
16:23 - 16:57	Moderate Risk	51.4
16:58 - 17:34	Moderate Risk	49.0
17:35 - 18:14*	Moderate Risk	45.9
≥ 18:15	High Risk	0.0

BODY COMPOSITION

AC (inches)	Health Risk Category	Points
≤ 29.0	Low Risk	20.0
29.5	Low Risk	20.0
30.0	Low Risk	20.0
30.5	Low Risk	20.0
31.0	Low Risk	20.0
31.5	Low Risk	20.0
32.0	Moderate Risk	17.6
32.5	Moderate Risk	17.1
33.0	Moderate Risk	16.5
33.5	Moderate Risk	15.9
34.0	Moderate Risk	15.2
34.5	Moderate Risk	14.5
35.0	Moderate Risk	13.7
35.5*	Moderate Risk	12.8
≥ 36.0	High Risk	0.0

MUSCLE FITNESS

Push-ups (reps/min)	Points	Sit-ups (reps/min)	Points	Push-ups (reps/min)	Points	Sit-ups (reps/min)	Points
≥ 38	10.0	≥ 41	10.0	21	8.3	26	6.8
33	9.5	38	9.5	20	8.2	25	6.4
32	9.4	37	9.4	19	8.1	24*	6.0
31	9.2	36	9.2	18	8.0	≤ 23	0.0
30	9.1	35	9.1	17	7.8		
29	9.0	34	9.0	16	7.5		
28	8.9	33	8.8	15	7.0		
27	8.8	32	8.5	14	6.5		
26	8.7	31	8.3	13	6.0		
25	8.6	30	8.2	12	5.5		
24	8.6	29	8.0	11*	5.0		
23	8.5	28	7.5	≤ 10	0.0		
22	8.4	27	7.0				

Minimum Component Values
Run time ≤ 18:14 mins:secs / Abd Circ ≤ 35.5 inches
Push-ups ≥ 11 repetitions/one minute / Sit-ups ≥ 24 repetitions/one minute

Composite Score Categories: Excellent ≥ 90.0 pts / Satisfactory = 75.0 - 89.9 / Unsatisfactory < 75.0

FEMALES 50 – 59 YEARS OF AGE

CARDIORESPIRATORY ENDURANCE

Run Time (mins:secs)	Health Risk Category	Points
≤ 12:53	Low-Risk	60.0
12:54 - 13:36	Low-Risk	59.8
13:37 - 14:00	Low-Risk	59.6
14:01 - 14:25	Low-Risk	59.3
14:26 - 14:52	Low-Risk	58.9
14:53 - 15:20	Low-Risk	58.4
15:21 - 15:50	Low-Risk	57.7
15:51 - 16:22	Low-Risk	56.8
16:23 - 16:57	Low-Risk	55.6
16:58 - 17:34	Low-Risk	54.0
17:35 - 18:14	Low-Risk	51.9
18:15 - 18:56	Moderate Risk	49.2
18:57 - 19:43*	Moderate Risk	45.5
≥ 19:44	High Risk	0.0

BODY COMPOSITION

AC (inches)	Health Risk Category	Points
≤ 29.0	Low Risk	20.0
29.5	Low Risk	20.0
30.0	Low Risk	20.0
30.5	Low Risk	20.0
31.0	Low Risk	20.0
31.5	Low Risk	20.0
32.0	Moderate Risk	17.6
32.5	Moderate Risk	17.1
33.0	Moderate Risk	16.5
33.5	Moderate Risk	15.9
34.0	Moderate Risk	15.2
34.5	Moderate Risk	14.5
35.0	Moderate Risk	13.7
35.5*	Moderate Risk	12.8
≥ 36.0	High Risk	0.0

MUSCLE FITNESS

Push-ups (reps/min)	Points	Sit-ups (reps/min)	Points	Push-ups (reps/min)	Points	Sit-ups (reps/min)	Points
≥ 35	10.0	≥ 32	10.0	19	8.4	≤ 19	0.0
30	9.5	30	9.5	18	8.3		
29	9.4	29	9.0	17	8.2		
28	9.3	28	8.9	16	8.1		
27	9.2	27	8.8	15	8.0		
26	9.1	26	8.6	14	7.5		
25	9.0	25	8.5	13	7.0		
24	8.8	24	8.0	12	6.5		
23	8.7	23	7.6	11	6.0		
22	8.6	22	7.0	10	5.5		
21	8.6	21	6.5	9*	5.0		
20	8.5	20*	6.0	≤ 8	0.0		

Minimum Component Values
 Run time ≤ 19:43 mins:secs / Abd Circ ≤ 35.5 inches
 Push-ups ≥ 9 repetitions/one minute / Sit-ups ≥ 20 repetitions/one minute

Composite Score Categories: Excellent ≥ 90.0 pts / Satisfactory = 75.0 - 89.9 / Unsatisfactory < 75.0

FEMALES 60+ YEARS OF AGE

CARDIORESPIRATORY ENDURANCE

Run Time (mins:secs)	Health Risk Category	Points
≤ 14:00	Low-Risk	60.0
14:01 - 14:52	Low-Risk	59.8
14:53 - 15:20	Low-Risk	59.5
15:21 - 15:50	Low-Risk	59.1
15:51 - 16:22	Low-Risk	58.6
16:23 - 16:57	Low-Risk	57.9
16:58 - 17:34	Low-Risk	57.0
17:35 - 18:14	Low-Risk	55.8
18:15 - 18:56	Low-Risk	54.2
18:57 - 19:43	Low-Risk	52.1
19:44 - 20:33	Moderate Risk	49.3
20:34 - 21:28	Moderate Risk	45.6
21:29 - 22:28*	Moderate Risk	40.8
≥ 22:29	High Risk	0.0

BODY COMPOSITION

AC (inches)	Health Risk Category	Points
≤ 29.0	Low Risk	20.0
29.5	Low Risk	20.0
30.0	Low Risk	20.0
30.5	Low Risk	20.0
31.0	Low Risk	20.0
31.5	Low Risk	20.0
32.0	Moderate Risk	17.6
32.5	Moderate Risk	17.1
33.0	Moderate Risk	16.5
33.5	Moderate Risk	15.9
34.0	Moderate Risk	15.2
34.5	Moderate Risk	14.5
35.0	Moderate Risk	13.7
35.5*	Moderate Risk	12.8
≥ 36.0	High Risk	0.0

MUSCLE FITNESS

Push-ups (reps/min)	Points	Sit-ups (reps/min)	Points	Push-ups (reps/min)	Points	Sit-ups (reps/min)	Points
≥ 21	10.0	≥ 31	10.0	10	6.0	19	8.3
19	9.5	28	9.5	9	5.7	18	8.2
18	9.4	27	9.4	8	5.3	17	8.0
17	9.0	26	9.0	7*	5.0	16	7.8
16	8.8	25	8.9	≤ 6	0.0	15	7.5
15	8.5	24	8.8			14	7.3
14	8.0	23	8.7			13	7.0
13	7.5	22	8.6			12	6.5
12	7.0	21	8.5			11*	6.0
11	6.5	20	8.4			≤ 10	0.0

Minimum Component Values
Run time ≤ 22:28 mins:secs / Abd Circ ≤ 35.5 inches
Push-ups ≥ 7 repetitions/one minute / Sit-ups ≥ 11 repetitions/one minute

Composite Score Categories: Excellent ≥ 90.0 pts / Satisfactory = 75.0 - 89.9 / Unsatisfactory < 75.0

Index

Page numbers in italics indicates illustrations, tables, and charts.

About the Author

Col. Stephen E. Wright, PhD, served in the United States Air Force for 30 years and is currently the Education Advisor and Deputy Commandant at the School of Advanced Air and Space Studies at Maxwell Air Force Base in Montgomery, Alabama. He is the author of *Aerospace Strategy for the Aerospace Nation* and numerous articles on Air Force issues. He lives in Montgomery, Alabama.

Notes

Notes

Notes

Notes

STACKPOLE BOOKS

Military Professional Reference Library